V...
WV...
for lots more I-95 info,
including gas prices

INTERSTATE

Drive I-95

Exit by Exit Info, Maps, History and Trivia

by Stan Posner and Sandra Phillips-Posner

You can buy more copies of Drive I-95 at:

 Our web site www.drivei95.com – credit cards and PayPal accepted

 Chain and independent book stores in the US and Canada by Title, Author or by number: ISBN 978-1894979-399

 Toll free 888-GUIDE95 (888-484-3395) – credit cards accepted

 On-line book stores

 Mail order coupon on the last page of this book – credit cards accepted

If you would like to receive our e-mail newsletter with extra tidbits, please send us a note at info@drivei95.com or fill in the subscription form on our web site.

Please feel free to contact us at:

TRAVELSMART
P.O. Box 43527 CSP Roxboro, Dollard des Ormeaux, Quebec, Canada H8Y 3P4
info@drivei95.com • ☎ 514-684-4020 • Fax: 866-329-2987

5th EDITION 2010
Copyright © 2010 by Stan Posner and Sandra Phillips-Posner

QUANTITY DISCOUNTS AVAILABLE FOR FUND-RAISING AND VOLUME PURCHASES

First Printing 2003
Second Printing 2004
Third Printing (2nd Edition) 2004
Fourth Printing (3rd Edition) 2005
Fifth Printing (4th Edition) 2007
Sixth Printing (5th Edition) 2010

All rights reserved. The use of any portion of this publication reproduced, transmitted in any form or by any means, electronic, mechanical, photocopying, recording or otherwise, or stored in a retrieval system without the proper consent of the Publisher is an infringement of copyright law, except for the inclusion of brief quotations in a review.

Drive I-95 accepts no advertising and is not beholden in any way to any commercial interest. Its reports are solely for the information and use of the readers of this publication. The contents of this book may not be used in advertising or for any commercial purpose of any nature, without permission of the author.

Although the material in this book is correct to the best of their knowledge, the authors accept no responsibility for any of the establishments mentioned in this book. All information is subject to change. Furthermore, errors and omissions, whether typographical, clerical or otherwise may occur within the body of this publication. The Publisher hereby disclaims any liability to any party for any loss or damage by errors or omissions within this publication, whether such errors or omissions result from negligence, accident or any other cause.

One or more images in this book may be copyrighted. We believe their use is covered by the "fair use" clause (Section 107) of the U.S. Copyright Law. If any copyright holder informs us in writing that the use is not fair, we shall remove the image in question.

Cataloguing in Publication Data
Posner, Stan, 1947-
Drive I-95 : exit by exit info, maps, history, and trivia / Stan Posner, Sandra Phillips-Posner.
(Interstate drive series)
ISBN 978-1894979-399
1. Interstate 95—Guidebooks.
2. Automobile travel—Atlantic States—Guidebooks.
3. Atlantic States—Guidebooks.
I. Phillips-Posner, Sandra, 1949-   II. Title. III. Series.
F106.P68 2003   917.504'44   C2003-903712-6

Cover Design by David Leblanc, Oneonone
Maps designed by Albert Albala (albert@mediatribe.net) and drawn by Albert Albala and a team consisting of: Stan Posner, Brandon Posner, Natalie Joseph, Julie Howick, Georgette Haddad and Khalil Atiyeh
Cover Photos: Stan Posner; R.I. Tourism
Photos taken by Stan Posner, Sandra Phillips-Posner and as noted by: Bram Eisenthal
Typography by Josiane Trépanier, Compographe
Symbols Page and **Photo Editing** by Stan Posner and Brandon Posner

Printed in Hong Kong

Table of Contents

☞ Radio Stations to Listen to as you Drive I-95 .... Outside Front Flap

☞ Drive I-95 Map Symbols.. Inside Front Flap

☞ How to Use This New Kind of Info-Map Guide .... Inside Front Cover

☞ Introduction and Overview Map 4

☞ Info-Maps - gas, food, motels, shopping, sights on each
side of the exits and a side road to avoid traffic or construction.................................. 5-81

☞ Stories of the Road - History, trivia, yummy home-cooked meals
and fun restaurants, comfy B & B's, places to romp with the kids or pets, malls,
museums, shopping. This can entertain you as you drive or offer
you a place to stop and stretch and discover someplace new 81-224

☞ Recipe - Bring home a taste of your trip... 225

☞ Campgrounds and RV parks on the I-95
- phone numbers, number of sites, distance from exit, directions 226-229

☞ Golf Courses along the I-95
- addresses, phone numbers, par, directions 230-233

☞ Auto mechanics on I-95 - Car trouble? These are garages
that still have a mechanic, with phone numbers, hours, towing 234-235

☞ Independent Motels and B&B's along I-95 - Want to give the locals
some business? - phone numbers, pets, truck/RV parking 236-237

☞ Acknowledgments.. 238

☞ Driving Memories - space to jot a few notes to remember places
or people you've met... 239-240

☞ Expense Log South - keep track of your mileage, gas, expenses,
motel reservations 241

☞ Expense Log North - keep track of your mileage, gas, expenses,
motel reservations 242

☞ Order Form - order another book for a friend, for a birthday,
as a thank you, as a hostess gift or for the holidays 243

☞ Motel Chain 800 Numbers - call before you leave or from your car......... Inside back cover

This book is dedicated to our Dads, Gaby Posner and Irv Phillips, who enjoyed driving and highway trips. We both spent many happy hours of our youth in the back seats of their cars looking forward to daily adventures. We would love to pass their/our road trip passion on to you.

Hi there road-trippers,

The drive is not a race. No one wins if they get there first; in fact we would say you lose, since you are missing out on so much fun along the way. Why not make the drive part of your vacation? A happy traveler wrote us, "We discovered several great attractions we otherwise would have missed out on if we had not purchased this great book. Are we ever glad we got it."

We've adding a whopping 182 new stories in this edition, and since we know food stops are important to you, we've fattened our waistbands and eaten through 163 restaurants. A fan posted that using this book, "You'll never have to settle for a hastily eaten fast food burger at a rest stop again!"

We are sure we have found things that will make you want to screech to a stop:

We can still taste the 5th best pizza in America at Bob & Timmy's on Federal Hill in Providence. Just down the road in CT you can board (for FREE) the Nautilus, the first submersible to make it to the North Pole. And in SC on the Edisto River, you can sleep overnight in a tree house with songbirds and owls as your only neighbors.

At Fowle's in MA, open since 1865, we flipped over their hash browns stuffed with cheddar, provolone, bacon, and onions served with sour cream. Buz, of Buz and Ned in Richmond VA, worked his way thru BBQ havens in 5 states and then merged all that expertise with Ned's 150-year old family recipe into his own scrumptious BBQ.

For fun, at Terrapin Adventures in MD you can experience the thrill of the 330' zip line. In GA you can board a shrimp trawler, help the crew and partake in the freshest possible shrimp boil. For extreme action, at Xtreme Indoor Karting in FL, you can feel like a race car driver.

To rest your weary bones, we cover a range of choices, from the Element in MA which is so "green" you can sit on your couch cushions or eat them, to the luxury oasis of the Mansion on Forsyth Park in Savannah with its Cirque du Soleil decor.

You can walk on the same ground as our patriots, at Lexington and at Concord's North Bridge, where in 1775 British regulars clashed with colonial militia and minute men for "the shot heard round the world". Did you know that along I-95, you can see Edison's phonograph, the Star Spangled Banner, Paul Revere's lantern, Eli Whitney's cotton gin and the trunk that George Washington carried throughout the War. If the drive is overwhelming, you can stop and worship at the Daytona Beach Drive-In Church, where you stay in your car (don't need to wear your Sunday best!) - and then head to the beach.

Hopefully these tidbits will entice you to read the stories to make the drive more enjoyable and to get out and discover someplace new.

Stan Sandra

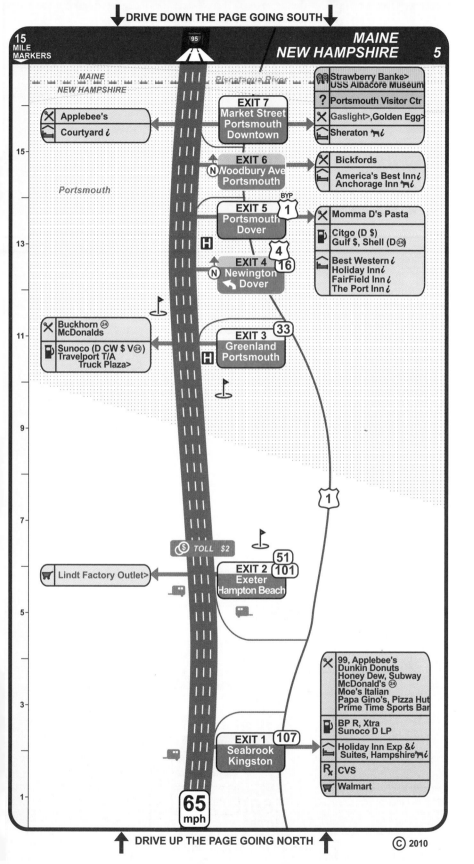

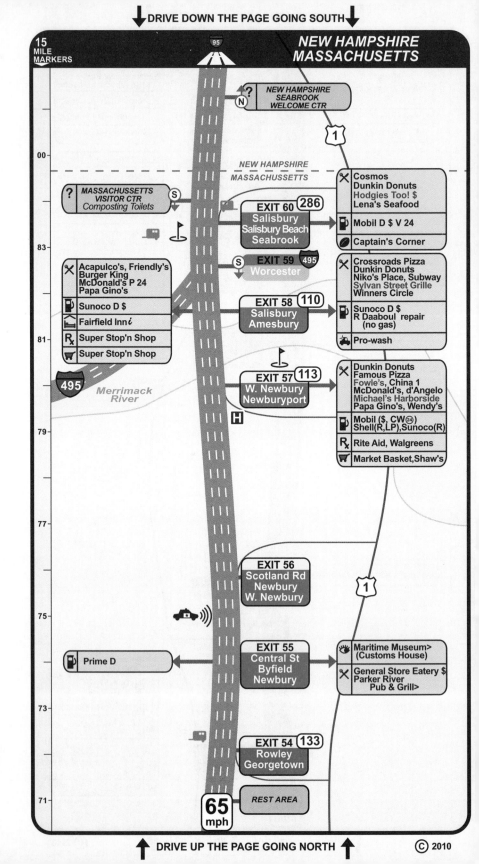

15 MILE MARKERS

NEW HAMPSHIRE MASSACHUSETTS

I-95

N ? NEW HAMPSHIRE
SEABROOK
WELCOME CTR

1

NEW HAMPSHIRE
MASSACHUSSETTS

? MASSACHUSSETTS VISITOR CTR Composting Toilets

S

00

83

| EXIT 60 | 286 |
| Salisbury
Salisbury Beach
Seabrook |

✕ Cosmos
Dunkin Donuts
Hodgies Too! $
Lena's Seafood

⛽ Mobil D $ V 24

Captain's Corner

S EXIT 59 495
Worcester

✕ Acapulco's, Friendly's
Burger King
McDonald's P 24
Papa Gino's

⛽ Sunoco D $

🛏 Fairfield Inn *i*

℞ Super Stop'n Shop

🛒 Super Stop'n Shop

| EXIT 58 | 110 |
| Salisbury
Amesbury |

✕ Crossroads Pizza
Dunkin Donuts
Niko's Place, Subway
Sylvan Street Grille
Winners Circle

⛽ Sunoco D $
R Daaboul repair
(no gas)

🚜 Pro-wash

81

495

Merrimack River

| EXIT 57 | 113 |
| W. Newbury
Newburyport |

H

✕ Dunkin Donuts
Famous Pizza
Fowle's, China 1
McDonald's, d'Angelo
Michael's Harborside
Papa Gino's, Wendy's

⛽ Mobil ($, CW㉔)
Shell(R,LP),Sunoco(R)

℞ Rite Aid, Walgreens

🛒 Market Basket,Shaw's

79

77

| EXIT 56 |
| Scotland Rd
Newbury
W. Newbury |

1

75

⛽ Prime D

| EXIT 55 |
| Central St
Byfield
Newbury |

✋ Maritime Museum>
(Customs House)

✕ General Store Eatery $
Parker River
Pub & Grill>

73

| EXIT 54 | 133 |
| Rowley
Georgetown |

71

65 mph

REST AREA

© 2010

15 MILE MARKERS

EXIT 53 97
Topsfield
Georgetown

1

70 —

EXIT 52
Topsfield Rd
Topsfield
Boxford

68 —

✕	Dunkin Donuts
Rx	CVS
🏠	Sheraton 🐾*i*

EXIT 51
Endicott Rd
Topsfield
Middleton

✕	Texas Roadhouse
Rx	CVS
🛒	Stop'n Shop

EXIT 50 1
Topsfield
Danvers

| ✕ | Four 66 Iron Chef |
| ⛽ | Gulf $, Mobil ($24) |

66 —

✕	Calitri's Italian Centre St Pizza
🛏	Comfort Inn*i* Motel 6 🐾*i* Extended Stay 🐾*i* Residence Inn 🐾*i* Towne Place 🐾*i*
🛒	Putnam Pantry Candies, Costco

EXIT 49 62
N Danvers
Middleton

EXIT 48
S Centre St
Danvers

64 —

| 🛒 | Union Jack |

EXIT 47 114
N Peabody
Middleton

✕	Bugaboo Creek Burger King, D'Angelo Macaroni Grill Market Basket McDonald's, Starbucks
⛽	Mobil, Shell $
🛏	Hilton Garden Inn Staybridge Suites
🛒	Trader Joe's

✕	Buffalo Bill's Dunkin Donuts Sunrise Pizza Subs Triple888 Vietnamese Thai, Fuji Sushi
⛽	Best D, Global Gas Gulf $, Sunoco D
🛏	Carriage House Plaza Motel *i*

EXIT 46 1
S Boston

62 —

1 **65 mph**

EXIT 45 128N
Gloucester
Left Exit
Northbound

✕	Bennigan's, Sonic Bertucci's, Wendy's Brothers Kouzina Carrabba's Italian Grill
⛽	7 Eleven Shell (D, R, $24)
🛏	Hampton*i* Holiday Inn*i* Homewood Suites 🐾*i* SpringHill Suites *i*

EXIT 44 1 129
Danvers
Boston
Everett
H

| ✕ | Karl's Sausage Kitchen Lynnfield Meat & Deli Polcari's Italian |

1

60 —

EXIT 43
Walnut St
Lynnfield
Saugus

| 🛏 | Sheraton 🐾*i* |

EXIT 42
Salem St
Wakefield

| ✕ | Montrose, Subway Dunkin Donuts |
| ⛽ | Sunoco ($24) |

58 —

H

EXIT 41
Main St
Lynnfield Ctr
Wakefield

✕	Meletharb Ice Cream Greg's Roast Beef Jade Gourmet
⛽	Shell (R, LP, $24)
🛒	Tedeschi Food

| ⛽ | Mobil $ |

EXIT 40 129
Wakefield Ctr
Wilmington

| ✕ | Bellino's Trattoria Gingerbread Construction Co Honeydew |

56 —

55 mph

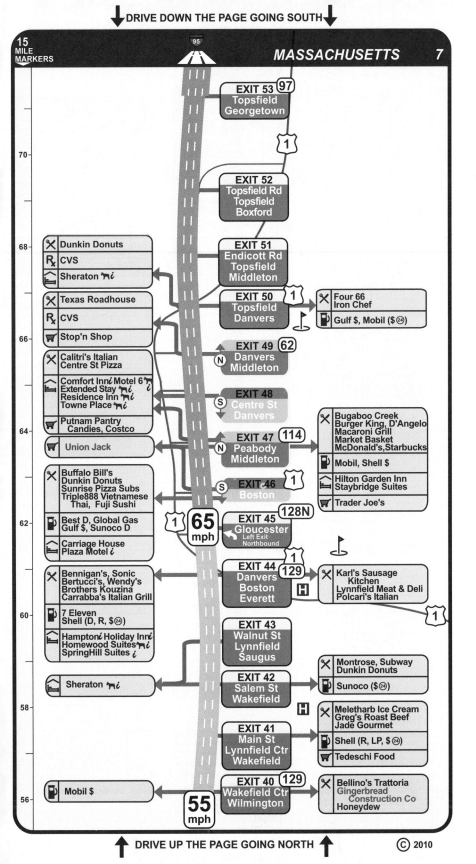

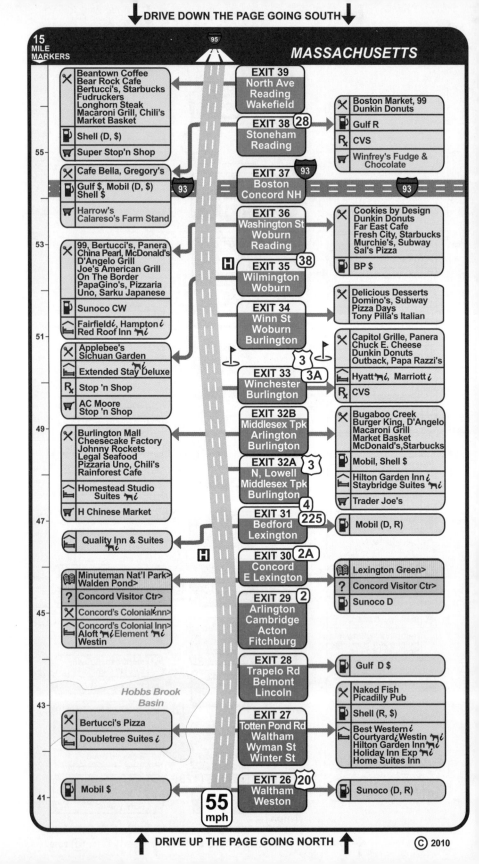

DRIVE DOWN THE PAGE GOING SOUTH

15 MILE MARKERS

MASSACHUSETTS

EXIT 39 North Ave Reading Wakefield
- Beantown Coffee, Bear Rock Cafe, Bertucci's, Starbucks, Fudruckers, Longhorn Steak, Macaroni Grill, Chili's, Market Basket
- Shell (D, $)
- Super Stop'n Shop

EXIT 38 (28) Stoneham Reading
- Boston Market, 99, Dunkin Donuts
- Gulf R
- CVS
- Winfrey's Fudge & Chocolate

EXIT 37 (93) Boston Concord NH
- Cafe Bella, Gregory's
- Gulf $, Mobil (D, $), Shell $
- Harrow's, Calareso's Farm Stand

EXIT 36 Washington St Woburn Reading
- Cookies by Design, Dunkin Donuts, Far East Cafe, Fresh City, Starbucks, Murchie's, Subway, Sal's Pizza
- BP $

EXIT 35 (38) Wilmington Woburn
- 99, Bertucci's, Panera, China Pearl, McDonald's, D'Angelo Grill, Joe's American Grill, On The Border, PapaGino's, Pizzaria Uno, Sarku Japanese
- Sunoco CW
- Fairfield i, Hampton i, Red Roof Inn

EXIT 34 Winn St Woburn Burlington
- Delicious Desserts, Domino's, Subway, Pizza Days, Tony Pilla's Italian

EXIT 33 (3A) Winchester Burlington
- Applebee's, Sichuan Garden
- Extended Stay Deluxe
- Stop 'n Shop
- AC Moore, Stop 'n Shop
- Capitol Grille, Panera, Chuck E. Cheese, Dunkin Donuts, Outback, Papa Razzi's
- Hyatt i, Marriott i
- CVS

EXIT 32B Middlesex Tpk Arlington Burlington
- Burlington Mall, Cheesecake Factory, Johnny Rockets, Legal Seafood, Pizzaria Uno, Chili's, Rainforest Cafe
- Bugaboo Creek, Burger King, D'Angelo, Macaroni Grill, Market Basket, McDonald's, Starbucks

EXIT 32A (3) N, Lowell Middlesex Tpk Burlington
- Homestead Studio Suites
- H Chinese Market
- Mobil, Shell $
- Hilton Garden Inn i, Staybridge Suites i
- Trader Joe's

EXIT 31 (4) (225) Bedford Lexington
- Quality Inn & Suites
- Mobil (D, R)

EXIT 30 (2A) Concord E Lexington
- Minuteman Nat'l Park>, Walden Pond>
- Concord Visitor Ctr>
- Concord's Colonial Inn>
- Concord's Colonial Inn>, Aloft i Element i, Westin
- Lexington Green>
- Concord Visitor Ctr>
- Sunoco D

EXIT 29 (2) Arlington Cambridge Acton Fitchburg

Hobbs Brook Basin

EXIT 28 Trapelo Rd Belmont Lincoln
- Gulf D $

EXIT 27 Totten Pond Rd Waltham Wyman St Winter St
- Bertucci's Pizza
- Doubletree Suites i
- Naked Fish, Picadilly Pub
- Shell (R, $)
- Best Western i, Courtyard i Westin i, Hilton Garden Inn i, Holiday Inn Exp i, Home Suites Inn

EXIT 26 (20) Waltham Weston
- Mobil $
- Sunoco (D, R)

55 mph

DRIVE UP THE PAGE GOING NORTH

© 2010

15 MILE MARKERS

95

MASSACHUSETTS

9

H

EXIT 25 90
Mass Pike

Charles River

90 90

EXIT 24 30
Newton 28
Waltham
Wayland

✕	Riverbend
⛽	Mobil R $
🏨	Marriott *i*
🚣	Charles River Canoe & Kayak

EXIT 23
Recreation Rd N

40

✕	99 Rest., Beacon's McDonald's (P) Dunkin Donuts Old Country Buffet Papa Gino's, Taco Bell

EXIT 22
Grove Street
M.B.T.A. Sta

🏨	Indigo 🛏*i*

S **NEWTON TRAVEL PLAZA**
MC, Honey Dew

EXIT 21 16
Newton
Wellesley
Washington St

H

⛽	Exxon R, Sunoco R

38

Charles River

EXIT 20 9
Boston
Worcester
Brookline

✕	Bickford's
🏨	Wingate 🛏*i*

36

EXIT 19
Highland Ave
Newton
Highlands
Needham

✕	Cookies by Design Mandarin Cuisine Mighty Subs, Panera d'Angelo
⛽	Hess
🏨	Sheraton Needham 🛏*i*

Cutler Lake

34

EXIT 18
Great Plain Ave
W Roxbury

H

EXIT 17 135
Needham
Natick

32

EXIT 16 109
Westwood
Dedham

✕	Bamboo, Chilis Bugaboo Creek Joe's, American Grill PF Chang's TGI Friday's
🏨	Fairfield *i* Holiday Inn *i* Residence Inn 🛏*i*
℞	CVS, Walgreens
🛒	Costco, Whole Foods

✕	Dunkin Donuts
⛽	Shell $
🏨	Budget Inn

30

EXIT 15 1
Norwood
Dedham

EXIT 14
East St
Canton St

🏨	Hilton

65 mph

EXIT 13
University
Ave

28

26

55 mph

© 2010

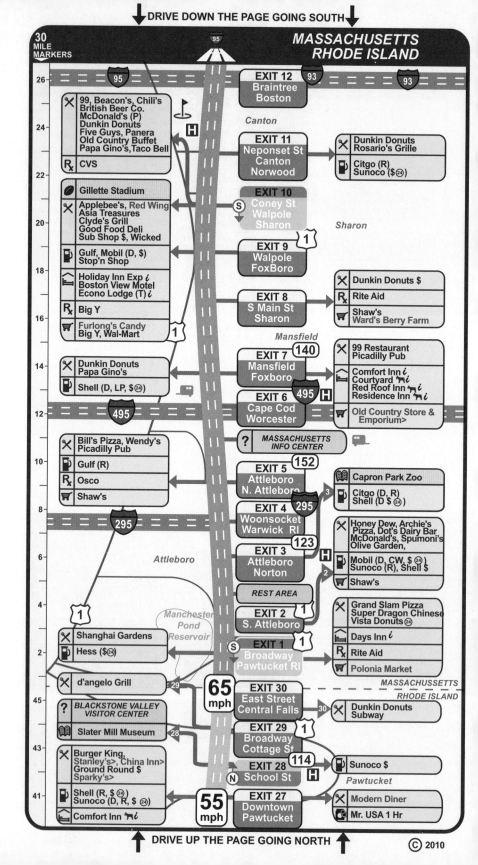

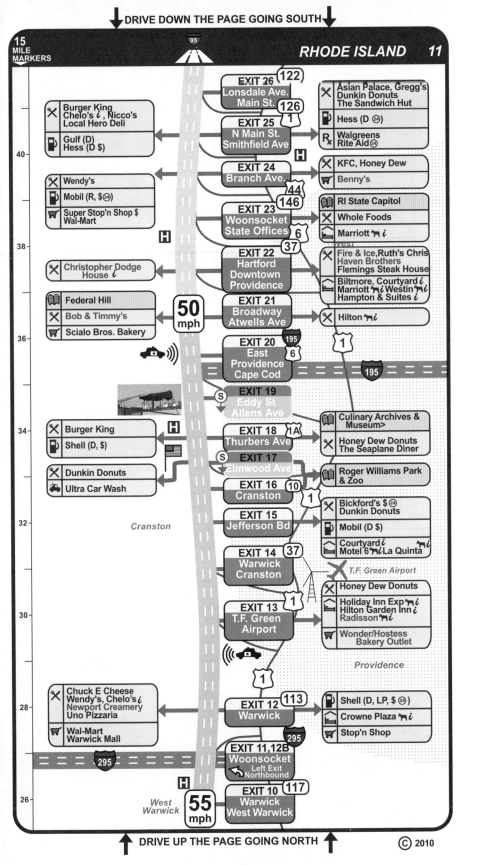

95

EXIT 26 122
Lonsdale Ave.
Main St.

EXIT 25 126 1
N Main St.
Smithfield Ave

Asian Palace, Gregg's
Dunkin Donuts
The Sandwich Hut

Hess (D 24)

Walgreens
Rite Aid 24

Burger King
Chelo's *i*, Nicco's
Local Hero Deli

Gulf (D)
Hess (D $)

H

40

EXIT 24 H
Branch Ave.

KFC, Honey Dew

Benny's

Wendy's

Mobil (R, $ 24)

Super Stop'n Shop $
Wal-Mart

EXIT 23 44 146
Woonsocket
State Offices 6 37

RI State Capitol

Whole Foods

Marriott 🛏 *i*

38

H

EXIT 22
Hartford
Downtown
Providence

West
Fire & Ice, Ruth's Chris
Haven Brothers
Flemings Steak House

Biltmore, Courtyard *i*
Marriott 🛏 *i* Westin 🛏 *i*
Hampton & Suites *i*

Christopher Dodge
House *i*

EXIT 21
Broadway
Atwells Ave

Hilton 🛏 *i*

Federal Hill

Bob & Timmy's

Scialo Bros. Bakery

50 mph

36

EXIT 20 195 6
East
Providence
Cape Cod

1

195

EXIT 19 S
Eddy St
Allens Ave

Culinary Archives &
Museum>

34

Burger King H

Shell (D, $)

EXIT 18 1A
Thurbers Ave

Honey Dew Donuts
The Seaplane Diner

Dunkin Donuts

Ultra Car Wash

EXIT 17 S
Elmwood Ave

EXIT 16 10
Cranston

Roger Williams Park
& Zoo

1

Cranston

32

EXIT 15
Jefferson Bd

Bickford's $ 24
Dunkin Donuts

Mobil (D $)

Courtyard *i*
Motel 6 🛏 *i* La Quinta 🛏 *i*

EXIT 14 37
Warwick
Cranston

✕ *T.F. Green Airport*

EXIT 13 1
T.F. Green
Airport

Honey Dew Donuts

Holiday Inn Exp 🛏 *i*
Hilton Garden Inn *i*
Radisson 🛏 *i*

Wonder/Hostess
Bakery Outlet

30

Providence

1

Chuck E Cheese
Wendy's, Chelo's *i*
Newport Creamery
Uno Pizzaria

Wal-Mart
Warwick Mall

EXIT 12 113
Warwick

Shell (D, LP, $ 24)

Crowne Plaza 🛏 *i*

Stop'n Shop

28

295

EXIT 11,12B
Woonsocket
⬅ Left Exit
Northbound

295

H

West Warwick

55 mph

EXIT 10 117
Warwick
West Warwick

26

© 2010

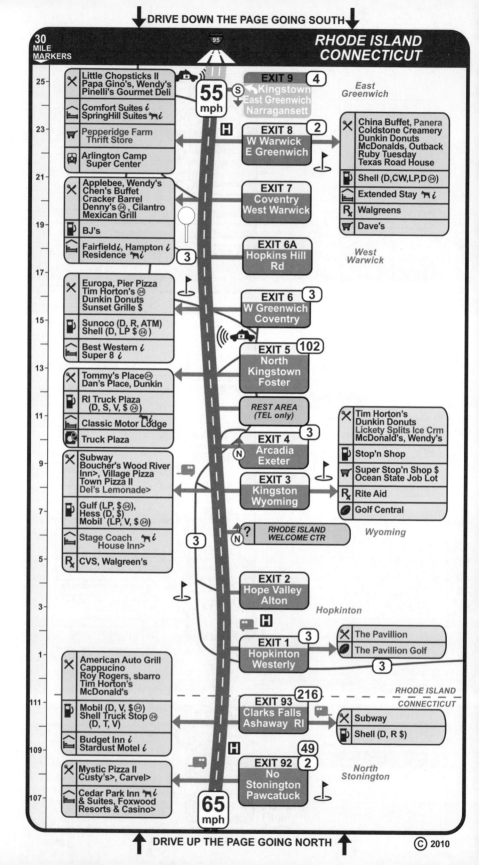

95

North Stonington

S ? CONNECTICUT WELCOME CENTER

1

106

Long Island

Sound

104

EXIT 91 234
No Main St
Stonington
Borough

✕ Noah's>

WEIGH STATION

? Mystic Tourist Info

📖 Mystic Seaport
Mystic Aquarium

✕ Ancient Mariner>
Starbucks, Friendly's
Equinox Diner, Five
Guys, Peking Tokyo
Go Fish, Steak Loft
Jamms Seafood
Kitchen Little>
McDonald's, Azu>
Capt Daniel Parker
Inne>, Mystic Pizza>

Mystic

102

✕ Dunkin Donuts
Starbucks, Subway
Thai One On

⛽ Shell ($ CW 24)

🏨 Best Western
Comfort Inn 🐾i
Days Inn i
Hampton Suites 🐾i
Residence Inn 🐾i

EXIT 90 27
Mystic

Mystic River

⛽ Mobil (D, $ 24)

🏨 Hyatt Place i Hilton 🏨
Howard Johnson i i
Econo Lodge 🐾i
Holiday Inn Exp
Whaler's Inn>

100

✕ Starbucks

🏨 Mystic Marriott i

EXIT 89
Allyn Street

🛒 Olde Mistick Village $
Franklin's Gen. Store

📖 USS Nautilus Mus.>

✕ Chinese Kitchen
Clam Bar, Taco Bell
NY Pizza, Village Inn
Russell's Ribs
KFC, Mirch Masala
Sal's Diner,Flanagan's
Groton Town House 24

⛽ Cory's (D,$ 24), Hess
Shell (D,$ 24)

🏨 Best Western i Super 8
Gold Star Motor Lodge
Groton Inn & Suites i
Hilton Garden Inn i
Days Inn & Suites i
Ramada 🐾i Windsor

🛒 Super Stop'n Shop $
Walmart

EXIT 88 117
Noank Groton
Long Point

H

1

98

65 mph

1

EXIT 87
Clarence B
Sharp Hwy
↰ Left Exit
Southbound

349

Groton
New England
Airport

✕ Applebee's, Olio, 99
Koto Japanese

🏨 Knights Inn i, Quality i
Hampton Inn i

🎳 Holiday Bowl

EXIT 86 184
US Sub Base 12
Gales Ferry

96

Groton

Thames River

✕ Portuguese Fisherman
Mr G's Pizza, New China
DJ's Campus Kitchen

⛽ Citgo (D, K, LP, $)
Shell (D, $)
Sunoco $

EXIT 85 1
Thames St
Downtown
Groton

🖐 Fort Griswold
Battlefield State Pk>

94

✕ Chili's, Golden Wok
Chucky Cheese
Outback

⛽ Sunoco ($ 24)

🏨 Holiday 🐾i Red Roof i
Red Carpet 🐾i
SpringHill Suites i

🛒 AC Moore,Shoprite
New London Mall

EXIT 84 32
Downtown
New London
Norwich

📖 Nathan Hale
Schoolhouse>

✕ Zavala>

🏨 Radisson> i

H

EXIT 83 32
Frontage Rd
Downtown
New London

92

55 mph

Long Island Sound

© 2010

DRIVE DOWN THE PAGE GOING SOUTH

15 MILE MARKERS

95

CONNECTICUT

EXIT 82A
Frontage Rd
New London

Chili's, Golden Wok
Chucky Cheese
Outback, Wendy's

Sunoco ($ 24)
Mobil (LP, $ 24)

Holiday Inn, Red Roof
Red Carpet
SpringHill Suites

AC Moore, Shoprite
Crystal Mall

Pizza Hut

Mobil ($, CW 24)

NSA Supermarket
Arrow Paper Party
Store

H

85

EXIT 82
Broad St
Waterford

Long Island

EXIT 81
Cross Rd

Sound

395

81

S

EXIT 80
Oil Mill Rd

Niantic River

395

Rodeway (T, V)

Wal-Mart

EXIT 76
Norwich
Plainfield

N

Children's Museum of
SE CT>

EXIT 75
Waterford

1

S

Flanders Fish, Frank's
Gourmet Grille
Flanders Pizza
King's Garden
McDonald's, Yummy
Pizza, The Shack
Nanami Japanese
Pizza Cuccina
Smokey O'Grady's

Shell (CW)

TriTown Foods

CVS, Rita Aid

Golf Driving Range

161

EXIT 74
Flanders
Niantic

Bickford's, KFC
Burger King (P)
Illiano's Grill, Starbucks
Shoreline Family Rest.

Mobil ($ 24), Citgo ($)
Corey's (D, R)

Best Value Inn
Hilltop, Days Inn
Motel 6
Sleep Inn & Suites

Super Stop'n Shop

Super Stop'n Shop

55 mph

East Lyme

1

EXIT 73
Society Rd

EXIT 72
Rocky Neck
State Park

Rocky Neck State Pk
(Beach)

EXIT 71
Four Mile
River Road

Long Island Sound

Florence Griswold
Museum

Boom, Hideaway
Andy's Deli, Subway
Hong Kong II Chinese
Old Lyme Inn
Koffee Works
Pizzeria Da Vinci

Shell (D, $)

Old Lyme Inn

Rite Aid

A & P

Old Lyme

1

156

EXIT 70
Old Lyme

Connecticut River

Otter Cove Restaurant

Comfort Inn

S

9

EXIT 69
Essex
Hartford

65 mph

DRIVE UP THE PAGE GOING NORTH

© 2010

DRIVE DOWN THE PAGE GOING SOUTH

95

CONNECTICUT 15

15 MILE MARKERS

	Cloud 9 Deli
	Citgo (D, CW), Irving, Mobil (LP)
EXIT 68 (S) Old Saybrook (1)	Burger King (P), Bella Sera Italian, Monkey Farm Cafe, Pasta Vista, Bagelz, Pat's Kountry Kitchen
EXIT 67 Old Saybrook Elm St (154)	Pizzaworks, Pizza Hut, Subway, Zhang's, Starbucks
	Gulf (D, K, R), Mercury, Sunoco $
	Executive Inn & Suites
EXIT 66 Spencer Plain Road (166)	Aleia's Bakery, Kumari, Alforno Pizza, Mindy K, Cuckoo's Nest Mexican, Pizza Palace, Luigi's, Tiberio's, Samurai Hibachi, Paesan's Pizza, Saigon City, Tiberio's
(N) CONNECTICUT WELCOME CENTER	
EXIT 65 Westbrook (153)	Citgo (D $), Days Inn, Super 8, EconoLodge, Benny's
EXIT 64 Horse Hill Road (145)	Cristy's, Cafe Routier, Denny's, Subway, Lenny & Joe's>, Cheryl's Corner Cafe, The Whole Enchilada, Westbrook Pizza
	Mobil (LP $ 24), Valero (LP $ 24), Westbrook Inn> i, Walgreen's, Tanger Outlet Center, Westbrook Antiques
63	Shell (D, LP, $24)
	Hammonasset Beach State Park
EXIT 62 Hammonasset State Park	Lenny & Joe's Fish Tale>
MADISON SERVICE AREA: Mcdonald's 24, Mobil (D 24)	
EXIT 61 Madison N Madison (79)	Cafe Allegre, Dunkin Donuts, Village Pizza, Starbucks, Subway, Savvy Tea Gourmet, Willoughby's Coffee, Gulf (LP), Shell $, Sunoco (R), CVS, Stop'n Shop
EXIT 60 (S) Mungertown Rd	Boss Pizza & Sub, First Garden Chinese, McDonald's, Wendy's, Nick & Tony's Apizza, Shoreline Diner, The Whole Enchilada, Dunkin Donuts, Citgo $, Shell (D $ 24), Mobil (LP $ 24)
EXIT 59 Goose Lane Guilford	Comfort Inn i

Cold Stone Creamery, Dunkin Donuts, Clinton Crossing Premium Outlets

EXIT 63 Clinton Killingworth (81)

65 mph

DRIVE UP THE PAGE GOING NORTH

© 2010

CONNECTICUT

DRIVE DOWN THE PAGE GOING SOUTH

15 MILE MARKERS

I-95

CONNECTICUT

EXIT 58 — **77** — Guilford North Guilford

EXIT 57 — Boston Post Rd

Long Island Sound

Guilford

- Henry Whitfield House>
- Ashley's Ice Crm Cafe, Guilford Bistro & Grille, C&C Pizza, Subway, The Place (seasonal), Friendly's, Naples Pizza
- BP $, Sunoco (D $), Hess (LP, $), Mobil (LP, $, CW ㉔)
- CVS, Rite Aid, Walgreens
- Foodworks, Candy Shop, Big Y, Wal-Mart
- 57 — Bishop's Orchards
- 56 — Rodeway Inn & Suites

Chowder Pot III, Friendly's, Popeye's, Subway, Starbucks, Willoughby's Coffee

Sunoco (D, $, K, BP), Mobil (CW ㉔), T/A Travel Ctr (TR㉔)

Amer. Best Value, Baymont & Suites

Stop'n Shop $

Stop'n Shop

Hoadley Creek

EXIT 56 — Leetes Is Rd Stony Creek

- Hole in the Wall, Lyn's Deli, Marco Pizza
- Branford Auto Ctr (R, $)
- Motel 6, Holiday Inn Exp
- Walgreens

Brothers Deli/Pizza, Gourmet Wok, Chuck's, Margarita's Grill, Parthenon Diner (ATM ㉔), Su Casa Mexican

Mobil (CW, D, LP $ ㉔), Exxon (D, $)

Days Inn

EXIT 55 — North Branford East Main St — **1**

Lake Saltonstall

65 mph

EXIT 54 — Branford Cedar St.

- Branford Townhouse, Dragon East, La Luna, Lenny's Indian Head>
- Citgo (R, D), Mobil ($, CW ㉔), Petrol Plus (R, U-Haul)

Born in America Pizza, Lion City Chinese

Brushy Hill Laundry

Krauszer's

Branford

BRANFORD SERVICE AREA
- McDonald's ㉔
- Mobil ㉔

- China Garden Buffet, Jersey Mike Subs, Kampai Japanese, Lo Monaco Italian, Moon Star, KFC, Siam Orchid Thai, Taco Bell, Pizza Wings, Quizno's, Starbucks, Subway, Wendy's

EXIT 53 — Short Beach — **1** — **142**
- Lukoil

East Haven

50 mph

EXIT 52 — East Haven No High St — **100** — **1**
- CVS, Walgreen's
- A & P ㉔, Wal-Mart

Tweed-New Haven Airport

EXIT 51 — East Haven Frontage Rd

F.J. Soleo's Italian, King China Buffet, RJ's Lunch, Wendy's

Forbes $

I-91

- Shore Line Trolley Museum>
- Boston Market, Chili's, Friendly's, Grace's Kitchen>
- Hess (D), Sunoco $ ㉔
- Quality Inn
- Xpect Discount

EXIT 50 — Woodward Ave Lighthouse Pt

EXIT 49 — Stiles St

A Touch of Ireland>

EXIT 48 — Hartford — **91** — Left Exit Northbound

EXIT 47 — Downtown New Haven — **34** — Left Exit Northbound

Yale University, Yale Ctr for British Art, Peabody Museum, Center Church on the Green

Frank Pepe's Libby's, Louis Lunch, Sally's Bentara

New Haven

EXIT 46 — Long Wharf Drive Sargent Drive

- Tourist Info (Seasonal)
- Food Trucks, Leon's

Brazi's Italian, Dunkin Donuts, Greek Olive, Johnny Salamis & Subs

Mobil (D, ATM, CW㉔)

La Quinta Premier Hotel & Suites >

IKEA

New Haven Harbor

55 mph

DRIVE UP THE PAGE GOING NORTH

© 2010

15 MILE MARKERS

CONNECTICUT 17

95

1

EXIT 45 10
Boulevard

EXIT 44 10
Kimberly Ave

West Haven

EXIT 43
Downtown West Haven

EXIT 42 162
Saw Mill Rd

EXIT 41
Marsh Hill Rd Orange

ORANGE SERVICE AREA
McDonald's (24) Original Pizza of Boston, Lavazza
Mobil (D 24)

EXIT 40
Old Gate Lane Woodmont Rd

EXIT 39
Milford

EXIT 38
Merritt Pkwy W Cross Pkwy

EXIT 37
High Street

EXIT 36
Plains Rd

EXIT 35
School House Rd Bic Drive

EXIT 34 1
Milford

EXIT 33 1 110
Ferry Blvd Devon

EXIT 32
W. Broad St Stratford

Stratford

EXIT 31
Honeyspot Rd

55 mph

West side (northbound listings)

- Dairy Queen, McDonald's (24), Tropical Krust, TownHouse Pizza
- Getty (ATM 24)
- China Sea, Salvadoreno
- First Fuel (D $), Xtra Gas $
- Krauszer's
- American Steak, Denny's, Dan's, Uncle Willie's BBQ, Friendly's, Subway, Texas Roadhouse
- Shell (LP $ 24)
- Best Western, Hampton Inn
- Wal-Mart
- On the Border, Outback Steak
- Courtyard
- AC Moore Arts & Crafts, Christmas Tree Shops
- Burger King, Panera, Hometown Buffet, Starbucks, Moe's, McDonald's (24), Arbys
- Mobil ($ CW)
- Rite Aid
- Fabric Factory Outlet, Westfield Mall, Wal-Mart, Honey-baked Ham
- Red Roof Inn, Residence Inn, SpringHill Suites
- Hong Kong Tokyo, McDonalds, Villa Pizza, 99
- Shaw's
- Shaw's, Wal-Mart
- Nat'l Helicopter Museum
- Dunkin Donuts, Acropolis Pizza
- Cumberland ($ 24)
- Hudson Paper Company Outlet
- Johnny's, Joe's Diner
- Citgo (D, R)
- VIP Car Wash

East side (southbound listings)

- Carvel, Panda House, Captain's Galley, Lorenzo's, Elm Diner, Nick's Luncheonette
- Sunoco (R 24), Citgo (24)
- Super 8
- Rite Aid
- Krauszer's
- Pizza Works, Saray, W Haven Duchess (24)
- King Chef, Pizza Palace
- Mobil (LP $ 24)
- EconoLodge
- Indian & Asian Groc.
- d'angelo, Gipper's, Cracker Barrel, Duchess, Wendy's (24)
- Sunoco $ (24), Pilot Truck Ctr (D 24), Secondi Citgo Plaza (D, TW 24), Shell ($ CW 24)
- Hilton Garden Quality, Mayflower Motel, Hyatt Place Milford Inn
- Original Toy Company
- Athenian Diner (24), Bella Napoli, Hooters, Friendly's, Pizzaria Uno
- Cumberland (24)
- Hwd Johnson Super 8
- Milford Green
- Pasquale, Subway, Rainbow Gardens, Gusto, The Corner
- Mobil (D, $, LP 24), Sunoco (D $)
- Hampton Inn
- Armellino's, Wendy's
- Citgo (LP)
- Fairfield Inn
- Ming Feng, bin100, Waterview Lunch, McDonald's (P,$ 24), Pizza Hut, Taco Bell, Bridgport Flyer (24)
- Angelo's Auto Ctr (D, R), Getty (D, $, LP)
- Devon Motel
- Walgreens
- Krauszer's $, WalMart, Ocean State Job Lot
- Danny's, Harborside, Assaggio, Subway
- Sunoco (R, LP 24)
- Gaetano's, Duchess Diner (24), Pickle Barrel, Zap's Pizza
- Gulf $
- Comfort Suites
- Stratford Antique Ctr

© 2010

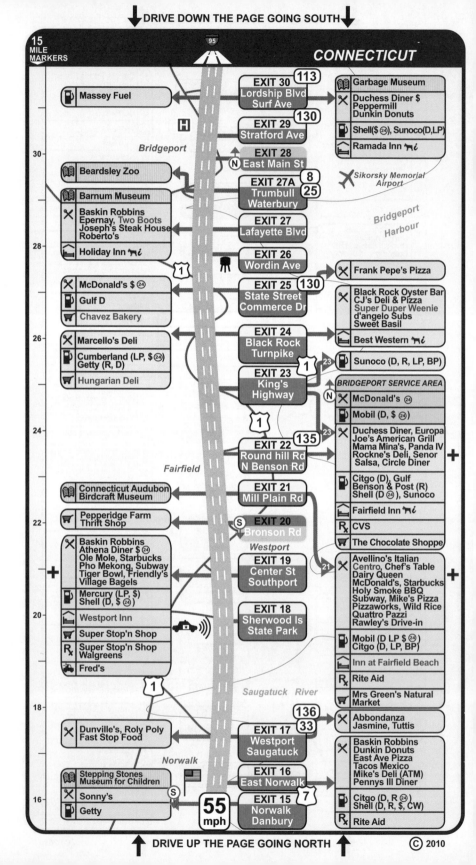

Norwalk
Harbor

Stepping Stones Museum for Children

Norwalk

Maritime Aquarium>

Bagelz, Dunkin Donuts Cosmo's, Sonny's Post Rd Diner, India House, Victoria's Deli Silver Star Diner $ Swanky Franks

EXIT 14 1
South Norwalk
Connecticut Ave

Celentano's Italian Cross Roads Pizza Dunkin Donuts El Charro, Kazu New Jade Lee

BP(D, $ 24), Getty C Gas (R $), Shell Sunoco (D, R, $)

Shell $ 24

Carvel, Pasta Fair Bertucci's Pizza, KFC Darien Diner, Centro McDonald's (P24)

EXIT 13 1
Post Road

DARIEN SERVICE AREA

Sunoco, Shell Mobil (R, LP, $)

EXIT 12 136
N Tokeneke Rd Rowayton

? CT Welcome Center

N McDonald's(P) +more

Doubletree i

Mobil (D 24)

Wal-Mart, Shoprite, Costco

Gofer Ice Cream Panera, Uncle's Deli Ching's Kitchen

EXIT 11 1
Boston Post Rd
Darien
Rowayton

Chuck's Steak House

BP (D $)

Gulf (R, LP)

EXIT 10
Noroton

S SERVICE AREA

CVS, Grieb's

McDonald's (P)

Standard (D, $) Shell (CW,$), BP (R,LP)

H

EXIT 9
Glenbrook

106 1

Mobil (D 24)

Water's Edge Smokey Joe's BBQ

Exit 9 Bagels, Stamford Pizza, McDonalds $ 24 Mi Terruno Stamford Rest & Pizza

Stamford

America's Best Value Stamford Motor Lodge

Gulf (LP, $ 24)

EXIT 8
Atlantic St
Elm St

Juliska Cafe Chef's Diner, Subway

Villa Italia, Taco Bell

Stamford Antique Area

Marriott i Holiday i

EXIT 7 137
Greenwich
Avenue

Hilton i

Hoyt Barnum House

Shell (D 24)

EXIT 6
Harvard Ave
West Ave

City Limits Diner

Super 8 i

H

Gulf (CW)

Baang Cafe, Tandoori McDonald's $ PieSano's Pizza Pomodoro Pizza Riverside Deli, Yangtze Hunan Cafe, Starbucks

EXIT 5 1
Riverside
Old
Greenwich

La Quinta Inn & Suites

Greenwich

Mobil (D, LP, $ 24) Getty $

CVS 24, Walgreen 24

EXIT 4
Indian Field
Rd
Cos Cob

Cos Cob
Harbor

A&P, Balducci's

Laundromat

H

Bush-Holley Historic Site

EXIT 3
Arch St
Greenwich

Bruce Museum of Arts and Science

Mobil

BSF Burgers Firehouse Deli Greenwich Lobster House, Fuzari's Pizza Vinnie's Lunch

1

**WEIGH
N STATION**

EXIT 2
Delavan Ave
Byram

Steilmann Ladies' European Fashion Costco

55 mph

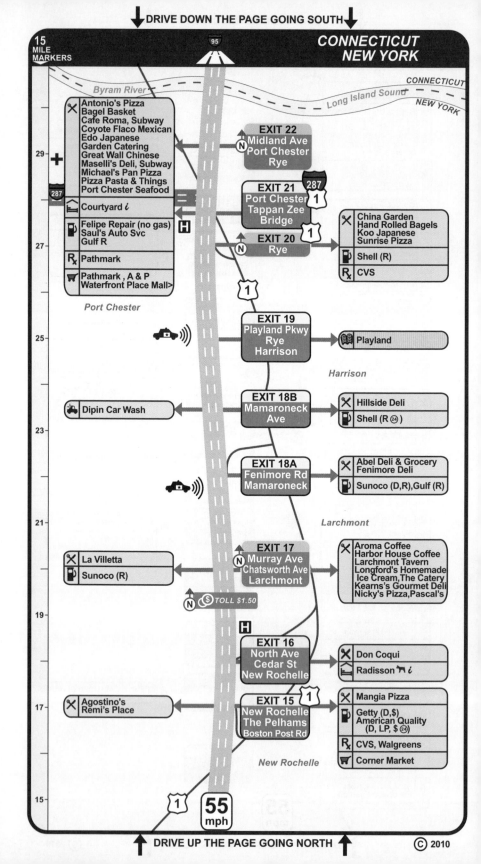

DRIVE DOWN THE PAGE GOING SOUTH

95

CONNECTICUT NEW YORK

15 MILE MARKERS

Byram River

CONNECTICUT

Long Island Sound

NEW YORK

29

287

Antonio's Pizza
Bagel Basket
Cafe Roma, Subway
Coyote Flaco Mexican
Edo Japanese
Garden Catering
Great Wall Chinese
Maselli's Deli, Subway
Michael's Pan Pizza
Pizza Pasta & Things
Port Chester Seafood

Courtyard *i*

Felipe Repair (no gas)
Saul's Auto Svc
Gulf R

Pathmark

Pathmark , A & P
Waterfront Place Mall>

Port Chester

EXIT 22
Midland Ave
Port Chester
Rye

EXIT 21
Port Chester
Tappan Zee
Bridge

287 1

1

EXIT 20
Rye

China Garden
Hand Rolled Bagels
Koo Japanese
Sunrise Pizza

Shell (R)

CVS

27

H

1

25

EXIT 19
Playland Pkwy
Rye
Harrison

Playland

Harrison

Dipin Car Wash

EXIT 18B
Mamaroneck
Ave

Hillside Deli

Shell (R 24)

23

EXIT 18A
Fenimore Rd
Mamaroneck

Abel Deli & Grocery
Fenimore Deli

Sunoco (D,R),Gulf (R)

21

Larchmont

La Villetta

Sunoco (R)

EXIT 17
Murray Ave
Chatsworth Ave
Larchmont

Aroma Coffee
Harbor House Coffee
Larchmont Tavern
Longford's Homemade
Ice Cream,The Catery
Kearns's Gourmet Deli
Nicky's Pizza,Pascal's

19

TOLL $1.50

H

EXIT 16
North Ave
Cedar St
New Rochelle

Don Coqui

Radisson *i*

17

Agostino's
Remi's Place

EXIT 15
New Rochelle
The Pelhams
Boston Post Rd

1

Mangia Pizza

Getty (D,$)
American Quality
(D, LP, $ 24)

CVS, Walgreens

Corner Market

New Rochelle

15

1

55 mph

DRIVE UP THE PAGE GOING NORTH

© 2010

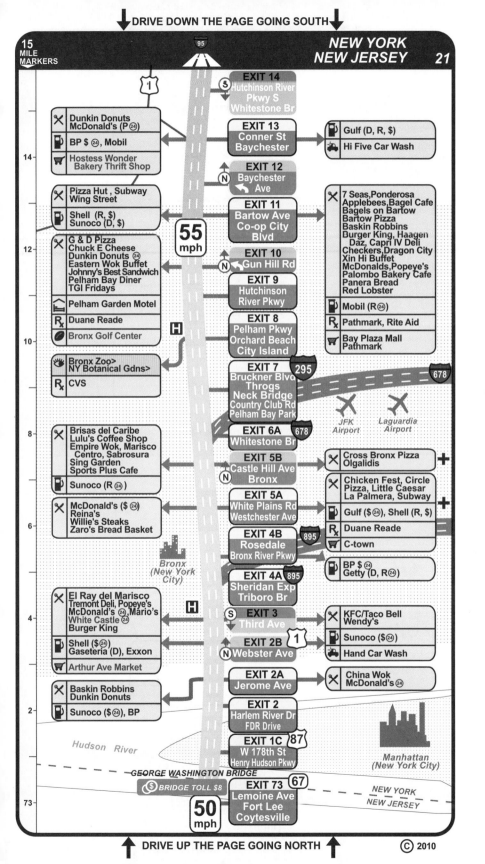

EXIT 14
Hutchinson River Pkwy S
Whitestone Br

Dunkin Donuts
McDonald's (P 24)
BP $ 24, Mobil
Hostess Wonder Bakery Thrift Shop

EXIT 13
Conner St
Baychester

Gulf (D, R, $)
Hi Five Car Wash

EXIT 12
Baychester Ave

Pizza Hut , Subway
Wing Street
Shell (R, $)
Sunoco (D, $)

EXIT 11
Bartow Ave
Co-op City Blvd

7 Seas, Ponderosa
Applebees, Bagel Cafe
Bagels on Bartow
Bartow Pizza
Baskin Robbins
Burger King, Haagen Daz, Capri IV Deli
Checkers, Dragon City
Xin Hi Buffet
McDonalds, Popeye's
Palombo Bakery Cafe
Panera Bread
Red Lobster

55 mph

EXIT 10
Gun Hill Rd

G & D Pizza
Chuck E Cheese
Dunkin Donuts 24
Eastern Wok Buffet
Johnny's Best Sandwich
Pelham Bay Diner
TGI Fridays
Pelham Garden Motel
Duane Reade
Bronx Golf Center

EXIT 9
Hutchinson River Pkwy

Mobil (R 24)
Pathmark, Rite Aid
Bay Plaza Mall
Pathmark

EXIT 8
Pelham Pkwy
Orchard Beach
City Island

H

Bronx Zoo>
NY Botanical Gdns>
CVS

EXIT 7
Bruckner Blvd
Throgs Neck Bridge
Country Club Rd
Pelham Bay Park

295

678

JFK Airport

Laguardia Airport

EXIT 6A
Whitestone Br

678

Brisas del Caribe
Lulu's Coffee Shop
Empire Wok, Marisco Centro, Sabrosura
Sing Garden
Sports Plus Cafe
Sunoco (R 24)

EXIT 5B
Castle Hill Ave
Bronx

Cross Bronx Pizza
Olgalidis

EXIT 5A
White Plains Rd
Westchester Ave

Chicken Fest, Circle Pizza, Little Caesar
La Palmera, Subway
Gulf ($ 24), Shell (R, $)
Duane Reade
C-town

McDonald's ($ 24)
Reina's
Willie's Steaks
Zaro's Bread Basket

EXIT 4B
Rosedale
Bronx River Pkwy

895

BP $ 24
Getty (D, R 24)

EXIT 4A
Sheridan Exp
Triboro Br

895

Bronx
(New York City)

H

El Ray del Marisco
Tremont Deli, Popeye's
McDonald's 24, Mario's
White Castle
Burger King
Shell ($ 24)
Gaseteria (D), Exxon
Arthur Ave Market

EXIT 3
Third Ave

S

KFC/Taco Bell
Wendy's
Sunoco ($ 24)
Hand Car Wash

EXIT 2B
Webster Ave

N

1

EXIT 2A
Jerome Ave

China Wok
McDonald's 24

Baskin Robbins
Dunkin Donuts
Sunoco ($ 24), BP

EXIT 2
Harlem River Dr
FDR Drive

Hudson River

EXIT 1C
W 178th St
Henry Hudson Pkwy

87

Manhattan
(New York City)

GEORGE WASHINGTON BRIDGE

BRIDGE TOLL $8

NEW YORK
NEW JERSEY

EXIT 73
Lemoine Ave
Fort Lee
Coytesville

67

50 mph

73

© 2010

DRIVE DOWN THE PAGE GOING SOUTH

15 MILE MARKERS
95
NEW JERSEY
80
EXIT 72
9
1
4
Fort Lee
Palisades Pwy
Fort Lee
H
EXIT 71
N
Broad Ave
Leonia
Engelwood
71
Teaneck Creek Conservancy
Marriott
EXIT 70
93
Leonia
Teaneck
9
EXIT 69
80 West
Left Exit Northbound
1
Hackensack
69
EXIT 68
Challenger Rd
Hackensack River
EXIT 18
46
Fort Lee
GW Bridge
Hackensack
116
?
VINCE LOMBARDI SERVICE AREA
Burger King, Nathan's
Cinnabon, TCBY
Popeye's
Sunoco (D24)
114
S
EXIT 17
3
Lincoln Tunnel
Secaucus
1
112
Secaucus
Meadowlands Sports Complex
Homestead Studio Suites, Courtyard
Radisson Suites
Secaucus Outlet Ctr
55 mph
EXIT 16E
3
Lincoln Tunnel
Secaucus
McDonalds (P)
Coach House Diner
Getty (LP)
Days Inn, Super 8
Holiday Inn Express
110
TOLL
ALEXANDER HAMILTON SERVICE AREA
S
Roy Rogers
Carvel
Sunoco (D24)
108
EXIT 15X
Secaucus Junction
SECAUCUS
EXIT 15
1
9
Newark
Jersey City
1
106
65 mph
Kearney

DRIVE UP THE PAGE GOING NORTH

© 2010

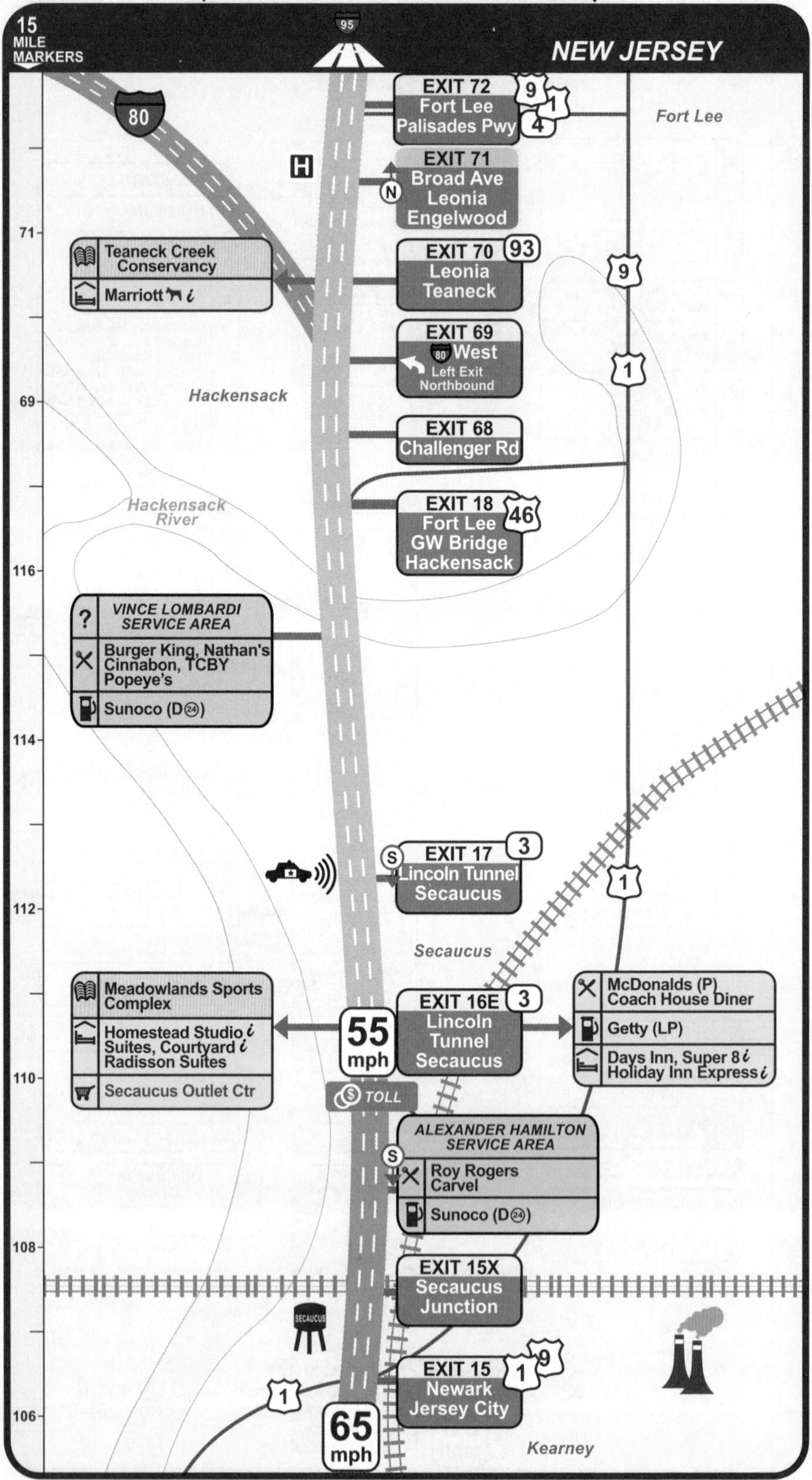

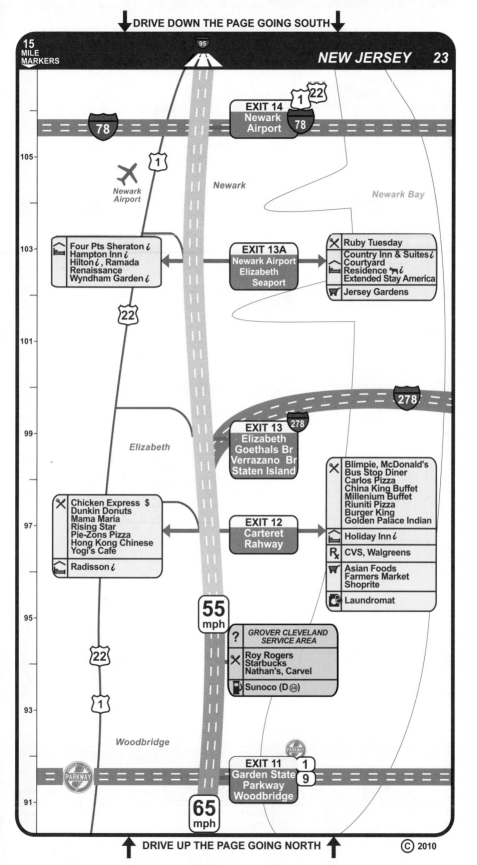

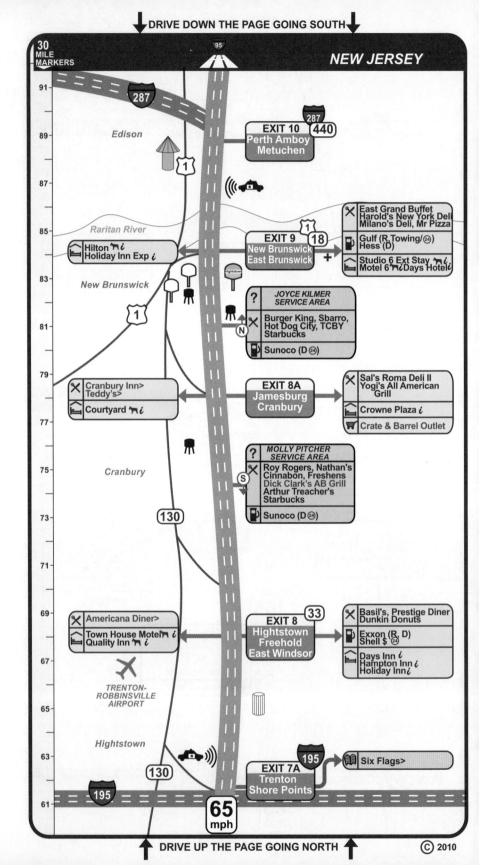

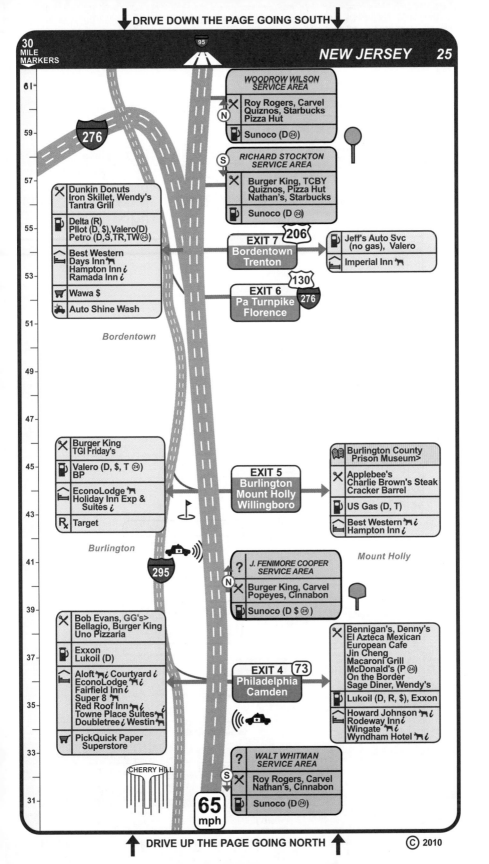

I-95

61 –
59 –

I-276

57 –
55 –
53 –
51 –
49 –
47 –
45 –
43 –
41 –
39 –
37 –
35 –
33 –
31 –

WOODROW WILSON SERVICE AREA
(N) ✕ Roy Rogers, Carvel
Quiznos, Starbucks
Pizza Hut
⛽ Sunoco (D 24)

RICHARD STOCKTON SERVICE AREA
(S) ✕ Burger King, TCBY
Quiznos, Pizza Hut
Nathan's, Starbucks
⛽ Sunoco (D 24)

✕ Dunkin Donuts
Iron Skillet, Wendy's
Tantra Grill
⛽ Delta (R)
Pilot (D, $), Valero (D)
Petro (D,S,TR,TW 24)
🛏 Best Western
Days Inn
Hampton Inn *i*
Ramada Inn *i*
🛒 Wawa $
🚗 Auto Shine Wash

Bordentown

EXIT 7 206
Bordentown
Trenton

⛽ Jeff's Auto Svc
(no gas), Valero
🛏 Imperial Inn

EXIT 6 130
Pa Turnpike 276
Florence

✕ Burger King
TGI Friday's
⛽ Valero (D, $, T 24)
BP
🛏 EconoLodge
Holiday Inn Exp &
Suites *i*
Rx Target

Burlington

I-295

EXIT 5
Burlington
Mount Holly
Willingboro

📖 Burlington County
Prison Museum>
✕ Applebee's
Charlie Brown's Steak
Cracker Barrel
⛽ US Gas (D, T)
🛏 Best Western *i*
Hampton Inn *i*

Mount Holly

J. FENIMORE COOPER SERVICE AREA
(N) ✕ Burger King, Carvel
Popeyes, Cinnabon
⛽ Sunoco (D $ 24)

✕ Bob Evans, GG's>
Bellagio, Burger King
Uno Pizzaria
⛽ Exxon
Lukoil (D)
🛏 Aloft *i* Courtyard *i*
EconoLodge *i*
Fairfield Inn *i*
Super 8
Red Roof Inn *i*
Towne Place Suites *i*
Doubletree *i* Westin
🛒 PickQuick Paper
Superstore

EXIT 4 73
Philadelphia
Camden

✕ Bennigan's, Denny's
El Azteca Mexican
European Cafe
Jin Cheng
Macaroni Grill
McDonald's (P 24)
On the Border
Sage Diner, Wendy's
⛽ Lukoil (D, R, $), Exxon
🛏 Howard Johnson *i*
Rodeway Inn *i*
Wingate *i*
Wyndham Hotel *i*

CHERRY HILL

WALT WHITMAN SERVICE AREA
(S) ✕ Roy Rogers, Carvel
Nathan's, Cinnabon
⛽ Sunoco (D 24)

65 mph

© 2010

↓ DRIVE DOWN THE PAGE GOING SOUTH ↓

30 MILE MARKERS

NEW JERSEY

95

31 —

Bellmawr

295

29 —
- Adventure Aquarium>
- Battleship New Jersey Museum>

EXIT 3 168
Camden
Philadelphia
Atlantic City

- Philly Diner
- Gulf (D, R, TR ㉔) Wawa ㉔
- Comfort Inn Holiday Inn *i*
- CVS ㉔

27 —
- Dunkin Donuts ㉔
- Italia Pizza, Wendy's
- Club Diner ㉔
- Primo Hoagies
- San Pedro Tierra Mexican
- Yummy Yummy Chinese

25 —
- Citgo (D, R)
- Shell (D, $ ㉔)
- Bellmawr Motor Inn *i*
- EconoLodge *i*
- Howard Johnson *i*
- Red Roof Inn *i*
- Super 8 *i*

23 —
- Walgreens ㉔
- Laundromat

21 —

Beaver Brook

19 —

Runnemede Lake

17 —

15 —
- Dunkin Donuts
- Shell (D, $ ㉔)
- Fresh Farm Stand (seasonal)

EXIT 2 322
Swedesboro
Chester, Pa

13 —

Swedesboro

295

JOHN FENWICK SERVICE AREA
- Burger King, Starbucks Nathans, TCBY
- Sunoco (D ㉔)

11 —

9 —
- Arthur Treachers
- Country Market Buffet
- Dunkin Donuts
- Magic Dragon
- Pepperoni's, Subway

CLARA BARTON SERVICE AREA
- Burger King, Cinnabon Nathans, Pizza Hut, TCBY
- Sunoco (D ㉔)

7 —
- Gulf (D)
- Coastal (D, K, LP, $)
- All American Plaza
- Valero (D,$,TR ㉔)
- Flying J Conoco (D, BP, $,RVD ㉔ *i*)
- Pilot Truck Stop (D, BP, $ ㉔)

$ TOLL

EXIT 40
Atlantic City

5 —
- Holiday Inn Exp *i*
- Quality *i*, Wellesley Inn & Suites
- Friendship Inn
- EconoLodge *i*
- Comfort Inn Suites *i*

EXIT 130
Penns Grove

- Applebee's
- McDonald's (P ㉔)
- Burger King (P)
- Cracker Barrel

3 —

Carney's Point

DUPONT

EXIT 1 49
Deepwater
Pennsville
Salem
295

- Exxon (D)
- Hampton Inn (T, RV)

1 —

Delaware River

65 mph

NEW JERSEY
DELAWARE

↑ DRIVE UP THE PAGE GOING NORTH ↑

© 2010

Delaware River

DELAWARE MEMORIAL BRIDGE

BRIDGE TOLL $3

EXIT 9
New Castle
Wilmington

Kalmar Nykel>
Our Lady Queen of Peace

McDonald's
Gordon's Pizza
Sunset BBQ

Universal (D, LP)
Shell (LP, $)

Rodeway, Motel 6
Superlodge

Bowlerama

Clarion Inn

Capriolli's>
Deep Blue>

Hotel Dupont>

50 mph

EXIT Landers Lane

EXIT 13 / 40 / 301
Newcastle
Dover
Wilmington

295

5C

Dragon Palace
Giovanni's Place
Primo Hoagies
Jessop's Tavern>

BP $, Citgo (D)

Rite Aid 24

Superfresh
Mike's Famous Harley

Burger King
Bagels Steaks Subs
Evergreen Chinese 24
Golden Dove Diner
Consentida II
McDonald's, Popeyes
Rascal's Seafood
Seasons Pizza
The Dog House Pizza
Subway, Wing's To Go

Exxon (D, BP, $ 24)
Sunoco (D, LP, $)
Wawa 24

Happy Harry's
Manor Pharmacy

Entenmann's Bakery Outlet

EXIT 5D / 295
Delaware Memorial Bridge
New Castle

NORTHBOUND KEEP RIGHT!
Do NOT get off at the 95/495 Exit. We will be following I-295 here across the Delaware Br and onto the NJ Turnpike

95 / 495

Bugaboo Creek, Chili's
Cheeseburger Paradise
Hot Spot, Cool Beans
Michael's Crabs

Country Inn & Suites
Courtyard, Hilton
Fairfield Inn
Days Inn
Homestead Studio Suites
Red Roof

EXIT 5C
Philadelphia
Left Exit
Southbound

40

Denny's
Dunkin Donuts
Oliver's, Pizza Hut

Getty (R), Shell (D,LP,$)

EconoLodge
Hampton Inn
Holiday Inn Exp

Sears Outlet

Christiana Skating Ctr

EXIT 5B / 141
Newport

EXIT 5A
Airport Rd

New Castle
Country Airport

4

3

H

EXIT 4 / 1 / 7
Christiana
Churchmns Cr

Christiana Mall

? DELAWARE HOUSE
Service Area & Vis. Ctr

Baja Fresh, Brioche Dorée
Famous Famiglia, Carvel
Burger King, Starbucks
Cinnabon, Popeye's

Exxon (D), Sunoco (D)

EXIT 3 / 273
Dover
Newark

Bob Evans, Wendy's
Boston Market
Olive Grill, Ciao Pizza
Red Robin
The Establishment

BP (CW)
Exxon (D, R, BP)

Ramada
Staybridge Suites
Towne Place Suites

Newark

1st State Diner
Matilda's Australian BBQ, Boston Market
Grotto Pizza
SAS Cupcakes
China Garden, Mario's Pizza, Caffe Gelato
Deer Park Tavern
TGI Friday's, Friendly's

Exxon $
Shell (D, R, $ 24)
Sunoco (D, $)
Texaco (D $)

Embassy Suites
Howard Johnson
Inn & Suites
Quality, Sleep Inn
Homewood Suites

EXIT 1 / 896
Newark
Middletown

Happy Harry's

Acme Supermarket

40

55 mph

DRIVE DOWN THE PAGE GOING SOUTH

15 MILE MARKERS

DELAWARE MARYLAND

Newark

TOLL $4

DELAWARE
MARYLAND

55 mph

EXIT 109
Elkton
Newark Del

279

Country Pride
Durham BBQ
Nick & Joe's Pizza
Subway

Mobil (D)
T/A Travel Ctr (D, S 24)
7 Eleven ($ 24)

Elk Forge B&B>*i*

Wawa $

Milburn Orchards

Cracker Barrel
Iron Skillet, KFC
McDonald's (P,T 24)
Taco Bell
Waffle House 24

Petro (TW, $ 24)
Shell (D, LP, $ 24)

Hawthorne Suites
Elkton Lodge *i* T
Hampton Inn *i*
Knights Inn
Motel 6, Days Inn

7

Elkton

40

Citgo (D, K, LP, $)
Mobil (R, NO GAS)

Fair Winds
Farm B&B>
Best Western

EXIT 100
North East
Rising Sun

272

Burger King
Dunkin Donuts
Frank's Pizza
McDonalds 24
Nauti-Goose>
Schroeder's Deli
Steak & Main>
The Cookery
Subway, Empire
Wellwood Club>
Woody's Crab House>

Flying J Travel Plaza
(D,S,BP, RVD 24 *i*)
Sunoco(D,LP,$ 24)

Comfort Inn *i*
& Suites
Holiday Inn Exp Suites

Eckerd's, Rite Aid
Walgreen's

Wal-Mart
Day Basket Factory>

North East

? CHESAPEAKE HOUSE
SERVICE AREA

Burger King $
Popeye's, Quiznos
Starbucks, Freshens
Cinnabon
Z Market

Exxon (D, R 24)
Sunoco (D, R, $ 24)

7

40

65 mph

DRIVE UP THE PAGE GOING NORTH

© 2010

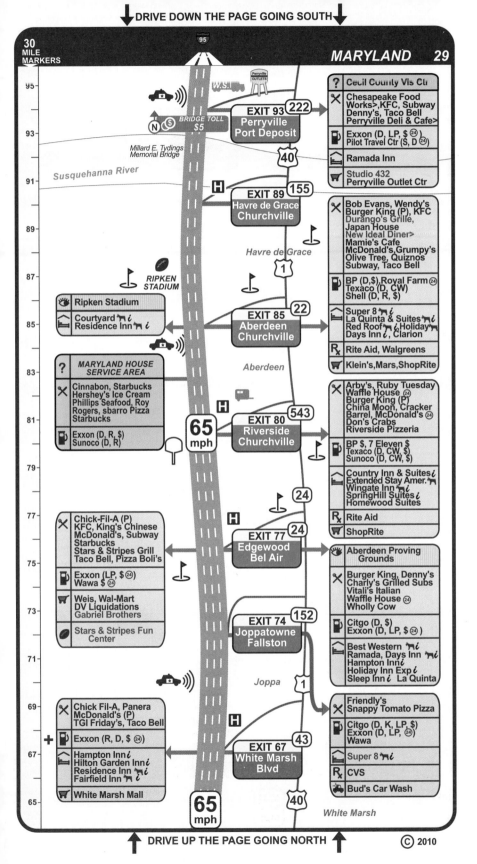

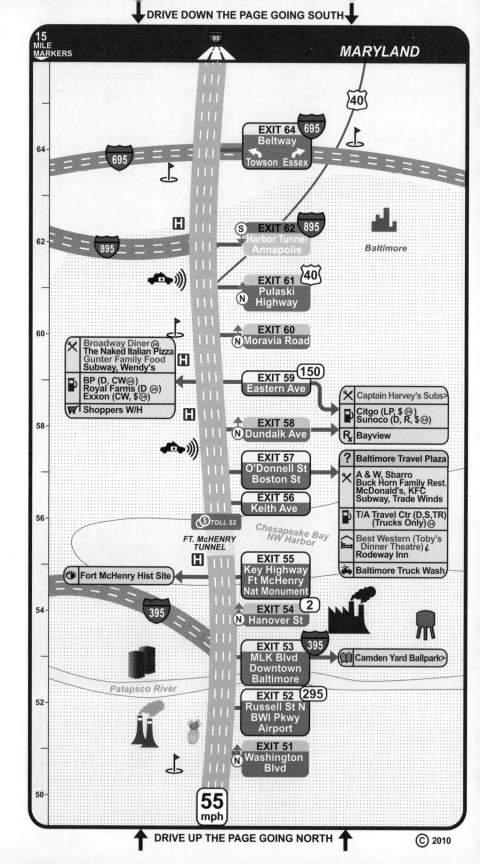

DRIVE DOWN THE PAGE GOING SOUTH

15 MILE MARKERS

95

MARYLAND

40

EXIT 64
695
Beltway
Towson Essex

64

695

EXIT 62
895
S Harbor Tunnel
Annapolis

Baltimore

62

895

EXIT 61
40
N Pulaski
Highway

EXIT 60
N Moravia Road

60

Broadway Diner ㉔
The Naked Italian Pizza
Gunter Family Food
Subway, Wendy's

H

BP (D, CW㉔)
Royal Farms (D ㉔)
Exxon (CW, $㉔)

Shoppers W/H

EXIT 59
150
Eastern Ave

Captain Harvey's Subs>

Citgo (LP, $ ㉔)
Sunoco (D, R, $㉔)

Bayview

H

EXIT 58
N Dundalk Ave

58

EXIT 57
O'Donnell St
Boston St

? Baltimore Travel Plaza

A & W, Sbarro
Buck Horn Family Rest.
McDonald's, KFC
Subway, Trade Winds

EXIT 56
Keith Ave

56

T/A Travel Ctr (D,S,TR)
(Trucks Only) ㉔

TOLL $2

Chesapeake Bay
NW Harbor

Best Western (Toby's
Dinner Theatre) ¿
Rodeway Inn

FT. McHENRY
TUNNEL

Baltimore Truck Wash

H

EXIT 55
Key Highway
Ft McHenry
Nat Monument

Fort McHenry Hist Site

395

EXIT 54
N Hanover St

2

54

EXIT 53
MLK Blvd
Downtown
Baltimore

395

Camden Yard Ballpark>

Patapsco River

EXIT 52
Russell St N
BWI Pkwy
Airport

295

52

EXIT 51
N Washington
Blvd

50

55
mph

DRIVE UP THE PAGE GOING NORTH

© 2010

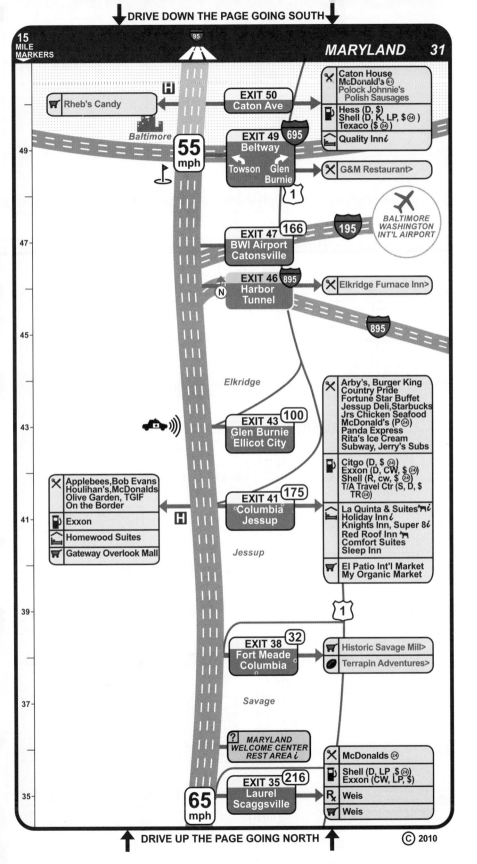

DRIVE DOWN THE PAGE GOING SOUTH

15 MILE MARKERS

MARYLAND 31

95

Rheb's Candy

Baltimore

55 mph

H

EXIT 50
Caton Ave

Caton House
McDonald's ④
Polock Johnnie's
Polish Sausages

Hess (D, $)
Shell (D, K, LP, $ ㉔)
Texaco ($ ㉔)

Quality Inn *i*

EXIT 49
Beltway
Towson ← Glen Burnie

695

49

G&M Restaurant>

1

EXIT 47
BWI Airport
Catonsville

166

195

47

BALTIMORE WASHINGTON INT'L AIRPORT

EXIT 46
Harbor Tunnel

895

N

Elkridge Furnace Inn>

45

895

Elkridge

EXIT 43
Glen Burnie
Ellicot City

100

43

Arby's, Burger King
Country Pride
Fortune Star Buffet
Jessup Deli,Starbucks
Jrs Chicken Seafood
McDonald's (P㉔)
Panda Express
Rita's Ice Cream
Subway, Jerry's Subs

Citgo (D, $ ㉔)
Exxon (D, CW, $ ㉔)
Shell (R, cw, $ ㉔)
T/A Travel Ctr (S, D, $ TR㉔)

Applebees,Bob Evans
Houlihan's,McDonalds
Olive Garden, TGIF
On the Border

Exxon

Homewood Suites

Gateway Overlook Mall

H

EXIT 41
°Columbia°
Jessup

175

41

La Quinta & Suites 🐾*i*
Holiday Inn *i*
Knights Inn, Super 8*i*
Red Roof Inn 🐾
Comfort Suites
Sleep Inn

El Patio Int'l Market
My Organic Market

Jessup

1

39

EXIT 38
Fort Meade
Columbia

32

Historic Savage Mill>

Terrapin Adventures>

Savage

37

? MARYLAND WELCOME CENTER REST AREA *i*

McDonalds ㉔

Shell (D, LP $㉔)
Exxon (CW, LP, $)

EXIT 35
Laurel
Scaggsville

216

35

Weis

Weis

65 mph

DRIVE UP THE PAGE GOING NORTH

© 2010

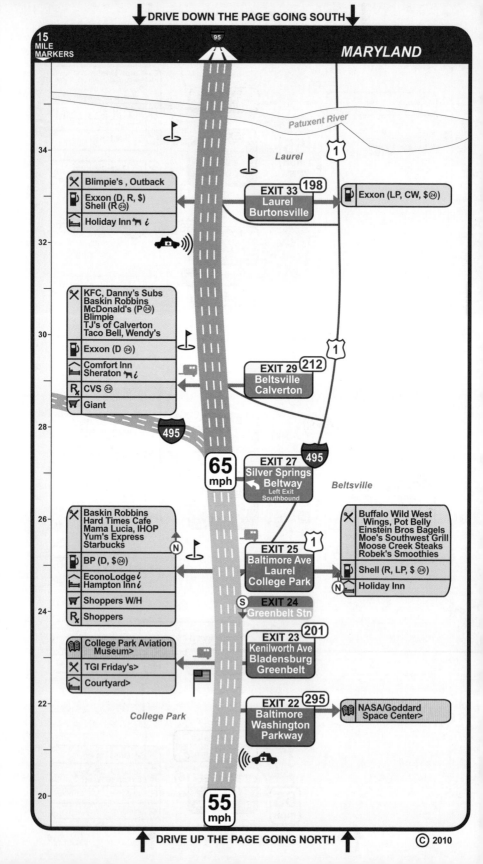

DRIVE DOWN THE PAGE GOING SOUTH

15 MILE MARKERS

95

MARYLAND

Patuxent River

Laurel

34

☓ Blimpie's , Outback
⛽ Exxon (D, R, $)
Shell (R 24)
🛏 Holiday Inn 🐾 *i*

EXIT 33 **198**
Laurel
Burtonsville

⛽ Exxon (LP, CW, $ 24)

32

☓ KFC, Danny's Subs
Baskin Robbins
McDonald's (P 24)
Blimpie
TJ's of Calverton
Taco Bell, Wendy's
⛽ Exxon (D 24)
🛏 Comfort Inn
Sheraton 🐾 *i*
Rx CVS 24
🛒 Giant

30

1

EXIT 29 **212**
Beltsville
Calverton

28

495

65 mph

EXIT 27 **495**
Silver Springs
Beltway
◤ Left Exit Southbound

Beltsville

26

☓ Baskin Robbins
Hard Times Cafe
Mama Lucia, IHOP
Yum's Express
Starbucks
⛽ BP (D, $ 24)
🛏 EconoLodge *i*
Hampton Inn *i*
🛒 Shoppers W/H
Rx Shoppers

Ⓝ

☓ Buffalo Wild West
Wings, Pot Belly
Einstein Bros Bagels
Moe's Southwest Grill
Moose Creek Steaks
Robek's Smoothies
⛽ Shell (R, LP, $ 24)
Ⓝ Holiday Inn

EXIT 25 **1**
Baltimore Ave
Laurel
College Park

Ⓢ **EXIT 24**
Greenbelt Stn

24

📖 College Park Aviation
Museum>
☓ TGI Friday's>
🛏 Courtyard>

EXIT 23 **201**
Kenilworth Ave
Bladensburg
Greenbelt

College Park

22

EXIT 22 **295**
Baltimore
Washington
Parkway

📖 NASA/Goddard
Space Center>

20

55 mph

DRIVE UP THE PAGE GOING NORTH

© 2010

15 MILE MARKERS

95

MARYLAND 33

Left Side	Exit	Right Side
✕ Atlantic Seafood, IHOP, Bojangles, Carvel, Five Guys, King Pollo, Papa John's, Quiznos, Cuisine of China, El Gran Chaparrel, Subway, Starbucks, Wendy's	**H** **EXIT 20** (450) Annapolis Rd Lanham Bladensburg	✕ Bojangles, Burger King, Jerry's Subs & Pizza, McDonald's(24), Paradise Cove, Red Lobster, Vocelli Pizza
		🛏 Best Western *i*, Days Inn *i*, Red Roof Inn *i*
19 — ⛽ 7 Eleven $, Shell (R, $ 24) 🛏 Sheraton Four Points Rₓ CVS 🛒 Foodway, National Wholesale Liquidators, Shoppers Warehouse	**EXIT 19** (50) Annapolis Washington	
17 — 🏟 FedEx Stadium ✕ China Restaurant	**EXIT 17** (202) Landover Rd Upper Marlboro Bladensburg	🛏 Holiday Inn Exp & Suites *i*, Radisson
	EXIT 16 Arena Drive	
15 — ✕ A&W, Carvel, Cameron's Seafood, Checkers, IHOP, Hunan Delight, Jerry's Sub & Pizza, Long John Silvers, McDonald's (P), Panda Exp, Wendy's ⛽ Texaco (D, $ 24), Exxon (D, $ 24) 🛏 Country Inn & Suites, Comfort Inn *i*, Motel 6	**EXIT 15** (214) Central Ave Largo Seat Pleasant	*Kettering*
13 — *Washingto DC* ←	**EXIT 13** Upper Marlboro Capital Heights	
11 — ✕ Eddie Leonard Carry Out, NY Fried Chicken ⛽ BP (R, $ 24), Citgo (R), Exxon (CW, $ 24), Sunoco (R, D, $ 24) 🛒 Murry's Warehouse Eddie Leonard	**EXIT 11** (4) Penn. Ave Upper Marlboro Washington	*Andrews Air Force Base*
9 — ✕ Drive thru Chicken, Subway (S) ⛽ Sunoco (D, CW, $ 24)	**H** **EXIT 9** (337) Allentown Rd Andrews AFB Morningside	✕ Baskin Robbins, Arby's, Checkers, Popeye's, McDonald's, Jiffy Pizza Gyros $, Eastern Carry-out ⛽ Texaco (D 24), Shell (R, $ 24) 🛏 Quality Inn *i*, Days Inn, Super 8 🛒 Plaza Latino, Wonder/Hostess Shop
7 — ✕ Subway (S) ⛽ Shell (D $) 🛏 Country Inn & Suites, Holiday Inn Exp	**H** **EXIT 7** (5) Branch Ave Waldorf Silver Hill	📖 Suratt House>

55 mph

© 2010

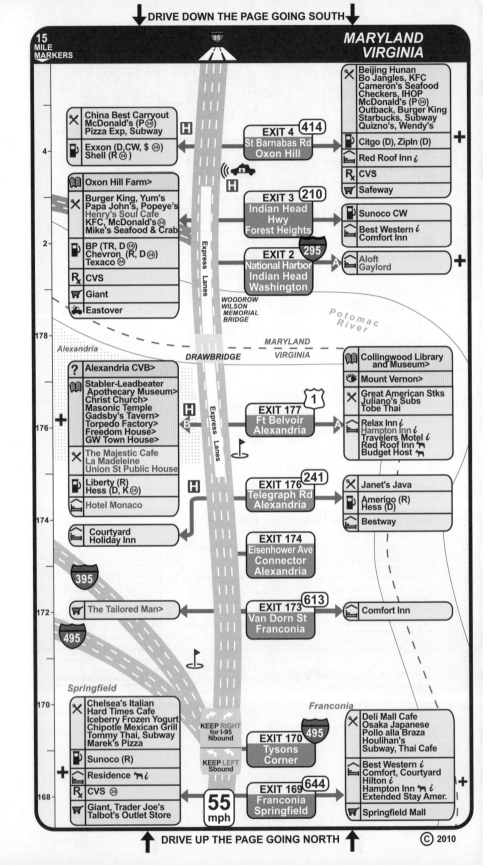

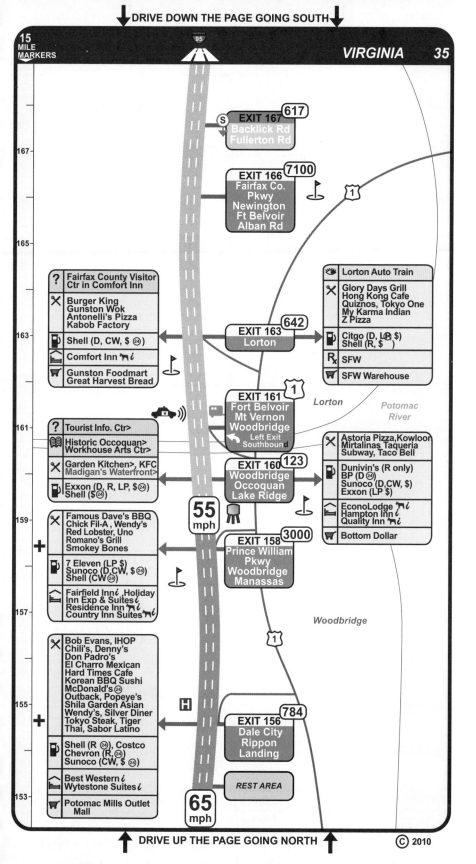

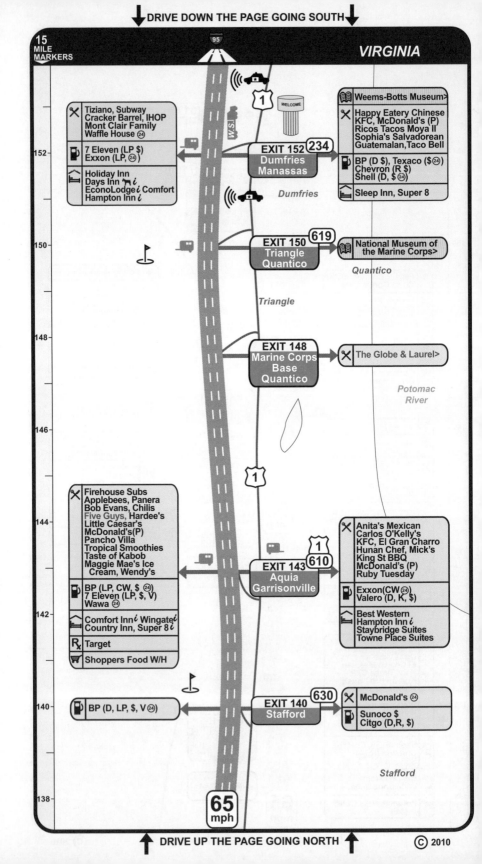

15 MILE MARKERS

VIRGINIA

95

EXIT 152 234
Dumfries
Manassas

Dumfries

Tiziano, Subway
Cracker Barrel, IHOP
Mont Clair Family
Waffle House (24)

7 Eleven (LP $)
Exxon (LP, (24))

Holiday Inn
Days Inn *i*
EconoLodge*i* Comfort
Hampton Inn *i*

Weems-Botts Museum>

Happy Eatery Chinese
KFC, McDonald's (P)
Ricos Tacos Moya II
Sophia's Salvadorean
Guatemalan,Taco Bell

BP (D $), Texaco ($(24))
Chevron (R $)
Shell (D, $ (24))

Sleep Inn, Super 8

EXIT 150 619
Triangle
Quantico

National Museum of
the Marine Corps>

Quantico

Triangle

EXIT 148
Marine Corps
Base
Quantico

The Globe & Laurel>

*Potomac
River*

1

Firehouse Subs
Applebees, Panera
Bob Evans, Chilis
Five Guys, Hardee's
Little Caesar's
McDonald's(P)
Pancho Villa
Tropical Smoothies
Taste of Kabob
Maggie Mae's Ice
Cream, Wendy's

BP (LP, CW, $ (24))
7 Eleven (LP, $, V)
Wawa (24)

Comfort Inn*i* Wingate*i*
Country Inn, Super 8 *i*

R_x Target

Shoppers Food W/H

EXIT 143 1 610
Aquia
Garrisonville

Anita's Mexican
Carlos O'Kelly's
KFC, El Gran Charro
Hunan Chef, Mick's
King St BBQ
McDonald's (P)
Ruby Tuesday

Exxon(CW (24))
Valero (D, K, $)

Best Western
Hampton Inn *i*
Staybridge Suites
Towne Place Suites

EXIT 140 630
Stafford

BP (D, LP, $, V (23))

McDonald's (24)

Sunoco $
Citgo (D,R, $)

Stafford

65 mph

DRIVE UP THE PAGE GOING NORTH

© 2010

15
MILE
MARKERS

95

1

EXIT 136 | 8700
Mountview Rd
Centreport Pkwy
Stafford Airport | 1

Falmouth

West side — Exit 136:

✕ Hardee's, Foster's Grille, Perkins, Pizza Hut, McDonald's (P), Ponderosa, Wendy's, Waffle House (24), Sam's Pizza & Subs

⛽ East Coast (D,K,LP,V), Shell (D, CW, $ (24))

🛏 America's Best Inn *i*, Days Inn *i* Super 8 *i*, Quality Inn *i*, Sleep Inn *i* Wingate, Travelodge *i*, Comfort Suites, Country Inn & Suites, Supervalue Inn

℞ Target

🛒 Target

East side — Exit 133:

✕ Ranchito El Pariso, Taco Mexico

⛽ Exxon (D, $, V (24)), Texaco (D, LP, CW, $)

🛏 Howard Johnson *i*, Motel 6

EXIT 133 | 17
Warrenton
Falmouth

Rappahannock River

S ? *VIRGINIA WELCOME CTR & REST AREA*

Fredericksburg

H

EXIT 130 | 3
Fredericksburg
Culpepper

1

West side — Exit 130:

✕ Applebee's, Aunt Sarah's, Burger King, Outback, Chili's, Fuddruckers, Joe's Crab Shack, Ruby Tuesday, IHOP, Red Horse BBQ, Starbucks, TGI Friday, Chipotle, Pancho Villa

⛽ Valero (LP $), Costco, Wawa (24), Exxon (D)

🛏 Best Western *i*, Hospitality House, Ramada *i* Super 8

🛒 Spotsylvania Mall, Central Park Mall, Wal-Mart, Costco

⚪ Funland

East side — Fredericksburg:

? Fredericksburg Vis Ctr>

🏛 Fredericksburg Museum>, Mary Washington House>, Hugh Mercer Apothecary>, Rising Sun Tavern>, James Monroe Mus.>

✕ Arby's, Bob Evans, Bistro Bethem>, Lone Star, Starbucks, Carl's Frozen Custard>, kybecca>, Carlos O'Kelly's Mexican, Subway, Shoney's, Wendy's, Friendly's, Kings Buffet, KFC, McDonald's, Vinny's Italian

⛽ Texaco (D, $, CW), BP (R, D, LP), Wawa (24), Shell (D, $ (24))

🛏 Best Western *i*, Quality Inn *i*, Courtyard>

Portsmouth

? Spotsylvania Cnty Vis Ctr>

✕ Bob Evans, KFC, Applebee's, Chick-fil-A, Cracker Barrel, Subway, El Charro, Chipotle, Firehouse Subs, Uno, Golden China, Chili's, McDonald's (P (24)), BK, Wendy's, Starbucks

⛽ Racetrac Truckstop (D, S, $), Exxon (CW (24))

🛏 Wytestone Suites *i*, Comfort Inn *i* Sleep *i*

🛒 Massaponax Outlets, SouthPoint Mall, Kolache House Bakery>, Wal-Mart

EXIT 126 | 1 17
Fredericksburg
Massaponax

East side — Exit 126:

✕ Arby's, Ruby Tuesday, Denny's, Friendly's, Golden Corral, McDonald's (P), Pancho Villa, Hooters, Pizza Hut, Taco Bell, Waffle House (24)

⛽ BP (D, R), Exxon (24), Chevron (D $), Citgo (D, $, LP (24)), Shell (CW, $ (24))

🛏 EconoLodge *i*, Fairfield *i* Days Inn *i*, Country Inn *i*, Ramada *i* Motel 6, Royal Inn *i* Super 8 *i*, Hampton & Suites *i*, Towne Place Suites

℞ Rite Aid

🛒 Food Lion

1

65
mph

© 2010

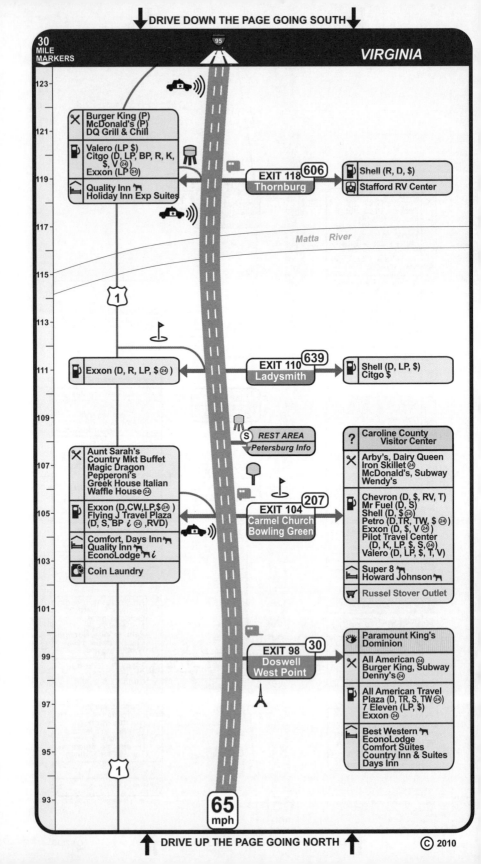

DRIVE DOWN THE PAGE GOING SOUTH

VIRGINIA

30 MILE MARKERS

95

123 —
121 —
119 —
117 —
115 —
113 —
111 —
109 —
107 —
105 —
103 —
101 —
99 —
97 —
95 —
93 —

Burger King (P)
McDonald's (P)
DQ Grill & Chill

Valero (LP $)
Citgo (D, LP, BP, R, K, $, V ㉔)
Exxon (LP ㉔)

Quality Inn
Holiday Inn Exp Suites

EXIT 118 (606)
Thornburg

Shell (R, D, $)
Stafford RV Center

Matta River

1

Exxon (D, R, LP, $ ㉔)

EXIT 110 (639)
Ladysmith

Shell (D, LP, $)
Citgo $

S REST AREA
Petersburg Info

? **Caroline County Visitor Center**

Aunt Sarah's
Country Mkt Buffet
Magic Dragon
Pepperoni's
Greek House Italian
Waffle House ㉔

Exxon (D,CW,LP,$ ㉔)
Flying J Travel Plaza
(D, S, BP i ㉔, RVD)

Comfort, Days Inn
Quality Inn
EconoLodge i

Coin Laundry

EXIT 104 (207)
Carmel Church
Bowling Green

Arby's, Dairy Queen
Iron Skillet ㉔
McDonald's, Subway
Wendy's

Chevron (D, $, RV, T)
Mr Fuel (D, S)
Shell (D, $ ㉔)
Petro (D,TR, TW, $ ㉔)
Exxon (D, $, V ㉔)
Pilot Travel Center
(D, K, LP, $, S, ㉔)
Valero (D, LP, $, T, V)

Super 8
Howard Johnson

Russel Stover Outlet

EXIT 98 (30)
Doswell
West Point

Paramount King's
Dominion

All American ㉔
Burger King, Subway
Denny's ㉔

All American Travel
Plaza (D, TR, S, TW ㉔)
7 Eleven (LP, $)
Exxon ㉔

Best Western
EconoLodge
Comfort Suites
Country Inn & Suites
Days Inn

1

65 mph

DRIVE UP THE PAGE GOING NORTH

© 2010

95

1

?	Ashland Vis. Center>
📖	Historic Ashland>
🍴	Applebee's, Wendy's Arby's, Buckhorn *Ashland Coffee & Tea>* Burger King, KFC *Homemades by Suzanne>* Jersey Mike's Subs McDonald's, Ponderosa Trackside Grill>, Iron Horse, Cracker Barrel Waffle House (24) Smoking Pig BBQ>
⛽	BP(CW,LP,$), Citgo(D) East Coast (D, LP, K, CW, $ V(24)), Shell (D,$) Exxon (LP, $ (24)) T/A Travel Ctr (D (24) S)
🏨	Apple Garden Inn Howard Johnson Inn & Suites, Hampton *i* Days Inn 🐎*i* Sleep *i* *Henry Clay Inn>* 🐎 Holiday Inn Exp Super 8 🐎*i* Motel 6 Quality Inn & Suites 🐎*i*
Rx	Rite Aid
🛒	Train Toy & Hobby>
🚌	McGeorge's RV Supercenter
🍴	Arby's, Cici's Pizza Jade Chinese, Sonic Jersey Mikes Subs Phat Boyz BBQ
⛽	7 Eleven $
🛒	Northcross Center Virginia Center Commons>
📖	Lewis Ginter Botanical Garden>
🍴	Dairy Queen, Hardee's Hawk's BBQ, Burger King, Frida's Mexican McDonald's (P) *River City Diner* Wendy's, Taco Bell Waffle House
⛽	7 Eleven (LP $) Exxon $, Shell (D, LP)
🏨	Holiday Inn *i*, Sleep *i* EconoLodge, Clarion Best Western Howard Johnson Exp
🛒	Food Lion, Wal-Mart
🍴	Little Caesar's Pizza Top's China
Rx	CVS, Ukrops
🛒	Ukrops
📖	Science Mus. of VA> Maymont
🍴	*Buz and Ned's BBQ* Bill's Virginia BBQ
⛽	Citgo (D $)
🏨	EconoLodge 🐎

65 mph

60 mph

55 mph

EXIT 92 (54) Hanover Ashland

⛽ Sunoco

EXIT 89 (802) Lewistown Rd

🍴	Country Pride Pizza Hut, Cinnabon Popeye's, Taco Bell
⛽	Shell (LP $) T/A Travel Ctr Mobil (D, TR, S, $ (24))

EXIT 86 (656) Atlee Elmont

🍴	Burger King, Marios China Star McDonalds (P) McLeans, Subway Mi Jalisco Mexican Pickle Barrel
⛽	Sheetz (LP, V(24)) Valero (D, LP, $(24) V)
Rx	CVS
🛒	Food Lion *Sansbury's Bakery*

EXIT 84 (295) Norfolk Rocky Mt NC Charlottesville

295

EXIT 83 (73) Parham Rd

Richmond

EXIT 82 (301) (2) Chamberlayne Ave

🍴	McDonald's (P)
⛽	Exxon (D, LP, V, $) Sunoco (D, (24) $)
🏨	Days Inn Super 8 🐎 *i*

EXIT 81 (N) (1)

🍴	Arby's, Friendly's KFC, Taco Bell La Casita, Wendy's Pizza Hut, Red House
⛽	Exxon (LP, $, CW, V) Texaco (LP, $) Wawa (24)
🏨	Travelodge 🐎 *i* Town Motel
Rx	Walgreens
🧺	Richmond Laundry

EXIT 80 (161) (N) Hermitage Rd Lakeside Ave

EXIT 79 (64) (195) Powhite Pkwy Charlottesville

64

Diamond Stadium

EXIT 78 (161) Boulevard

🍴	Kitchen 64
⛽	BP (D, K, LP, $)
🏨	Holiday Inn 🐎 *i*

1

© 2010

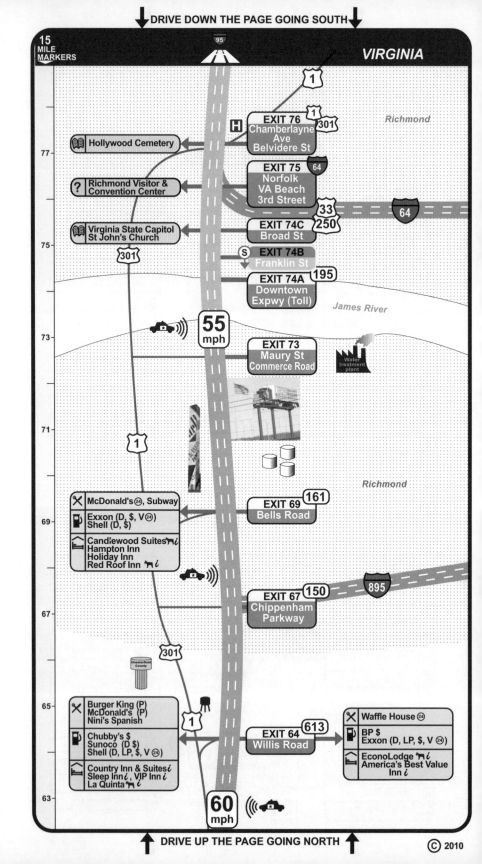

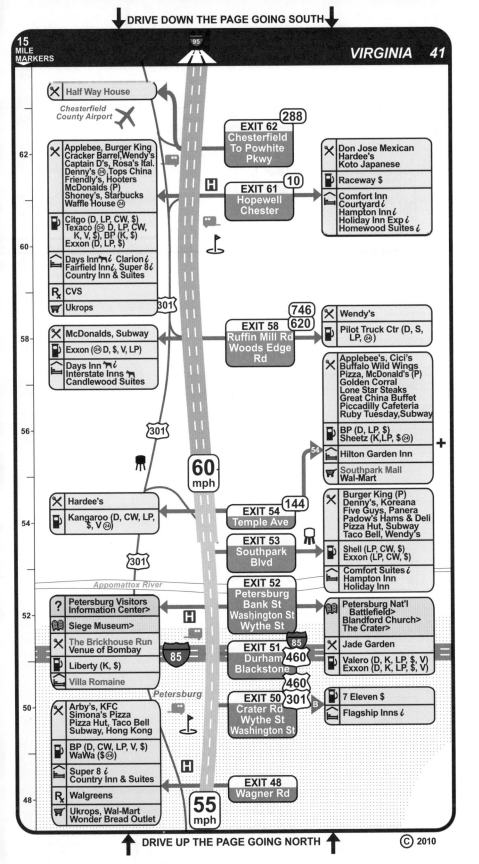

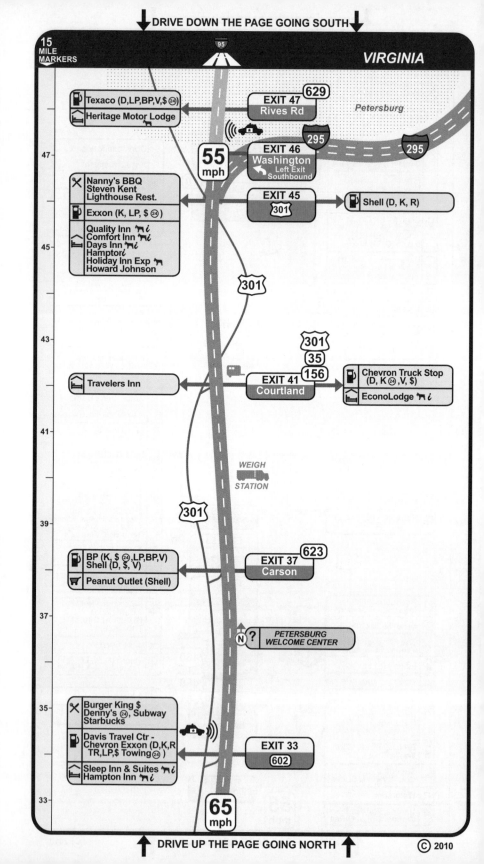

DRIVE DOWN THE PAGE GOING SOUTH

95

VIRGINIA

15 MILE MARKERS

Petersburg

Texaco (D,LP,BP,V,$ 24)
Heritage Motor Lodge

EXIT 47 629
Rives Rd

295
295

55 mph

EXIT 46
Washington
Left Exit
Southbound

47 —

Nanny's BBQ
Steven Kent
Lighthouse Rest.

Exxon (K, LP, $ 24)

Quality Inn
Comfort Inn
Days Inn
Hampton
Holiday Inn Exp
Howard Johnson

EXIT 45
301

Shell (D, K, R)

45 —

301

43 —

301
35
156

Travelers Inn

EXIT 41
Courtland

Chevron Truck Stop
(D, K 24, V, $)
EconoLodge

41 —

WEIGH
STATION

39 —

301

BP (K, $ 24,LP,BP,V)
Shell (D, $, V)
Peanut Outlet (Shell)

EXIT 37 623
Carson

37 —

N ?
PETERSBURG
WELCOME CENTER

35 —

Burger King $
Denny's 24, Subway
Starbucks

Davis Travel Ctr -
Chevron Exxon (D,K,R
TR,LP,$ Towing 24)

Sleep Inn & Suites
Hampton Inn

EXIT 33
602

33 —

65 mph

DRIVE UP THE PAGE GOING NORTH

© 2010

EXIT 31 40
Stony Creek
Waverly

- Carter's Grill & Diner
  Tastee Hut BBQ
- Shell (D, K, R, ㉔ Towing/ ㉔)

EXIT 24
645

EXIT 20 631
Jarratt

- Blimpie's
  Granny's Fried
  Chicken, Pizza Hut Exp
- Exxon ($, V ㉔)
  Texaco (D, K, $, V)

301

EXIT 17 U.S. 301

- Knights Inn
  Resté Motel

13
- Shell (LP, V)
  Texaco (D, K, LP, V, Racing Fuel)

Emporia Greensville Regional Airport

Emporia

- Applebee's, Arby's
  Blimpie's, Wendy's
  Burger King, Hardee's
  Cracker Barrel, KFC
  Carolina BBQ
  Long John Silver's
  McDonald's (P)
  Subway, Taco Bell
  Wong's Garden

- BoJangles, Shoney's
  Pueblo Viejo
  Sadler Plaza Buffet
  Five Guys, Quiznos
- Petro (K, $), Exxon $
  Sadler Travel Plaza -
  Shell (S, D, TR ㉔,V)
  Race-in (D $)
- Best Western
  Days Inn
  Hampton
  Holiday Inn Exp Suites
  Quality Inn
  Sleep Inn

EXIT 13 614
Emporia

EXIT 12 U.S. 301
N

EXIT 11 58
Emporia
Norfolk
South Hill

- BP (D, $, LP)
  Exxon $, Citgo,
  Texaco(CW,LP,$ ㉔ V)
- Fairfield Inn & Suites
  US Inn
  Country Inn & Suites
- Rx Rite Aid
- Food Lion $
  Wal-Mart

EXIT 8 301
Emporia

- Anderson's Pharmacy>
  Logan's Diner>
  Huddle House
- Exxon $
  Simmons Travel -
  BP (S,D,TR,BP,$㉔)
- Super 8

EXIT 4 629
Skippers

- Shell (LP $)
- EconoLodge

- McDonald's ㉔
- Love's Truck Stop (D, S, K, LP, $ ㉔ RVD)
- Good Earth Peanut Co

301

65 mph

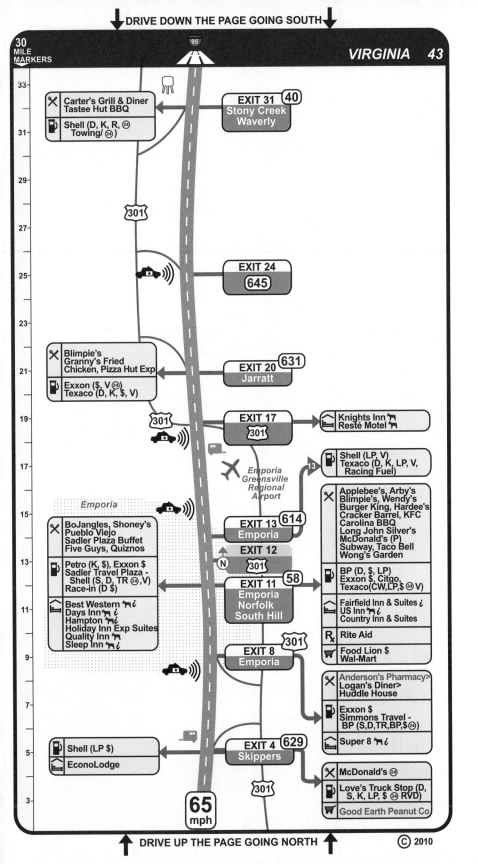

© 2010

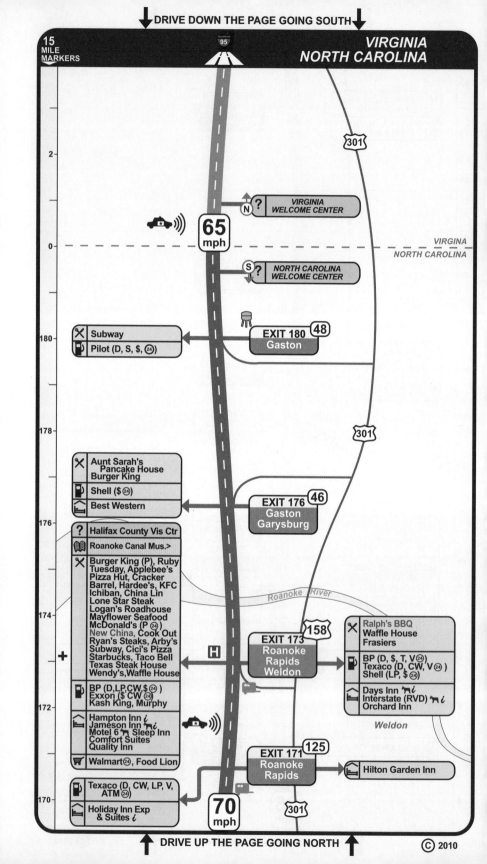

DRIVE DOWN THE PAGE GOING SOUTH

VIRGINIA
NORTH CAROLINA

95

15 MILE MARKERS

301

N ? VIRGINIA WELCOME CENTER

65 mph

VIRGINIA
NORTH CAROLINA

S ? NORTH CAROLINA WELCOME CENTER

EXIT 180 48
Gaston

Subway
Pilot (D, S, $, 24)

301

Aunt Sarah's Pancake House
Burger King
Shell ($ 24)
Best Western

EXIT 176 46
Gaston
Garysburg

? Halifax County Vis Ctr
Roanoke Canal Mus.>
Burger King (P), Ruby
Tuesday, Applebee's
Pizza Hut, Cracker
Barrel, Hardee's, KFC
Ichiban, China Lin
Lone Star Steak
Logan's Roadhouse
Mayflower Seafood
McDonald's (P 24)
New China, Cook Out
Ryan's Steaks, Arby's
Subway, Cici's Pizza
Starbucks, Taco Bell
Texas Steak House
Wendy's, Waffle House

Roanoke River

EXIT 173 158
Roanoke
Rapids
Weldon

Ralph's BBQ
Waffle House
Frasiers
BP (D, $, T, V 24)
Texaco (D, CW, V 24)
Shell (LP, $ 24)
Days Inn 🐾 i
Interstate (RVD) 🐾 i
Orchard Inn

Weldon

H

BP (D,LP,CW,$ 24)
Exxon ($ CW 24)
Kash King, Murphy
Hampton Inn i
Jameson Inn 🐾 i
Motel 6 🐾 Sleep Inn
Comfort Suites
Quality Inn
Walmart 24, Food Lion

EXIT 171 125
Roanoke
Rapids

Hilton Garden Inn

Texaco (D, CW, LP, V, ATM 24)
Holiday Inn Exp & Suites i

70 mph

301

DRIVE UP THE PAGE GOING NORTH

© 2010

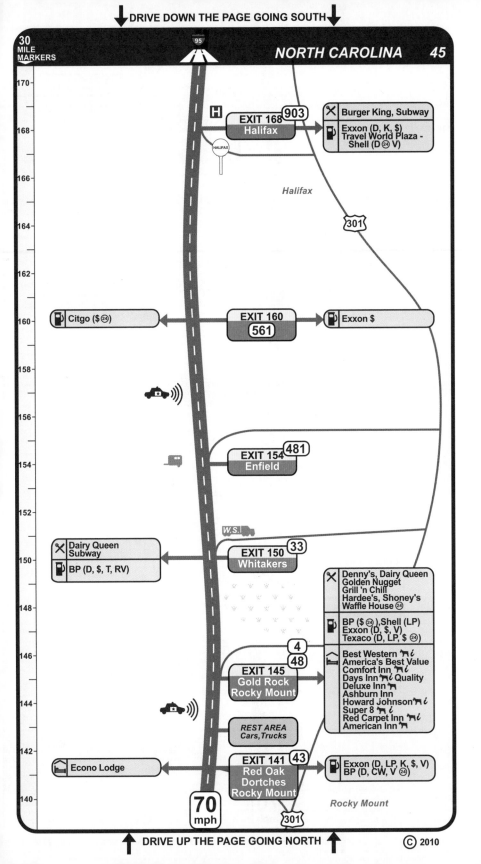

95

H

EXIT 168
Halifax   903

HALIFAX

Burger King, Subway

Exxon (D, K, $)
Travel World Plaza -
Shell (D 24 V)

Halifax

301

Citgo ($ 24)

EXIT 160
561

Exxon $

EXIT 154   481
Enfield

W.S.

Dairy Queen
Subway

BP (D, $, T, RV)

EXIT 150   33
Whitakers

Denny's, Dairy Queen
Golden Nugget
Grill 'n Chill
Hardee's, Shoney's
Waffle House 24

BP ($ 24), Shell (LP)
Exxon (D, $, V)
Texaco (D, LP, $ 24)

4
48

EXIT 145
Gold Rock
Rocky Mount

Best Western
America's Best Value
Comfort Inn
Days Inn Quality
Deluxe Inn
Ashburn Inn
Howard Johnson
Super 8
Red Carpet Inn
American Inn

REST AREA
Cars, Trucks

Econo Lodge

EXIT 141   43
Red Oak
Dortches
Rocky Mount

Exxon (D, LP, K, $, V)
BP (D, CW, V 24)

Rocky Mount

301

70 mph

© 2010

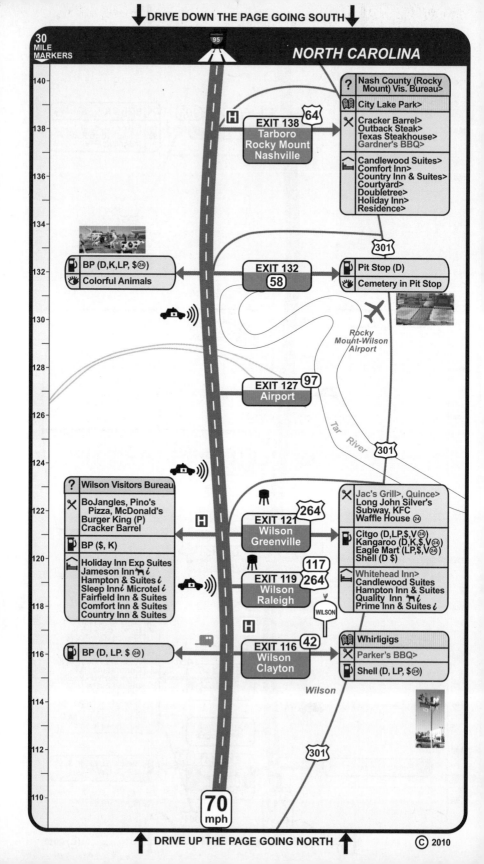

95

NORTH CAROLINA

30 MILE MARKERS

140

138

136

134

132

130

128

126

124

122

120

118

116

114

112

110

? Nash County (Rocky Mount) Vis. Bureau>

City Lake Park>

✕ Cracker Barrel>
Outback Steak>
Texas Steakhouse>
Gardner's BBQ>

🛏 Candlewood Suites>
Comfort Inn>
Country Inn & Suites>
Courtyard>
Doubletree>
Holiday Inn>
Residence>

H EXIT 138 64
Tarboro
Rocky Mount
Nashville

301

BP (D,K,LP, $ 24)
Colorful Animals

EXIT 132 58

Pit Stop (D)
Cemetery in Pit Stop

301

Rocky Mount-Wilson Airport

EXIT 127 97
Airport

Tar River

301

? Wilson Visitors Bureau

✕ BoJangles, Pino's Pizza, McDonald's Burger King (P) Cracker Barrel

BP ($, K)

🛏 Holiday Inn Exp Suites
Jameson Inn 🐾 i
Hampton & Suites i
Sleep Inn i Microtel i
Fairfield Inn & Suites
Comfort Inn & Suites
Country Inn & Suites

H EXIT 121 264
Wilson
Greenville

✕ Jac's Grill>, Quince>
Long John Silver's
Subway, KFC
Waffle House 24

Citgo (D,LP,$,V 24)
Kangaroo (D,K,$,V 24)
Eagle Mart (LP,$,V 24)
Shell (D $)

EXIT 119 117 264
Wilson
Raleigh

WILSON

🛏 Whitehead Inn>
Candlewood Suites
Hampton Inn & Suites
Quality Inn 🐾 i
Prime Inn & Suites i

H

BP (D, LP. $ 24)

EXIT 116 42
Wilson
Clayton

Whirligigs

✕ Parker's BBQ>

Shell (D, LP, $ 24)

Wilson

301

70 mph

© 2010

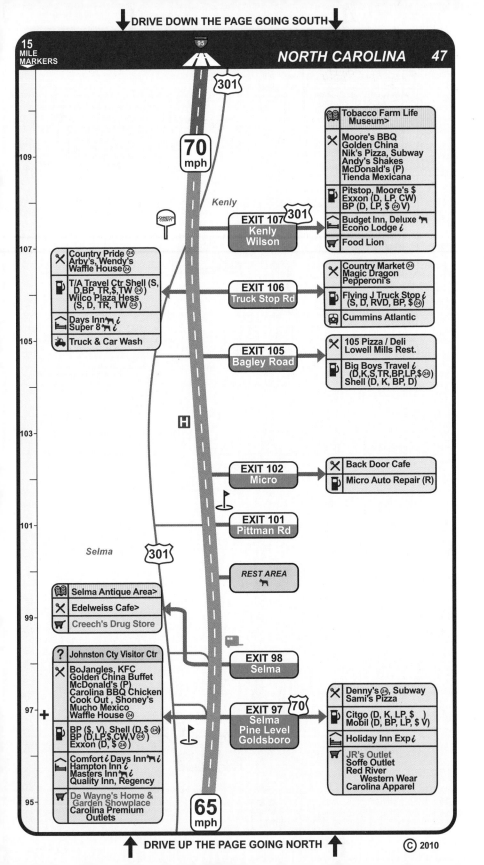

DRIVE DOWN THE PAGE GOING SOUTH

95

301

70 mph

Kenly

JOHNSTON COUNTY

Tobacco Farm Life Museum>

Moore's BBQ
Golden China
Nik's Pizza, Subway
Andy's Shakes
McDonald's (P)
Tienda Mexicana

Pitstop, Moore's $
Exxon (D, LP, CW)
BP (D, LP, $ 24 V)

Budget Inn, Deluxe
Econo Lodge *i*

Food Lion

EXIT 107 301
Kenly
Wilson

109-

107-

Country Pride 24
Arby's, Wendy's
Waffle House 24

T/A Travel Ctr Shell (S, D,BP TR,$,TW 24)
Wilco Plaza Hess (S, D, TR, TW 24)

Days Inn *i*
Super 8 *i*

Truck & Car Wash

EXIT 106
Truck Stop Rd

Country Market 24
Magic Dragon
Pepperoni's

Flying J Truck Stop *i*
(S, D, RVD, BP, $ 24)

Cummins Atlantic

105-

EXIT 105
Bagley Road

105 Pizza / Deli
Lowell Mills Rest.

Big Boys Travel *i*
(D,K,S,TR,BP,LP,$ 24)
Shell (D, K, BP, D)

103-

H

EXIT 102
Micro

Back Door Cafe

Micro Auto Repair (R)

101-

EXIT 101
Pittman Rd

Selma

301

REST AREA

Selma Antique Area>

Edelweiss Cafe>

Creech's Drug Store

99-

? Johnston Cty Visitor Ctr

BoJangles, KFC
Golden China Buffet
McDonald's (P)
Carolina BBQ Chicken
Cook Out , Shoney's
Mucho Mexico
Waffle House 24

EXIT 98
Selma

97-

BP ($, V), Shell (D,$ 24)
BP (D,LP,$,CW,V 24)
Exxon (D, $ 24)

Comfort *i* Days Inn *i*
Hampton Inn *i*
Masters Inn *i*
Quality Inn, Regency

EXIT 97 70
Selma
Pine Level
Goldsboro

Denny's 24, Subway
Sami's Pizza

Citgo (D, K, LP, $)
Mobil (D, BP, LP, $ V)

Holiday Inn Exp *i*

JR's Outlet
Soffe Outlet
Red River
Western Wear
Carolina Apparel

95-

De Wayne's Home &
Garden Showplace
Carolina Premium
Outlets

65 mph

DRIVE UP THE PAGE GOING NORTH

© 2010

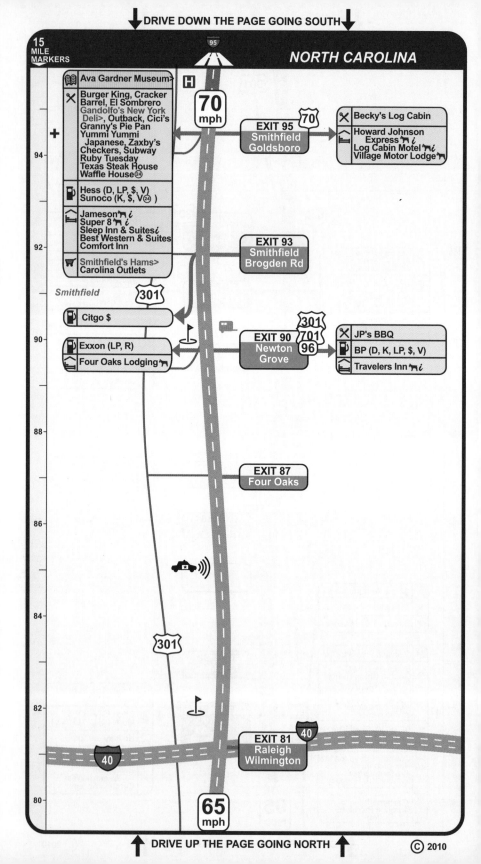

DRIVE DOWN THE PAGE GOING SOUTH

95

15 MILE MARKERS

NORTH CAROLINA

Ava Gardner Museum>

H

70 mph

Burger King, Cracker Barrel, El Sombrero
Gandolfo's New York Deli>, Outback, Cici's
Granny's Pie Pan
Yummi Yummi
Japanese, Zaxby's
Checkers, Subway
Ruby Tuesday
Texas Steak House
Waffle House㉔

Hess (D, LP, $, V)
Sunoco (K, $, V㉔)

Jameson 🐎 i
Super 8 🐎 & i
Sleep Inn & Suites i
Best Western & Suites
Comfort Inn

Smithfield's Hams>
Carolina Outlets

Smithfield

301

Citgo $

Exxon (LP, R)
Four Oaks Lodging 🐎

EXIT 95
Smithfield
Goldsboro

70

Becky's Log Cabin

Howard Johnson
Express 🐎 i
Log Cabin Motel 🐎 i
Village Motor Lodge 🐎 i

EXIT 93
Smithfield
Brogden Rd

EXIT 90
Newton
Grove

301
701
96

JP's BBQ

BP (D, K, LP, $, V)

Travelers Inn 🐎 i

EXIT 87
Four Oaks

301

EXIT 81
Raleigh
Wilmington

40

40

65 mph

DRIVE UP THE PAGE GOING NORTH

© 2010

95

NORTH CAROLINA 49

30 MILE MARKERS

Marker	West side		Exit	East side

- 80

✕ Burger King, KFC
Domino's, China #8
McDonald's (P, $ ㉔)
Pizza Hut, Subway
El Charro Mexican

- 78

⛽ Mule City (D,R,$ ㉔)
Exxon (LP), Pure (D,$)

🛏 Days Inn 🐾 ⓘ

℞ Kerr

🛒 Pound Cake Co.>
Food Lion

- 76

EXIT 79 50
Benson
Newton Grove

✕ Waffle House ㉔
Papa's Pizza

⛽ BP (D, $)
Citgo (D, $)

EXIT 77
Hodges
Chapel Road

✕ Subway ㉔

⛽ Pilot Truck Stop (㉔ S, D, TR, $)

- 74

✕ Milestone Diner ㉔
Dairy Queen, Quizno's

⛽ Sadler Travel Shell
(S, D, TR, RVD, $ ㉔)
Texaco $

🅷

EXIT 75
Jonesboro
Road

- 72

❓ Dunn Area Tourism

📖 Lee Airborne Museum>

✕ BoJangles, BK
Dairy Freeze
Sagebrush, Taco Bell
Yamato's>, Subway
Triangle Waffle

- 70

⛽ Exxon (D, $, V)
Hess (D, K, LP, $)

🛏 Quality Inn
Holiday Inn Exp ⓘ
Jameson Inn 🐾 ⓘ
Simply Divine B&B>
Hampton Inn
Super 8

🛒 IGA

- 68

EXIT 73 55 421
Dunn
Clinton

✕ Andy's Cheesesteaks
Panda House, Wendy's
Zane's Clubhouse
Grill, Cracker Barrel

🛒 Food Lion

EXIT 72
Pope Road

🛏 Comfort Inn ⓘ
Red Carpet Inn ⓘ

EXIT 71
Long Branch Rd

✕ Hardee's ㉔

⛽ Citgo Truck/Auto Plaza
(㉔ D, LP, S, $)

EXIT 70
1811

🛏 Relax Inn

- 66

✕ Brass Lantern Steak
Double T

⛽ Pure (D, LP)
BP (CW, K, LP, $)

🛏 Express Inn Dunn 🐾

- 64

72

EXIT 65 82
Godwin
Falcon

- 62

📖 Averasboro Civil War
Battlefield Museum>

71

⛽ Epco (D, LP, $ ㉔)
Smith's Car/Truck Rpr

65

⛽ BP (D, LP, $, V ㉔ ⓘ)

61

- 60

301

EXIT 61
Wade

⛽ 61 Truck Stop Citgo
(D, K, $, TR, V ㉔)

EXIT 58 13 295
Newton
Grove

✕ Waffle House ㉔
Quiznos

🛏 Days Inn 🐾 ⓘ

- 58

BUS 95

Ⓢ **EXIT 56** 301
Fayetteville
Ft Bragg
Pope AFB

- 56

✕ Subway

⛽ Epco Gas (D, K, LP, $)
Kangaroo (LP, $ ㉔ V)

EXIT 55
Murphy Rd

- 54

301

❓ Fayetteville CVB>

📖 Cape Fear Botanical
Gardens>

🎨 Fascinate-U
Children's Museum>
Climbing Place>
Docks at the Capitol>

🛒 Soffe Outlet>

- 52

EXIT 52 24
Fayetteville
Clinton

- 50

65 mph

© 2010

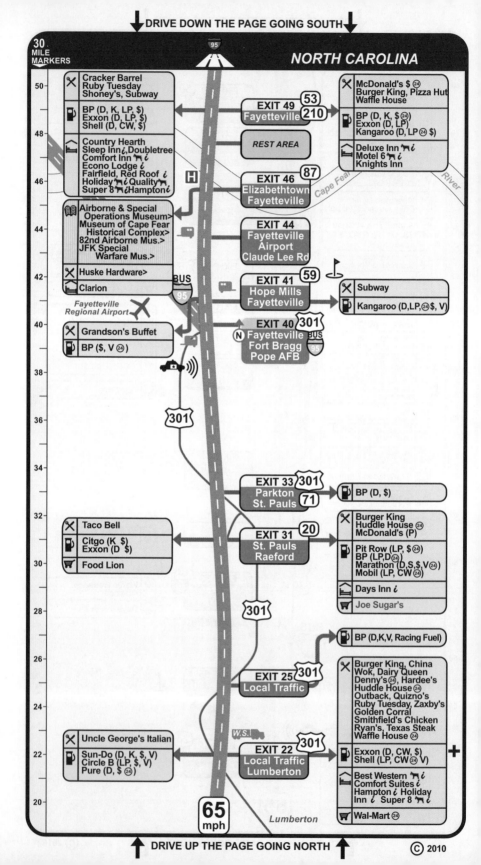

DRIVE DOWN THE PAGE GOING SOUTH

95

NORTH CAROLINA

30 MILE MARKERS

50 —

✕ Cracker Barrel
Ruby Tuesday
Shoney's, Subway

⛽ BP (D, K, LP, $)
Exxon (D, LP, $)
Shell (D, CW, $)

48 —

🛏 Country Hearth
Sleep Inn𝒊,Doubletree
Comfort Inn 🐾 𝒊
Econo Lodge 𝒊
Fairfield, Red Roof 𝒊
Holiday 🐾𝒊 Quality 🐾
Super 8 🐾𝒊 Hampton𝒊

46 —

🏛 Airborne & Special
Operations Museum>
Museum of Cape Fear
Historical Complex>
82nd Airborne Mus.>
JFK Special
Warfare Mus.>

44 —

✕ Huske Hardware>
🛏 Clarion

42 —

*Fayetteville
Regional Airport* ✈

40 —

✕ Grandson's Buffet
⛽ BP ($, V ㉔)

38 —

301

36 —

34 —

EXIT 49 53 210
Fayetteville

REST AREA

EXIT 46 87
Elizabethtown
Fayetteville

EXIT 44
Fayetteville
Airport
Claude Lee Rd

EXIT 41 59
Hope Mills
Fayetteville

Ⓝ **EXIT 40** 301
Fayetteville
Fort Bragg
Pope AFB

H

Cape Fear

River

✕ McDonald's $ ㉔
Burger King, Pizza Hut
Waffle House

⛽ BP (D, K, $ ㉔)
Exxon (D, LP)
Kangaroo (D, LP ㉔ $)

🛏 Deluxe Inn 🐾 𝒊
Motel 6 🐾 𝒊
Knights Inn

✕ Subway
⛽ Kangaroo (D,LP,㉔$, V)

BUS 95

✕ Taco Bell
⛽ Citgo (K $)
Exxon (D $)
🛒 Food Lion

32 —

30 —

EXIT 33 301
Parkton 71
St. Pauls

⛽ BP (D, $)

EXIT 31 20
St. Pauls
Raeford

✕ Burger King
Huddle House ㉔
McDonald's (P)

⛽ Pit Row (LP, $ ㉔)
BP (LP,D㉔)
Marathon (D,S,$,V㉔)
Mobil (LP, CW ㉔)

🛏 Days Inn 𝒊
🛒 Joe Sugar's

28 —

301

26 —

⛽ BP (D,K,V, Racing Fuel)

EXIT 25 301
Local Traffic

✕ Burger King, China
Wok, Dairy Queen
Denny's㉔, Hardee's
Huddle House ㉔
Outback, Quizno's
Ruby Tuesday, Zaxby's
Golden Corral
Smithfield's Chicken
Ryan's, Texas Steak
Waffle House ㉔

24 —

22 —

✕ Uncle George's Italian
⛽ Sun-Do (D, K, $, V)
Circle B (LP, $, V)
Pure (D, $ ㉔)

W.S.

EXIT 22 301
Local Traffic
Lumberton

⛽ Exxon (D, CW, $)
Shell (LP, CW㉔ V)

🛏 Best Western 🐾 𝒊
Comfort Suites 𝒊
Hampton 𝒊 Holiday
Inn 𝒊 Super 8 🐾 𝒊

🛒 Wal-Mart ㉔

20 —

65 mph

Lumberton

DRIVE UP THE PAGE GOING NORTH

Ⓒ 2010

? Lumberton CVB

✕ Cracker Barrel, Lung Wah, Fullers BBQ San Jose Mexican

🛢 Shell (D, $, K)

🛏 Country & Suites Days Inn 🐾 *i* America's Best Value*i* Fairfield Inn*i* Econo Lodge, Comfort*i*

🛒 Tienda Carniceria El Ranchero #2

EXIT 20 41
Lumberton 211
Red Springs

H

Lumberton

✕ Burger King, Mikoti, Two Guys Grill Little Caesar's McDonald's (P) Hardee's (24) Kami Shoney's, Subway Village Station 1893 Waffle House (24)

🛢 Liberty (LP, $) Citgo (24) $) Exxon (D, $, V)

🛏 Deluxe Inn, Ramada Howard Johnson*i* Fairfield Inn

🛒 Merita Bakery Outlet Food Lion>

EXIT 19
Carthage Rd

✕ Los Molcajetes Taqueria Mexican

🛢 Exxon (D, $)

🛏 Knight's Inn 🐾 *i* Motel 6 🐾

✕ Mi Casita

🛢 BP ($, V)

🛏 Traveler's Inn 🐾

19

EXIT 17 72
Lumberton 711
Pembroke

🚕)))

Lumberton Municipal Airport ✈

📖 Lumberton Riverwalk Britt Park

✕ Burger King, Hardee's Huddle House (24) Little China, Subway McDonald's (P)(24) Papa Bill's Old Fashioned BBQ Ruby Tuesday Waffle House(24)Wendy's

🛢 Atkinson (D, $, V) Dobbs Place (D, $ (24) GoGas (D (24)), BP (D) Mobil (R, D, $ (24) Dobbs Exp (CW, $ (24))

🛏 Budget Inn 🐾 Atkinson Inn & Suites

Rₓ CVS

🛒 Food Lion

EXIT 13 74
Laurinburg
Rockingham
Wilmington

🚩

301

EXIT 10 301
Fairmont

EXIT 7
McDonald
Raynham

N ? *NORTH CAROLINA WELCOME CENTER*

301

65
mph

© 2010

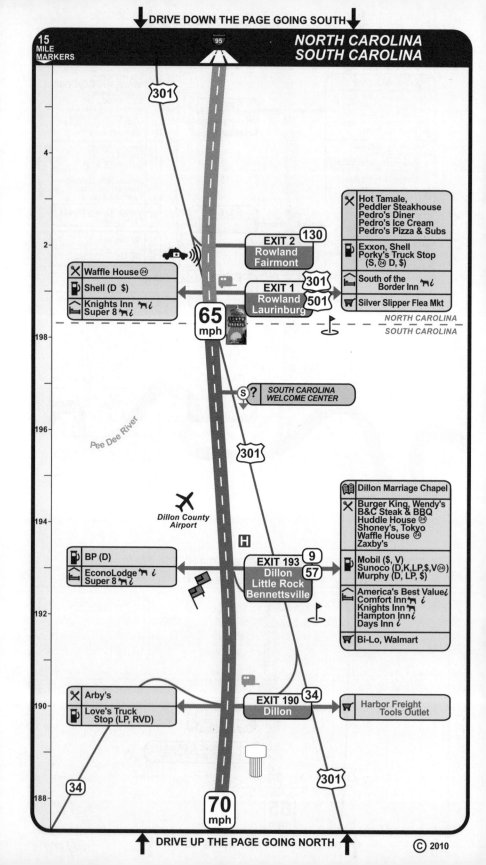

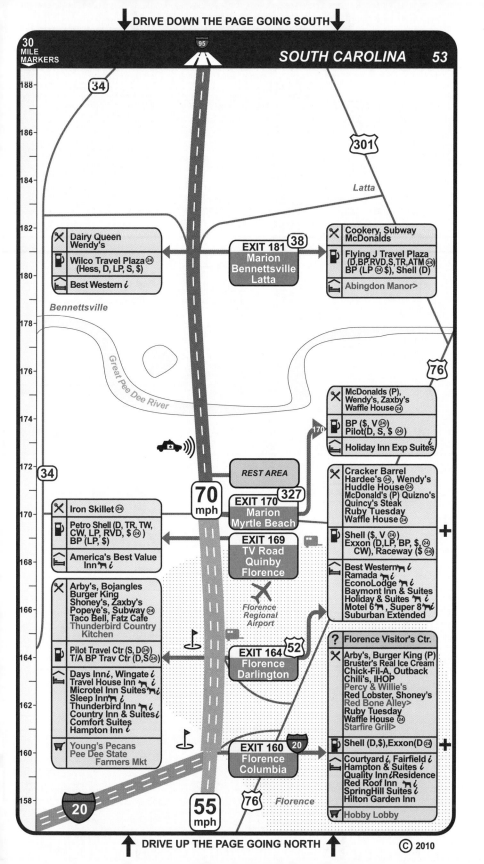

95

34

301

Latta

188
186
184
182
180
178
176
174
172
170
168
166
164
162
160
158

76

Bennettsville

Great Pee Dee River

34

EXIT 181 38
Marion
Bennettsville
Latta

✕ Dairy Queen
Wendy's

⛽ Wilco Travel Plaza 24
(Hess, D, LP, S, $)

🛏 Best Western i

✕ Cookery, Subway
McDonalds

⛽ Flying J Travel Plaza
(D,BP,RVD,S,TR,ATM 24)
BP (LP 24 $), Shell (D)

🛏 Abingdon Manor>

✕ McDonalds (P),
Wendy's, Zaxby's
Waffle House 24

⛽ BP ($, V 24)
Pilot(D, S, $) 24

🛏 Holiday Inn Exp Suites i

170

REST AREA

70 mph

EXIT 170 327
Marion
Myrtle Beach

EXIT 169
TV Road
Quinby
Florence

✕ Cracker Barrel
Hardee's 24, Wendy's
Huddle House 24
McDonald's (P) Quizno's
Quincy's Steak
Ruby Tuesday
Waffle House 24

⛽ Shell ($, V 24)
Exxon (D,LP, BP, $,
CW), Raceway ($ 24)

🛏 Best Western i
Ramada 🐾 i
EconoLodge 🐾 i
Baymont Inn & Suites
Holiday & Suites i
Motel 6 🐾 , Super 8 🐾 i
Suburban Extended

+

✕ Iron Skillet 24

⛽ Petro Shell (D, TR, TW,
CW, LP, RVD, $ 24)
BP (LP, $)

🛏 America's Best Value
Inn 🐾 i

✕ Arby's, Bojangles
Burger King
Shoney's, Zaxby's
Popeye's, Subway 24
Taco Bell, Fatz Cafe
Thunderbird Country
Kitchen

⛽ Pilot Travel Ctr (S, D 24)
T/A BP Trav Ctr (D,S 24)

🛏 Days Inn i, Wingate i
Travel House Inn 🐾 i
Microtel Inn Suites 🐾 i
Sleep Inn 🐾 i
Thunderbird Inn 🐾 i
Country Inn & Suites i
Comfort Suites
Hampton Inn i

🛒 Young's Pecans
Pee Dee State
Farmers Mkt

EXIT 164 52
Florence
Darlington

Florence
Regional
Airport

EXIT 160 20
Florence
Columbia

? Florence Visitor's Ctr.

✕ Arby's, Burger King (P)
Bruster's Real Ice Cream
Chick-Fil-A, Outback
Chili's, IHOP
Percy & Willie's
Red Lobster, Shoney's
Red Bone Alley>
Ruby Tuesday
Waffle House 24
Starfire Grill>

⛽ Shell (D,$),Exxon(D 24)

🛏 Courtyard i, Fairfield i
Hampton & Suites i
Quality Inn i Residence
Red Roof Inn i
SpringHill Suites i
Hilton Garden Inn

🛒 Hobby Lobby

+

20

76

Florence

55 mph

© 2010

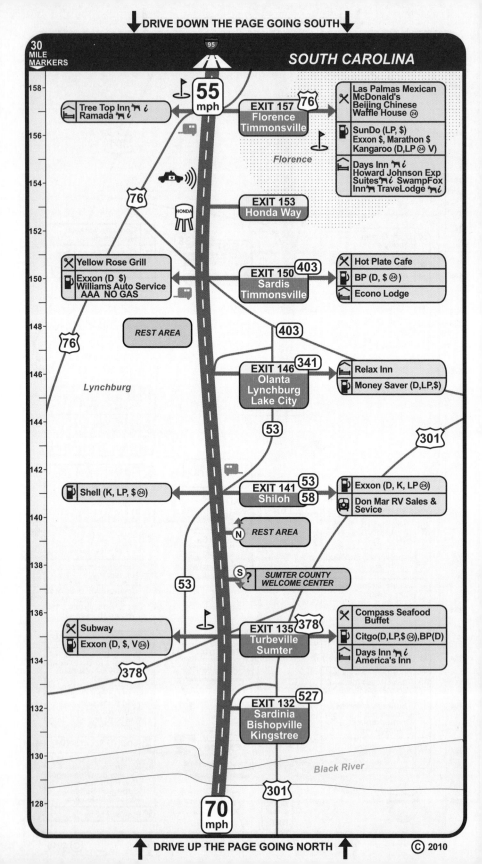

DRIVE DOWN THE PAGE GOING SOUTH

I-95

30 MILE MARKERS

SOUTH CAROLINA

158 -
156 -

55 mph

Tree Top Inn, Ramada

EXIT 157 76
Florence
Timmonsville

Las Palmas Mexican
McDonald's
Beijing Chinese
Waffle House (24)

SunDo (LP, $)
Exxon $, Marathon $
Kangaroo (D,LP (24) V)

Days Inn
Howard Johnson Exp
Suites SwampFox
Inn TraveLodge

Florence

154 -

76

EXIT 153
Honda Way

HONDA

152 -

150 -

Yellow Rose Grill
Exxon (D $)
Williams Auto Service
AAA NO GAS

EXIT 150 403
Sardis
Timmonsville

Hot Plate Cafe
BP (D, $ (24))
Econo Lodge

148 -

REST AREA

403

76

146 -

Lynchburg

EXIT 146 341
Olanta
Lynchburg
Lake City

Relax Inn
Money Saver (D,LP,$)

144 -

53

301

142 -

Shell (K, LP, $ (24))

EXIT 141 53
Shiloh 58

Exxon (D, K, LP (24))
Don Mar RV Sales &
Sevice

140 -

N **REST AREA**

138 -

S ? **SUMTER COUNTY
WELCOME CENTER**

53

136 -

Subway
Exxon (D, $, V (24))

EXIT 135 378
Turbeville
Sumter

Compass Seafood
Buffet
Citgo(D,LP,$ (23)),BP(D)
Days Inn
America's Inn

134 -

378

132 -

EXIT 132 527
Sardinia
Bishopville
Kingstree

130 -

Black River

301

128 -

70 mph

DRIVE UP THE PAGE GOING NORTH

© 2010

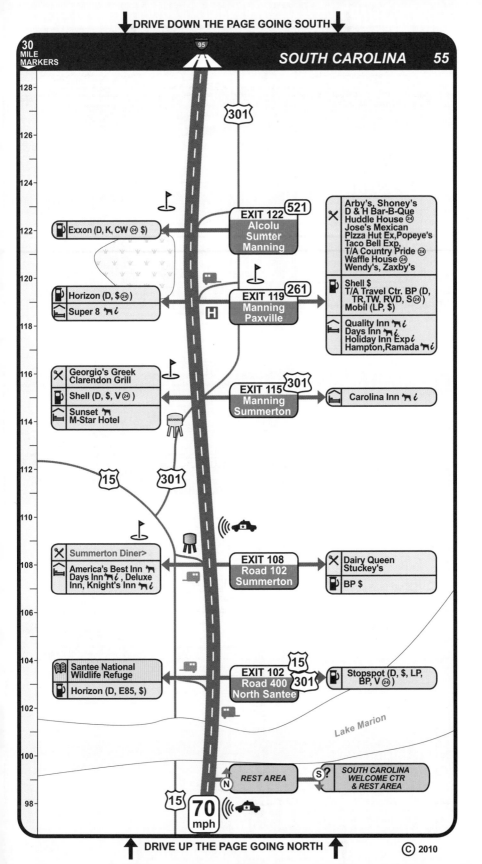

DRIVE DOWN THE PAGE GOING SOUTH

30 MILE MARKERS

SOUTH CAROLINA

95

98

EXIT 98
Eutawville
Santee — 6

210

Santee State Park>
Elloree Heritage Mus>

Burger King, Wendy's
Clark's Family Rest.
Cracker Barrel, TCBY
Lone Star BBQ>
Maurice's Gourmet
  BBQ, McDonald's (P)
Peking Chinese
Noble Roman's Pizza
Waffle House (24)

EXIT 97 — 301
Orangeburg

? Santee Cooper Cty
Tourist Information

Bojangles
Coaster Seafood
Huddle House (24)
KFC, Pizza Hut (24)
La Fogata Mexican
Shoney's, Thai House
Subway, Theo's Italian
Captain's Quarters

96

Citgo (K, $)
Exxon (LP, $)
Hess (D, K, $)
Horizon (D, K, $)
Shell (D, R, $ (24))

EXIT 93 — 15 US
Santee
Elloree
Holly Hill

BP $, Citgo
Smith's Chevron (LP, BP, $ (24))
Mobil (D, $, CW, V)

94

92

Clark's Inn, Holiday Inn
Baymont & Suites
Lake Marion Inn
Elloree B&B>
Country Inn & Suites
Quality Inn & Suites
State Park Cabins>

15

Best Western
Whitten Inn
Hampton Inn
Howard Johnson
Ramada
Super 8
Travelodge

90

Exxon (D, LP, $)

EXIT 90 — 176 US
Holly Hill
Cameron

Piggly-Wiggly
Russell Stover Outlet
Smith's

88

26 — 210

86

EXIT 86 — 26
Charleston
Columbia

84

82

Shell (D, $, V)

EXIT 82 — 178
Harleyville
Bowman

Dairy Queen, Wendy's

BP $
Wilco Travel Plaze Hess
(D, LP, S, V (24))

Peach Tree Inn

80

15

78

Huddle House (24)
Taco Bell

BP, Shell (D, $, V (24))

Country Hearth
Days Inn
Southern Inn
Super 8

EXIT 77 — 78
St. George
Branchville

Empire Chinese
Giorgio's Greek & Ital.
Hardee's, KFC
McDonald's (P) (24)
Pizza Hut, Subway
TCBY, Waffle House (24)
Mi Rancho Mexican

Exxon $, Monoco $
Horizon (K, $, E85 (24))

America's Best Value
Inn, Comfort
Econo Lodge
Quality Inn

Reid's

76

74

*PARKING AREA
(No Services)*

72

70

Edisto River

15

68

70 mph

DRIVE UP THE PAGE GOING NORTH

© 2010

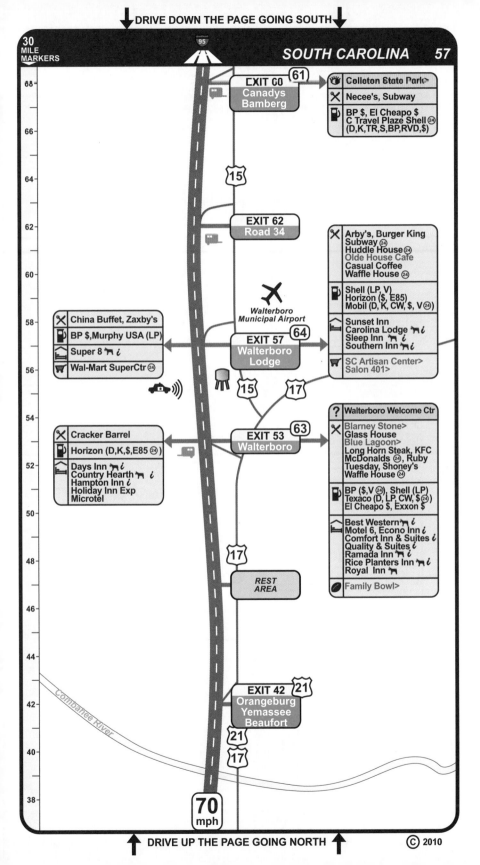

30 MILE MARKERS

68

EXIT 60
Canadys
Bamberg — 61

Colleton State Park>
Necee's, Subway
BP $, El Cheapo $
C Travel Plaze Shell 24
(D,K,TR,S,BP,RVD,$)

66

15

64

EXIT 62
Road 34

62

Arby's, Burger King
Subway 24
Huddle House 24
Olde House Cafe
Casual Coffee
Waffle House 24

60

Shell (LP, V)
Horizon ($, E85)
Mobil (D, K, CW, $, V 24)

China Buffet, Zaxby's
BP $,Murphy USA (LP)
Super 8
Wal-Mart SuperCtr 24

58

EXIT 57
Walterboro
Lodge — 64

Walterboro Municipal Airport

Sunset Inn
Carolina Lodge
Sleep Inn
Southern Inn

SC Artisan Center>
Salon 401>

56

15   17

54

Walterboro Welcome Ctr

Cracker Barrel
Horizon (D,K,$,E85 24)
Days Inn
Country Hearth
Hampton Inn
Holiday Inn Exp
Microtel

EXIT 53
Walterboro — 63

Blarney Stone>
Glass House
Blue Lagoon>
Long Horn Steak, KFC
McDonalds 24, Ruby
Tuesday, Shoney's
Waffle House 24

52

BP ($,V 24), Shell (LP)
Texaco (D, LP, CW, $ 24)
El Cheapo $, Exxon $

Best Western
Motel 6, Econo Inn
Comfort Inn & Suites
Quality & Suites
Ramada Inn
Rice Planters Inn
Royal Inn

50

Family Bowl>

48

17

REST AREA

46

44

EXIT 42
Orangeburg
Yemassee
Beaufort — 21

42

21

40

17

Combahee River

38

70 mph

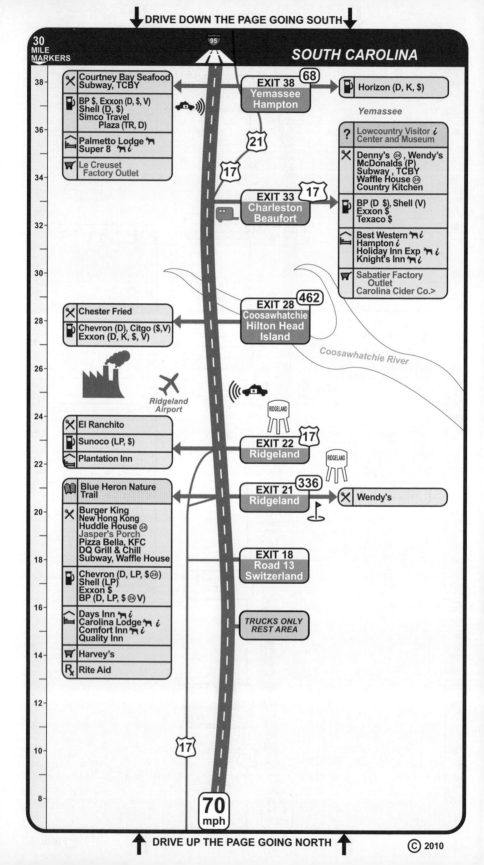

DRIVE DOWN THE PAGE GOING SOUTH

95

30 MILE MARKERS

SOUTH CAROLINA

Marker	Left side	Exit	Right side
38	Courtney Bay Seafood, Subway, TCBY	**EXIT 38** Yemassee Hampton	Horizon (D, K, $)
	BP $, Exxon (D, $, V), Shell (D, $), Simco Travel Plaza (TR, D)		*Yemassee*
36	Palmetto Lodge, Super 8	21	Lowcountry Visitor Center and Museum
34	Le Creuset Factory Outlet	17	Denny's, Wendy's, McDonalds (P), Subway, TCBY, Waffle House, Country Kitchen
		EXIT 33 Charleston Beaufort	BP (D $), Shell (V), Exxon $, Texaco $
32			Best Western, Hampton, Holiday Inn Exp, Knight's Inn
30			Sabatier Factory Outlet, Carolina Cider Co.>
28	Chester Fried	**EXIT 28** Coosawhatchie Hilton Head Island	
	Chevron (D), Citgo ($,V), Exxon (D, K, $, V)		*Coosawhatchie River*
26			
24	*Ridgeland Airport*	RIDGELAND	
	El Ranchito	17	
22	Sunoco (LP, $)	**EXIT 22** Ridgeland	RIDGELAND
	Plantation Inn		
21	Blue Heron Nature Trail	**EXIT 21** Ridgeland	Wendy's
20	Burger King, New Hong Kong, Huddle House, Jasper's Porch, Pizza Bella, KFC, DQ Grill & Chill, Subway, Waffle House		
18	Chevron (D, LP, $), Shell (LP), Exxon $, BP (D, LP, $ V)	**EXIT 18** Road 13 Switzerland	
16	Days Inn, Carolina Lodge, Comfort Inn, Quality Inn	*TRUCKS ONLY REST AREA*	
14	Harvey's		
	Rite Aid		
12			
10	17		
8			

70 mph

DRIVE UP THE PAGE GOING NORTH

© 2010

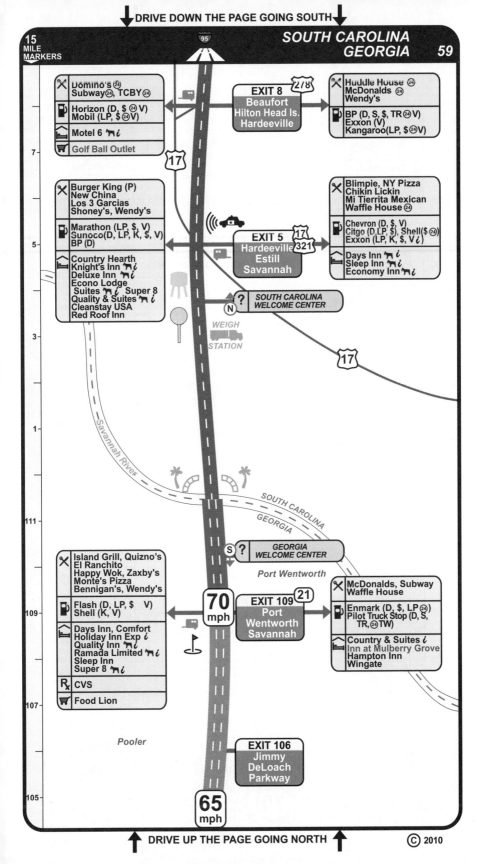

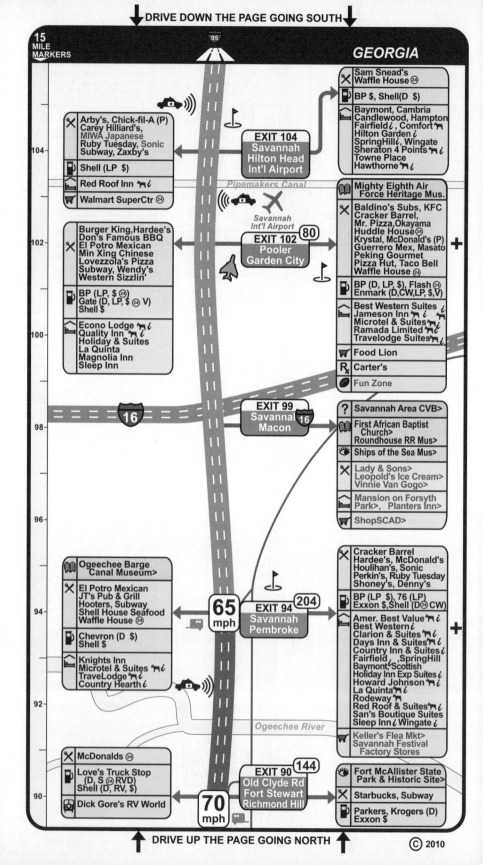

DRIVE DOWN THE PAGE GOING SOUTH

15 MILE MARKERS

I-95

GEORGIA

EXIT 104
Savannah
Hilton Head
Int'l Airport

✕ Arby's, Chick-fil-A (P)
Carey Hilliard's,
MIWA Japanese
Ruby Tuesday, Sonic
Subway, Zaxby's

⛽ Shell (LP $)

🛏 Red Roof Inn 🐾𝑖

🛒 Walmart SuperCtr ㉔

Pipemakers Canal

Savannah Int'l Airport

✕ Sam Snead's
Waffle House ㉔

⛽ BP $, Shell(D $)

🛏 Baymont, Cambria
Candlewood, Hampton
Fairfield 𝑖, Comfort 🐾
Hilton Garden 𝑖
SpringHill𝑖, Wingate
Sheraton 4 Points 🐾 𝑖
Towne Place
Hawthorne 🐾𝑖

EXIT 102
Pooler
Garden City 80

✕ Burger King, Hardee's
Don's Famous BBQ
El Potro Mexican
Min Xing Chinese
Lovezzola's Pizza
Subway, Wendy's
Western Sizzlin'

⛽ BP (LP, $ ㉔)
Gate (D, LP, $ ㉔ V)
Shell $

🛏 Econo Lodge 🐾𝑖
Quality Inn 🐾𝑖
Holiday & Suites
La Quinta
Magnolia Inn
Sleep Inn

📖 Mighty Eighth Air
Force Heritage Mus.

✕ Baldino's Subs, KFC
Cracker Barrel,
Mr. Pizza, Okayama
Huddle House ㉔
Krystal, McDonald's (P)
Guerrero Mex, Masato
Peking Gourmet
Pizza Hut, Taco Bell
Waffle House ㉔

⛽ BP (D, LP, $), Flash ㉔
Enmark (D,CW,LP, $,V)

🛏 Best Western Suites 𝑖
Jameson Inn 🐾 𝑖
Microtel & Suites 𝑖
Ramada Limited 🐾𝑖
Travelodge Suites🐾𝑖

🛒 Food Lion

℞ Carter's

🎡 Fun Zone

I-16

EXIT 99
Savannah
Macon 16

? Savannah Area CVB>

📖 First African Baptist
Church>
Roundhouse RR Mus>

🐚 Ships of the Sea Mus>

✕ Lady & Sons>
Leopold's Ice Cream>
Vinnie Van Gogo>

🛏 Mansion on Forsyth
Park>, Planters Inn>

🛒 ShopSCAD>

📖 Ogeechee Barge
Canal Museum>

✕ El Potro Mexican
JT's Pub & Grill
Hooters, Subway
Shell House Seafood
Waffle House ㉔

⛽ Chevron (D $)
Shell $

🛏 Knights Inn
Microtel & Suites 🐾𝑖
TraveLodge 🐾𝑖
Country Hearth 𝑖

65 mph

EXIT 94
Savannah
Pembroke 204

✕ Cracker Barrel
Hardee's, McDonald's
Houlihan's, Sonic
Perkin's, Ruby Tuesday
Shoney's, Denny's

⛽ BP (LP $), 76 (LP)
Exxon $,Shell (D㉔ CW)

🛏 Amer. Best Value 🐾 𝑖
Best Western 𝑖
Clarion & Suites 🐾𝑖
Days Inn & Suites 🐾𝑖
Country Inn & Suites 𝑖
Fairfield 𝑖, SpringHill 𝑖
Baymont𝑖,Scottish
Holiday Inn Exp Suites 𝑖
Howard Johnson 🐾𝑖
La Quinta 🐾𝑖
Rodeway 🐾
Red Roof & Suites🐾𝑖
San's Boutique Suites
Sleep Inn 𝑖 Wingate 𝑖

🛒 Keller's Flea Mkt>
Savannah Festival
Factory Stores

Ogeechee River

✕ McDonalds ㉔

⛽ Love's Truck Stop
(D, S ㉔ RVD)
Shell (D, RV, $)

🚌 Dick Gore's RV World

70 mph

EXIT 90
Old Clyde Rd
Fort Stewart
Richmond Hill 144

🖐 Fort McAllister State
Park & Historic Site>

✕ Starbucks, Subway

⛽ Parkers, Krogers (D)
Exxon $

DRIVE UP THE PAGE GOING NORTH

© 2010

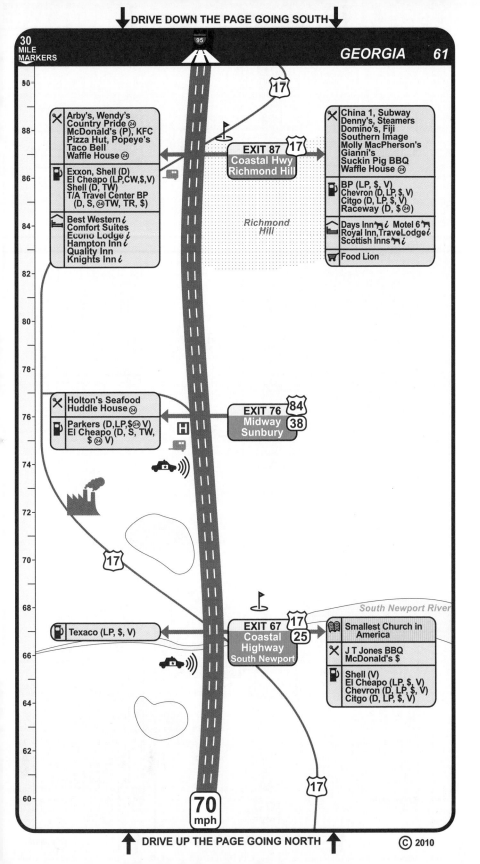

17

EXIT 87 17
Coastal Hwy
Richmond Hill

Richmond Hill

Arby's, Wendy's
Country Pride 24
McDonald's (P), KFC
Pizza Hut, Popeye's
Taco Bell
Waffle House 24

Exxon, Shell (D)
El Cheapo (LP,CW,$,V)
Shell (D, TW)
T/A Travel Center BP
(D, S, 24 TW, TR, $)

Best Western *i*
Comfort Suites
Econo Lodge *i*
Hampton Inn *i*
Quality Inn
Knights Inn *i*

China 1, Subway
Denny's, Steamers
Domino's, Fiji
Southern Image
Molly MacPherson's
Gianni's
Suckin Pig BBQ
Waffle House 24

BP (LP, $, V)
Chevron (D, LP, $, V)
Citgo (D, LP, $, V)
Raceway (D, $ 24)

Days Inn *i* Motel 6
Royal Inn, TraveLodge *i*
Scottish Inns *i*

Food Lion

EXIT 76 84
Midway 38
Sunbury

Holton's Seafood
Huddle House 24

Parkers (D,LP,$24 V)
El Cheapo (D, S, TW,
$ 24 V)

17

EXIT 67 17
Coastal 25
Highway
South Newport

Texaco (LP, $, V)

South Newport River

Smallest Church in
America

J T Jones BBQ
McDonald's $

Shell (V)
El Cheapo (LP, $, V)
Chevron (D, LP, $, V)
Citgo (D, LP, $, V)

17

70 mph

© 2010

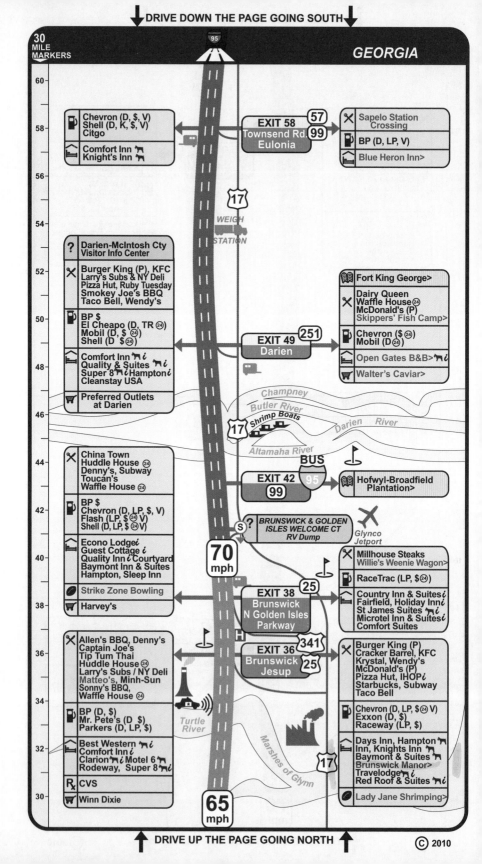

DRIVE DOWN THE PAGE GOING SOUTH

30 MILE MARKERS

GEORGIA

95

60

58
- Chevron (D, $, V)
- Shell (D, K, $, V)
- Citgo
- Comfort Inn
- Knight's Inn

EXIT 58 57 / 99
Townsend Rd.
Eulonia

- Sapelo Station Crossing
- BP (D, LP, V)
- Blue Heron Inn>

56

17

54
WEIGH STATION

52
- **?** Darien-McIntosh Cty Visitor Info Center
- Burger King (P), KFC
  Larry's Subs & NY Deli
  Pizza Hut, Ruby Tuesday
  Smokey Joe's BBQ
  Taco Bell, Wendy's

- Fort King George>
- Dairy Queen
  Waffle House (24)
  McDonald's (P)
  Skippers' Fish Camp>

50
- BP $
  El Cheapo (D, TR (24))
  Mobil (D, $ (24))
  Shell (D $ (24))

- Chevron ($ (24))
  Mobil (D (24))

EXIT 49 251
Darien

48
- Comfort Inn
  Quality & Suites
  Super 8 / Hampton
  Cleanstay USA

- Open Gates B&B>
- Walter's Caviar>

- Preferred Outlets at Darien

46
Champney
Butler River
Shrimp Boats
Darien River
17
Altamaha River

44
- China Town
  Huddle House (24)
  Denny's, Subway
  Toucan's
  Waffle House (24)

BUS 95
- Hofwyl-Broadfield Plantation>

EXIT 42 99

42
- BP $
  Chevron (D, LP, $, V)
  Flash (LP, $ (24) V)
  Shell (D, LP, $ (24) V)

? BRUNSWICK & GOLDEN ISLES WELCOME CT RV Dump

Glynco Jetport

40
- Econo Lodge
  Guest Cottage
  Quality Inn / Courtyard
  Baymont Inn & Suites
  Hampton, Sleep Inn

70 mph

- Millhouse Steaks
  Willie's Weenie Wagon>
- RaceTrac (LP, $ (24))

- Strike Zone Bowling
- Harvey's

38
EXIT 38 25
Brunswick
N Golden Isles
Parkway

- Country Inn & Suites
  Fairfield, Holiday Inn
  St James Suites
  Microtel Inn & Suites
  Comfort Suites

36
- Allen's BBQ, Denny's
  Captain Joe's
  Tip Tum Thai
  Huddle House (24)
  Larry's Subs / NY Deli
  Matteo's, Minh-Sun
  Sonny's BBQ
  Waffle House (24)

H

EXIT 36 341 / 25
Brunswick
Jesup

- Burger King (P)
  Cracker Barrel, KFC
  Krystal, Wendy's
  McDonald's (P)
  Pizza Hut, IHOP
  Starbucks, Subway
  Taco Bell

34
- BP (D, $)
  Mr. Pete's (D $)
  Parkers (D, LP, $)

Turtle River

- Chevron (D, LP, $ (24) V)
  Exxon (D, $)
  Raceway (LP, $)

32
- Best Western
  Comfort Inn
  Clarion / Motel 6
  Rodeway, Super 8

Marshes of Glynn

17

- Days Inn, Hampton
  Inn, Knights Inn
  Baymont & Suites
  Brunswick Manor>
  Travelodge
  Red Roof & Suites

- **Rx** CVS

30
- Winn Dixie

- Lady Jane Shrimping>

65 mph

DRIVE UP THE PAGE GOING NORTH

© 2010

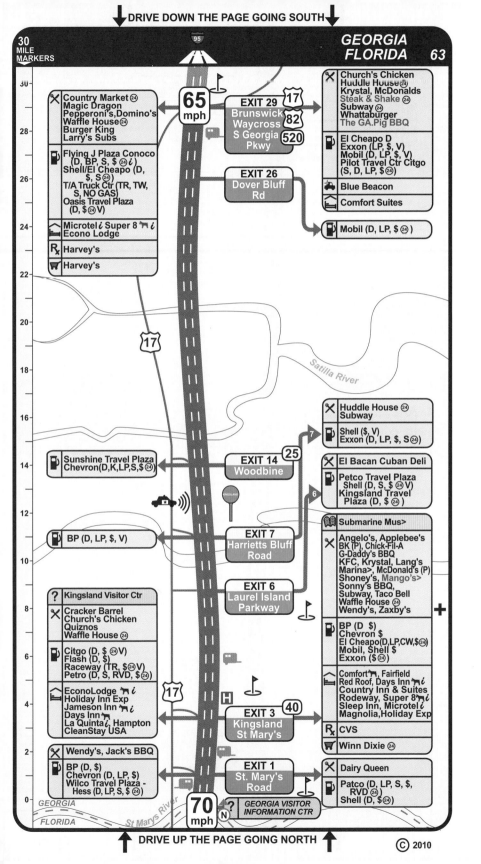

65 mph

70 mph

EXIT 29
Brunswick
Waycross
S Georgia
Pkwy
17
82
520

EXIT 26
Dover Bluff
Rd

EXIT 14 25
Woodbine

EXIT 7
Harrietts Bluff
Road

EXIT 6
Laurel Island
Parkway

EXIT 3 40
Kingsland
St Mary's

EXIT 1
St. Mary's
Road

17

GEORGIA VISITOR
INFORMATION CTR

Left side

✗ Country Market ㉔
Magic Dragon
Pepperoni's, Domino's
Waffle House ㉔
Burger King
Larry's Subs

⛽ Flying J Plaza Conoco
(D, BP, S, $ ㉔ i)
Shell/El Cheapo (D,
$, S ㉔)
T/A Truck Ctr (TR, TW,
S, NO GAS)
Oasis Travel Plaza
(D, $ ㉔ V)

🛏 Microtel i Super 8 🐴 i
Econo Lodge

℞ Harvey's

🛒 Harvey's

⛽ Sunshine Travel Plaza
Chevron(D,K,LP,S,$ ㉔)

⛽ BP (D, LP, $, V)

? Kingsland Visitor Ctr

✗ Cracker Barrel
Church's Chicken
Quiznos
Waffle House ㉔

⛽ Citgo (D, $ ㉔ V)
Flash (D, $)
Raceway (TR, $ ㉔ V)
Petro (D, S, RVD, $ ㉔)

🏠 EconoLodge 🐴 i
Holiday Inn Exp
Jameson Inn 🐴 i
Days Inn 🐴
La Quinta i, Hampton
CleanStay USA

✗ Wendy's, Jack's BBQ

⛽ BP (D, $)
Chevron (D, LP, $)
Wilco Travel Plaza -
Hess (D, LP, S, $ ㉔)

Right side

✗ Church's Chicken
Huddle House ㉔
Krystal, McDonalds
Steak & Shake ㉔
Subway ㉔
Whattaburger
The GA.Pig BBQ

⛽ El Cheapo D
Exxon (LP, $, V)
Mobil (D, LP, $, V)
Pilot Travel Ctr Citgo
(S, D, LP, $ ㉔)

🚜 Blue Beacon

🛏 Comfort Suites

⛽ Mobil (D, LP, $ ㉔)

✗ Huddle House ㉔
Subway

⛽ Shell ($, V)
Exxon (D, LP, $, S ㉔)

7

✗ El Bacan Cuban Deli

⛽ Petco Travel Plaza
Shell (D, S, ㉔ V)
Kingsland Travel
Plaza (D, $ ㉔)

6

📖 Submarine Mus>

✗ Angelo's, Applebee's
BK (P), Chick-Fil-A
G-Daddy's BBQ
KFC, Krystal, Lang's
Marina>, McDonald's (P)
Shoney's, Mango's>
Sonny's BBQ
Subway, Taco Bell
Waffle House ㉔
Wendy's, Zaxby's

⛽ BP (D $)
Chevron $
El Cheapo(D,LP,CW,$㉔)
Mobil, Shell $
Exxon ($ ㉔)

🏠 Comfort 🐴, Fairfield
Red Roof, Days Inn i
Country Inn & Suites
Rodeway, Super 8 🐴 i
Sleep Inn, Microtel i
Magnolia, Holiday Exp

℞ CVS

🛒 Winn Dixie ㉔

✗ Dairy Queen

⛽ Patco (D, LP, S, $,
RVD ㉔)
Shell (D, $ ㉔)

Satilla River

KINGSLAND

H

St Marys River

GEORGIA
FLORIDA

© 2010

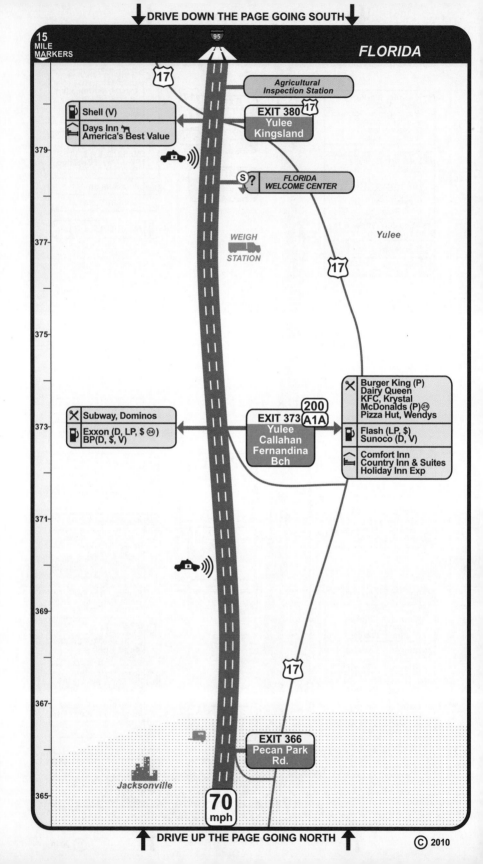

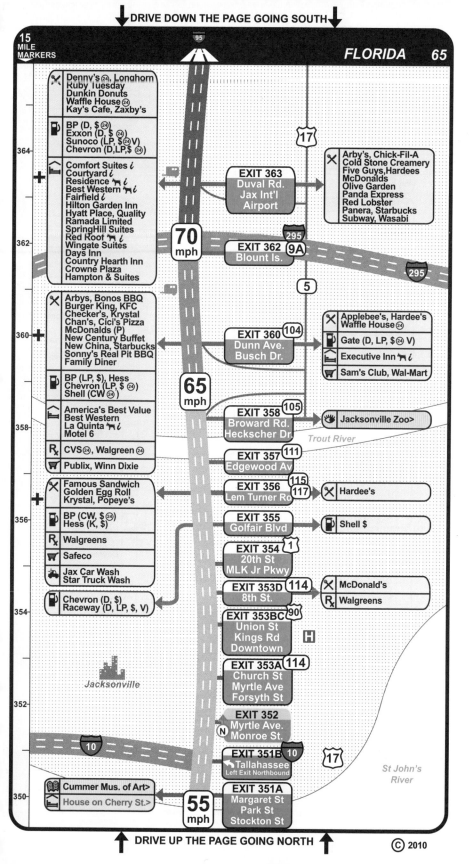

Denny's (24), Longhorn
Ruby Tuesday
Dunkin Donuts
Waffle House (24)
Kay's Cafe, Zaxby's

BP (D, $) (24)
Exxon (D, $) (24)
Sunoco (LP, $) (24) V)
Chevron (D,LP,$) (24)

Comfort Suites i
Courtyard i
Residence i
Best Western i
Fairfield i
Hilton Garden Inn
Hyatt Place, Quality
Ramada Limited
SpringHill Suites
Red Roof i
Wingate Suites
Days Inn
Country Hearth Inn
Crowne Plaza
Hampton & Suites

Arbys, Bonos BBQ
Burger King, KFC
Checker's, Krystal
Chan's, Cici's Pizza
McDonalds (P)
New Century Buffet
New China, Starbucks
Sonny's Real Pit BBQ
Family Diner

BP (LP, $), **Hess**
Chevron (LP, $) (24)
Shell (CW) (24)

America's Best Value
Best Western
La Quinta i
Motel 6

CVS (24), **Walgreen** (24)

Publix, Winn Dixie

Famous Sandwich
Golden Egg Roll
Krystal, Popeye's

BP (CW, $) (24)
Hess (K, $)

Walgreens

Safeco

Jax Car Wash
Star Truck Wash

Chevron (D, $)
Raceway (D, LP, $, V)

Jacksonville

Cummer Mus. of Art>
House on Cherry St.>

70 mph

65 mph

55 mph

95

17

EXIT 363
Duval Rd.
Jax Int'l
Airport

295
EXIT 362 9A
Blount Is.

295

5

EXIT 360 104
Dunn Ave.
Busch Dr.

EXIT 358 105
Broward Rd.
Heckscher Dr.
Trout River

EXIT 357 111
Edgewood Av

EXIT 356 115 117
Lem Turner Rd

EXIT 355
Golfair Blvd

EXIT 354 1
20th St
MLK Jr Pkwy

EXIT 353D 114
8th St.

EXIT 353BC 90
Union St
Kings Rd
Downtown
H

EXIT 353A 114
Church St
Myrtle Ave
Forsyth St

EXIT 352
Myrtle Ave.
Monroe St. N

10

EXIT 351B 10 17
Tallahassee
Left Exit Northbound

St John's River

EXIT 351A
Margaret St
Park St
Stockton St

Arby's, Chick-Fil-A
Cold Stone Creamery
Five Guys,Hardees
McDonalds
Olive Garden
Panda Express
Red Lobster
Panera, Starbucks
Subway, Wasabi

Applebee's, Hardee's
Waffle House (24)

Gate (D, LP, $) (24) V)

Executive Inn i

Sam's Club, Wal-Mart

Jacksonville Zoo>

Hardee's

Shell $

McDonald's
Walgreens

Mile markers:
364 - 362 - 360 - 358 - 356 - 354 - 352 - 350

DRIVE DOWN THE PAGE GOING SOUTH

15 MILE MARKERS

FLORIDA

95

✕ Bistro Aix	**EXIT 350** San Marco Blvd	📖 Museum of Science & History>
🛒 Peterbrooke Chocolatier		🏠 River City Brewing>
		🏈 Kids Kampus>

5 | **55 mph** | Ⓢ **EXIT 349** Downtown to Beaches | Jacksonville | 1

EXIT 348 Philips Hwy (1)

349-

| 🏠 Scottish Inns ℹ Super 8 | | |

1A

✕ McDonalds, Taco Bell	**EXIT 347** Emerson St. 126	🔋 Shell (R, $) Chevron (D, $)
🔋 Gate (D, V) Hess (D, K, CW, V)		
🏠 Emerson Inn		
🛒 Sunbeam Bakery Shop		

347-

✕ Baskin Robbins Burger King, Taco Bell Dunkin Donuts Sonny's BBQ	Ⓗ **EXIT 346** University Blvd 109	✕ Capt D's, Happy Garden, Krystal Ying's Chinese
🔋 BP (D, $) RaceTrac (LP, $⑳V)		🔋 BP (CW) Shell (LP, $⑳)
🏠 Days Inn Ramada, Super 8	**EXIT 345** Bowden Rd University Blvd 109 Ⓗ	✕ Asian Taste, Bono's BBQ, Blimpie Donair House Godfathers Pizza

345-

| | | 🔋 Gate (D, K, LP, $) Hess (D, V) |
| | | 🛒 Bosnia Market |

| ✕ Applebee's, Hardee's Chick-Fil-A (P) Cracker Barrel McDonald's⑳ Waffle House⑳ Sonic, Wendy's | Ⓗ **EXIT 344** Butler Blvd Jax Beaches 202 | 📖 Mayo Clinic> |
| | | 🏠 Best Western Hampton Holiday Inn Exp Homestead Studio Radisson, Marriott |

343-

🔋 BP (D, CW, $⑳) Shell (LP⑳ V)		
🏠 Courtyard, La Quinta Extended Stay Deluxe Jameson Inn Microtel & Suites Towne Place Suites Red Roof, Wingate	Jacksonville	✕ Arby's, Hardee's Krystal
		🔋 Gate (D, LP, $, V) Shell (D, CW, $)
🛒 Edwinn Watts Golf Superstore	**EXIT 341** Baymeadows Rd 152	🏠 Comfort Suites Holiday Inn Embassy Suites HomeStead Studio Baymeadows Inn

341-

1

| ✕ Bamboo Creek Asian Burger King Denny's, KFC Larry's Giant Subs McDonalds, Pagoda Red Lobster, Wendy's Renna's Pizza | 5 Ⓝ **EXIT 340** Southside Blvd 115 | |
| 🔋 Shell (LP, $⑳) | **EXIT 339** Phillips Hwy 1 | ✕ Arby's, Mcdonald's Bono Pit BBQ Buca di Beppo Burger King (P), Taco Bell, Istanbul Grille Olive Garden |

339-

| 🏠 Homewood Suites La Quinta, Studio 6 Sun Suites 🐾ℹ | | 🔋 Kangaroo (D, LP⑳) |
| | 1 | 🛒 The Avenues Mall |

Jacksonville

295

| | 1 | |
| | **EXIT 337** Orange Park 295 | |

337-

✕ Bamboo Wok, Chili's Brooklyn Pizza McDonald's, NY Deli Panera, Sushi House		5
🔋 Gate (D, LP, $⑳V) Shell (D, LP, CW, $⑳)		
🏠 Hampton Inn & Suites	**EXIT 335** St Augustine Rd	✕ Applebee's Starbucks
℞ Walgreens $		🏠 Courtyard
🛒 Publix $	**65 mph**	

335-

DRIVE UP THE PAGE GOING NORTH

© 2010

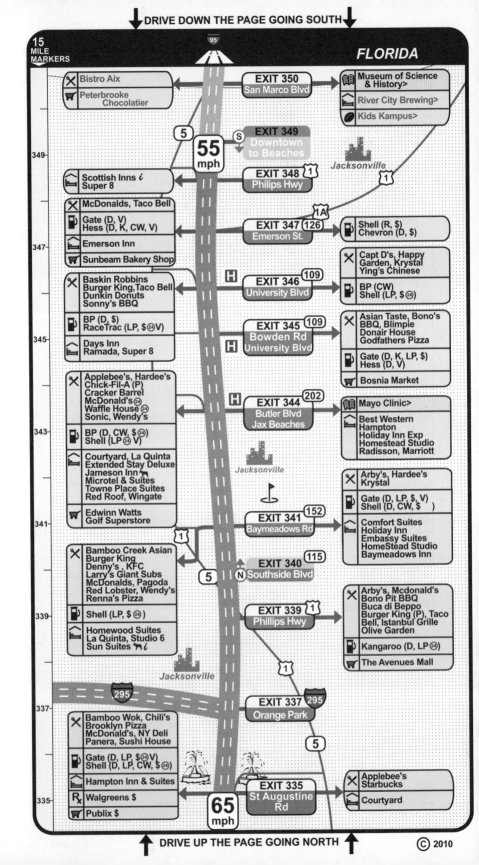

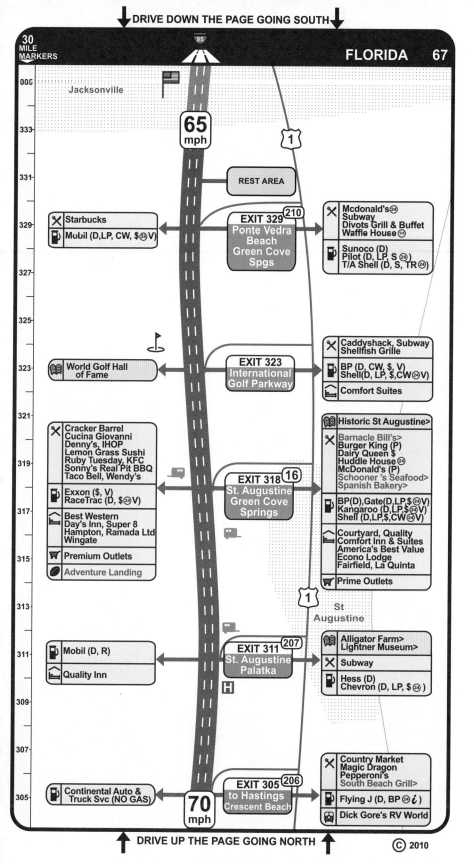

65 mph

Jacksonville

000

333

331 — REST AREA

329 — **EXIT 329** 210
Ponte Vedra Beach Green Cove Spgs

Starbucks
Mobil (D, LP, CW, $24 V)

Mcdonald's 24
Subway
Divots Grill & Buffet
Waffle House 24

Sunoco (D)
Pilot (D, LP, S 24)
T/A Shell (D, S, TR 24)

327

325

323 — **EXIT 323** International Golf Parkway

World Golf Hall of Fame

Caddyshack, Subway
Shellfish Grille

BP (D, CW, $, V)
Shell(D, LP, $,CW 24 V)

Comfort Suites

321

Historic St Augustine>

319 — **EXIT 318** 16
St. Augustine Green Cove Springs

Cracker Barrel
Cucina Giovanni
Denny's, IHOP
Lemon Grass Sushi
Ruby Tuesday, KFC
Sonny's Real Pit BBQ
Taco Bell, Wendy's

Barnacle Bill's>
Burger King (P)
Dairy Queen $
Huddle House 24
McDonald's (P)
Schooner's Seafood>
Spanish Bakery>

Exxon ($, V)
RaceTrac (D, $24 V)

BP(D),Gate(D,LP,$24 V)
Kangaroo (D,LP,$ 24 V)
Shell (D,LP,$,CW 24 V)

317

Best Western
Day's Inn, Super 8
Hampton, Ramada Ltd
Wingate

Courtyard, Quality
Comfort Inn & Suites
America's Best Value
Econo Lodge
Fairfield, La Quinta

315

Premium Outlets

Adventure Landing

Prime Outlets

313

St Augustine
1

311 — **EXIT 311** 207
St. Augustine Palatka

Mobil (D, R)

Quality Inn

Alligator Farm>
Lightner Museum>

Subway

Hess (D)
Chevron (D, LP, $ 24)

309

H

307

305 — **EXIT 305** 206
to Hastings Crescent Beach

Continental Auto & Truck Svc (NO GAS)

70 mph

Country Market
Magic Dragon
Pepperoni's
South Beach Grill>

Flying J (D, BP 24 i)

Dick Gore's RV World

© 2010

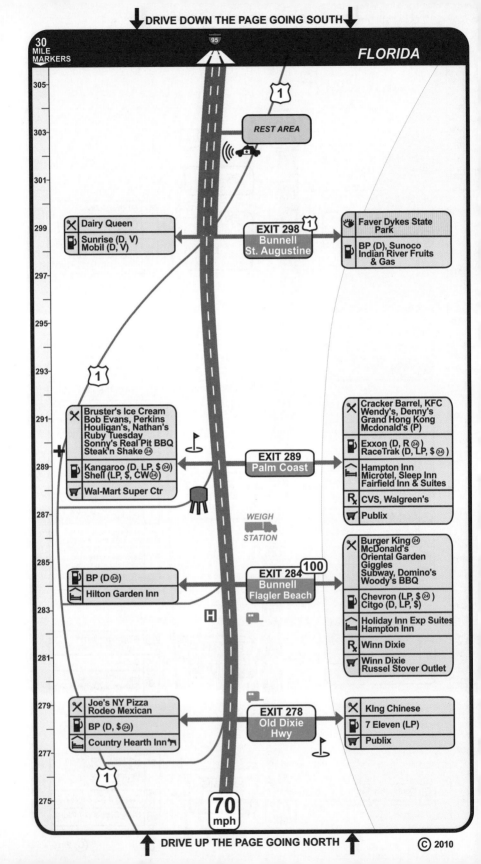

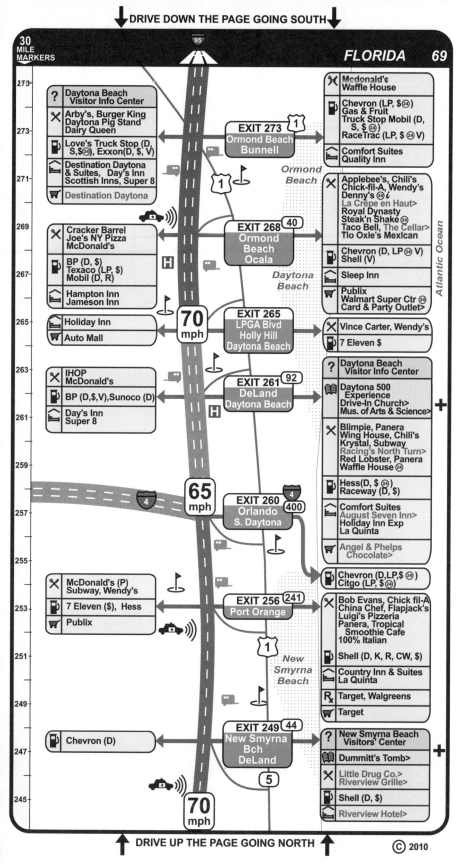

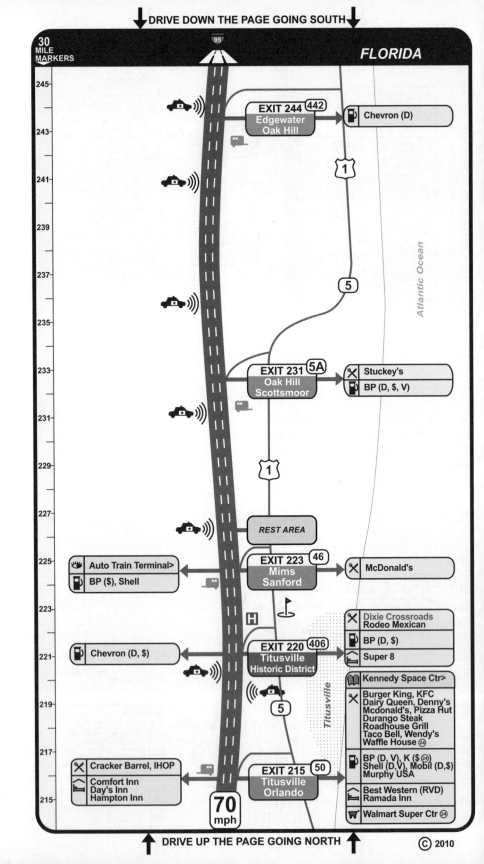

DRIVE DOWN THE PAGE GOING SOUTH

95

FLORIDA

30 MILE MARKERS

EXIT 244 (442)
Edgewater
Oak Hill → Chevron (D)

1

Atlantic Ocean

5

EXIT 231 (5A)
Oak Hill
Scottsmoor → Stuckey's
BP (D, $, V)

1

REST AREA

Auto Train Terminal>
BP ($), Shell ← **EXIT 223** (46)
Mims
Sanford → McDonald's

H

Chevron (D, $) ← **EXIT 220** (406)
Titusville
Historic District

Dixie Crossroads
Rodeo Mexican
BP (D, $)
Super 8

Kennedy Space Ctr>

Burger King, KFC
Dairy Queen, Denny's
Mcdonald's, Pizza Hut
Durango Steak
Roadhouse Grill
Taco Bell, Wendy's
Waffle House (24)

5

Titusville

BP (D, V), K ($ (24))
Shell (D,V), Mobil (D,$)
Murphy USA

Cracker Barrel, IHOP
Comfort Inn
Day's Inn
Hampton Inn ← **EXIT 215** (50)
Titusville
Orlando →

Best Western (RVD)
Ramada Inn

Walmart Super Ctr (24)

70 mph

DRIVE UP THE PAGE GOING NORTH

© 2010

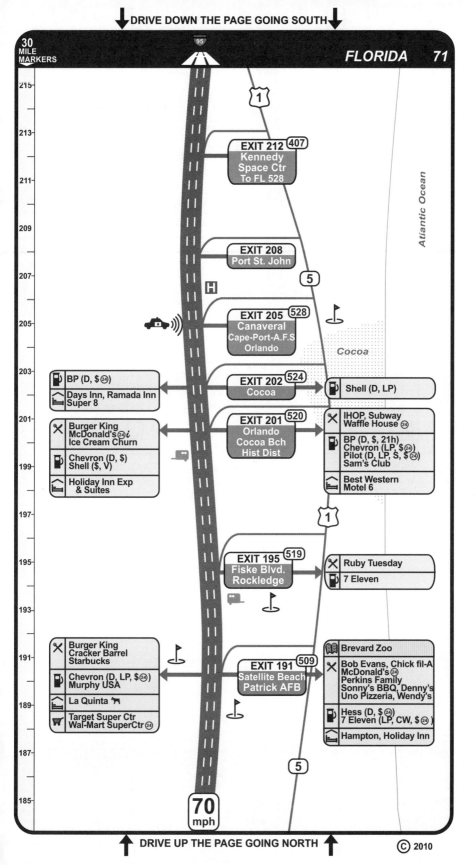

95

215

213

1

EXIT 212 407
Kennedy
Space Ctr
To FL 528

211

209

EXIT 208
Port St. John

207

5

Atlantic Ocean

H

205

EXIT 205 528
Canaveral
Cape-Port-A.F.S
Orlando

Cocoa

203

BP (D, $ 24)
Days Inn, Ramada Inn
Super 8

EXIT 202 524
Cocoa

Shell (D, LP)

201

Burger King
McDonald's 24 i
Ice Cream Churn

Chevron (D, $)
Shell ($, V)

Holiday Inn Exp
& Suites

EXIT 201 520
Orlando
Cocoa Bch
Hist Dist

IHOP, Subway
Waffle House 24

BP (D, $, 21h)
Chevron (LP, $ 24)
Pilot (D, LP, S, $ 24)
Sam's Club

Best Western
Motel 6

199

197

1

195

EXIT 195 519
Fiske Blvd.
Rockledge

Ruby Tuesday

7 Eleven

193

191

Burger King
Cracker Barrel
Starbucks

Chevron (D, LP, $ 24)
Murphy USA

La Quinta

Target Super Ctr
Wal-Mart SuperCtr 24

EXIT 191 509
Satellite Beach
Patrick AFB

Brevard Zoo

Bob Evans, Chick fil-A
McDonald's 24
Perkins Family
Sonny's BBQ, Denny's
Uno Pizzeria, Wendy's

Hess (D, $ 24)
7 Eleven (LP, CW, $ 24)

Hampton, Holiday Inn

189

187

185

70 mph

© 2010

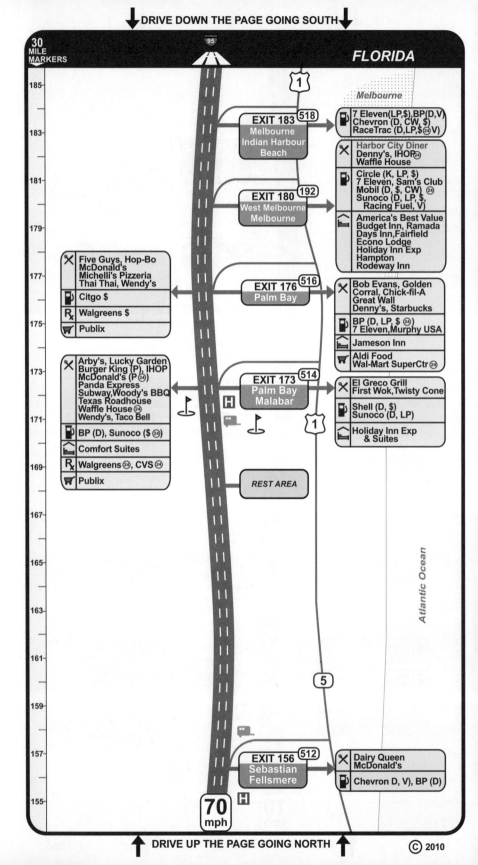

DRIVE DOWN THE PAGE GOING SOUTH

30 MILE MARKERS

I-95

FLORIDA

Melbourne

EXIT 183 (518)
Melbourne
Indian Harbour
Beach

7 Eleven(LP,$), BP(D,V)
Chevron (D, CW, $)
RaceTrac (D,LP,$⑳V)

Harbor City Diner
Denny's, IHOP⑳
Waffle House

EXIT 180 (192)
West Melbourne
Melbourne

Circle (K, LP, $)
7 Eleven, Sam's Club
Mobil (D, $, CW) ⑳
Sunoco (D, LP, $,
Racing Fuel, V)

America's Best Value
Budget Inn, Ramada
Days Inn, Fairfield
Econo Lodge
Holiday Inn Exp
Hampton
Rodeway Inn

Five Guys, Hop-Bo
McDonald's
Michelli's Pizzeria
Thai Thai, Wendy's

Citgo $

Walgreens $

Publix

EXIT 176 (516)
Palm Bay

Bob Evans, Golden
Corral, Chick-fil-A
Great Wall
Denny's, Starbucks

BP (D, LP, $ ⑳)
7 Eleven, Murphy USA

Jameson Inn

Aldi Food
Wal-Mart SuperCtr ⑳

Arby's, Lucky Garden
Burger King (P), IHOP
McDonald's (P⑳)
Panda Express
Subway, Woody's BBQ
Texas Roadhouse
Waffle House ⑳
Wendy's, Taco Bell

BP (D), Sunoco ($ ⑳)

Comfort Suites

Walgreens ⑳, CVS ⑳

Publix

EXIT 173 (514)
Palm Bay
Malabar

El Greco Grill
First Wok, Twisty Cone

Shell (D, $)
Sunoco (D, LP)

Holiday Inn Exp
& Suites

REST AREA

Atlantic Ocean

(5)

EXIT 156 (512)
Sebastian
Fellsmere

Dairy Queen
McDonald's

Chevron D, V), BP (D)

70 mph

DRIVE UP THE PAGE GOING NORTH

© 2010

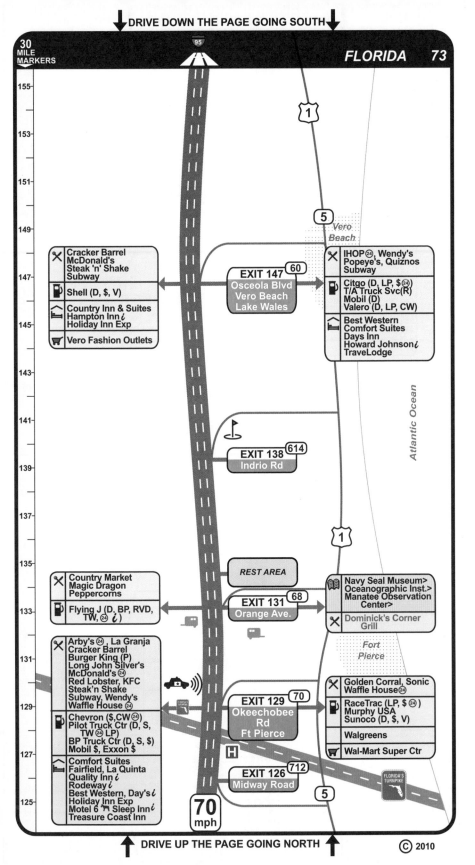

DRIVE DOWN THE PAGE GOING SOUTH

95

FLORIDA

30 MILE MARKERS | 73

155
153
151
149
147
145
143
141
139
137
135
133
131
129
127
125

1

5

Vero Beach

✕ Cracker Barrel
McDonald's
Steak 'n' Shake
Subway

⛽ Shell (D, $, V)

🛏 Country Inn & Suites
Hampton Inn *i*
Holiday Inn Exp

🛒 Vero Fashion Outlets

EXIT 147 60
Osceola Blvd
Vero Beach
Lake Wales

✕ IHOP㉔, Wendy's
Popeye's, Quiznos
Subway

⛽ Citgo (D, LP, $㉔)
T/A Truck Svc(R)
Mobil (D)
Valero (D, LP, CW)

🛏 Best Western
Comfort Suites
Days Inn
Howard Johnson*i*
TraveLodge

🚩

EXIT 138 614
Indrio Rd

Atlantic Ocean

1

REST AREA

✕ Country Market
Magic Dragon
Peppercorns

⛽ Flying J (D, BP, RVD,
TW, ㉔ *i*)

EXIT 131 68
Orange Ave.

📖 Navy Seal Museum>
Oceanographic Inst.>
Manatee Observation
Center>

✕ Dominick's Corner
Grill

Fort Pierce

✕ Arby's ㉔, La Granja
Cracker Barrel
Burger King (P)
Long John Silver's
McDonald's ㉔
Red Lobster, KFC
Steak'n Shake
Subway, Wendy's
Waffle House ㉔

⛽ Chevron ($,CW㉔)
Pilot Truck Ctr (D, S,
TW ㉔ LP)
BP Truck Ctr (D, S, $)
Mobil $, Exxon $

🛏 Comfort Suites
Fairfield, La Quinta
Quality Inn *i*
Rodeway *i*
Best Western, Day's*i*
Holiday Inn Exp
Motel 6 🐾 Sleep Inn*i*
Treasure Coast Inn

✕ Golden Corral, Sonic
Waffle House㉔

⛽ RaceTrac (LP, $㉔)
Murphy USA
Sunoco (D, $, V)

Walgreens

🛒 Wal-Mart Super Ctr

EXIT 129 70
Okeechobee
Rd
Ft Pierce

H

EXIT 126 712
Midway Road

5

FLORIDA'S
TURNPIKE

70
mph

DRIVE UP THE PAGE GOING NORTH

© 2010

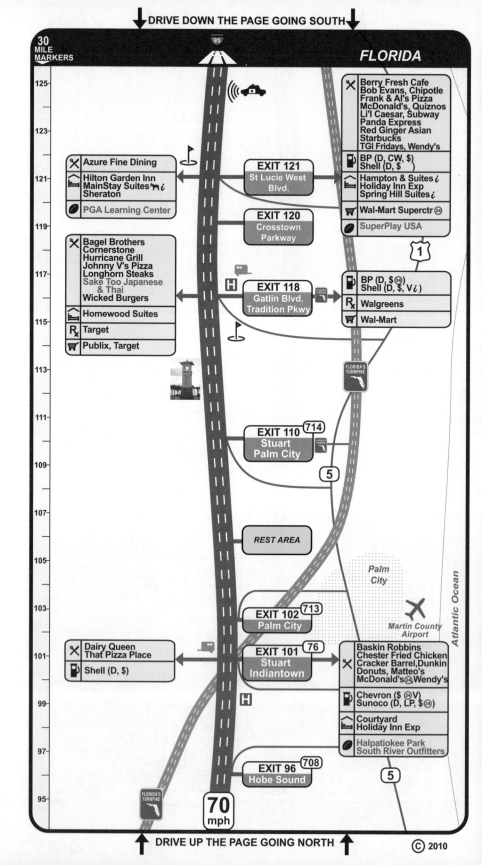

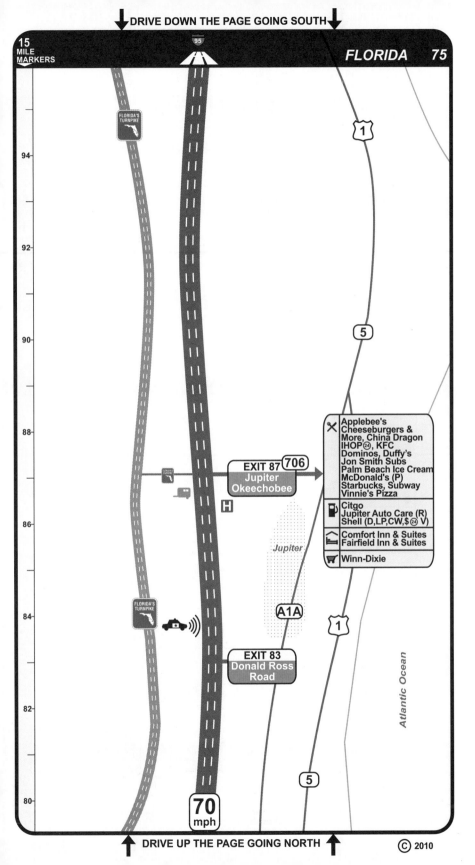

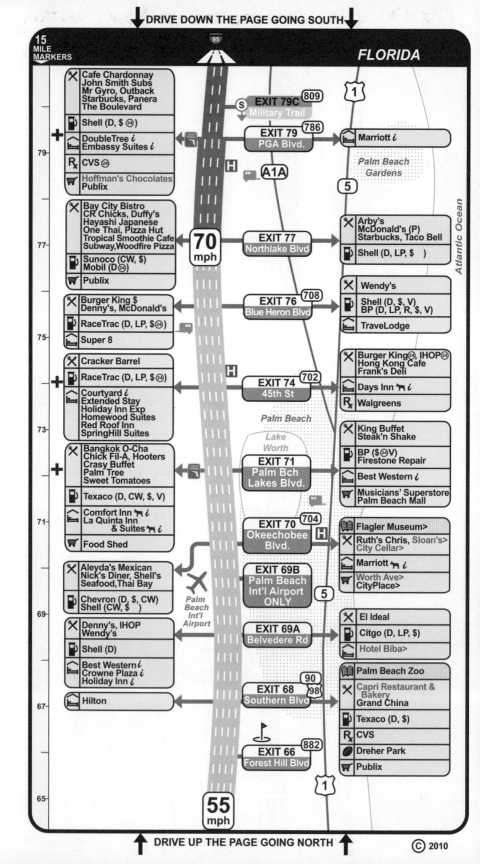

DRIVE DOWN THE PAGE GOING SOUTH

95

15 MILE MARKERS

FLORIDA

1

EXIT 79C (809)
Military Trail

S

Cafe Chardonnay
John Smith Subs
Mr Gyro, Outback
Starbucks, Panera
The Boulevard

Shell (D, $ 24)

DoubleTree *i*
Embassy Suites *i*

CVS 24

Hoffman's Chocolates
Publix

EXIT 79 (786)
PGA Blvd.

Marriott *i*

Palm Beach Gardens

5

H

A1A

Bay City Bistro
CR Chicks, Duffy's
Hayashi Japanese
One Thai, Pizza Hut
Tropical Smoothie Cafe
Subway, Woodfire Pizza

Sunoco (CW, $)
Mobil (D 24)

Publix

70 mph

EXIT 77
Northlake Blvd.

Arby's
McDonald's (P)
Starbucks, Taco Bell

Shell (D, LP, $)

Burger King $
Denny's, McDonald's

RaceTrac (D, LP, $ 24)

Super 8

EXIT 76 (708)
Blue Heron Blvd.

Wendy's

Shell (D, $, V)
BP (D, LP, R, $, V)

TraveLodge

Cracker Barrel

RaceTrac (D, LP, $ 24)

Courtyard *i*
Extended Stay
Holiday Inn Exp
Homewood Suites
Red Roof Inn
SpringHill Suites

H

EXIT 74 (702)
45th St

Burger King 24 **IHOP** 24
Hong Kong Cafe
Frank's Deli

Days Inn 🐾 *i*

Walgreens

Palm Beach

Lake Worth

Bangkok O-Cha
Chick Fil-A, Hooters
Crasy Buffet
Palm Tree
Sweet Tomatoes

Texaco (D, CW, $, V)

Comfort Inn 🐾 *i*
La Quinta Inn
& Suites 🐾 *i*

Food Shed

EXIT 71
Palm Bch
Lakes Blvd.

King Buffet
Steak'n Shake

BP ($ 24 V)
Firestone Repair

Best Western *i*

Musicians' Superstore
Palm Beach Mall

EXIT 70 (704)
Okeechobee
Blvd.

H

Flagler Museum>

Ruth's Chris, Sloan's>
City Cellar>

Marriott 🐾 *i*

Worth Ave>
CityPlace>

EXIT 69B
Palm Beach
Int'l Airport
ONLY

5

Aleyda's Mexican
Nick's Diner, Shell's
Seafood, Thai Bay

Chevron (D, $, CW)
Shell (CW, $)

Palm Beach Int'l Airport

Denny's, IHOP
Wendy's

Shell (D)

Best Western *i*
Crowne Plaza *i*
Holiday Inn *i*

EXIT 69A
Belvedere Rd

El Ideal

Citgo (D, LP, $)

Hotel Biba>

Hilton

EXIT 68 (90)(98)
Southern Blvd

Palm Beach Zoo

Capri Restaurant &
Bakery
Grand China

Texaco (D, $)

CVS

Dreher Park

Publix

EXIT 66 (882)
Forest Hill Blvd

1

55 mph

DRIVE UP THE PAGE GOING NORTH

© 2010

Atlantic Ocean

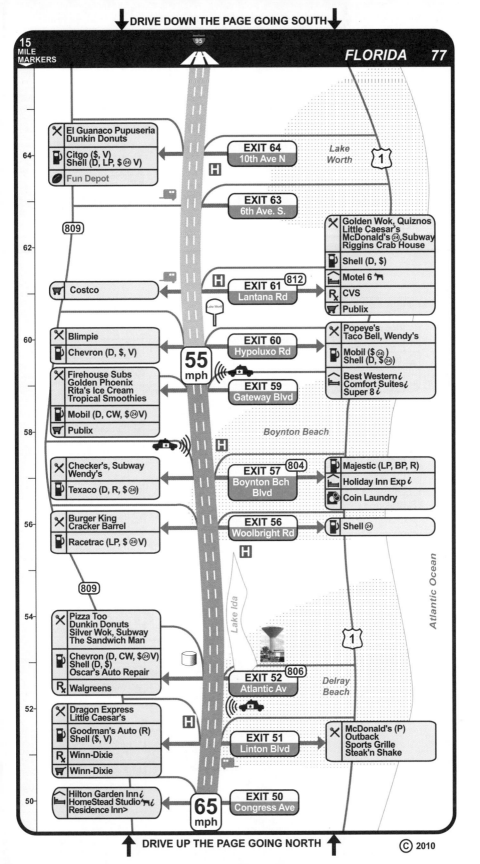

64

El Guanaco Pupuseria
Dunkin Donuts

Citgo ($, V)
Shell (D, LP, $ 24 V)

Fun Depot

H

EXIT 64
10th Ave N

Lake Worth

1

EXIT 63
6th Ave. S.

809

Golden Wok, Quiznos
Little Caesar's
McDonald's 24, Subway
Riggins Crab House

Shell (D, $)

Motel 6

CVS Rx

Publix

62

Costco

H

EXIT 61
Lantana Rd

812

60

Blimpie

Chevron (D, $, V)

EXIT 60
Hypoluxo Rd

Popeye's
Taco Bell, Wendy's

Mobil ($ 24)
Shell (D, $ 24)

55 mph

EXIT 59
Gateway Blvd

Best Western i
Comfort Suites i
Super 8 i

Firehouse Subs
Golden Phoenix
Rita's Ice Cream
Tropical Smoothies

Mobil (D, CW, $ 24 V)

Publix

58

Boynton Beach

H

Checker's, Subway
Wendy's

Texaco (D, R, $ 23)

EXIT 57
Boynton Bch Blvd

804

Majestic (LP, BP, R)

Holiday Inn Exp i

Coin Laundry

56

Burger King
Cracker Barrel

Racetrac (LP, $ 24 V)

EXIT 56
Woolbright Rd

Shell 24

H

809

54

Pizza Too
Dunkin Donuts
Silver Wok, Subway
The Sandwich Man

Chevron (D, CW, $ 24 V)
Shell (D, $)
Oscar's Auto Repair

Walgreens Rx

Lake Ida

1

EXIT 52
Atlantic Av

806

Delray Beach

52

Dragon Express
Little Caesar's

Goodman's Auto (R)
Shell ($, V)

Winn-Dixie Rx

Winn-Dixie

H

EXIT 51
Linton Blvd

McDonald's (P)
Outback
Sports Grille
Steak'n Shake

50

Hilton Garden Inn i
HomeStead Studio i
Residence Inn>

65 mph

EXIT 50
Congress Ave

Atlantic Ocean

© 2010

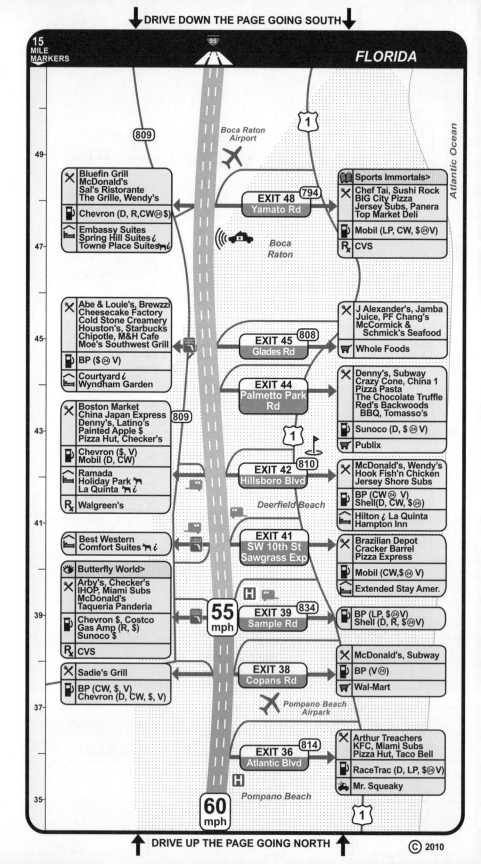

DRIVE DOWN THE PAGE GOING SOUTH

95

FLORIDA

15 MILE MARKERS

Boca Raton Airport

1

49

Bluefin Grill
McDonald's
Sal's Ristorante
The Grille, Wendy's

Chevron (D, R, CW⊘ $)

Embassy Suites
Spring Hill Suites *i*
Towne Place Suites ⊁*i*

EXIT 48
Yamato Rd
794

Boca Raton

47

Sports Immortals>

Chef Tai, Sushi Rock
BIG City Pizza
Jersey Subs, Panera
Top Market Deli

Mobil (LP, CW, $⊘V)

CVS

Abe & Louie's, Brewzzi
Cheesecake Factory
Cold Stone Creamery
Houston's, Starbucks
Chipotle, M&H Cafe
Moe's Southwest Grill

BP ($⊘ V)

Courtyard *i*
Wyndham Garden

EXIT 45
Glades Rd
808

45

J Alexander's, Jamba
Juice, PF Chang's
McCormick &
Schmick's Seafood

Whole Foods

EXIT 44
Palmetto Park Rd

Denny's, Subway
Crazy Cone, China 1
Pizza Pasta
The Chocolate Truffle
Red's Backwoods
BBQ, Tomasso's

809

43

Boston Market
China Japan Express
Denny's, Latino's
Painted Apple $
Pizza Hut, Checker's

Chevron ($, V)
Mobil (D, CW)

Ramada
Holiday Park ⊁*i*
La Quinta ⊁*i*

Walgreen's

1

Sunoco (D, $⊘ V)

Publix

EXIT 42
Hillsboro Blvd
810

McDonald's, Wendy's
Hook Fish'n Chicken
Jersey Shore Subs

BP (CW⊘ V)
Shell(D, CW, $⊘)

Hilton *i* La Quinta
Hampton Inn

Deerfield Beach

41

Best Western
Comfort Suites ⊁*i*

EXIT 41
SW 10th St
Sawgrass Exp

Brazilian Depot
Cracker Barrel
Pizza Express

Mobil (CW,$⊘ V)

Extended Stay Amer.

Butterfly World>

Arby's, Checker's
IHOP, Miami Subs
McDonald's
Taqueria Panderia

Chevron $, Costco
Gas Amp (R, $)
Sunoco $

CVS

55 mph

H

EXIT 39
Sample Rd
834

BP (LP, $⊘V)
Shell (D, R, $⊘V)

39

Sadie's Grill

BP (CW, $, V)
Chevron (D, CW, $, V)

EXIT 38
Copans Rd

McDonald's, Subway

BP (V⊘)

Wal-Mart

37

Pompano Beach Airpark

Arthur Treachers
KFC, Miami Subs
Pizza Hut, Taco Bell

EXIT 36
Atlantic Blvd
814

RaceTrac (D, LP, $⊘V)

Mr. Squeaky

H

Pompano Beach

60 mph

1

35

DRIVE UP THE PAGE GOING NORTH

© 2010

Atlantic Ocean

809

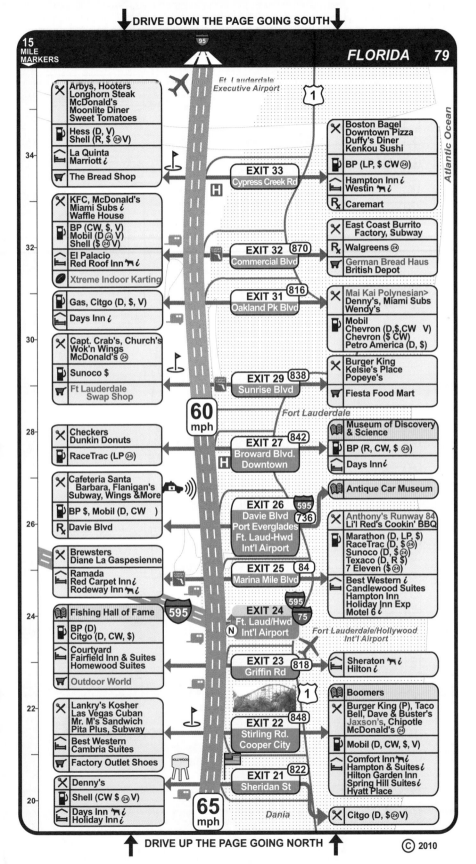

Ft. Lauderdale Executive Airport

1

34

Arbys, Hooters Longhorn Steak McDonald's Moonlite Diner Sweet Tomatoes

Hess (D, V) Shell (R, $ 24 V)

La Quinta Marriott i

The Bread Shop

Boston Bagel Downtown Pizza Duffy's Diner Kenkou Sushi

BP (LP, $ CW 24)

Hampton Inn i Westin 🐾 i

Rx Caremart

EXIT 33 Cypress Creek Rd

H

32

KFC, McDonald's Miami Subs i Waffle House

BP (CW, $, V) Mobil (D 24 V) Shell ($ 24 V)

El Palacio Red Roof Inn 🐾 i

Xtreme Indoor Karting

EXIT 32 870 Commercial Blvd

East Coast Burrito Factory, Subway

Rx Walgreens 24

German Bread Haus British Depot

31

Gas, Citgo (D, $, V)

Days Inn i

EXIT 31 816 Oakland Pk Blvd

Mai Kai Polynesian> Denny's, Miami Subs Wendy's

Mobil Chevron (D,$,CW V) Chevron ($ CW) Petro America (D, $)

30

Capt. Crab's, Church's Wok'n Wings McDonald's 24

Sunoco $

Ft Lauderdale Swap Shop

Burger King Kelsie's Place Popeye's

Fiesta Food Mart

EXIT 29 838 Sunrise Blvd

60 mph

Fort Lauderdale

28

Checkers Dunkin Donuts

RaceTrac (LP 24)

EXIT 27 842 Broward Blvd. Downtown

H

Museum of Discovery & Science

BP (R, CW, $ 24)

Days Inn i

26

Cafeteria Santa Barbara, Flanigan's Subway, Wings &More

BP $, Mobil (D, CW)

Rx Davie Blvd

EXIT 26 595 Davie Blvd 736 Port Everglades Ft. Laud-Hwd Int'l Airport

Antique Car Museum

Anthony's Runway 84 Li'l Red's Cookin' BBQ

Marathon (D, LP, $) RaceTrac (D, $ 24) Sunoco (D, $ 24) Texaco (D, R $) 7 Eleven ($ 24)

Brewsters Diane La Gaspesienne

Ramada Red Carpet Inn i Rodeway Inn 🐾 i

EXIT 25 84 Marina Mile Blvd

Best Western i Candlewood Suites Hampton Inn Holiday Inn Exp Motel 6 i

24

Fishing Hall of Fame

595

BP (D) Citgo (D, CW, $)

Courtyard Fairfield Inn & Suites Homewood Suites

Outdoor World

EXIT 24 595 Ft. Laud/Hwd 75 N Int'l Airport

Fort Lauderdale/Hollywood Int'l Airport

Sheraton 🐾 i Hilton i

EXIT 23 818 Griffin Rd

1

Boomers

22

Lankry's Kosher Las Vegas Cuban Mr. M's Sandwich Pita Plus, Subway

Best Western Cambria Suites

Factory Outlet Shoes

HOLLYWOOD

EXIT 22 848 Stirling Rd. Cooper City

Burger King (P), Taco Bell, Dave & Buster's Jaxson's, Chipotle McDonald's 24

Mobil (D, CW, $, V)

Comfort Inn 🐾 i Hampton & Suites i Hilton Garden Inn Spring Hill Suites i Hyatt Place

20

Denny's

Shell (CW $ 24 V)

Days Inn 🐾 i Holiday Inn i

EXIT 21 822 Sheridan St

65 mph

Dania

Citgo (D, $ 24 V)

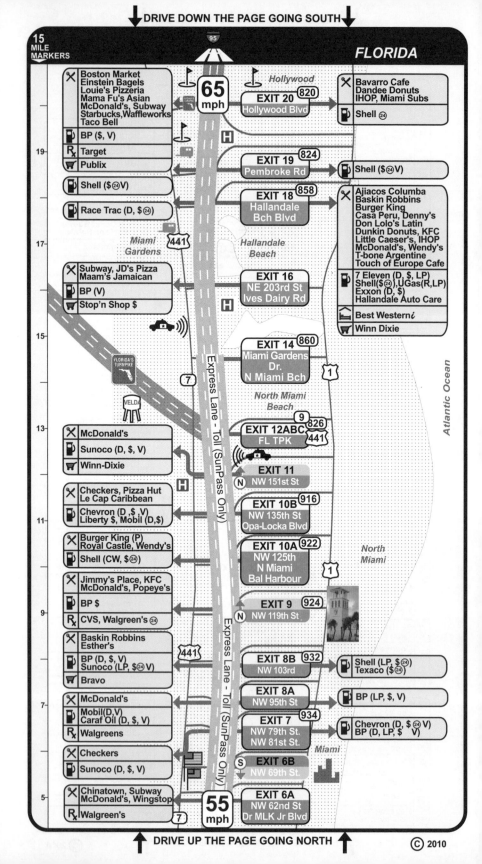

DRIVE DOWN THE PAGE GOING SOUTH

95

15 MILE MARKERS

FLORIDA

Hollywood

65 mph

H

| Boston Market, Einstein Bagels, Louie's Pizzeria, Mama Fu's Asian, McDonald's, Subway, Starbucks, Waffleworks, Taco Bell |
| BP ($, V) |
| Target |
| Publix |

19

EXIT 20 (820) Hollywood Blvd

Bavarro Cafe, Dandee Donuts, IHOP, Miami Subs
Shell (24)

| Shell ($ 24 V) |
| Race Trac (D, $ 24) |

EXIT 19 (824) Pembroke Rd

Shell ($ 24 V)

Miami Gardens 441

17

Hallandale Beach

EXIT 18 (858) Hallandale Bch Blvd

Ajiacos Columba, Baskin Robbins, Burger King, Casa Peru, Denny's, Don Lolo's Latin, Dunkin Donuts, KFC, Little Caeser's, IHOP, McDonald's, Wendy's, T-bone Argentine, Touch of Europe Cafe

| Subway, JD's Pizza, Maam's Jamaican |
| BP (V) |
| Stop'n Shop $ |

EXIT 16 NE 203rd St Ives Dairy Rd

H

7 Eleven (D, $, LP), Shell($ 24),UGas(R,LP), Exxon (D, $), Hallandale Auto Care

Best Western *i*
Winn Dixie

15

FLORIDA'S TURNPIKE

7

VELDA

EXIT 14 (860) Miami Gardens Dr. N Miami Bch

1

North Miami Beach

13

| McDonald's |
| Sunoco (D, $, V) |
| Winn-Dixie |

EXIT 12ABC 9 (826) FL TPK 441

EXIT 11 N NW 151st St

| Checkers, Pizza Hut, Le Cap Caribbean |
| Chevron (D ,$,V), Liberty $, Mobil (D,$) |

H

EXIT 10B (916) NW 135th St Opa-Locka Blvd

| Burger King (P), Royal Castle, Wendy's |
| Shell (CW, $ 24) |

EXIT 10A (922) NW 125th N Miami Bal Harbour

North Miami

1

| Jimmy's Place, KFC, McDonald's, Popeye's |
| BP $ |
| CVS, Walgreen's 24 |

9

EXIT 9 (924) N NW 119th St

| Baskin Robbins, Esther's |
| BP (D, $, V), Sunoco (LP, $ 24 V) |
| Bravo |

441

EXIT 8B (932) NW 103rd

Shell (LP, $ 24), Texaco ($ 24)

EXIT 8A NW 95th St

BP (LP, $, V)

7

| McDonald's |
| Mobil(D,V), Caraf Oil (D, $, V) |
| Walgreens |

EXIT 7 (934) NW 79th St. NW 81st St.

Chevron (D, $ 24 V), BP (D, LP, $ V)

Miami

| Checkers |
| Sunoco (D, $, V) |

EXIT 6B S NW 69th St.

5

| Chinatown, Subway, McDonald's, Wingstop |
| Walgreen's |

7

55 mph

EXIT 6A NW 62nd St Dr MLK Jr Blvd

Express Lane - Toll (SunPass Only)

Atlantic Ocean

DRIVE UP THE PAGE GOING NORTH

© 2010

441

✈ Miami Int'l Airport

195
112

EXIT 4
Miami Beach
Miami Int'l Airport

195

7

1

EXIT 3A 836
Miami Int'l Airport

West Miami

H

S

Miami

EXIT 3B
NW 8th St
Port of Miami
Orange Bowl

395

Atlantic Ocean

EXIT 2D 395
Miami Beach
← Left Exit Southbound

EXIT 2B
NW 2nd St
Arenas

N

✕ Area 31

🏨 Epic Hotel 🐾
Marriott
Hyatt Regency

441

EXIT 2AC 1
Biscayne Blvd
Downtown
↙ Left Exit Southbound

✕ Cafe Cubana,Wendy's
Chick Grill, La Moon
McDonald's, Subway
Moe's SW Grill

⛽ Citgo(R,$24V),Chevron

✕ La Baguette,
Papa John's
Tapas de Rosa
Taqueria el Mexicano
Versailles>

⛽ Shell (D $ 24 V)

🛒 Presidente Market

EXIT 1B 41
SW 7th
Brickell Ave.

🏨 Urbano, Starlite East

Rx CVS

🛒 Publix

Coral Gables

7

55 mph

S **EXIT 1A**
SW 25th
Rickenbacker
Cswy
Key Biscayne

📖 Vizcaya
Museum of Science &
Planetarium

1

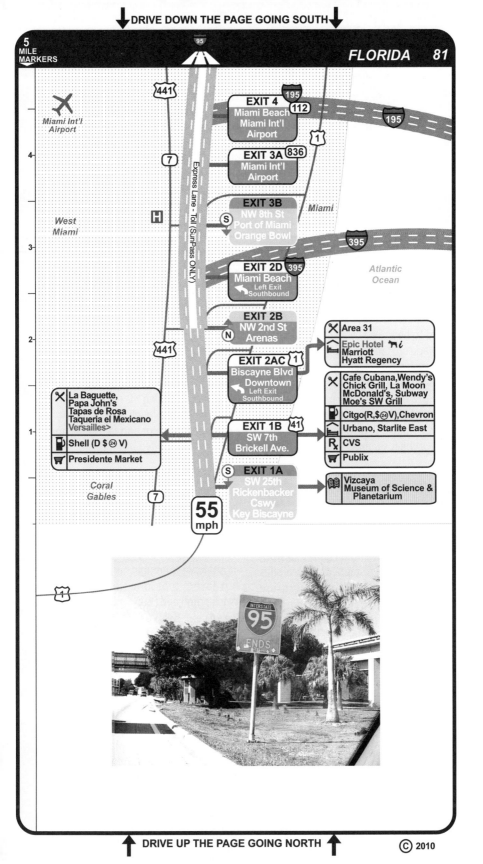

First Road Trip?

Over 100 years before we started down I-95, Dr. Horatio Nelson Jackson left San Francisco in a 20-horsepower 2-cylinder cherry red Winton touring car that had no roof or windshield. A 31-year-old retired doctor from Vermont, he accepted a $50 wager that he could drive a car all the way to NYC in less than 3 months. Jackson hired a 22 year-old bicycle repairman, Sewall K. Crocker, to accompany him. Starting in June 1903, he arrived in NYC 63 days later, having achieved speeds as high as 30 mph. And so the American road trip was born .

The back seat of the vehicle named "Vermont" was removed to make room for a block and tackle with 150 ft of hemp rope, a shotgun, rifle, pistols, ammunition, rubber rain coats and a small Kodak camera to record his trip. After 15 miles his first blowout occurred (first of many problems and mechanical failures), and he had to be towed by a cowboy and a horse!

Jackson, Crocker and Bud, a goggle-wearing bulldog purchased in Iowa, splashed through streams, got stuck in buffalo wallows, bounced over railroad trestles to cross major rivers, and frightened horses on the dusty trails. And as he moved eastward, his quest slowly became a national sensation, with thousands lining the streets of towns (tipped off by the telegraph of his approach) as he whizzed through at 20 mph.

On August 7, he arrived home. Just as he drove the Vermont into the stable, the drive chain snapped in two.

NEW HAMPSHIRE

Exit 7: Greater Portsmouth Visitor's Center – Organize your visit here by using their computer to book motels, check out restaurants or local sites. There's a mail drop and a bathroom to use. To learn this city, you can pick up the booklet to stroll the Harbour Trail (on your own or with a guide) winding your way through 71 sites downtown and in waterfront areas to discover history, architecture, tugboats, maritime fun, horticulture, museums, 17th C. homes where George Washington and John Hancock were guests - and even a submarine. When the center is closed you can still pick up pamphlets in the foyer. ☀ May-Oct M-F 8:30-5, S&S 10-5 (Oct-May M-F 8:30-5). 500 Market St. *i* portsmouthchamber.org ☎ 603-436-3988 or 603-610-5510.

Exit 7>: Strawbery Banke Museum – We're not sure how this amazing living history spot escaped our Northern radar, but we loved it. You can explore 4 centuries of life through 43 original buildings that were brought here - from the Wm Pitt Tavern that John Hancock, George Washington and Paul Revere passed through to Abbott's grocery store dealing with rationing during WWII or the Shapiro Home, where Jewish Russian immigrants lived in the

1920's. Costumed role players bring history to life, recounting the stories of the people who lived and worked in these buildings, sometimes with live demonstrations of hearth cooking, coopering, or

making chicken soup. There's plenty of landscape to walk around in and a daily garden tour of a kitchen garden, victory garden or Victorian garden. Indoors there's a gallery and a discovery center to learn about games, crafts, chores and pastimes. An extensive gift shop has local Squamscot sodas: birch beer, root beer (and diet), fruit bowl and creamy maple. ◑ May-Oct 10-5. 14 Hancock St. *i* strawberybanke.org ☎ 603-433-1100.

Exit 7: USS Albacore – Built right here at the Portsmouth Naval Base, this sub served the US Navy from 1953-1972 and never fired a weapon or went to war. Her motto Praenuntius Futuri (Forerunner of the Future) explained her experimental mission: to be constantly redesigned and readapted into new prototypes. You

can explore (self-guided audio on board) all 205 ft of the fastest submarine of her time as she pioneered the teardrop design which became the model for many countries. This lab afloat tested new control systems, dive brakes, sonar, escape mechanisms and hydrodynamics. The indoor museum has Navy memorabilia. ◑ end May - Oct 9:30-5:30, Oct - May Th-M

9:30-4 (closed mid Jan - mid Feb). 600 Market St. *i* ussalbacore.org ☎ 603-436-3680.

Exit 7>: Portsmouth Gas Light Co. – This was the utility company building built in 1837. In fact, if you look closely on the eastern wall, you can still see original brick charred by an ages old fire. On 3 levels you can enjoy casual dining, music and dancing. In the Street Level Restaurant you'll find homemade clam chowder, Thai spring rolls, Japanese miso salad, lobster stuffed haddock, grilled chicken pasta, Cajun sausage ragout, maple bourbon short ribs and grilled ears of corn. The basement level Brick Oven Pizza Pub was originally excavated by hand using a five-gallon pickle bucket. Its wood-fired brick oven burns New England hard woods (a cord a week), which gives their pizza a unique smoky flavor. You can down calzones, pasta, salads and Sun-Th there's a lunch pizza buffet for only $5.99. The Deck is the city's largest courtyard venue and the 3rd floor is the night club. ◑ M-Th 11:30-10, F 11:30-11, Sat 11-11, Sun 11-9. 64 Market St. *i* portsmouthgaslight.com ☎ 603-430-9122.

Exit 7: John Paul Jones was the father of the US Navy, and he captained the Ranger (built here in Portsmouth), the first American warship to fly the Stars and Stripes, which scored the first Revolutionary sea victory with the capture of a British warship, the Drake. His famous battle came in 1779 on the Bon Homme Richard (named by France to honor Benjamin Franklin and his Poor Richard's Almanac) against the British Serapis. Two of his cannon were hit broadside, blowing up some crew and the deck above them. The British then knocked out the remainig guns one by one. With his ship leaking badly, he rammed the Serapis and boarded her deck. His ship timbers were on fire, so he was asked to surrender. That was when he uttered his famous reply, "I have not yet begun to fight". And he hadn't. A crew member managed to throw a grenade into their ammunition, blowing up that ship. After 3 1/2 hours of a savage moonlit battle, the British commander surrendered. Then they watched as Jones' ship disappeard into the deep blue.

Exit 2>: Lindt Chocolate Outlet – Wow, what a pitstop. The company started way back in 1845 in Zurich, and then acquired the famous Rudolf Lindt's company in1899 (he invented the "conche" melting method). This European chocolate shop offers you all the Lindt classics plus all kinds of Lindor truffles (fill your own bag of truffles $6.50/lb) and some

Ghirardelli. Bars might be 2/$2.69 in white chocolate with coconut, intense mint, chili or dark chocolate in 70%, 85%, and 95%. Clear bags of 2nds are $6.99 lb. - and the chocolate still tastes just as wonderful at these low prices. ◑ M-Sat 9-6, Sun 12-5 ☞ Exit 2, then follow Rte 101 west for 3.7 mi. to Exit 11. Left turn to 3 Portsmouth Ave. *i* lindt.com ☎ 603-772-3614.

Mile 1 Northbound: New Hampshire Welcome Center – You can figure out where you are by checking out the topographical map of NH, QC, VT or MA here. Grab a motel coupon book, use the vending machines or picnic area, have them help you with your car trouble, and take advantage of the restrooms. ◑ Daily 24h ☎ 603-474-5211.

MASSACHUSETTS

Mile 84: Massachusetts Visitor Information Center – Here's a "green" rest area with composting toilets (closed after dark). You can find out about the State, pick up motel coupon booklets (outside when closed), get help with car trouble, use a fax machine, have a picnic on their tables, buy gifts and take your pet for a run. Internet available as well as an ATM outside. ◑ Daily 8-6, Memorial Day to Labor Day, also F-Sun 8-10. ☎ 800-742-5306 or 978-465-6555.

Exit 60: Hodgie's Too! – It's fun for anyone of

any age to stop for real ice cream at this 19-year old stand run by a husband and wife team. The ice cream is made here, and even though they have a repetoire of 90 crazy flavors, French vanilla is still the favorite. Be forewarned of gigantic sizes, as 1 scoop = everyone else's 3 scoops and a 1/4 kiddie is a small. Fun flavors are: frozen pudding (with dried fruits and rum extracts), candy store, bumbleberry swirl, cider donut, dirt pie (coffee, chocolate, oreo crumbs), Indian pudding and Kermit cow, and toppings are: grapenuts, crunch, brownie, nerds, cookie dough and fat free or sugar free hot fudge (why bother?). The most asked question: "What is thundercloud?" (double rich chocolate). There's a peanut lovers' sundae with fudge, Reeses pieces and peanut butter. The Hodgie Special is 12 scoops with fudge, caramel, banana, pineapple, strawberry and whipped cream. ◑ Apr, May, Sept, Oct 11:30-9, Memorial Day-Labor Day 11:30-10. 136 Rabbit Rd. ☎ 978-463-0214.

Payback Time

It was on the balcony of the Old State House that the Declaration of Independence was read out in 1776 by William Greenleaf. In 1976, when Queen Elizabeth came for the bicentennial celebrations and was standing on the very same balcony, she was given a cheque for $35,000 to cover the cost of the tea that had been thrown in the harbor. (She never cashed it).

MAP PG 5-7

Exit 58: Sylvan Street Grille – There's something for everyone at this 20-year-old friendly family resto, including TV's to watch your favorite shows. The food goes from 21 shareable appetizers (Philly cheesesteak eggrolls), a dozen salads (Tex-Mex), burgers and paninis to a triple decker turkey club, chicken pot pie and ribeye steak. Then the world tastes start: macadamia nut crusted chicken, roasted eggplant ravioli, scallop pie, Oriental chicken or seafood pesto. Sandra actually started with Mama Louanne's famous brickle pie (vanilla and coffee ice cream, heath bar, marshmallow, cookie crust), while Stan oogled the banana pizza. No time to stop? Check out their online menu and order from the car. ● M-Sat 11:30-11:30, Sun 9-10:30. 12 Sylvan St. *i* sylvanstreetgrille.com ☎ 978-774-1724.

Exit 57>: Fowle's – This schizophrenic building, housing both a coffee shop and a news stand, has been open since 1865. Sandra flipped over their house special hash browns stuffed with cheddar, provolone, bacon, and onions served with sour cream on the side. The corned beef for the hash is cooked on the premises and

mixed with those hash browns - yum. There's omelettes with sprouts, cilantro, and topped with toasted almonds or lemon-raspberry french toast or a strawberry parfait for breakfast! Lunch offers up a California like menu with soups, salads and healthy sandwiches (on triple seed or cinnamon swirl bread): pesto or left coast veggie, tomato, spinach and cheese or Cuban and hot Italian. Locals get their coffee fix here, and they're known for their lemon-raspberry smoothie made with Brigham's ice cream, and if you need one, hot fudge sundaes or frappes. ● M-F 6:30-3, S&S 7-4. 17 State St. ☎ 978-463-8855.

Exit 57>: Michael's Harborside – Yes it's at harborside, and you can eat on the deck. Around 30 years, there are favorites they cannot take off the menu: the breadcrumb topped baked haddock or the seafood scampi with shrimp, scallops, garlic, mushrooms and tomatoes. Other offerings have been crispy coconut shrimp, chicken in mango sauce or Louisiana crab cake, but you can also have meatloaf, pot roast or ribs.

We liked the interesting salads - one had butternut squash ravioli. Desserts are by the local Alden Merrell bakery: strawberry shortcake or a "turtle" one are local favorites, or try banana bread pudding. ● Sun-Th 11:30-9 F&S 11:30-10. ☞ RT onto Rte 113E for 2 1/2mi. into town, LT on Market St for 3 blocks. 1 Tournament Wharf. *i* michaelsharborside.com ☎ 978-462-7785.

Got Haggis?

Exit 46: Union Jack – Okay you Brits, you probably didn't know that for the past 25 years you could have stopped here and gotten your meat pies, pork bridies and banger rolls for lunch and washed it all down with fiery ginger beer. You could've cooked up dessert with Bird's custard powder or just have had a Cadbury bar. In-between courses could include Heinz treacle, spotted dick or baked beans, Chivers jelly, mushy peas, Irish cheddar, marmalade, Branston pickle, Haywood's onions and of course, marmite. Wash it all down with a giant bag of 960 Taylors of Harrowgate teabags. If you need them, there's kilts and kilt socks. ● T-Sat 10-5, Sun 12-5. 134 Newbury St. ☎ 978-535-6256.

NEW! **Exit 40:** The Gingerbread Construction Company – The name belies the fact that there are no gingerbread houses here (only on holidays). What you will find are 20 varieties of muffins (yes, a gingerbread-filled one, banana cream with heath bar toffee, carrot filled with walnuts and raisins, pineapple coconut, strawberry shortcake or fresh fruit). Some of these come in loaves. For the car there's brown-

ies, bags of candies (coconut crunch, chocolate rocks, sugar-free chocolate peanuts, gummi penguins) and cookies: chocolate pecan, white chocolate with macadamia nuts and ginger bread, of course, and smoothies or coffee to go with it all. ◗ M-F 6-6, S&S 6-5. 52 Main St. *i* gingerbreadusa.com ☎ 781-246-2200.

NEW! **Exit 38B:** Harrows – Around since 1938, the restaurant may have closed, but the famous chicken pies live on in the 2nd generation (Wally and Dan). They are made fresh daily from fresh chickens which cook slowly overnight and are then smothered in flavorful scratch gravy, firm carrots and potatoes and poured into lovely pastry. They come cold or frozen in 4 sizes: individual ($5.25), 2-3 servings ($11.75), 4 servings (15.95) and jumbo 6

servings ($19.25). If you want to gobble them up in the car, call 1 1/2 hours ahead and they will heat them up for you. Also on the take-out menu are mashed potatoes, squash, cranberry sauce, chicken gravy, chicken salad, chicken soup, apple or blueberry pie. We loved the chicken pies. ◗ Daily 10-7:30 pm. 126 Main St. *i* chickenpie.com ☎ 781-944-0410.

NEW! **Exit 38B:** Calareso's Farm Stand – Here you have a family business that's been around for over 50 years. Pick up some healthy fruits and veggies for the car or check out the heat-and-serve food: grilled panini, meatballs marinara, chicken parmigiana, stuffed shells, 3-bean salad, spinach hummus, sliced cold cuts, cheeses, tabboulah, olives. There's bread (sourdough, sweet bread, Tuscan bread) for sandwich making and sweets for dessert: whoopie pie, black and white cookies, apple strudel puffs, ginger snaps, banana bread, blueberry muffins, apple cider donuts, chocolate cream pie and bags of cookies. ◗ Mon-S 8-8, Sun 8-7. 122 Main St. ☎ 781-944-6010.

NEW! **Exit 38N or 37S:** Winfrey's – To find a chocolate oasis on the road is always a dream. This one started out as a home fudge business so a couple could become stay-at-home parents for twin boys while using their fudge stove to heat their

home. Nowadays they are up to 25 flavors of fudge (even penuchi) and 5 retail stores. They can satisfy any chocoholic with chocolate covered twinkies or Jordan crackers, non-pareils, raspberry jells or the new raspberry truffle. There's old-fashioned puff candy, chocolate macadamia popcorn, and you can create boxes of all dark or all caramels or all fudge. There's sugar-free almonds, butter creams, peanut brittle, toasted coconut, vanilla caramel, almond buttercrunch, cashew clusters, dipped pineapple, periwinkles (look like turtles), covered ginger and chocolate covered potato chips and pretzels. ◗ M&T 9:30-6, W-F 9:30-8, Sat 9:30-5, Sun 11-5. 41 Main St. *i* winfreyscom ☎ 781-279-7448.

MAP PG 7-8

Exit 31>: Lexington Battle Green and Visitor Center – It was on the morning of April 19th, 1775 that 77 farmers and tradesmen, as part of the Lexington militia, assembled on the Common to defend their town. They wanted to prevent about 750 British light infantry from destroying a supply of arms in Concord. Captain John Parker, whose statue

stands proudly on the Green today, was quoted as saying "Stand your ground; don't fire unless fired upon; but if they mean to have a war, let it begin here." Captain Parker, noticing he was outnumbered, ordered his men to disperse and not to fire. As they started to leave, a shot of unknown origin rang out and the British fired a return volley killing 8 Minutemen and wounding 10 with 1 Redcoat wounded.

George Washington wrote in his diary "the first blood was spilt in the dispute with Great Britain". The Revolutionary War had started. After the battle, Samuel Adams exclaimed to John Hancock, "What a glorious morning for America!" (see Concord for the next part of the battle).

Lexington Visitors Center: First take a look at the historic diorama depicting the battle on the Green, ask about tours and then check out the things you can see, find places to sleep, eat and use the clean rest rooms. Ask about the Liberty Ride Trolley (*i* libertyride.us) with 15 stops amongst Lexington and Concord. There's a gift shop. 1875 Massachusetts Ave. ◗ Daily Apr-Nov 9-5; Dec-Mar 10-4 *i* lexingtonchamber.org ☎ 781-862-1450.

Exit 30>: Concord Visitor Center – Right in town, get all the info you need to scope out this historical area and take advantage of the rest rooms (7am-8pm even when center closed). From Apr-Oct there are guided walking tours Fri and Mon at 11, Sat & Sun 11 & 1 and by appt. From Apr-Oct, Dr Joel Andrews and his team (*i* concordguides.com ☎ 978-287-0897) offer comprehensive tours too. ◗ Apr-Oct 10-4. 58 Main St. *i* concordcfhamberofcommerce.org ☎ 978-369-3120.

Exit 30>: Concord's Colonial Inn – This elegant 1716 restaurant sitting musket distance from "the shot heard 'round the world" (was an arms storehouse during the Revolution) still dishes up tastes from back then: flavorful Yankee pot roast with divine mashed potatoes or yummy chicken pot pie; we sure hope Paul Revere got to taste the corn bread, which is made fresh all day long. However, the seasonal menus go well beyond that, with dishes like butternut squash risotto with shaved parmesan and toasted nuts (see the recipe on page 225) or pecan and mushroom stuffed trout and standards like: lobster/shrimp/crab/bisque, black bean & ale chile (made with prime rib) or Rhode Island Jonah crab cakes. Desserts can offer up Indian pudding, but we lapped up the 20th century creme brule. Come here for Sunday brunch - you may bump into Louisa May Alcott. If you're too full to travel, you can sleep at the Inn, but you may share your room with ghosts. ◗ M-Sat 7:30-11, 11:30-2, 5-8:30, Sun 10:30-2, 4-8:30. 48 Monument Sq. *i* concordscolonialinn.com ☎ 978-369-9200 or 800-370-9200.

Searching for Weapons of Mass Destruction

Exit 30>: Minute Man National Historic Park and the Old North Bridge – On April 19, 1775 British regulars clashed with colonial militia and minute men at Lexington, Concord's North Bridge, and on the road back to Boston. Many years later these events were called "the shot heard round the world" by Ralph Waldo Emerson. The skirmishes began the war for independence, which lasted more than 8 years. Here, you can walk the ground where it all occurred and the US began.

On April 18, 1775, General Thomas Gage gave orders to about 700 British soldiers to go out to Concord to seize and destroy military supplies known to be stockpiled in the town. His orders to Lt. Col. Smith, the British officer who was to lead the expedition, were as follows:

"Sir: Having received intelligence, that a quantity of Ammunition, Provision, Artillery, Tents and small arms, have been collected at Concord, for the Avowed Purpose of raising and supporting a Rebellion against His Majesty, you will march with the Corps of Grenadiers and Light Infantry, put under your command, with the utmost expedition and secrecy to Concord, where you will seize and destroy all Artillery, Ammunition, Provision, Tents, Small Arms, and all military stores whatever. But you will take care that the Soldiers do not plunder the inhabitants, or hurt private property."

Sometime after 9 am around Concord's North Bridge, the militiamen saw smoke coming from the area of the town (burning military supplies) and believing the town was being set on fire, marched down upon the bridge. The British soldiers were outnumbered 4 to1, so they retreated to the east side of the bridge, and quickly organized for defense. The colonials continued their advance down Punkatesset Hill until the British fired and killed 2 minute men. Maj. John Buttrick of Concord then gave the order "Fire, fellow soldiers, for God's sake, fire!" and for the first time Americans fired a volley into the lines of British soldiers and 2 were killed. According to one British officer, "Captain Laurie made us retire to this side of the bridge, which by the bye he ought to have done at the first for the rebels were so near..."

The battle continued for 16 miles on the road all the way back to Boston with the British running the gauntlet of colonial fire where a musket seemed to be hiding behind every tree. ◗ The grounds of Minute Man National Historical Park are open sunrise to sunset. Minute Man Visitor Center: Don't miss the excellent short movie."Road to Revolution". There are a couple of exhibits, tours and talks and a gift shop. See if you can find the "real Paul Revere" on a horse. 270 North Great Rd ◗ Apr-Oct 9-5; Nov 9-4; Closed Dec-Mar. *i* nps.gov/mima ☎ 781-674-1920. North Bridge Visitor Center (inside 1911 Buttrick Mansion) 174 Liberty St. Expect to find Ranger programs, a bookstore. gardens, the "Hancock" cannon and a 10 min. video about the cannon. ◗ Apr-Oct 9-5, Nov 9-4, Dec-Mar 11-3. *i* nps.gov/mima ☎ 978-369-6993.

MAP PG 8

Exit 30>: Minute Man Statue (inside Minute Man National Historic Park) – This famous statue represents the citizen-soldier: a farmer who has his left hand on his plow and his right hand on his musket in order to defend his land and liberty. He was ready to fight at a moment's notice. Though the statue is supposed to be any farmer, when local Concord man, Daniel Chester French, was planning the statue he made sketches of some of the descendants of Isaac Davis of Acton, who was one of the few killed at the Old North Bridge. This statue became the logo for the National Guard, and is the one you see on the 2000 Massachusetts quarter. It is also on US Savings Bonds and was on War Bonds during WWII.

French won a contest to design a monument for the 100th anniversary of the battle (in 1875). In a historical twist, Civil War cannons were melted down to cast the bronze statue. French later created many other pieces of art, including Lincoln in the Lincoln Memorial. You can see it off an I-95 Exit. ◗ Grounds of Minute Man National Historical Park are open sunrise to sunset.

Exit 30>: Walden Pond State Reservation – It really exists, and it looks pretty much like it did when Henry David Thoreau hung out there - even down to a replica of his house where he practiced his experiment in simplicity. The vegetation is lush with berry bushes, sumac, pitch pine, hickory, oak and birds twittering (kingfishers, black birds, chickadees, red-tailed hawks, migratory ducks and geese) and common sightings of squirrels, chipmunks and rabbits with skunks, raccoons and red foxes active at night.

Thoreau lived here on the shores of this kettle hole for 2 years and kept a journal

of his thoughts which was published as "Walden" in 1854, which helped inspire awareness and respect for the natural environment and is considered the birthplace of the conservation movement. He also taught school, expanded his family's pencil-making business, and worked at carpentry, stone masonry and gardening. He and his family were also instrumental in helping runaway slaves get to Canada. Route 126, Visitor Center, 915 Walden St. ◗ Apr-Oct 7-8pm, Nov-Mar 8-5. *i* www.mass.gov/dcr/parks/walden/ ☎ 978-369-3254.

Exit 30: Element – When walking into this gorgeous new green concept hotel our jaws dropped. The LEED certified sleek extended-stay suites have been built with low VOC paints, flooring made from 25% recycled content, CFL/LED bulbs, bed frames from certified forests, art mounted on recycled tires, soap & shampoo dispensers, Energy Star GE appliances and water efficient fixtures. You can sit on your

couch cushions or eat them - they're made from soy.

Functionally, the 359-degree TV (with a DVD player below and plug & play docking station) swivels to face the bed, desk or sofa. By the glass-topped desk (you can see what you left in the drawers), there's a jack pack for all of your electronic toys, an ergonomic chair and a recycle bin. For fun, the room has a white board to write notes-to-self, and magnetized maid messages which stick to the outside of the door. In the open-concept great room (lobby), natural light infuses a social gathering space, with lots of white tables on which to open up your laptops, and you can eat the complimentary hot breakfast on them or at bar stools or couches. In the parking lot, hybrid cars get priority spots. Element Lexington by Westin, 727 Marrett Road - B. *i* elementhotels.com ☎ 781-761-1750.

NEW! **Exit 24:** Charles River Canoe & Kayak – Just fall off this exit and into the water of the Charles River. You can take a cooling break in a kayak ($14-$20/hr), canoe ($16/hr), paddleboat ($18-$20/hr) or rowboat ($18/hr) and glide 3 miles up or down river with 1-4 persons aboard (even have infant vests). You can also take lessons or buy a boat. This site always was a place for fun -

decades ago it was an amusement park (Notice the design of the rental building) and amphitheater. ◑ (Apr-beginning Nov) daily M-F 10-1 hr. before sunset, S&S 9-1 hr. before sunset. *i* paddleboston.com ☎ 617-965-5110.

NEW! **Exit 19:** Cookies by Design – Though this is a gift basket franchise, it still bakes up fresh cookies for you to munch on on the road. Flavors are simple: oatmeal raisin, peanut butter, chocolate chip, millennium (oatmeal chocolate chip with pecans and Hershey pieces) and the cute-named snickerdoodle (sugar cookie with cinnamon). The colored/designed cookies for the baskets are adorable, so you may want to order them for a gift on your trip. 54 Highland Ave. (Other location: Exit 36 in Woburn). ◑ M-F 9-6, Sat 10-3 *i* cookiesbydesign.com ☎ 866-8-CRUMBS or 781-444-8230.

NEW! **Y'er Out!**

Rob Barry's been throwing at Fenway Park since 1981, and his collegues agree that he has the best arm in the baseball business. His strike zone isn't where you'd think: Barry throws peanuts to fans. His Dad (who had a 30-plus year career as a Fenway vendor) got him into the business when he was 13. He once threw peanuts from the 1st base side to a friend in the stands behind the 3rd base line. That toss, which flew across the pitcher's line of vision, resulted in a time out, and eventually inspired a "Sports and Leisure" question in the Genus 5 Edition of Trivial Pursuit.

Exit 10 S or 9 N: Furlong's Cottage Candies – Stock up for the trip at this 80-year-old homemade chocolate store. They are famous for stemmed cherries dipped into fondant and chocolate. Stan likes the cream centers - they offer 18 different ones (pineapple, ice cream drop, pistachio, coconut), but for Sandra it's the buttercrunch. There's raspberry truffles, dipped marshmallows, chocolate covered nuts or apricots (there's also orange peel, ginger, prunes).

People who love hard and chewy candy will enjoy molasses sponge, peanut butter bolsters and caramash. Sugar free treats are here, and most everything can be shipped home. ☞ Nbound - 2 mi N on US 1; Sbound - W up Coney St. to US 1, RT to 1355 Providence Hwy (US 1). ☎ 781-762-4124.

SOLDIERETTE?

Exit 9: Robert Shurtlieff was a brave soldier, a hero who fought in the Revolutionary War, and he was wounded twice in battle. He was not only a hero, but he was a she. Deborah Sampson didn't like the husband-to-be her Mom had chosen for her. To run

MAP PG 9-10

away, be able to travel alone, and satisfy her need for adventure she joined the Army! Sampson bound her breasts, deepened her voice and went so far to avoid being detected that when she was wounded in the thigh, she dug the bullet out herself. She eventually was discovered by an Army doctor when she suffered a high fever, yet she managed to get an honorary discharge, and none other than patriot Paul Revere helped her get a pension. A monument to Deborah Sampson stands in her home town of Sharon.

~~~~~~

Exit 9>: Red Wing – Way back in 1951, Joe and George Campanario started deep frying seafood in this 1933 wooden Worchester Club Car. Third generation Liam Murphy has taken over from 2nd-generation Joe and George, so he's at the helm buying fresh fish and clams daily and processing them through a filtering machine. The light batter and freshness of the clams (their specialty) or seafood, the homemade soups, the 19 kinds of pizza and Italian food is the combo that keeps everyone coming back to belly up to the same wooden counter. ☞ S on US 1 for 2 mi. 2235 Rte 1 ● Tues-Sat 11:30-10, Sun 12-8. *i* redwingdiner.com ☎ 508-668-0453.

Exit 8: Ward's Berry Farm – If you want to pick up fresh food for the car, you can't get much fresher than a farm stand store. In season there's strawberries, blueberries, raspberries, tomatoes, cucumbers, edamame, peas, peaches, squash and corn, etc. They make fresh fruit juices and smoothies and offer a sandwich bar, and Mrs. Ward bakes 6 kinds of pies and preserves. In the fridge there's quick lunch food: garlic hummus, chicken grapenut salad, oriental noodles, eggplant parmigiana, Hungarian mushroom soup or Mrs. Ward's meatballs.

In season, you can pick berries or pumpkins or take hay rides. There's even an indoor

petting zoo cared for by the local 4H club and an outdoor playground, including toy tractors.

Jim and Bob Ward's dad purchased land in 1981 for his "retirement"; he bought 7,000 blueberry bushes to start a farm. Neither Jim nor Bob had any farming experience, but when their father died they decided to run the 150-acre farm. ● M-F 9-7, S&S 9-6 (Jan-Mar M,Th & F 9-6, S&S 9-5). ☎ 781-784-3600.

Exit 7>: Old Country Store & Emporium – The 2nd generation of the Zecher family adheres to the 150-year old business' name. As you enter the wooden room with pickle barrels, long lost candy (non pareils, squirrel nuts, bit-o-honey, caramel corn, homemade fudge, Boston baked beans), it evokes the past, and so does the organized clutter through the warren of rooms filled with potato bins, curio cabinets, fireplace accessories, candles, wooden coat racks, place mats, braided rugs, wrought iron

hardware, gadgets, a rocking chair attic and tons of funny signs. See if you can find the soda fountain, apothecary wall unit or the player pianos - the kids will love them. ● M-Sat 10-6, Sun 12-5. ☞ Rte 140 south 2 mi, RT on School St for 1.6 mi underneath I-495, then RT on Otis St. 26 Otis St. *i* oldcountrystoreonline.com ☎ 508-339-8128.

Mile 9 Northbound: Massachusetts Tourist Information Center Nbound – Here's a place to stop and ask questions about things to do in the state (and Maine, NH, VT). Pick up brochures, motel coupon booklets and take advantage of freshly brewed coffee and bathrooms. There's vending machines and a picnic and pet walk area. ◗ Sept-May Daily 8-4; Mem Day-Labor Day 7-7. ☎ 508-339-8300.

Exit 3: Capron Park Zoo – If the kids need a bit of an airing, why not let them run about in this intimate zoo with a rain forest display, a nocturnal building and more. Go see the rare white lion Ramses, river otters and Visayan warty pigs. You can actually come in for a Zoo Snooze - spend the night in your tent, experience 2 behind-the-scenes tours plus supper and breakfast (1-12 persons $250). The park around the zoo is a nice place for a picnic lunch, and the kids will love the elephant poo products. ◗ Daily 10-5. ☞ E along South Ave (Rte 123) to County St., LT and follow to zoo in Capron Park at 201 County St. *i* capronparkzoo.com ☎ 774-203-1840.

NEW! **Exit 2:** Polonia Market –We're suckers for East European food, so we came back twice to buy the kabanos, a thin smoked length of pork sausage that we break off and eat in chunks. You can buy the fixings for sandwiches, since they have all the polish deli meats (kielbasa

too) and breads, homemade stuffed cabbage and bigos, and round off a meal with: jarred dill pickles, cucumber salad, red cabbage, sweet pickled peppers and go for the babkas or cheese danish for dessert. Other groceries abound: sour cherry syrup, plum butter, herrings, packaged Appetita soups, etc. 736 Broadway ◗ T& W 10-6, Th-Sat 10-5, Sun 12:30-3. ☎ 401-727-8400.

RHODE ISLAND

Exit 29S or 28N>: Blackstone Valley Visitor Center – Well, here not only do you get a clean bathroom, and brochures, but a gift shop with original items by Rhode Island artists (and no tax!): hats, soaps, jewelry, pottery, handmade gift cards, prints, purses, straw brooms and RI coffee syrup. There is an art gallery exhibit and a film about the rise and fall of the American Industrial Revolution. Map freaks will love the floor map of the Blackstone Valley. ◗ Daily 9-5. ☞ Visitor Center is across the street from the Slater Mill Museum below. 175 Main St. *i* tourblackstone.com ☎ 800-454-2882 or 401-724-2200.

Exit 28N or 29S>: Slater Mill Living History Museum – In 1789, 21-year-old Samuel Slater left England with some knowledge of textile machinery,

having been a manager in the Arkwright Mills in Derbyshire. With financial support from Moses Brown, he built this water-powered mill, and within the year was able to produce cotton yarn. One of these machines could supply a weaver with the same amount of yarn as 10 hand weavers.

This was the first water-powered factory in America, and it helped transform the area so much that by 1820 processing cotton became the backbone of Rhode Island's economy. Besides the mill, the museum displays the history of US textile manufacturing, including a real live cotton gin.

On site is the Wilkinson Mill, built of rubble stone in 1810 and it is used as a machine shop and textile mill. Moved to the site is the Sylvanus Brown House (1758), which is now used for spinning and weaving demonstrations and which sports a textile and dye garden. ◑ June Oct, T-Sun 10-4, May S&S 10-4 ☞ Sbound: exit 29, RT at 2nd stop sign to Broadway. RT at light to Exchange St, LT next light to Roosevelt Ave. Nbound: exit 28, LT bottom of ramp, thru the light, down the hill, bear right across river and RT to Roosevelt Ave. 67 Roosevelt Ave. *i* slatermill.org ☎ 401-725-8638.

Exit 27>: Modern Diner – This Sterling Streamliner opened in 1941. What's cute about the menu here is that it is schizophrenic - the oldsters can still have their classic menu, featuring their famous "Jimmie Gimmie" (2 poached eggs on an English muffin with sliced tomatoes, topped with melted cheese and bacon), while the youngsters trek in for the modern twist on it: "Eggs St. Nick" (2 poached eggs with fried onions and leeks set in a potato skin).

Daily lunch specials (meatloaf, liver & onions), fresh burgers, remain the same, but brunch on the weekends will bring butterscotch almond coconut pancakes, custard French toast with Kentucky bourbon sauce or lobster Benedict. ◑ M-Sat 6-2, Sun 7-2. ☞ George St. (Rte 1) S, bearing LT at the fork. 364 East Ave. ☎ 401-726-8390.

Exit 27>: China Inn – Around since 1976, it was rated the best in RI by all the major news outlets, so expect a delish Mandarin or Szechuan meal here. The pork dumplings are a favorite, and so is the General Tao chicken or the sesame chicken on broccoli, which is sweet and hot. House specialities are aparagus chicken, salt and pepper calamari, banana chicken or shredded pork in chili sauce. The Wor Bar (shrimp, scallops, lobster, chicken on crunchy sizzling rice) still has us licking our lips. ◑ M-Th 11:30-10, F 11:30-11, Sat 12-11, Sun 12-10. ☞ 0.3 mi N on George St as it turns into Park. Stop and park when it ends on Main St. Restaurant is to left at 285 Main St. ☎ 401-723-3960.

Exit 27>: Stanley's – In 1932, in the midst of the Depression, Stanley F. Kryla created a regional comfort food with quality beef topped with loads of fried onions and pickles.

Yummy Stanley-burgers have stood the test of time, even under the watch of the next owner, Gregory Raheb. The menu has 15 variations on that burger along with sandwiches, homemade soup and chili, Friday fish specials and Quebec-style fries topped with shredded mozzarella and gravy. You can wash them all down with a RI "cabinet" - a shake, (traditional flavor is coffee). Notice the fabulous new/old re-design by famous diner guru Morris Nathanson. ◑ M-Th 11-8, F&S 11-9. ☞ see Sparky's. 535 Dexter St. (other location 371 Richmond St, Providence) *i* stanleyshamburgers.com ☎ 401-726-9689.

Exit 27>: Sparky's – John Chippis (3rd generation), the newest "Sparky", started a 50-year-club for all the regulars who come back here for the hot wieners (not hot dogs, not frankfurters), which are smaller, spicier and are layered with a special meat sauce, mustard and onions, so all the flavors blend

together as one. In RI this is known as the New York system, and they wash them down with coffee milk. You can order burgers, sandwiches, etc., but why bother? ◑ Sat-Th 7-3, F 7-7. ☞ N on George St, RT onto East Ave. Stay left for 3 blocks as it turns on to Summer St. LT on Goff for 1 block, RT on Dexter St for 1/2 mi. 548 Dexter St. ☎ 401-726-9086.

Exit 24: Benny's – Started in 1924 as an automobile supply store, this

MAP PG 10-11

business evolved In the 50's and 60's (due to its reputation for great customer service) into a chain of 32 discount variety stores in RI, MA and CT. It covers housewares, hardware, sporting goods, electronics, toys, bikes, fishing and marine gear and stuff for your lawn and garden. For your trip, you might need a car pillow, paper goods, a lunch box, an ice chest, folding seats or no-spill drink bottles. Kids can keep busy with puzzles, maze games, word searches, dot-to-dot, jump rope, travel sized games, coloring books or badminton, balls, and sand toys for the beach. Hey, they still offer free lay away! ◗ M-Sat 8-9, Sun 9-6. 66 Branch Ave. *i* hellobennys.com ☎ 401-861-5995.

Exit 23>: Rhode Island State Capitol – Built 1895-1904 and based on the US capitol, it features many treasures. The most famous is the full-length portrait of George Washington by Gilbert Stuart, but there's also a reproduction of the Liberty Bell, one of the original copies of the Declaration of Independence (given to each of the colonies) and two cannons, the Gettysburg Gun which was struck by three Confederate shells during Pickett's Charge at

the Battle of Gettysburg on July 3, 1863, and the Civil War cannon, used in the Battle of Bull Run. Most important, though, is the Royal Charter of 1663, referring to the principle of religious liberty and tolerance upon which Roger Williams founded the State. See if you can find these words inscribed over the South doorway: "To hold forth a lively experiment that a most civil state may stand and best be maintained with full liberty in religious concernment". Independent Man, the 11 ft bronze statue on top of the dome, originally named "Hope," has been standing

there since 1899. He has braved RI blizzards and hurricanes, and has been struck by lightning 27 times. A symbol of freedom and independence, he holds a spear in his right hand and the State symbol, an anchor, lies at his feet. Do you know the real name of Rhode Island is the State of Rhode Island and the Providence Plantations? 82 Smith St. ◗ M-F 8-4:30. FREE tours 9-1. *i* www.rilin.state.ri.us/statehousetour/index.htm ☎ 401-222-3983.

Exit 22C: Christopher Dodge House – You can't get much closer to I-95 than this 1865 brick Italianate home which is also near the magnificent State Capitol. You can walk from here to downtown, to the Providence Mall or the FREE fitness center. This home has 15 rooms, each with a fireplace and fan and a heat/AC unit for your comfort. 11 W. Park St. *i* providence-suites.com ☎ 401-351-6111.

Exit 22>: Haven Bros. – Haven Bros. Diner, which stands night duty on the corner of City Hall, began in 1888 as a wooden lunch wagon by Anna Coffey Haven, who passed it to her sons Tom and Henry.

In 1986, city planners were trying to attract new business downtown and tried to give the diner the boot because of its "unattractive" quality, so by a Mayor's order it was moved 3 blocks away. The people of Providence protested, and the mayor's office was flooded with requests pleading for the diner to stay at City Hall. "I never realized that so many people would care so much about a truck that sells hot dogs", exclaimed Mayor Paolino. The 18-wheeler was allowed back to its privileged spot (with its electricity hook-up

to a lamppost), and the mayor helped celebrate its 100th anniversary in 1988 with a hot dog and champagne party.

Between 5pm and 3am Sun-Th and 5 pm-4 am F & S, you can join senators, cops, truck drivers, bar hoppers, hospital shift workers and motorcyclists for the burgers, (veggie ones too), shakes, fried eggs, grilled cheese, chili dogs, and beans. Corner of Dorrence and Fulton. ☎ 401-861-7777.

Exit 22>: John Brown House Museum – America's grandest mansion of the time (1788), a 3 story Georgian, was built by this businessman, patriot, politician, China trade pioneer and slave trader (60% of the slave trade in the mid 18th century was through RI). Brown invested heavily in privateers, and was the one who in 1775 sold the US Navy its first ship, the USS Providence.

This home passed to his daughters, their families (his grandson John Francis Brown was Gov. of RI - his cradle is here) and then became the winter residence of the elegant Gammell family in the 2nd half of the 19th century. Afterwards, in the early 20th, it became the mansion of Marsden Perry, a real estate and trolley mogul. Notice the leather wall covering and 4 walls of WPA murals of Washington's Inauguration. ◐ Apr-Dec T-F 1-2, Sat 10-4; Jan-Mar F&S 10-4 ☞ E on Memorial Blvd as it curves right, LT on Washington Pl. 2 blocks to Benefir St, RT for 1/3 mi to Power St. 52 Power St. *i* rihs.org ☎ 401-273-7507.

Exit 22>: Fire & Ice – The fire in the name relates to the huge 35-foot grill in the middle of the restaurant that is used to cook your meal. The ice is the bed where all of the ingredients rest. You choose your meal by meandering down the ice trail choosing amongst the 18 raw meats and seafood (sirloin, lamb, shrimp), 40 veggies, pastas and 15 sauces. You then hand your ingredients to one of the chefs and stand around the circular grill with the rest of the crowd watching carefully to make sure you get the right meal back.

The place is popular, noisy and hopping (you could bring a crying baby here without it getting noticed!). One price for all you can eat. ◐ M-Th 11:30-10, F 1130-11, S 11:30-11, Sun 10-10. 42 Providence Place. *i* fire-ice.com ☎ 401-270-4040.

Exit 21: Federal Hill – If you pine for family-style Italian food the way mamma would have made it, this Italian district dishes up the goods. For an inexpensive meal head to Angelo's Civita Farnese, 141 Atwells Ave. (☎ 401-621-8171 *i* angelosonthehill.com), where the marble table tops you see were bought used in 1924. The 3rd generation offers daily menus (escarole & beans, baked pork chops,  roast chicken), but you can always get a meatball sandwich, veal & peppers and homemade macaroni.

Foodies will love Venda Ravioli at #265 (☎ 401-421-9105 *i* vendaravioli.com) with its huge oval counter of prepared dishes (rolled eggplant, stuffed portobello mushrooms, frittata), cheeses, dried salamis and 150 pastas (lobster ravioli). Open since 1917, Scialo Bros. Bakery at #257 (☎ 877-421-0986 *i* scialobakery.com) is the place for desserts. Luigi ran it for 70 years, and now daughters Carol and Lois bake in the same brick ovens: cannoli, sfogliatelle, biscotti, anise slices and (available by the slice) cassata cake, tiramisu, zuppa inglese, torrone, etc.

Others known on the block are Caseta Pizzaeria, with its "Wimpy Skippy" sandwich stuffed with spinach, cheese and pepperoni, and the upscale Constantino's, or go to Tony's for your grocery needs.

However if you want the 5th best pizza in America (GQ mag), go one block north to Bob & Timmy's (32 Spruce St ☎ 401-453-2221 *i* bobandtimmys.com) and scarf down the spinach and mushroom wood-grilled melt-in- your-mouth version (we can still taste it). We're also still drooling over the Hill special pasta wtih chicken, sun-dried tomatoes, mushrooms in a rich smoked Gouda cream sauce (enough for 4 people).

The Big Blue Bug

Mile 35.5, between exits 18 and 19 on the W side: Get the kids ready to catch a glimpse of the 9 ft high, 58 ft long big blue bug named "Nibbles Woodaway" which overlooks the highway. This hurricane-proof 2 ton termite, 928 times the size of the household variety, must be hard to get rid of - it's been sitting on top of the New England Pest Control Building for 30 years. The steel wire-mesh-fiberglass creature is not only a landmark on the road, but also a movie star, having appeared

in *Dumb and Dumber* and on the *Oprah Winfrey Show*.

The company dresses it for holidays: Uncle Sam hat for July 4, witch's hat and broom for Halloween, and a red blinking nose and antlers for Christmas.

Exit 18>: Culinary Archives & Museum – This window into our gastronomic past owes much to Chicago Chef Louis Szathmary's personal collections. You would expect rare cookbooks (Paul Fritzsche's collection of 7,500), but there's also restaurant appliances, cruise ship menus, the evolution of the stove, food posters, chef's uniforms, a New England Tavern and the History of the First Stomach: eating habits of our Presidents. Delight in the birth of the diner, which started out in Provi-dence in 1872 in horse-drawn canteens to serve night workers - the precursor to our fast food. You can oogle the drawings and photos of famed RI diner designer

Exit 22: Women of the world should be thankful that in 1794 Nehemiah and Seril Dodge, Providence goldsmiths, developed the process for plating base metal with gold. Most of the sparkly gold costume jewelry that adorns us today can be traced back to their invention. Until the late 20th century, RI had been Costume Jewelry Capital of the world.

Father of Religious Freedom in America

Roger Williams always sought "freedom for the Souls of Men". Just about everyone and all nations of his time thought that religious freedom and civic order could not co-exist. While back in London in 1644, he published "The Bloudy Tenent of Persecution", calling for religious freedom for all, including the Paganish, Jewish, Turkish, or Antichristian. Parliament ordered all copies burned, as his ideas were considered naive and dangerous.

Even though Anglicanism was the national religion in England, he managed in 1663 to get Charles II to grant Rhode Island a charter confirming that no one would be "molested, punished, disquieted, or called in question, for difference in opinion in matters of religion."

His ideas were included, more than a century later, in the First Amendment to the U.S. Constitution.

MAP PG 11

Morris Nathanson, who created much of what we know as neon/stainless diner decor, or follow the menus of the chang-ing American palate. ●T-Sun 10-5. ☞ E 1 block, RT on Allens Ave for 1 mi, LT on Harborside. 315 Harborside Blvd. *i* www.culinary.org ☎ 401-598-2805.

Exit 16N or 17S: Roger Williams Zoo and Park – Open in 1872, one of the country's oldest zoos teems with foliage, giving you a sense of meeting animals in the wild (you can even walk through a rainforest). Get up close to a dromedary camel and watch bisons graze. Meet George and Gracie - the moon bears, find the tree kangaroos, and listen to the laughing kookaburra. See if you can spot the golden lion tamarins, and we know you will have no trouble finding the elephants (watch their daily bath) or giraffes. Experience the "Journey through the Wild" daily programs. Beside the zoo the 120 year-old Roger Williams Park, probably the most beautiful park along I-95, is perfect for a rest stop. Take a ride through it looking for the little wooden bridge, the swan paddleboats, the statuary, the Victorian carousel, Hasbro playground (accessible), indoor botanical gardens (T-Sun 10-4) and decide where you want to play.  ● Zoo: Daily 9-4, Park: dawn-dusk). 1000 Elmwood Ave. *i* rwpzoo.org ☎ 401-785-3510 (zoo), 401-785-9450 (park).

Exit 13>: Radisson – This hotel is a teaching unit of the nearby Johnson & Wales University (largest culinary arts school in the world). Part of these enthusiastic students' internships is to work in the various departments, including front desk, sales, maintenance, banquets and even housekeeping. The restaurant in this hotel also rotates culinary students through, and yes they have to wash dishes. 2081 Post Rd. *i* radisson.com/warwickri ☎ 401-739-3000.

Exit 13: Wonder/Hostess Bakery Outlet – A discount snack stop is always welcomed by everyone in the car. Favorites from your youth are there as low as 5/$3.89. You can pick from fudge brownies, Twinkies, Hohos, Devil Dogs, Coffee Cakes, Yodels, Hostess cupcakes or Sno Balls, Honey Buns, Ring Dings, fruit pies, Fruit and Grain cereal bars or 100-calorie snacks. You can buy bread, peanut butter and jam to make sandwiches, Miss Cubbison's cookies, Utz chips, puddings, instant soups, and there's even sugar free snacks: chocolate creme cookies and wafers. ● M-F 9-6, Sat 9-5. 1150 Jefferson Blvd. *i* bakeryoutlets.com ☎ 401-738-7956 X 14 or 800-247-6564.

Exit 12B S or 11 N: Warwick Mall – Kids will love the Carousel food court, and you'll all enjoy Rhode Island's famous Newport Creamery for "cabinets" (milk  shakes). Coffee is the local favorite flavor, but there's also Strawberry Banana Chip, Cappuccino Crunch and Choc O' Nutster. Macy's, and JC Penney are the anchors, and there's Lane Bryant, Old Navy, Abercrombie & Fitch for the clothes, Aldo for shoes, The Disney Store and 8 jewelers. ● M-Sat 10-9, Sun 11-6 DIR.: Take I-295 N, get off at exit 2. *i* warwickmall.com ☎ 401-739-7500.

Exit 8: Panera Bread – When we find great tasting quick meals, we have to let you know. This bakery/cafe chain's artisanal breads are the star here. The stuff they put on them - asiago roast beef, chipotle chicken, is yummy too. We love the combos: daily soups (broccoli cheddar and low fat ones) with a 1/2 sandwich, or the interesting salads: Asian sesame chicken, Fuji apple chicken or paninis (frontega chicken is popular) There's bagels (cinnamon crunch, everything), sinful cookies, french-style desserts (pineapple upside down cake, wild blueberry scones, pecan braid, macadamia nut blondie) and designer coffees or teas. We can't leave without buying the asiago cheese bread to take home. *i* panerabread.com.

Farm Turnovers, 3-Layer Cakes and Texas Toast, which is still 20% of their line.

In the 60's, in Switzerland, she flipped over their little fish-shaped crackers, and today Goldfish remain one of their leading icon products. In 1961 Rudkin sold out to Campbell Soup and became the first woman on their board. In 1963, Margeret Rudkin's "The Pepperidge Farm Cookbook" became the first cookbook to ever make it onto the NY Times bestseller list. If you want to try her products, at this discount shop you can really score some deals. Senior saver days are Tues & Wed. ◗ Mon-Fri 9:30-6, Sat 9:30-6, Sun 12-5. 691 Quaker Lane, Quaker Valley Mall *i* pepperidgefarm.com ☎ 401-828-3070.

> *NEW!* Rhode Island was one of the the only states that rejected and did not ratify the 18th Amendment to the US Constitution prohibiting the sale of alcoholic beverages. Rhode Island rumrunners subsequently made a tidy profit ferrying liquor ashore from beyond the three-mile limit.

NEW! GOING AGAINST THE GRAIN

Exit 8: Pepperidge Farm Thrift Shop – Milano cookie alert. Seventy year ago, Marge Rudkin's (who lived on Pepperidge Farm in Fairfield CT) youngest son had allergies and couldn't eat most commerical processed foods. Going against the grain, she started a bread business in the height of the Great Depression. While bread prices were $.10, she had the nerve to sell her premium loaves for $.25. She sold them in CT, and her Wall St. husband carried them on the train to his job in NYC and sold them in specialty shops there.

By 1940 production was up to 1,000,000 loaves. On a visit to Belgium, Rudkin noticed the unique fancy chocolate cookies which were sold to the Belgian Royal House. She bought the US rights, and the Distinctive Cookies were born: Milano, Brussels and Bordaux are still some of the most popular. She foresaw the frozen food revolution and bought a bakery to produce Pepperidge

Mile 9 Northbound: Rhode Island Welcome Center – You are always welcome to pick up any flyers on the State, motel coupon booklets or check out the hotel rates in the area. Ask for travel info, use the clean rest rooms, try the vending machines (profits go to the RI Assoc. of the Blind), use the ATM, walk your pets or enjoy the picnic area. ◗ Daily 8:30-6 (restrooms open 7-6). ☎ 401-539-3031.

Exit 3: The Stagecoach House Inn – Imagine what stagecoach drivers and travelers in 1796 (when this was built) would have thought of the Jacuzzi tubs in their rooms. Have a soak, romance by the fireplace and enjoy your breakfast on the deck overlooking Wood River listening to the waterfall. Near-

by there's 8 golf courses (6 within 5 mi). 1136 Main St. *i* stagecoachhouse.com ☎ 888-814-9600 or 401-539-9600.

NEW! Exit 3: Del's Frozen Lemonade – You will come across green-and-yellow roadside signs advertising this local treat. Angelo DeLucia started it in 1948 using a recipe that his grandfather brought from Italy. The cup of half-melted snow is a blend between Italian ices and a Slurpee, and is refreshing for both its icy texture and the tart flavor (which comes from real lemons, not processed syrup). It has virtually no name recognition outside of RI. "I don't really know why it never caught on in other places," said Bruce DeLucia, Angelo's son. "Maybe we just like to keep things to ourselves around here." ◗ Memorial Day-Labor Day 10-9. 1135 Main St. *i* dels.com ☎ 401-491-9655.

NEW! Exit 3: Lickety Splits – Local (since 1924!) Bliss Bros. ice cream is served up here in a large assortment from their 60 hard and 40 soft flavors. Some wild ones: pomegranate chip, purple cow (black raspberry, white and chocolate chips), dinosaur crunch and ones with no sugar: coffee, caramel pecan, moose tracks (fudge swirl and mini peanut butter cups) or no-fat frozen yogurt: kahlua fudge, wildberry crumble. There's sorbet, sherbet, real root beer floats and of course, coffee cabinets (shakes). 39 Kingston Rd ◗ Apr-Oct Sun-Th 12-9:30, F&S 12-10:30. ☎ 401-539-9047.

Exit 1: The Pavilion Restaurant and Golf – You can drive some balls or play 18-hole mini-golf here, and then dine at a nice restaurant. Practice your chipping, lob shots and driving on 9 target greens and then eat some greens, subs, steak, veal or pasta. ◗ Daily 10-dusk (golf); M-Sat 11-10, Sun 8am-10pm (food). ☞ 1/4 mi. S on Rte 3, LT on Frontier Rd to #15. *i* thepavilionrestaurant.com ☎ 401-377-9900.

CONNECTICUT

Mile 108 Sbound: Connecticut Welcome Center – It always pays to stop at Welcome Centers for their clean rest rooms, motel coupon booklets and friendly advice. This one has a canine rest area, truck parking, vending machines and picnic tables. ◗ Daily 8-5. ☎ 860-599-2056.

Exit 90: Mystic & Shoreline Visitors' Information Center – They'll help you find a motel or something fun to do in Mystic (discount tickets to the Seaport), if you'd only stop in and ask. The booklets for motel coupons are here, and there's a mailbox outside. When it is closed, you can use the FREE hotel reservation phones located outside, and pick up the popular tourist site flyers. You can experience the area on a segway (☎ 203-453-5799 *i* segwaytoursandrentals.com) ◗ Sept-Nov & May M-Sat 9:30-5, Sun 10-5; Dec-Mar 10-5, June-Aug M-Sat 9-6, Sun 10-5. *i* mysticinfo.com ☎ 860-536-1641.

Exit 90: Mystic Aquarium & Institute for Exploration – The sea lion (Coco, Surfer, Boomerang and pup Jeffy) show is bound to please the whole family. Ever wonder what it would be like to touch a whale? In their Beluga Contact Program you can go into the water with a whale: you'll hear it breathe, spout and vocalize and get to touch it. Besides all their exotic fish, underwater explorer Dr. Robert Ballard's team's findings are on view. Walk through the Fluorescent Coral exhibit and find out how fluorescence is being used for research projects to find cures and treaments for Alzheimer's and cancer. Check out the Sting Ray Touch Pool or sign up for an encounter program with African penguins or sharks. ◗ Apr-Oct 9-6, Nov & Mar 9-5, Dec-Feb 10-5. 55 Coogan Blvd. *i* mysticaquarium.org ☎ 860-572-5955.

MAP PG 11-12

Exit 90: Mystic Seaport – Step back in time in this 19th century maritime village offering you everything from tall ships to boarding the very last wooden whale ship. See a scale model of the area in 1876, figureheads from the bows of ships, a planetarium, a visitors' gallery overlooking a restoration in progress and the world's largest collection of nautical photography. The permanent seafaring exhibit covers immigrants, traders, explorers, fishermen, artists and vacationers on oceans, lakes and rivers. Try to catch

the dead horse ceremony, and leave time for the large museum and book shop. Second day is FREE. ◗ Apr-Oct 9-5, Nov-Mar Th-Sun 10-4. ☞ S on CT 27 (Greenmanville Ave.) to 75 Greenmanville Ave. *i* mysticseaport.org ☎ 888-9seaport (860-572-5315) or 860-572-0711.

Exit 90: Franklin's General Store – Smack in the middle of Mystic Village, this shop has authentic New England wares. Stan adores the 21 flavors of fudge: rocky road (marshmallows & walnuts), praline (caramel/pecan/vanilla), Mystic (heath bar) crunch, tiger butter (vanilla, peanut butter and chocolate), etc. However you

can find wooden toys, hot sauces, mustards, maple syrup, steak sauces, fuzzy navel jam, nautical lamps, funny signs, cheeses for the car (and picnic baskets) and even duck food to feed the ducks in the village. ◗ summer M-Sat 10-8 (winter 10-6), Sun 11-6 *i* mysticfudge.com ☎ 800-585-0676 or 860-536-1038.

Exit 90>: Ancient Mariner – The trend toward retro classics works for us. We enjoy chowing down on chicken pot pie, shepherd's pie, cheese fondue, Yankee pot roast or mac 'n cheese, with a Whoopie pie or banana split for dessert. However, in this downtown Mystic place you can also opt for fried calamari with snow peas and red peppers (nice bite), sesame seared tuna with Asian veggies, a lobster BLT, clam roll po' boy or tuna tartare. Entertainment most Wed-Sun eves. 21 W. Main St. ◗ Daily 11-10. *i* ancientmarinermystic.com ☎ 860-536-5200.

Exit 90>: Whaler's Inn – Mystic flourished as a ship-building center, and at this Inn you can still see sailing schooners pass beneath the Bascule Drawbridge, one block away. This Inn, perfectly located in the heart of downtown Mystic, is made up of 5 buildings which have served as boarding houses or hotels for over 100 years. The "1865 House" is a historic Victorian, while Noank and Stonington share a large porch and are good for families. The newest, Hoxie House, overlooks the

Mystic River. Zagat rated for gourmet dining, Bravo Bravo is housed on the main level. ☞ South on Rte 27 (Greenmanville Rd) for 1.25 mi., turn right on East Main St to 20 East Main St. *i* whalersinnmystic.com ☎ 800-243-2588 or 860-536-1506.

Between Exit 89-90, Mile 100 Northbound only: Hoxie Scenic Overlook – Look out over Mystic Seaport and imagine it in its heyday, busy with fishing, sealing and whaling, with more than a dozen shipyards building sloops, schooners, brigs, ships and steamers. It was the 2nd busiest (after Boston), launching ships during the Civil War. The bluff on the right was the scene of a Pequot Indian War. Looking east, you can see in the distance, at Mystic Seaport (originally George Greenman & Bros Shipyard), the masts of the 1841 Charles W. Morgan, a whaling ship, the square-rigged 1882 Joseph Conrad, the sailing schooner L.A. Dunton and many more.

NEW **Exit 89>:** Captain Daniel Packer Inne – Since 1756, this building has been owned by the same family. Sure, you can now enjoy live music every night in their pub, but back then Captain Packer would regale weary travelers with tales of the high seas. The next morn he would transport them, their horses and stage-coaches across the Mystic River on his rope ferry. On the opposite shore,

while bidding them a fond farewell, he'd pick up another group of travelers. The inne remains, with its Colonial style, beams, mantles and original fireplaces in every room. Certainly you could have a shrimp cocktail or clam chowder, but wouldn't you rather try the lobster lollipops with plum dijon sauce or wild boar sausage with apples and caramelized onion chutney or fig and pancetta salad? A local favorite is the lemon peppered chicken, but we veered toward the veal homard scaloppini with lobster meat, shallots and mushrooms and the hazelnut chicken with butternut squash in a Frangelico tarragon cream sauce on cranberry/almond rice. For dessert the Xango, banana cheesecake in a deep fried tortilla drizzled with caramel sauce was deliciously crunchy and not sweet or greasy. ☞ As you exit turn left (southbound) or right (northbound) and take Allyn St to light (Rte 1). LT onto Rte 1 and RT onto Water st (just before you get to downtown) to 32 Water St. ◑ 11-4, 5-10. *i* danielpacker.com ☎ 860-536-3555.

Exit 89>: Azu – This is a buzzing place - a friendly local hangout for all ages and all appetites, from small "bites" to adventurous dinner plates. You can nibble on shrimp fritters, hot and sweet bbq ribs, crispy stacked onion rings, or chow down on lamb lollipops, lobster mac and cheese, fig/blue cheese pizza, pasta Bolognese or fish tacos. The name? - it's a play on comments about busy nights: "What a zoo!". ☞ S on Allyn St, LT on Library St 400 yds to W Main St, bear left to 3234 W. Main St. ◑ M-Th 11:30-9, F 11:30-10, Sat 7am-10, Sun 7am-9pm. ☎ 860-536-6336.

Exit 88: Mystic Marriott and (Elizabeth Arden) Red Door Spa – What we have here is the known luxury of a Marriott hotel, and this one not only has a Starbucks in the lobby, the Octogan steakhouse for lobster bisque, raw bar and Kobe steak (try the chili rub or 3 others) for dinner but a decadent Red Door Spa attached to it. What better way to make your drive more relaxing than to come in and get all those kinks smoothed out of your body with a a choice of 7 massages, 11 facials (how about champagne and rose?) done on an ergonomic heated table, cozy warm cocoon towel wraps and eye pillows to soothe. Spa ◑ Summer: M-Sat 8-8, Sun 8-7. Rest year: M-Th 8-7, F&S 8-8, Sun 8-6. 625 North Rd. *i* reddoorsalons.com ☎ (hotel) 866-449-7390 or 860-446-2600; (spa) 860-446-2500.

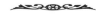

Exit 86>: USS Nautilus and U.S. Navy Submarine Force Museum – The story of the US Navy's "Silent Service" and "sharks of steel" is depicted here, starting from Bushnell's Turtle, which served in the American Revolution. David Bushnell, from CT, developed a hand powered submarine called the Turtle, which

MAP PG 13

tried to attach a 150-lb explosive charge to the British HMS Eagle hull in the NY harbor. The attempt failed. Learn about the modern Seawolf, Los Angeles and Ohio class submarines and get hands-on in a control room (from the USS Bill Fish) or try one of the 3 periscopes. The highlight of your experience here is boarding the Nautilus, the U.S.'s first nuclear powered submersible and the first ship to make it to the North Pole. You must go to see how the men slept, figure out where they kept their clothes and gear and imagine 120 of them cooped up here. ◑ May-Oct, Wed-Mon 9-5, Nov-Apr, Wed-Mon 9-4. ☞ Rte 12N 1.7 mi. to the sub base. LT on Crystal Lake Rd., follow signs. 1 Crystal Lake Rd. FREE *i* ussnautilus.org ☎ 800-343-0079 or 860-694-3174.

⚜

Exit 86: Olio – Superb modern Italian food worth getting off an exit for. Starters can be crisp calamari served with marinara sauce and a chipotle mayonnaise, a lobster-stuffed artichoke or a grilled steak bruschetta. Pastas are original, like open faced lobster, shrimp, scallop ravioli or gnocchi with shrimps, sun dried tomatoes, asparagus and saffron cream sauce. Mains run the gamut from veal francaise with spinach, tomatoes, risotto in a white wine garlic sauce to crab cakes with lobster chive sauce

NEW!!

Exit 86: USS Nautilus was the first ship in the world to reach the North Pole. It was the first nuclear powered submarine, and it navigated the 60,000 miles on a lump of uranium the size of a golf ball. You can actually go aboard it right here.

or a nicely executed roast chicken and mashies. There's grilled pizzas, burgers and lovely salads too, and save room for the banana split. ◑ M-Th 11:30-9, F & S 11:30-10, Sun 4:30- 9. ☞ Sbound exit becomes Kings Hwy; Nbound RT on CT 12 to Kings Hwy. 33 Kings Highway. ☎ 860-445-6546.

Exit 86: Holiday Bowl – For over 43 years families have been enjoying wholesome fun bowling here on 32 lanes. Stop for a nice break for as little as $1.99 a game (M-W 9 pm-12, Sun 9-noon), or for weekend (Sat or Sun 12-3) pizza, pop and pins, for the family (for $54.95). Or the kids might just play in the arcade. The Laneside Grill has a menu with pizza, quesadillas, burgers or Philly cheesesteak, and you can wash it all down with a mug of root beer. ◑ Sun 9am-11pm, Mon 9am-1am, T-Th 9-12am, Fri & Sat 9am-2am. ☞ Follow exit to Rte 1 S (Long Hill Rd), turn right on King's Highway to 27 King's Highway. *i* holidaybowlgroton.com ☎ 860-445-6500.

Our Most Famous Traitor Slept Here

Exit 85: America's most famous traitor, Benedict Arnold, arrived on Sept 6,1781 with 1,700 British soldiers and attacked Fort Griswold. The 140 American soldiers were able to withstand 2 battles, but succumbed to the 3rd. Lt. Col. William Ledyard surrendered by offering his sword to a British officer, who accepted it and then drove it right through him. A massacre followed this act, with 80 Americans killed after this offer to surrender. Dear Benedict, a native of Connecticut, kept busy by setting fire to New London, burning down 150 buildings, supposedly with pleasure. This was one of Britain's last actions in the North.

MAP PG 13-14

Exit 83N or 84S>: Zavala – As you walk in here, you feel like you've stepped into a boisterous Mexican backyard party. You realize the food is authentic when you can start with a delicious cactus salad (tomato, cilantro, onion, cheese) or even fried cactus. Popular is the Ninos Envueltos, a steak rolled with cheese and mushrooms in a tomato pepper cream sauce (yum) or the Yucatan Cochinita Pibil, which is tender  pork slow cooked in annatto sauce and wrapped in a banana leaf. The pan seared scallops in coconut and tequila lime broth sounded great, and you can wash it all down with over 80 choices of tequila or Mexican sodas or beers. If you must, there's typical Tex-Mex too, and end your meal with Mexican Pastel de Tres Leches, flan or a banana Presidente. See if you can get a table in the back overlooking the harbor. ◗ M-F 11-8:30, S&S 4-8:30. ☞ Follow Water St to town til it comes to a T at State St. 2 State St., New London. ☎ 860-437-1891.

Exit 83N or 84S>: Nathan Hale Schoolhouse – Revolutionary War notable Nathan Hale was a teacher in New London (and East Haddam). "He was a happy and faithful teacher, everybody loved him. He was sprightly, kind, intelligent and ever so handsome." In July, 1775 he closed the schoolhouse and joined the patriots. In  the summer of 1776, George Washington was desperate for information on the British, so he asked for a volunteer to spy on them. Nathan Hale exchanged his uniform for a plain brown suit and broadbrimmed hat, and grabbing his Yale diploma, pretended to be a schoolmaster. He crossed the L.I. Sound and headed for Manhattan, where he was captured on September 21, 1776.

The intelligence reports found on his person caused British General William Howe to order him hanged the next morn without trial. His dying words have turned him into one of the most famous patriots, "I only regret that I have but one life to lose for my country." ◗ May-Oct W-Sun 11-4. ☞ See Zavala. corner of Water St. & State St. *i* connecticutsar.org ☎ 860-873-3399.

Exit 82: Crystal Mall – With its signature Waterford Crystal chandelier, this mall has 130 options on 2 floors. Jazz up your vacation at Frederick's of Hollywood, buy Euro fashions at H&M (for kids too), find backseat ideas at the Game Stop, make a Build-a-Bear for cuddling, and for active gear - Champs or Eastern Mountain Sports. There's Spencer Gifts for well, gifts. ◗ M-Sat 10-9, Sun 12-6. ☞ N on Hartford Turnpike (Rte 85), LT for Nbound travelers, 1/4 mi. *i* shopsimon.com/Mall/?id=334 ☎ 860-442-8500.

Exit 70: The Florence Griswold Museum – In the 1890's, Florence Griswold was forced to take in boarders to save her family home. By sheer providence Henry Ward Ranger, an established artist, was looking to start up an art colony in an area similar to one in Giverny, France. The lands around Miss Florence's home were lush with salt marshes, gnarled oaks, rock outcroppings and orchards, all bathed in the morning mist off the ocean and fabulous evening "slanted light".

Through the years over 200 artists (Childe Hassam, John Henry Twachtman, Willard Metcalf) lived and worked here in a communal setting, with Miss Florence acting as birth mother to the Lyme Art Colony, creators of American Impressionism. Look for the "wiggle game" drawings, where one artist would scribble random lines and another had to turn it into a cartoon. The dining room is famous for its painted doors and panels which were created by the "Hot Air Club". The paintings displayed here and in the new river front gallery are a living record captured on canvas in the very place they were created. ◐ T-Sat 10-5, Sun 1-5. 96 Lyme St. *i* florencegriswoldmuseum.org ☎ 860-434-5542.

Exit 70: Old Lyme Inn – If you require an elegant stop along your journey, here you could enjoy a beautifully refurbished inn with large antique bedecked rooms. In the refined restaurant, you can graze on smoked duck confit with black truffle mushroom sauce, butternut squash and sweet potato soup, rack of lamb, swordfish medal-

lions with blood orange mojo, pistachio cous cous and mango salsa and flamed prime steaks. Leave room for the chocolate velvet mousse cake and creme brule. 85 Lyme St. *i* oldlymeinn.com ☎ 800-434-5352 or 860-434-2600.

Exit 67N or 68S: Pat's Kountry Kitchen – Voted CT's Best Family dining for 9 years, famous for its clam hash recipe (invented 25 years ago when her son Gary spilled the clam broth by mistake), Pat's is decorated with kitchen gadgets, blue and white "delft" plates and a teddy bear collection. Lori and Gary are now running the place, and still serve comfort food like chicken pot pie, yankee pot roast, stuffed flounder with vegetables and the local favorite red flannel hash (yum - with pastrami and corned beef). The homemade soups could be RI clam chowder or the wow spicey pork and cabbage (you can buy them frozen to go), and the homemade dessert standards are the chocolate bread pudding,

banana or chocolate cream pie, fruit pies and sugar free options. Lighter fare includes gorgonzola salad with walnuts and craisins, grilled veggie salad or grilled chicken with eggplant. ◐ closed Wed, Sun brunch 12:30-2, M, T, Th, F, Sat 7am-9pm. 70 E. Mill Rock Rd. ☎ 860-388-4784.

Mile 65 Nbound: Connecticut Welcome Center – It always pays to stop at Welcome Centers for their clean rest rooms, motel coupon booklets and friendly advice. This one has a canine rest area. ◐ Memorial Day to Labor Day: Daily 8-4; Oct-May Th-Sun 8-1. ☎ 860-399-8122.

Exit 65: Tanger Outlets – Here's 65 outlets with variety for all: Casual Male XL, Levi's, Rockport, Children's Place, Hollister (CA gear), Pepperidge Farm and more. It has a homey village architecture reminiscent of a New England train station, and for fun you can check out both a restored 1902 cruising yawl and the last working steam engine in the state. AAA members can get a savings book and more if you join Tanger Club. ◐ Apr-Dec M-Sat 10-9, Sun 10-6; Jan-Mar Sun-Th 10-6, F&S 10-9. *i* tangeroutlet.com ☎ 860-399-8656.

Exit 65>: Westbrook Inn – Finding this 1876 antique-filled elegant inn built by a sea captain (which housed seaman, travelers and later on NYC vacationing actors) near an exit is a treat. The extra bonus here is that you can go to the beach down the street (they'll give you towels, chairs, umbrella), take their bikes for a ride or enjoy their grounds and gazebo. Many rooms have beautifully carved-wood gas fireplaces. ☞ 0.4 mi S on Essex Rd, RT on Boston Post Rd to 976 Boston Post Rd.

i westbrookinn.com ☎ 800-342-3162 or 860-399-4777.

Exit 63: Clinton Crossing Premium Outlets – Names, names names, they're all here: Barneys, Saks Off 5th, J. Crew, BCBG, Max Azria, Juicy Couture, Banana Republic, Waterford Wedgwood, Dooney & Bourke, Le Creuset, Cole Haan, Bose, Lindt chocolate (yum!) and about 75 more. Join the VIP Shoppers club for special discounts and sales, and 50+ get 10% off on Tues. ◗ M-Sat 10-9, Sun 10-6 (Jul&Aug Sun 10-8). *i* premiumoutlets.com ☎ 860-664-0700.

ROUND AND ROUND

There are now less than 200 antique wooden carousels left in the U.S., and

Connecticut is lucky to have 12 locations with carousels, 5 of which are the antique wooden ones. Along I-95 you can have fun hopping on and off 5 of them: Exit 28: Beardsley Zoo Carousel, 1875 Noble Ave, Bridgeport ☎ 203-394-6565; Exit 50: Lighthouse Point Park, 2 Lighthouse Rd, New Haven ☎ 203-946-8327; Exit 62: Lenny and Joe's Fish Tale Restaurant, 1301 Boston Post Rd, Madison ☎ 203-245-7289; Exit 71: Carousel at Old Lyme, 75 Hartford Ave. Sound View Beach (eve only) ☎ 860-434-3908; Exit 83: Ocean Beach Park, 1225 Ocean Ave., New London ☎ 860-447-3031.

Exit 62: Lenny & Joe's Fish Tale Restaurant – In 1979, Lenny and Joe

opened up a roadside clam stand with 4 picnic tables and offered overly generous portions with friendly service, and it has

grown to 2 restaurants offering the freshest fish and seafood in a casual atmosphere. The portions are definitely shareable, and you won't have to negotiate what to eat if you just order the seafood platter, which has clam strips, scallops, shrimp and scrod. Whole clams with "firm, flavorful bellies" are a specialty.

In the summer there's a lobster shack offering fresh lobster or chunky buttery lobster rolls, and the ice cream stand opens. This location has outdoor seating and a carousel for the kids. ◗ Sun-Th 11-9, F & S 11-10. ☞ S towards Hammonasset State Park, LT at Boston Post Rd (Rte 1). 1301 Boston Post Rd. (Other location at Exit 64: Westbrook, 86 Boston Post Rd. ☎ 860-669-0767). *i* ljfishtale.com ☎ 203-245-7289.

Exit 57: Bishop's Orchards – Just like it used to be back in 1871, you can buy fresh farm products and home baking at this 5th generation market. Over 200 acres of fruits and veggies are grown for sale, and in season you can pick your own. Beyond produce, you can plan a meal amongst stuffed chicken, veal riblets, 5 veggie ravioli, sushi and 2 dozen fresh soups (asparagus brie, Hungarian mushroom) accompanied by a wheat ciabatta roll or multigrain bread. Finish off the picnic with their famous apple cider  and apple donuts, pies (apple cranberry, chocolate lemon) or banana bread. Some llamas, alpacas or goats are housed on the

MAP PG 14-15

left side of the main building. ◑ M-Sat 8-7, Sun 9-6. ☞ 1/2 mi. E on US 1. 1355 Boston Post Rd. *i* bishopsorchards.com ☎ 203-458-PICK.

Exit 54>: Lenny's Indian Head Inn – This wooden structure, set on the marshes with its well worn varnished wooden booths, is your Kodak shot of a New England seafood shack. The food is worth the detour off I-95 just to taste Grandma Georgianna Moon's tangy clam soup recipe and their magical way of deep frying fish without you being able to discern that oil was involved. The platter with clams, shrimps, scallops and scrod was not only huge but delicious. The dippable zuppa d'clams is a popular starter.

     This is a 45-year-old 2nd generation family business, with such attention to freshness that some days the boys of the family, Tom and Chris, are out fishing for your dinner. Carnivores please note: there are steaks, burgers, wings, and ribs. There's an outdoor deck in warm weather. Cash only (ATM in front). ☞ Cedar St. S 1/2 mi. to the end. LT at Main St., take R fork as it turns into S Main St. RT at Montowese St. (Rte 146) for 1.4 mi. 205 S Montowese St. *i* LennysNow.com ☎ 203-488-1500.

Exit 52S or 51N>: Grace's Kitchen – If you want casual dining with home-style Italian cooking as found in Italy, order off the daily white board menu here (lots of

seafood, since they hail from an Italian island). The vodka sauce, no matter what they put it on, is wow; chicken a la Grace (tomatoes, mushrooms, ham topped with cheese) was a standout, calamari a la Grace (marsala, olives, artichoke, tomato on pasta) is a highlight too. The printed menu (really reasonable prices) has the requisite

grinders, pasta, pizza (16 kinds, including escarole & beans or stuffed with chicken scampi), daily homemade soups and stuffed breads too. ☞ Sbound - LT on N High St for 200 yds, LT on Saltonstall Pkwy for 1 mi. Nbound - straight off exit onto Saltonstall Pkwy to 251 W. Main St. ◑ M-Sat 9-9:30. *i* graceskitchenonline.net ☎ 203-315-1911.

Exit 48>: Touch of Ireland Guest House – Their motto, "Where the kettle is always on for a welcoming cup of tea",

gives you an indication of the warmth of the owners of this conveniently located Inn - in walking distance to Yale and the center of town. The address is on Whitney St., since Eli himself once owned all the land around here and ran some gun factories. He would've loved their homemade muffins, fresh fruit parfait and baked cheddar eggs for breakfast. 670 Whitney Ave. *i* touchofirelandguesthouse.com ☎ 866-787-7990 or 203-787-7997.

Exit 47>: Little Italy – It is definitely worth a detour into New Haven to eat on Wooster St. for amazing pizza. There is a continuing rivalry between the lovers of

NEW! Eli Whitney, Hero of the South - and the North

Exit 47: The assembly line was first used at Brewster's Carriage Factory on Wooster St. in 1809. James Brewster, applying Eli Whitney's principles of mass production, made New Haven carriages the equal of British models. So first Whitney revolutionized the South with the invention of the cotton gin, and then he revolutionized the North.

Pepe's (Frank Pepe Pizzeria Napoletana #157 or The Spot #163) version or Sally's (#237), but you should note that pizza sauce is in their blood, since they're actually 3rd cousins. They use over a ton of coal a week in original coal-fired ovens, which adds to the unique taste of both pizza parlors. In 1925 Frank Pepe, a baker, started a trend by spreading sauce on top of his bread. Pepe's now makes about a dozen varieties, but the signature pizza is the one with fresh clams.

Flora Consiglio, widow of Salvatore Consiglio (Frank Pepe's nephew) who opened Sally's in 1938, offers her oblong pizza with its thin crispy crust in a decor that hasn't changed in decades. If either restaurant offers seasonal specialties like broccoli rabe, zucchini or yellow squash, do try them.

Consiglio's (#165), also from 1938, serves classic veal, pasta, and chicken and

a daily polenta. You can try Tre Scalini (#100), which offers white-tablecloth dining with dishes ranging from rigatoni in vodka sauce to lamb chop with figs and pine nuts. Tony & Lucille's I (#127) opened in 1953, and was so popular for calzones, etc. that it outgrew its 40-seat trattoria and opened #II across the street (#150) in 1977 with seating for 100.

Tradition dictates that after you've eaten, you waddle down the street to Libby's (#139) for dessert. After 88 years, this has become the Ben & Jerry's of canoli, with about 16 flavors: pistachio, heath bar, raspberry, cappuccino and canoli pignole (pine nuts). The 4th generation is now making the Italian ices in 28 flavors, and sure, there's all your favorite traditional Italian desserts too, like hazelnut and pignolati cookies. *i* pepespizzeria.com, sallysapizza.net, consiglios.com, trescalinirestaurant.com

Exit 47>: Center Church on the Green – When this church was moved off the green in 1813, they placed it over a section of the green's graveyard. If you go down to the basement, you can walk amongst the grave markers and table stones (for the richer folks) dating from 1687 to 1812. Benedict Arnold's 1st wife is here (he took the 2nd one and hightailed it to England), and so is Reverend James Pierpont, a founder of Yale college. ◗ Apr-Oct Th & Sat 11-1. 250 Temple St. *i* newhavencenterchurch.org/crypt.html ☎ 203-787-0121.

Exit 47>: Louis' Lunch (The birthplace of the hamburger sandwich) – In 1900, a customer asked Louis Lassen for a meal on the run. He cooked some chopped beef and toast on a vertical cast iron grill. Today you can take a bite of history cooked on that very grill (they sure knew how to build them in those days), but remember - only onions, cheese or tomato are acceptable garnishes (no mustard or ketchup here). This century-old family business holds such a special place in the hearts and stomachs of the locals that when it was threatened with demolition, many helped preserve it. When 3 of its walls were moved, supporters sent 3rd generation Ken Lassen, Louis' grandson, thousands of bricks from every corner of the globe for the 4th wall. ◗

T & W 11-3:45, Th-Sat 12-2am (closed Aug). ☞ Rte 34 (LT if Nbound) to Downtown. Keep R, take Exit 1, Service Rd to Church St, RT 2 blocks, LT to Crown St. 261-263 Crown St. *i* louislunch.com ☎ 203-562-5507.

Exit 47>: Yale Peabody Museum of Natural History – The star of this

small museum is the 67 ft brontosaurus skeleton. He's there along with Triceratops, Stegosaurus and others in the Great Hall of Dinosaurs under Rudolph F. Zallinger's famous mural "The Age of Reptiles".

The museum's collections began in the 1870's, when O.C. Marsh (George Peabody's nephew) led four Yale expeditions to the American West searching for fossils. There's classic dioramas of animals - timber wolf, bighorn sheep and polar bear. At the bison one, we learned that the U.S. Government encouraged the elimination of the herds of buffalo to control the Plains Indians whose culture and economy depended on them.

The rest of the museum is filled with the birds and minerals of CT, evolutionary human origins, CT Indians and the spooky hall of ancient Egypt, with real "live" dead mummies. ◐ M-Sat 10-5, Sun 12-5. ☞ LH exit, then off at exit 1. Service Rd to Church St., RT. In 7 blocks, it turns into Whitney Ave. Pkg lot just past the museum. 170 Whitney Ave. *i* peabody.yale.edu ☎ 203-432-5050.

NEW! **Exit 47>:** Bentara – What a treat to find Malaysian food with its crispy/soft, cold/hot, spicy/sweet tastes. Hasni Ghazali started cooking at his mother's restaurant in Kuala Lampur and then, lucky for us, left his large family and started cooking here. The waitress is very helpful

in deciphering the menu, and we were glad she led us to our favorite of the night - the peanut-based mee soup istimewa with chicken and egg noodles with that bite at the end. You work your way through griddle breads, salads made of kang kong, tofu, bean sprouts, jicama and then coconut curries, wok fried goreng kicap (2 soys), rendang with lemon grass and coconut milk or specialties like Hasni's mother's famous Malaysian breakfast, which you can have for supper. 76 Orange St. ◐ M-Sat 11:30-3, 5-9:30, Sun 3-9. *i* bentara.com ☎ 203-562-2511.

Exit 47>: Yale University – You can say you "went to Yale" after taking the FREE campus walking tour. The student-led 75 min. tour covers the history, architecture and traditions (rub the foot of the statue of Theodore Dwight Woolsey for good luck) as you walk on the same ground as many U.S. Presidents through Old Campus, College courtyards and Sterling Memorial Library, and get a glimpse of a Gutenberg bible in the Beinecke Rare Book & Manuscript Library. You can also pick up a self-guided walking tour map called the Blue Trail for $1, and a kid's (6-11) architectural treasure hunt or art tour map. ◐ Walks: M-F 10:30 & 2, S&S 1:30.; center M-F 9-4:30, S&S 11-4. Yale Visitor Center, 149 Elm St. *i* yale.edu/visitor ☎ 203-432-2300.

Exit 47>: Yale Center for British Art – Opened in 1977, this small museum houses the most comprehensive collection outside the UK of British paintings, drawings, rare books and sculpture, from the end of the middle Ages to the present. Kids might like the supernatural room, including the Man with the Snake or The Farmer's Wife doing "oopsy"; fashionistas might be charmed by Lord Granville, who sports today's ladies' fashions: 3/4 culottes edged in ribbon, ballet slippers and a short coat with fur trim. ◐ T-Sat 10-5, Sun 12-5. 1080 Chapel St. *i* yale.edu/ycba FREE ☎ 203-432-2800.

NEW! **Exit 46:** Premiere Hotel and Suites – This friendly hotel, in an odd area right off the highway, looks like a little neighborhood - you even get your own entrance and porch. There are full kitchens (with an area event calendar posted there),

some have fireplaces or 2 stories, and there's a pool and spa tub. There's a daily shuttle service, and they will even do your grocery shopping. Not only do you get a buffet breakfast included, but there's light dinners too, from Mon-Thurs. 3 Long Wharf Dr. *i* newhavensuites.com ☎ 866-458-0232 or 203-777-5337.

NEW! **Exit 46:** Leon's – Started in 1938 by Leon and Anna Varipapa, this restaurant had been a New Haven go-to place for family celebrations and special nights out, due to its gourmet home cooking. Now rejuvenated in its beautiful new home - in a quirk of fate, the building was built in the early 80's by the chef's great-grandfather Leon, grandfather Eddie and great uncle Eugene - with spectacular water views. The 4th generation chef/owner, Eddie Varipapa, is still serving their famous signature dishes. The family's pane cotto (saut1ed greens, beans, rustic bread), chicken zingara (gypsy chicken) made with Italian fennel sausage, onions, garlic and potatoes, steak Leon, which is pan saut1ed with garlic, scallions, and white wine, and clas-

sic Sicilian escarole saut1ed with garlic, toasted pignoli nuts, capers, anchovies, and olives are all there along with a nightly "Goodie List" covering shrimps (maybe Limoncello), chops, pastas, lobster and more.

There's live entertainment Fri night and outdoor dining. ◗ M-Sat 11:30-10:30, Sun 10:30-10:30. 501 Long Wharf Dr. *i* leonsrestaurant.com ☎ 203-562-5366 (LEON).

NEW! **Exit 46:** Mobile Food Trucks – There are about 8 vans parked daily right off this exit selling mostly Mexican food, but a bit of hot dogs, burgers, roses and flags (of all things?). Names painted on the sides are: Ixtapa, Tacos, Tripletas & more, Sweeney's Hot Dogs, Mexicali, Tapalonia, La Pincerra Co., Flagman and Roses. They've been there for years, and there are always familes lining up to eat, dining in the car enjoying a great view of the New Haven Harbor.

Exit 44>: Captain's Galley – Some of our new-found favorite seafood dishes were discovered in this family restaurant. Firstly, seafood a la vodka, which doesn't taste like vodka but more like light cheesy, tomatoey, creamy and full of shrimp, lobster and scallops served on pasta; secondly, lobster pie, which is chunks of lobster in puff pastry covered with lobster bisque sauce. Their RI clam chowder was chunky and deliciously spicy, and so were the mussels, and even their simple broiled fish platter was yummy. Carnivores will be happy to know that their roast beef has won awards. The portions are big enough for a family of 4 (sharing charge). ◗ Sun-Th 11:30-9, F&S 11:30-9:30. ☞ LT onto Kimberley Ave .3 mi, LT at 2nd light (First Ave., turns into Beach St.) for 1.2 mi. 19 Beach St., West Haven. *i* captainsgalleyct.com ☎ 203-932-1811.

Exit 44>: Nick's Luncheonette – Some towns are lucky enough to have a friendly hangout where all the locals go to chow down. Nick's is that kind of place, with a buzzing, hopping, elbow-to-elbow party going on. Your basic breakfast and lunch menu is there, but they do get creative too, and offer delicious Reese's pieces or banana pancakes, a Greek omelette and

MAP PG 16-17

kielbasa or grilled pastrami and eggs. Do not miss their home fried potatoes - take

some to go, if you have no time to stop and eat. ◗ M-F 5-3, Sat 5-1:30, Sun 5-1:30. ☞ LT onto Kimberley Ave for .3 mi, LT at 2nd light (First Ave.). 423 First Ave. ☎ 203-937-9036.

Exit 41 W: A.C. Moore – This is arts and crafts supply heaven. For keeping kids busy in the car, there's wooden puzzles, origami paper, crafts sets, paint by numbers and doll house miniatures. The best deal we found were wooden models (truck, ship, plane) for $.99. The aisles are chock full of scrapbooking supplies, baby & bridal decor, knitting and embroidery needs (bibs and towels to sew on), stained glass, a tole painting corner, cake making and even a red hat lady section. Perhaps you might want to buy some blank sweat shirts or T-shirts for the gang to paint on. ◗ M-Sat 9-9, Sun 10-6. Christmas Tree Plaza. Other location: Exit 82S or 83N, New London. *i* acmoore.com ☎ 860-447-1277.

NEW! **Exit 40:** The Original Toy Company Factory Outlet – Whoa boy, discount toys right on an exit - parents, this is your stop. You never know what might be here, but it will range amongst: puzzles, games, baby toys, arts & crafts, puppets, blocks,

sand and water, wooden toys and - trampolines. 230 Woodmont Rd. ◗ M-F 9-5, Nov & Dec Sat 9-3. *i* theoriginaltoycompany.com ☎ 800-899-4258.

Exit 39: Fabric Factory Outlet – If you want to pick up a few yards of gorgeous fabric for your home, this shop has ends of bolts (and full ones) of famous names (Schummacher, Kravat, Brunschwig & Fils, Robert Allen, P. Kaufman, Waverly) at deep discount prices ($8-$25/yd, lots around $12-$18) which they get from hotels, jobbers and manufacturers. There are a couple of sale areas: one to the left at 20%-50% off, and a few shelves to the right. There's a designer on hand if you have a house nearby. 1250 Boston Post Rd. across from the CT Post Mall. ☎ 203-877-3380.

Exit 39: Boston Post Rd. – This old road runs parallel to I-95, from New Haven to NY, and still bears the same name as it did 300 years ago. It was just a wilderness trail when on January 22, 1673, the first mail on the continent was sent from NY to Boston, taking the rider "only" two weeks! America's earliest highway became part of the King's Highway, which traveled very much the same route as I-95 from Maine to Florida. By 1730 it took "only" 4 weeks to post a letter from Boston to Williamsburg. Many of the revolutionary heros used this road to achieve the goals of Independence. Paul Revere rode to NY on it to report how he and 49 other men "painted as Indians" boarded 3 English ships and dumped 342 chests of tea into the Boston Harbor. Samuel Adams and his cousin John Adams (later President) traversed this road back and forth from Boston to Philadelphia and the First Continental Congress. General George Washington rode up it from Philadelphia to British-held Boston trying to figure out how he would combine the ragged units of volunteers into a coordinated fighting army. When the British left Boston, Washington raced with his men on horseback down the road to try to save NYC, but failed. The road was then filled in droves with military men deserting the army. But in 1789 Washington, now as President, rode the road in triumph with cheering crowds greeting him in every town along the way.

MAP PG 17

Pay for Your Trip - Find Buried Treasure

Exit 37>: Milford Chamber of Commerce – Take a break, go to a beach, have  a meal or walk around one of the longest and most photogenic town greens in CT, with its duck pond, stone bridge and waterfall. You can pick up the FREE booklet "Milford's Favorite Walks", and heading W on N Broad St, you'll pass: **1**. Rainbow Gardens #117 Broad (see story); **2**. Howes Drug #78 Broad; **3**. 90+ year-old Arciuolo's Shoes #74 Broad; **4**. Park Lane Deli #50-4 Broad; **5**. Hebert Jewelers #14 Broad; and go around the corner to **7**. Milford Photo, #22 River St. for every single photographic need you might have (*i* milfordphoto.com), or grab a bite for the car at **8**. Villa Gourmet #11 River St. On the way up River St, stop to enjoy **6**. the waterfall.

Captain Kidd and other pirates sailed and hid along the CT coast, so it is said that buried treasure is hiding on Charles Island where they camped out. The tiny island that Indians called "Poquahaug" is a mile off Milford's appropriately named Silver Sands Beach, and can be reached at low tide by foot. Make sure you come back before the tide comes in. Chamber of Commerce - marked CofC on map: 5 Broad St. ● Tues-Fri 8:30-4:30. *i* milfordct.com ☎ 878-0681.

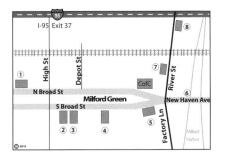

Exit 37>: The Corner Restaurant – It is rare to find a gourmet brunch spot, and this one, around 13 years with its friendly service and decorated with collectibles, gets high marks. We could hardly make a choice amongst the crispy goat cheese over grilled tomato on an English muffin with poached eggs and bernaise sauce, or similarly (instead of the cheese) have pan seared crab cakes or African hash made of spicy beef and lentils on top. There's spiced Indian pulled duck with bacon in a tortilla with scrambled eggs or the shareable trio of strawberry banana french toast, apple cinnamon raisin and cream cheese stuffed toast - and - a slice of their "tres leche" cake soaked in sweet cream and topped with strawberries. We need to go back here often. ● M-F 7:30-2:30, Sat & Sun 7-12:30. 105 River St. ☎ 203-882-1150.

Exit 37N or 36S>: Rainbow Gardens – Meals made here are with love and humor: Start with Appeteasers like the Lovin' Spoonful soup and hit the raspberry chicken salad explosion, which drapes fresh fruit (berries, oranges apples, grapes) over chicken with Gorgonzola, almonds slices, and a raspberry vinaigrette. Endless Pastabilities offers up When in Rome, a 4-cheese lasagna in Bolognese meat sauce while the Hungry Cowboy is a burger with bacon, bbq sauce and cheddar. Beauty & the Beef is a yummy peppercorn-grilled filet of beef with roasted peppers, Gorgonzola and garlic mashies, and how could we not mention the Ventura Highway - smoked spice rubbed Pacific rim salmon with jasmine rice. 117 N. Broad St. *i* rainbowgardens.org ☎ 203-878-2500.

Exit 36: Gusto – If you want to know what Italian food tastes like in Italy, let Riccardo (whose Momma and family are still back in Sardinia) cook for you. You could start with fresh mozzarella, tomatoes, greens, onions, with a warm balsamic dressing or eggplant rollotini (yum!). Pasta is light and varied, from cavatelli, orecchiette to gnocchi, including one with broccoli rabe and sausage, and there's brick oven pizzas too (truffle oil, gorgonzola, prosciutto). The classic mains include shrimp scampi, veal and grilled fish. A baci ball dessert was the perfect ending (and shareable), or have a fruit sorbet (lemon, mango, coconut) to wash it all down. ● M-F 11:30-10, Sat 4-10, Sun 4-8:30. ☞ S on Plains Rd to 255 Boston Post Rd. *i* gustotrattoria.com ☎ 203-876-7464.

Exit 34: Ocean State Job Lot – Many of us have a love affair with a bargain, and stores, starting with the Five and Dime years ago, have realized that. Job lot refers to closeouts, overruns, package changes of stock that need liquidating; these used to be picked up by independent jobbers who re-sold the low priced items for low prices. This business, now with 95 locations, started in North Kingstown, RI in 1977, and is a department store of options: household (blender $15, light bulb $1.30), pet (crate $35), garden (knee pads $3, rake $5), clothing (ladies' tops $4), food (canned salmon 14.75 oz $3), hardware (work gloves 2/$3), stationery (calendar $1.50), health (travel walker $20), etc. ● M-Sat 8-9, Sun 9-8. 545 Bridgeport Ave. *i* oceanstatejoblot.com ☎ 203-878-9547.

Exit 32: Hudson Paper Company – Craft lovers will love this real wholesale outlet which is open to the public for all

things paper. Since 1908, it's still run by the same family and is still making some boxes on a circa-1880 machine. Looking for hat boxes, gift boxes, Chinese take-out boxes, rolls of wrapping paper (Sandra's favorite) and tablecloths, bubble wrap, clear bags and ribbon (sometimes a clearance cart in the door-

way) - they have them all. There's one room for party needs (in the left back there's clearance), paper place mats, plastic serving stuff - you just never know what you might score here. Kids might like to see the ostriches, ducks and geese out back. ● M-Sat 9-5. ☞ W on W. Broad St., under RR bridge, LT into lot behind bldg. 1341 W. Broad St. *i* hudsonpaper.com ☎ 203-378-8759.

Exit 31: Stratford Antique Center – Just what every antique fan needs for a pit stop on your drive - a 16,500 sq. ft. blue building right off an exit full of 200 deal-

ers. Opened in 1992, the booths are neatly organized and laden with furniture, glassware, artwork, housewares, toys, jewelry, lamps, brass, mirrors, Christmas decorations, vintage clothing, figurines, and perhaps a kitchen sink. The owners urge dealers not to overprice items, instead making them affordable and enticing. ● Daily 10-5. 400 Honeyspot Rd. *i* stratfordantique.com ☎ 203-378-7754.

Exit 30>: Garbage Museum – You are greeted here by a giant trashosaurus, and in the tiny exhibit area you learn about recyled soda bottles (PET), which can be made into carpets, a bench, or fuzz on tennis balls. They

will run one of their 6 short cartoons for you - just ask. Kids will enjoy the garbage treasure hunt, but the best part is upstairs. Enter an ordinary-looking door to the extraordinary sight of a constant stream of trucks dumping mountains of cans, paper and plastic, and the people sorting conveyor belts of trash. You will think twice about your waste after this stop.

◗ Sept-June W-F 12-4; Jul & Aug T-F 10-4. ☞ Down Lordship Rd .5 mi, RT on Honeyspot Extension to 1410 Honeyspot Rd. Extension *i* crra.org ☎ 203-381-9571.

Exit 27>: The Barnum Museum –

Here's your chance to run away from your car trip and join the circus for a moment. Kids and kids-at-heart will be fascinated by the life and legacies of P.T. Barnum - entrepreneur, politician, journalist and showman. Learn the story of Tom Thumb (and Mrs Tom - Lavinia Warren), and see their carriages, furniture and clothing. Discover Jenny Lind, "the Swedish Nightingale", William Brinley's miniature hand-carved 5-ring circus and Baby Bridgeport, the elephant. You can see the splendor of a room in Barnum's home and wallow in the eccentricities of his multi-faceted life. ◗ T-Sat 10-4:30, Sun 12-4:30. ☞ Nbound: 5th light, LT on Main St. Sbound: stay in R lane, RT on State St., 2nd light RT to Main. 820 Main St. *i* barnum-museum.org ☎ 203-331-1104.

Exit 27A>: Beardsley Zoo – Before you leave, print out one of the themed scavenger hunts from their web site, then take a break here (at this 1922 Olmstead designed zoo) and see who's first to finish the challenges. Of the 120 species to enjoy, the newest is Naka, a female Amur (Siberian) tiger, part of the Special Survival Plan, since only about 44 of these great cats survive.

Pass by the Tropics Rainforest with a free flight aviary, a New England farmyard with goats to feed or bunnies to pet, Alligator Alley and a pop-up prairie dog exhibit. North and South American animals include a maned wolf, toucan, otters, ocelots, and one of the smallest primates: a pygmy marmoset. Don't forget a ride on the carousel. ◗ Daily 9-4. ☞ Rte 8 & 25 for 2 1/2 mi. to Exit 5 (Boston Ave). LT at light to 1875 Noble Ave. *i* beardsleyzoo.org ☎ 203-394-6565.

NEW **Exit 27>:** Two Boots – What funky fun to walk into this intense red and green combo of New Orleans (mardi gras beaded wall) with slick 50's diner trappings. The food combo is of Italy's pizzas (boot one) with hot Louisiana (boot two) Cajun popcorn (that's crawfish to you). Expect po' boys, of course (blackened catfish, creole chicken), and do wash them down with local Freaky Dog sodas. Be warned - the creatively mixed pizzas say "mild sauce available on request" - but they bite back (with sopressata, Cajun ham, bbq shrimp, crawfish) and are named after Bette Middler, Newman, Mel Cooley, Big Maybelle et al. ◗ M-W 12-10, Th 12-1, F 12-2, Sat 4-2, Sun 4-9. 281 Fairfield Ave. *i* twoboots.com ☎ 203-331-1377.

NEW **Exit 25:** Chaves Bakery – What we have here is a big bright newly located schizophrenic bakery that bakes Portuguese (feijao, mimos, natas $1.03), Italian (canoli, small $1.08) and a touch of French (cream puffs, small $1.03) sweets at rea-

sonable prices. Three revolving displays show off the decorated cakes, but it's the linzer tortes, pink and blue teddy bear cookies, donuts, muffins, shortcake trifles, individual lemon meringue pies, black and white cookies, character cupcakes (Cookie Monster, clowns), Hershey cakes and pound cakes ($7.25) that bring 'em in. Sure, there's fresh Portuguese and Italian breads and rolls, and even European rye and Boar's Head cold cuts for sandwiches, but why

MAP PG 17-18

bother - just have cake for lunch. 1365 State St. ◑ M-Sat 6am-7pm, Sun 7-4 ☎ 203-333-6254.

Exit 24: Hungarian Deli – This area is saturated with Hungarians who settled

here, so the food at this place is authentic. In the fridge, you can buy (ask them to heat to eat) beef, veal or szekely goulash, paprika chicken and dumplings (our favorite), stuffed cabbage or sauerkraut. You can start with sour cherry soup or herring and end with cherry or poppyseed strudel. There's cold cuts for sandwiches, schnitzel, fried meatballs and a hot goulash soup. Grocery items like stuffed peppers, red cabbage, or gooseberry and lingonberry jam line the shelves. ◑ M-Sat 9-6, Sun 10-4. 849 King's Highway E. ☎ 203-696-2322.

Exit 24: Super Duper Weenie – When Gourmet magazine rated this place "one of America's 10 best hot dog joints", we had to investigate. The split and grilled dogs will tickle your taste buds no matter where you are from, because they salute all the regions.

The New Yorker has sauerkraut, onion sauce, mustard and hot relish, while the Chicagoan has the required lettuce, tomato, mustard, celery salt, hot relish and pickle, and if you're from Dixie, you can eat the one with meat chili and cole slaw. If you must, there is also grilled chicken, veggie burgers, sausages, tuna salad, burgers, grilled cheese and nuggets. All of their condiments are home-made. Their crispy salt and pepper fries are great with everything, and they have freshly brewed tea, Boylan beverages and homemade soup in season (go early - they sell out fast).

◑ M-Th 11-4, F&S 11-8, Sun 11-6. ☞ take the roundabout to the S of I-95, bearing right down Black Rock Turnpike. Look left as you leave the roundabout. 306 Black Rock Turnpike *i* superduperweenie.com ☎ 203-334-DOGS.

NEW! **Exit 21>:** The Inn at Fairfield Beach – It's all beachy staircases and balconies when you first drive up to this family-run Inn, perfectly situated just steps away from the CT shoreline and a few blocks from downtown Fairfield. Each themed room (artist, nautical, safari, Greek) is white and airy and sports its own kitchenette. The Seagrape Cafe is right next door, and you can catch your own lobster in the tank or use the cafe for room service. They even offer a mobile spa which comes to you - have a massage

and then slip off to beddie-bye, ahhh. 1160 Reef Rd *i* innatfairfieldbeach.com ☎ 203-255-6808.

NEW! **Exit 21:** Centro – The zingy red/green/yellow/blue decor and customer artwork cheerfully invite you to partake in a meal to go (have a picnic in the gazebo next door or at the beach 1/4 mile away) or to sit down and enjoy their authentic Italian food (trips to Italy each year to learn more). After 20 years, they know you might want to start light with a warm chicken and pear salad (walnuts, cranberries, Gorgonzola) or have some Roma beans, pancetta, and arugula. Sandra flipped over the chicken and porcini mushroom risotto while Stan scarfed down the classic spaghetti (pastas are homemade here) with Tuscan meatballs. There's paninis, hanger steak, thin crust pizza or perhaps bowties with chicken, spinach, sun-dried tomatoes with a 3-cheese sauce, and even Arthur

Ave. mozzarella (See NY Exit 2B or 3). (Other location on I-95: Exit 13, Norwalk, CT). ◑ Lunch: M-Sat 11:30-3, Dinner: M-Th 5-10, Fri & Sat 5-10:30, Sun 5-9:30. 1435 Post Rd *i* centroristorante.com ☎ 203-255-1210.

Exit 21>: Connecticut Audubon Birdcraft Museum – Step back in time in this 95-year-old preserved museum with its display windows stuffed with  all kinds of lifelike CT birds. Follow through the small rooms with wildlife dioramas, the Bedford Collection of African animals and then take a stroll through the paths of the songbird sanctuary. ◑ T-F 9-1 (6 acre sanctuary open daily dawn to dusk). Admission by donation. ☞ Head E through town, LT at Old Post Rd which is also Unquowa Rd. to 314 Unquowa Rd. *i* ctaudubon.org ☎ 203-259-0416.

Exit 19>: Westport Inn – If you need a bit of coastal elegance in your life, this large inn has spacious balcony rooms overlooking the indoor pool, a fitness center and a bistro, and accepts pets as members of your family. If you call ahead you can add indulgences: red satin sheets, rose petals or a chocolate basket. ☞ 1 mi W on Post Rd to 1595 Post Rd. E. *i* westportinn.com ☎ 800-446-8997 or 203-259-5236.

Exit 14N or 15S: Stepping Stones – For children ages 1-10 or children at heart (couldn't get Stan out of here), you can explore in Waterscape through pools, cascades, a streambed, a vortex and a fog machine. Practice conservation in the Rainforest Adventure using 40 multi-sensory games and problem solving activities in this newly enlarged fun museum.

Exits 16-14: During the French and Indian War, 1754-1763, Col. Thomas Fitch led the troops from Norwalk. His sister Elizabeth arrived to see him off, and was dismayed by their dishevelled uniforms. To spiff them up, she took some chicken feathers and placed one in each man's cap.

They rode to Fort Crailo near Albany, NY, where Brit. Army Surgeon Richard Shuckburgh, amused by their garb, exclaimed "Now stab my vitals, they're macaronis!" (A slang term for dandies who affected foreign mannerisms and fashions). He wrote a derogatory verse about them called a "New England Noodle". Everyone sing along now...

"Yankee Doodle went to town
A-ridin' on a pony
He stuck a feather in his cap
And called it macaroni. "

A doodle was a put-down to mean simpleton or a do-little. The tune used was popular in Britain with many different verses, but one sheet music version that has survived goes:

"Brother Ephraim sold his Cow
And bought him a Commission;
And then he went to Canada

To fight for the Nation;
But when Ephraim he came home
He proved an arrant Coward,

He wouldn't fight the Frenchman there
For fear of being devour'd."

The Americans wound up liking the tune and turned the derision around, making it their principal battle theme of the Revolution, and eventually a greater symbol of humiliation to the British than it had been to the Americans. It was actually played victoriously in 1781 as the beaten British forces filed out of Yorktown to end the Revolutionary War.

MAP PG 18

Figure out the principles of motion, gravity and velocity with race cars, light and machines and have fun with bubbles. In Healthyville see how the brain controls the body, test your senses on a sidewalk of sounds, sights and textures, hop on a skeleton-bike to see how your bones work and learn through the interactive model of the digestive tract - gulp! ◐ Daily 10-5. ☞ Nbound: Exit 14N - 1st light, LT onto West Ave. Sbound: Exit 15 - down hill, RT onto West Ave. Entrance at rt at light in Matthews Park, 303 West Ave. *i* steppingstonesmuseum.org ☎ 203-899-0606.

Exit 14: Swanky Frank's – Back in 1949, Frank Christiano lost this hot dog stand in a poker game. Too bad for him, because this business is still open (cousin Lou) 63 years later selling their yummy grilled or deep fried dogs with famous hot mustard (grandpa's recipe) paired with crispy fries. On a Saturday this stand goes through 300 lbs. of fresh potatoes. They make their own cole slaw, macaroni salad and onion rings, and to top the dogs, you can slather on grandpa's chile, cheese, sauerkraut, green onions or bacon. If you don't want hot dogs, chow down on Philly steaks, fried seafood, patty melt, mac 'n cheese or meatloaf, and wash it all down with local Norwalk Freaky Dog

soda (cola, diet, lemon up, roof beer, lickin lemonade). ◐ W-Sat 11-8, Sun-T 11-4. 182 Connecticut Ave. ☎ 203-853-DOGS.

Exit 14N/15S>: The Maritime Aquarium at Norwalk has been built inside a 19th

century foundry overlooking the harbor. Notice the Tango vessel which was pedalled across the Atlantic, and try to find the poison dart frog. There's the required shark (up to 9 ft long) aquarium, a touch tank (sea stars, snails, spider crabs), a river habitat, coral reef with tropical fish, and if you get there at the right time you can catch the seal feeding. Check out the interesting shipbuilding area, the IMAX theater and a neat jellies tank. If you haven't seen river otters (an albino one!) or sea turtles, they're here too and a chock-full gift shop. There are even exploration cruises you can join.

◐ Daily 10-5. ☞ S on West St. into Norwalk 1/2 mi., LT on Washington St., LT on N. Water St. to 10 N. Water St. *i* maritimeaquarium.org ☎ 203-852-0700.

NEW! **Exit 13:** Rip Van Winkle Lanes – Get off the road and stretch your muscles throwing a couple of balls down these lanes built in a 1940's airplane hangar. You can grab a bite at the same time (breakfast sandwiches, buffalo chicken sandwich, smoked turkey wrap, sausage & pepper sub, pizza, sliders, Chicago hot dogs, wings, BLT's and Sandra's fave - soft pretzels). Ask about the Pizza Bowl, good for 4-6 people for 2 hours of bowling, including shoes, pizza and soda. Things get revved up on Fri & Sat nights with Xtreme bowling. ◐ M 12-11 T-Th 9-11, Fri 12-1am, Sat 12-1am, Sun 12-10. 701 Connecticut Ave *i* ripvanwinklelanes.amfcenters.com ☎ 203-838-7501.

Mile 12.5 Nbound: Connecticut Welcome Center – Pick up info on the State, motel coupon booklets and use the clean rest rooms. This one has a pet walk, a stamp machine, ATM and one of the busiest McDonald's in the US, because it is the first service area on I-95 since upper

NJ. There's Original Pizza of Boston and Lavazza for coffee, smoothies, salads (Greek, chef), sandwiches (roast beef, turkey) and lots of pastries: cheese danish, brownies, eclairs, black & white cookies, cheesecake. ◐ Summer Daily 8-5. Restaurants open 24 hrs. ☎ 203-655-8289.

Exit 8: Chef's Diner – This narrow diner's been around for 63 years, and the new

owner still keeps up the made-from-scratch routine. Jump on a stool or into a booth and have some homemade soups, meatloaf, roast beef and turkey dinner or a pizza burger. The breakfast egg on roll is $1.75, and be careful if you order the "Mouth on Fire Omelette" or ask for the chile on your dog - they're Hot! ◐ M-Sat 6-3, Sun 7-3. ☞ S on Canal St off exit, LT onto Jefferson. 127 Jefferson St. ☎ 203-324-CHEF.

NEW! **Exit 6:** City Limits Diner – The partners of this gourmet restaurant masquerading as a diner also run a few high class restos in Manhattan, so that would explain the great chefs (Peter Assue

and his wife, pastry chef Tracy Assue) who work here and the Morris Nathanson design. Their chunky, rich and fabulous chicken noodle soup (angel hair noodles, shredded chicken) is really like Jewish penicillin, and regulars will not let them take it off the menu, yet you'll also find Provencal fish soup.

Try not to fill up on the delish corn bread, and you can't go wrong by starting with the smoked chicken and corn quesadilla or steamed pork dumplings and then going on to the veal meatloaf and mashies, turkey chile or sesame crusted tuna. Fish is bought by same Manhattan purveyor, so it's always fresh (yellowfin tuna salad on potato rye bread or sesame crusted tuna are really popular), and burgers are ground in-house daily from chuck, hanger and sirloin. Breakfast is served all day. People come here just to buy the pastries and breads. You can order ahead online for pickup or just stop in for home-made ice cream treats, including milk shakes, egg creams, root beer floats and even knockout chocolate pudding. ◐ Sun-Th 7-11, Fri &Sat 7-12. 135 Harvard Ave. *i* citylimitsdiner.com ☎ 203-348-7000.

Exit 4>: Bush-Holley Historic Site – Erected in 1730, this home became the center of CT's 1st art colony from 1890-1920. American Impressionists John Henry Twachtman and J. Alden Weir encouraged others like Theodore Robinson and Childe Hassam to work here, painting the waterfront views, life in the village square and scenery. Over 200 artists followed, living here and sharing communal meals along with lively discussions. The home also showcases the Bush family, including slaves' attic sleeping quarters. The visitors' center has changing FREE art exhibits. ◐ Mar-Dec tours only W-Sun, 1, 2, 3pm; Jan & Feb F-Sun only. ☞ N on Indian Field Rd, quick RT onto Sound Shore Drive to end, RT on Strickland Road to 39 Strickland Rd. Parking lot on Left under I-95 overpass. *i* hstg.org ☎ 203-869-6899.

Exit 3: Bruce Museum of Arts and Science – This gem of a museum has little hors d'oeuvres which are sure to please the palate of many in your car. It mixes up 19th and 20th century American paintings, minerals of the world (some in drawers with fun names like "It's a bad hair day"), the mammals and birds of New England, decorative arts and Native American cultures. Children and adults alike love the cave-like mineral gallery with its

MAP PG 19

fluorescent niche, the wigwam (listen to native story-telling), live-animal marine touch tank and the 1,200-lb touchable meteorite. ● T-Sat 10-5, Sun 1-5. ☞ RT at end of ramp (LT if from N). Follow Arch St. and it turns into Museum Dr. 1 Museum Dr. *i* brucemuseum.org ☎ 203-869-0376.

Exit 2>: Steilmann Ladies' European Fashion – This is a real outlet store tucked on the side of their office. Tons of samples in sizes 6-8 in exclusive European

fashions (Steilmann, emozioni, Apanage, Gerry Weber, Damo) fill the middle. There is also regular sized merchandise (sizes 4-16), all at least 30% off. Don't miss the back left corner that has the best markdowns, at 50% off the last sale price. Add yourself to the list for special sales. ● Fr-Wed 11-6, Th 11-7. ☞ W on Delavan Ave for 0.6 mi to end, RT on N Main St. to 354 N. Main St. ☎ 914-939-1500.

FREE FOOD

We have stayed in almost every brand of motel on the I-95 exits, and the FREE breakfasts seem to come out of the same commissary: bagels, cream cheese, jams, peanut butter, sliced bread, 3 kinds of cold cereal, packs of hot oatmeal and hot cocoa, apples, bananas, muffins, orange juice, coffee, cold French toast to be microwaved or a waffle-maker. Occasionally there will be a burst of excitement when we see hard boiled eggs, biscuits and gravy, scrambled eggs, bacon, or packaged ham/egg or sausage patties on English muffins. It is interesting to note, though, that when you stay in the higher priced hotels, you never get a FREE breakfast!

Exit 19: Playland Amusement Park – Built in 1928 with Art Deco structures, this is America's first totally planned amusement park, sporting 50 rides for children and adults, a beach, boardwalk, swimming pool, lake boating, picnic area, free entertainment, mini golf, indoor ice-skating and FREE admission. What a concept - you only pay for the rides you want to go on!

The Dragon Coaster, even after 82 years, still plunges you 128 feet into the mouth of a dragon. The Carousel was constructed in 1915 with its 66 elaborate horses and 3 chariots, which circle the rare Gavioli band organ with monkey ornaments. The Derby Racer is one of only 2 known original rides of this type in the U.S., and gallops along at 25 mph, imitating the motion of

real steeplechase steeds. Besides the fun rides, there's fun foods like funnel cakes, Dippin Dots ice cream, Nathan's hot dogs or Carvel soft custard. ● Closed Mon. Varies daily between 12-11, May-Sept. *i* ryeplayland.org ☎ 914-813-7000.

Exit 13: Wonder Hostess Bakery Thrift Shop – If someone in the car has the munchies, you might as well stop at a factory outlet store like this one and get some snacks as low as 5/$3.89. You can pick from fudge brownies, Twinkies, Hohos, Devil Dogs, Coffee Cakes, Yodels, Hostess cupcakes or Sno Balls, Honey Buns, Ring Dings, fruit pies or Fruit and Grain cereal bars. You can buy bread, peanut butter and jam to make sandwiches, Utz chips, puddings, instant soups and there's 100-calorie and sugar free snacks: chocolate creme cookies and wafers. ● M-Sat 8:30-6, Sun

MAP PG 19-21

Did he Get a Busy Signal?

On April 3, 1973 people were amazed at the sight of Martin Cooper talking on a wireless device at the corner of 56th St. & Lexington Ave. He recalls that the prototype Dyna-Tac cell phone, which took 3 months to build, weighed almost 1 kg, and Cooper has said "The battery lifetime was 20 minutes, but that wasn't really a big problem because you couldn't hold that phone up for that long." The 1st call he made was to taunt his counterpart Joel Engel at Bell labs.

9-5. ☞ LT on Tillotson Ave., LT on Conner St. (Sbound, RT on Conners at gas station). Pass Hollers Ave., plant is on left, store behind it. *i* bakeryoutlets.com ☎ 718-325-9775.

When is a gas station more than a gas station?

Gas stations sure have come a long way since they diversified beyond selling fan belts and spare tires. Now it is unusual to see one without a mini-mart attached. However, if you really look around, you'll be surprised at the things you might find: fireworks, country hams, live bait, live crabs and fishing gear, a peanut outlet, key making, fresh jumbo eggs, dry cleaning, muscadine cider, trees, DVD vending machines, firewood, guns, shrimp meal, clay, car detailing, bird houses, bows & arrows and very interesting take-out food: hot boiled peanuts, Claxton fruit cakes, or fried gizzards and livers. One even had a mart with a drive through window, so you don't even have to get out to pick up your milk, cigarettes, etc. The strangest one had a sign that said "Armed guard after hours". We're suggesting you skip that one.

What color were George Washington's hair and eyes?

Reddish brown hair and blue eyes

Exit 10: Bronx Golf Center – Who would've thought that you could go golfing on an exit in the Bronx? The driving range has ball specials from M-F 9-1, S & S 8-10am, where for $5 you get 51 balls instead of 34. There is miniature golf for

family fun ($6 for seniors), and batting cages if you need to expend some of that driving tension. ● M-Th 9-8, F 9-9, S 8-9, Sun 8-8. ☞ Sbound: Exit 11, stay on service rd., RT on Gun Hill Rd. 1825 E. Gun Hill Rd. ☎ 718-379-6666.

Ciao-ing Down

Exit 3 or 2B>: Arthur Avenue and Market – For about 100 years, this street has been the heart of the Bronx Italian community. Third generation stores still abound: Madonia Brothers Bakery, #2348 (718-295-5573); Cosenza's Fish, #2354 (718-364-8410); Teitel Brothers, #2372 (718-733-9400); Randazzo's Seafood, #2327 (718-367-4139) and then Calandra's Cheese, # 2314 (718-365-7572); Calabria Pork #2338 (718-367-5145) and many more.

The famous market at #2344 is a cornucopia of Italiana: Peter's Meat Market is a favorite "meating place", Boiano Fruits, Mt. Carmel Gourmet Food for gourmet items (chestnuts in liqueur, Torrone nougat, cipolline in balsamic vinegar,) Nick's Variety for all your kitchen needs, and leave room for lunch at Mike's Deli. ☞ North on 3rd Ave for 2 blocks, RT on E Tremont to Arthur Ave.

Sandra was saved in 1987 when the hamburgers and cheeseburgers became available frozen in grocery stores. Wash the burgers down with a chocolate thick shake, so thick you need a spoon to eat it. Sometimes she will weaken and have a side of the fried clam strips or chicken rings. Yum! ☞ N. on Webster Ave. *i* whitecastle.com

---

What's in a Name?

How did officers address the Marquis Marie-Joseph-Paul Yves Roch Gilbert de Motier Lafayette during the Revolutionary War? They called him Gilbert. And what did Gilbert call his son - George Washington Lafayette.

Exit 2B Nbound: White Castle – Sandra has had a lifelong addiction to their signature Sliders - burgers so soft , they melt in your mouth. These are teeny 3 bite, 100% beef burgers cooked on a bed of fried onions with the buns on top, absorbing the delicious flavor.

White Castle, the first hamburger chain, started in 1921 in Wichita, KS with a medieval motif; early restaurants sported rooftop battlements and a turret. Way back in 1931, they began to use frozen beef patties to assure quality, and developed the crush-resistant cardboard cartons, which keep the burgers both hot and looking good. In 1949, after an employee suggestion, 5 evenly spaced holes were added (or subtracted?) to their burgers, which

permitted the onion flavor to permeate, the burger to cook faster and eliminated turning, which increased productivity. By 1961 White Castle had served 1 billion hamburgers, more than any other hamburger chain in the U.S. The burgers started out at *5 cents*, and have only made it to *64 cents*.

A TASTE OF ITALY

Giovanni da Verrazzano, an Italian explorer, navigated this part of the New World for France before paddling on up as far as Newfoundland, noticing Manhattan Island along the way. The Verrazano Narrows there were named after him, and later the bridge from Brooklyn to Staten Island. His explorations established King Francis I's claim to the New World, so Verrazzano was sent back for two more voyages. Unfortunately, on his final trip he stopped off at an island, probably Guadeloupe (little bit of a vacation?), in the West Indies and was gobbled up by cannibals.

NEW JERSEY

Exit 70: Marriott Glenpointe – If you enjoy the luxury of a full service Marriott but don't want to spend NYC prices for it, stay here at the top of NJ. By car it's only 1/2 hour to central Manhattan, but even better: leave the car in the free lot and hop on the bus ($3.50) on the corner. Luxuriate in the oversized rooms, take some down time in the pool or gym or plan a spa day - a good balance to the frantic Big Apple activities. 100 Frank W. Burr Blvd., just W of the exit. *i* teaneckmarriott.com ☎ 201-836-0600.

Exit 70>: Teaneck Creek Conservancy – Originally a dumping ground when I-95 was built, this creek and 46 acres  around it have been brought back to life as a nature and art park, with 3 trails for walking, jogging and nature watching. A labyrinth was built with the I-95 rubble consisting of 7 circuits of stones, and notice the eco-art sculptures. Take a driving break and listen to the birds twittering. ◐ dawn to dusk. ☞ W off the exit up the hill past the Marriott, RT on Teaneck Rd for 300 yds to 20 Puffin Way. *i* teaneckcreek.org ☎ 201-836-2403.

Between Exit 18 & 17 Nbound & Sbound, Mile 116: Vince Lombardi Service Area – Look for the hotel/motel boards with phones to call for reservations, and don't forget to pick up your motel coupon booklets and use the clean bathrooms. This service area has a travel information center. ◐ (Vis Ctr) Daily 8-3:45. ☎ 201-943-8757.

Vince Lombardi's most famous quote was "Winning isn't everything; it's the only thing.", and that motto drove him as a coach from the NY Giants to the Green Bay Packers (5 NFL titles and the first 2 Super Bowls). His lifetime coaching record was an outstanding 94-34-6. ◐ 24 hrs. ☎ 201-943-1171.

Exit 16W Sbound or 17 Nbound>: Secaucus Outlet Stores – You can ask for a booklet with map at any of the buildings you find here. Originally an "outlet" meant the factory store located in a small area in a plant where companies could get rid of surplus, unsold, out-of-season goods at bargain prices to their employees or the locals. It was popularized in the 1970's, when clever businessmen banded together to form the "outlet mall" to sell surplus stock.

The Secaucus area is a receiving and distribution center for Metropolitan NYC firms. Outlets sell the current season's merchandise at 40-60% off. If you visit Secaucus in the summer you will find summer clothes, whereas regular malls are already focusing on back-to-school and fall merchandise. You will discover brands like: Gucci, Liz Claiborne, Kenneth Cole, DKNY Jeans, Anne Klein, Tommy Hilfiger, Juicy Couture, Calvin Klein and Eileen Fisher.

Since so many of these goods are manufactured in places like Singapore, South Korea, Hong Kong and China, Secaucus is about the closest you'll get to the factory without flying to Asia. ◐ M-W 10-6, Th 10-8, F & S 10-7, Sun 11-6. Area map with store listings: *i* http://harmon meadow.com/pages/ secaucuspage.html ☎ 877-688-5382 or 201-348-4780.

The Missing Link

The lower part of the New Jersey Turnpike is not really part of I-95, though logically people use it as such, so we have drawn it that way (I-95 really goes through Pennsylvania, but the signage is poor or missing, so we feel motorists will get lost). It has been discussed for many years to include the NJ Turnpike as part of I-95, but the southern 51 miles are still not even part of the Interstate system and remain solely a state road.

New! Between Exit 15E & 16E Sbound, Mile 111.6: Alexander Hamilton Service Area – Don't forget to come and pick up your FREE motel coupon booklets which offer great deals along the way. There's a lit up hotel/motel board with phones to call for reservations.

Alexander Hamilton was Washington's aide-de-camp during the Revolutionary

MAP PG 21-22

War, was elected to the Continental Congress, wrote the Federalist Papers which helped get the Constitution ratifed (and was one of our first constitutional lawyers), was the first Treasurer-Secretary of the U.S, and founded the Bank of New York. His famous duel with Aaron Burr was fought near here in Weehawken NJ. John Adams described Hamilton as the "most restless, impatient, artful, indefatigable and unprincipled intriguer in the United States." Many also felt the same about Burr. Jefferson said, "I never thought him an honest, frank-dealing man, but considered him as a crooked gun, or other perverted machine, whose aim or shot you could never be sure of". Jefferson added that he was "A great man in little things, he is really small in great ones".

On July 11, 1804, on the Weehawken Dueling Grounds, Burr shot Hamilton, who fired into the air either as a reflex after being shot or purposely to avoid shooting Burr. Hamilton was rowed back across the river to NYC, where he died the next day in great pain. Burr was indicted for murder, but was never prosecuted. ◐ 24 hrs. ☎ 201-863-3345.

Exit 13A: Jersey Gardens – Not only is this NJ's largest outlet mall, but for kids it houses Jeepers, with arcade games, bumper cars, air hockey, a climbing jungle and a wee train. Sandra's favorite DSW Shoe Warehouse is in

here, and how about "As Seen on TV"? Clothing stores abound: Neiman Marcus Last Call, H&M, Daffy's, Filene's Basement, Juicy Couture, Quiksilver Factory Store, Tommy Clearance, Victoria Secret Outlet, Ashley Stewart (Plus size) and the Children's Place Outlet or Justice for Girls. Travelers might like the Aquamassage. If you live over 40 mi. away, ask for a FREE License to Shop coupon book at the Concierge desk. ◐ M-Sat 10-9, Sun 11-7. *i* jerseygardens.com ☎ 877-729-8258 or 908-354-5900.

NEW! Women's Rights Heroine

Alice Stokes Paul (1885-1977) was a feminist, suffragist, political strategist and a Jersey girl. In 1922 the New York Times called her one of the 12 most famous women in the US. Her triumphs for equality:

- Organized massive pro-suffrage demonstrations, the most famous of which took place in March 1913, prior to Woodrow Wilson's inauguration

- Authored the Equal Rights Amendment in 1923 and worked 54 years for its passage - Initiated the inclusion of sex equality in the UN Charter

- Led a coalition that succeeded in adding equal gender rights to Title VI of the 1964 Civil Rights Act.

Between Exit 12 & 11 Sbound, Mile 92.9: Thomas Edison Service Area – Look for the hotel/motel boards with phones to call for reservations, and don't forget to pick up your motel coupon booklets and use the clean bathrooms.

Thomas Alva Edison did his inventing very close to here in Menlo Park and W. Orange. Known as the inventor of the incandescent electric lamp (light bulb), he also patented 1,368 other inventions in diverse fields, including: the phonograph, motion picture machine, stock ticker, paraffin paper (first used for wrapping candies), carbon telephone transmitter "button", which led to the microphone and then to the solid state "diode" or transistor used in today's electronic devices, fluoroscope (for X-rays), pre-cast cement, iron ore rolling machine, dictating machine and thousands more. ◑ 24 hrs. ☎ 732-750-8779.

Between Exit 11 and 12 Nbound, Mile 92.9: Grover Cleveland Service Area – Look for the hotel/motel boards with phones to call for

Exit 8: Battle of Monmouth – On June 27, 1778, the main British army under Sir Henry Clinton abandoned Philadelphia and was headed to New York with a baggage caravan that was 12 miles long. Washington saw this as an opportunity for a surprise attack on an exposed, strung out enemy.

General Charles Lee, leading the attack, scattered his 5,000 men. When advised that the advantage would be lost if he didn't apply more force to the enemy, he replied "Sir, you do not know the British soldiers. We cannot stand against them". His lines soon fell apart.

George Washington, coming in from Valley Forge with the main army of 8,500, met Lee's men in retreat. For once, the ordinarily restrained commander in chief let himself go and "swore 'til the leaves shook on the trees". Soldiers stopped in their tracks and stared at the stately man on the large white horse who began darting up and down the line, personally turning back the retreat.

A young Marquis de Lafayette remembered the moment for the rest of his life. Washington rode "all along the lines amid the shouts of the soldiers, cheering them by his voice and example and restoring to our standard the fortunes of the fight. I thought then, as now, that never had I beheld so superb a man". Washington relieved Lee of his command. By the time he had the army turned around, his great white horse had died from exhaustion.

The battle was a political triumph for the Continental Army, for they had met the British in an open field and forced them to retreat. Monmouth was the last major battle in the North. It left enough of an impression on London that they recognized a stalemate and shifted their attention to the South. Washington took satisfaction in knowing that his men would turn and follow when he called.

reservations, and don't forget to pick up your motel coupon booklets and use the clean bathrooms. Grover Cleveland was President of the U.S. twice - the only one to ever do that! He first won in 1884, lost the re-election to Benjamin Harrison (although he actually won a larger popular majority, he received fewer electoral votes), then regained the Presidency in 1892.

He started out as a lawyer in Buffalo, NY, became Mayor of Buffalo and later Governor of NY. Cleveland was not comfortable with the amenities of the White House, writing "I must go to dinner, but I wish it was to eat a pickled herring, a Swiss cheese and a chop at Louis' instead of the French stuff I shall find.". He was the only President married in the White House, marrying 21-year-old Frances Folsom in June 1886 (he was 49).

He was thought of as an honest politician in a time when graft, bribery and corruption ran rampant. (What, you thought things were different back then?) After leaving the White House, Cleveland lived in retirement in Princeton, N.J. til his death on June 24, 1908. ◑ 24 hrs. ☎ 732-634-2923.

Between Exit 8A and 9 Nbound, Mile 78.7: Joyce Kilmer Service Area – Look for hotel/motel boards with phones to call for reservations, and don't forget to pick up your motel coupon booklets and use the clean bathrooms.

MAP PG 23-24

Joyce Kilmer was an editor, critic, lecturer and soldier, and was best known as a poet, especially for his poem called "Trees". "Trees" was written at Kilmer's home in Mahwah, NJ on Feb. 2, 1913; it was written in a little notebook in the afternoon, while looking out a window which overlooked a wooded hill. It was dedicated to Kilmer's mother-in-law (wow!), who was well-loved by all her family. ◗ 24hrs. ☎ 732- 254-4225.

Trees (For Mrs. Henry Mills Alden)

I think that I shall never see
A poem lovely as a tree.
A tree whose hungry mouth is prest

Against the earth's sweet flowing
*   breast;*
A tree that looks at God all day,
And lifts her leafy arms to pray;
A tree that may in Summer wear
A nest of robins in her hair;
Upon whose bosom snow has lain;
Who intimately lives with rain.
Poems are made by fools like me,
But only God can make a tree.

Exit 8A>: Crate & Barrel Outlet Store – Nesters will be delighted by the deals at this real outlet store. After the rainbow of dishes and wine glasses, you may discover the wall of vases up to 2' tall, rugs, or fabric marked down from $32 to $4.95 a yard. There are items you could not live without: striped napkins, storage bins, cafe ware, planters, place mats or cupcake carriers. The warehouse room on the right is filled with upholstered furniture at least 30% - 50% off and marked down each Monday morn an additional 10%. Don't miss the "Last Hurrah" shelves for drop dead prices. 315 Cranbury Half Acre Rd. ◗ M-Sat 10-6, Sun 11-5. *i* crateandbarrel.com ☎ 609-819-0200.

$$$ Books on Audio

We are audio book junkies. Once you get hooked, long road trips go by so fast, and you actually don't mind traffic jams. Here's 2 suggestions of how to buy them inexpensively. Cracker Barrel Old Country Stores help us get our fix by offering about 75-100 titles on CD (a few tapes) to choose from, including best sellers, with a money saving deal. You buy one at prices from $9.99 to $59.99, and when you finish the book, you return it at any other Cracker Barrel down the road, and they give you back your money minus $3.49 for each week you've had it. You can mail them back if you've forgotten to return one. *i* crackerbarrel.com

Secondly, *i* audible.com offers you more than 75,000 titles that you can download for $14.95 for 1 book/magazine/news-paper per month or $22.95 for 2 titles. (You could finally make your way through the Sunday NY Times this way). They play on most handheld devices or you can burn them onto a CD, and you can listen in the car on your CD player or with a tape or MP3 adapter.

Exit 8A>: Teddy's – You can find the regulars on their designated stools each morn creating the day's verbal newspaper. The rest of the townies are being served by 46-year veteran Janice or friendly Ellen (30+ yrs) on weekends, and they're chowing down on the eggs, real home fries with scrapple, creamed chipped beef or the local favorite - pork roll. Teddy (58 years here) might even be at the cash 5am right through lunch - be it meat loat sandwich, liverwurst, pot roast, cabbage rolls, Reuben, tuna stuffed tomato or the triple deckers. ◑ M-W 5am-7pm, Th & F 5-8, Sat 5-2, Sun 5-noon. ☞ W on Rte 32 (Fosgate Dr) for 0.8 mi, LT on Rte 130 for 1.6 mi, RT on N Main St for 1.1 mi to 49 Main St. ☎ 609-655-3120.

Exit 8A>: Cranbury Inn – Since 1780 travelers have been stopping by for their sustenance, but today that meal might include filet mignon in wild mushroom cream sauce, osso bucco, shrimp scampi or roast turkey dinner. You'll be happy if you start with their crab cake or the famous 3-cheese onion  soup (loved it) and we enjoyed the honey mustard house dressing. The room has Colonial charm with its knotty pine walls and original chairs, and you just might see your grandma's dinner plates amongst those bordering the ceiling. ◑ Lunch M-Sat 11-4; Dinner M-Th 5-9, F&S 5-10, Sun 2-9. ☞ W on Rte 32 (Fosgate Dr) for 0.8 mi, LT on Rte 130 for 1.6 mi, RT on N Main St for 1.4 mi to 21 S. Main St. *i* thecranburyinn.com ☎ 609-655-5595.

Between Exit 8A & 8 Sbound, Mile 71.7: Molly Pitcher Service Area – Look for the hotel/motel boards with phones to call for reservations, and don't forget to pick up your motel coupon booklets and use the clean bathrooms. This service area has a travel information center. ☎ 609-655-1610.

The Battle of Monmouth (see story) produced a heroine, Mary Ludwig, who followed her husband John Hays to war. In the 100 degree temperature, the soldiers were dropping from thirst, so Mary used an artillery bucket filled with spring water to offer drinks to the troops. Soldiers seeing her moving across the terrain called "Here comes Molly with her pitcher!". She also nursed the wounded that day. When her husband fell beside a cannon he was manning, she took the rammer staff and worked the rest of the day swabbing and loading the gun under heavy fire. Folklore has it that Gen. Washington himself thanked the barefooted, powder-stained "Molly Pitcher" and issued her a warrant as a non-commissioned officer. You can see the paintings of this story in the entrance to this service area. ◑ 24 hrs. ☎ 609-655-4330.

MAP PG 24

His Son, His Enemy

William Randolph Franklin was the illegitimate son of Benjamin Franklin (raised as a member of his family), and was the last Royal Governor of NJ, having used Benjamin's influence to secure the position. Though they had worked together through the 1760's, William was as much a loyalist as his father a patriot. William was imprisoned in Burlington in 1776, and chose exile to England when American independence was won. "Nothing has ever hurt me so much...as to find myself deserted in my old age by my only son". Benjamin never forgave William for his disloyalty. William was eager to revive his "affectionate intercourse and connexion" with his father at war's end, but Ben would not hear of reconciliation.

NEW! **Exit 8A:** Dick Clark American Bandstand Grill – How nice to find a sit-down restaurant at the Molly Pitcher Travel Plaza. It's fun to hang out in, since it is festooned with TV monitors of Dick's old shows and his memorabilia: Dick's Times Square New Year's Eve jacket and press pass, an Elvis window with hat, jacket shirt, '45's, photos, "We are the World" sheet music, a Bob Dylan gold record, Phillies jersey autographed by Madonna or a giant Decca record on the ceiling. See if you can find the piece of wooden fence from Graceland.

The menu strives for a slice of America: starting with spicy Buffalo wings, Southwest egg rolls (chicken, black beans, veggies, cheese), a "Studio" club sandwich,

Newport tuna melt, pulled BBQ pork with Dick's own BBQ sauce, Kansas City steak 'n eggs, NJ Flyer, rasta pasta, New England pot roast and at the "soda shop": Lovin' Spoonful (chocolate brownie, vanilla ice cream, peanuts), berry berry cocoa pop (pineapple, coconut, strawberry, raspberry) and NY cheesecake. We liked their salted and peppered french fries. For car munching, there's a fridge in front for Bandstand to go-go - cute. ◑ M-Th 7am-8pm, F,S,S 7am-9pm ☎ 609-655-4330.

TRUCK STOPS

It really is a myth that if you see trucks parked at a restaurant, you know the food is good. What you know is that there is room to park trucks there, and you will find basic cooking, not exotic fare. However, you should stop at one of the many humongous truck plazas along the way,

just for the fun of it. First of all, the gas prices are usually excellent. If you need to take a shower, wire money, buy long distance phone cards, play video games, use the internet, shop for travel/auto products, or perhaps just chat with truckers, these places are fascinating.

Exit 8>: The Americana Diner – Open for 25 years, it's the details that set this diner apart from others on the road: the in-house butcher and baker, the freshly squeezed orange juice and a twist of lemon in your water glass. For breakfast, they've created 16 omelets (Memphis has pulled pork, onions, cheddar) or create your own, filet mignon Benedict, and banana Foster waffles. The menu will satisfy anyone in your car - corn beef and pastrami sandwiches (and 25 more), 12 burgers (Santa Monica with avocado, arugula,

grilled onion, dijon balsamic dressing), the popular Szechwan honey sesame chicken or apricot chicken (apricot brandy sauce, mint, pecans, scallions), penne with vodka sauce and fish 'n chips. You can check out the online menu and use the curbside pickup. There's a frequent diner's club points program. ◑ M-Th 6am-1am, F&S 6am-2am, Sun 6am-12am. ☞ Follow Rte 33 E 3/4 mi, LT on Rte 133 to Rte

130 S. 359 Rte. 130N. *i* americanadiner.com ☎ 609-448-4477.

Between Exit 7A & 7 Southbound, Mile 58.7: Richard Stockton Service Area – Look for the hotel/motel boards with phones to call for reservations, and don't forget to pick up your motel coupon booklets and use the clean bathrooms. Richard Stockton, not a well known name, was an American hero who was born in Princeton on October 1, 1730. He was the first signer of the Declaration of Independence from NJ, and was a well respected lawyer from a wealthy distinguished family.

In the autumn of 1776, as a member of the Continental Congress, he was sent to Saratoga, NY to give a report on the state of the army. He wrote that the NJ soldiers were "marching with cheerfulness, but (a) great part of the men (are) barefooted and barelegged... There is not a single shoe or stocking to be had in this part of the world, or I would ride a hundred miles through the woods and purchase them with my own money".

For his efforts upon his return, he was captured by the British and put in prison. Though he had escaped death twice before in his life (once by a thug in Edinburgh and again when he missed a ship that later sunk), his confinement was so severe that his constitution never recovered. As if this wasn't enough, his lands and animals were destroyed, his papers and library burnt and his fortune greatly reduced. He died an invalid in Princeton on February 28, 1781. ◗ 24 hrs. ☎ 609-585-1155.

Exit 7A>: Six Flags – If you need to bribe the kids to be quiet in the back seat, this 140-acre park has Bulin's Jungle and Wiggles World, 13 roller coasters including El Toro, the steepest drop wooden coaster and Kingda Ka, the tallest and fastest on earth, or you can soar over Gotham city in Batman the Ride. If you want to visit the park efficiently, you can sign up for Flash Pass, which allows you to reserve your ride time so you get on more rides with less waiting time. You can also buy guided V.I.P. Tours.

On hot days there's Hurricane Harbor, with 20 speed slides, a million gallon wave pool, and for the folks - the longest lazy river. Or try the 350-acre, 4.5 mile world's largest drive-thru safari, with 1,200 animals from six continents and its Exploration Station, an interactive adventure. ☞ I-195 E. 10 mi. to Exit 16A (Rte 537 W), follow 1/2 mi. to entrance. *i* sixflags.com ☎ 732-928-1821.

Between Exit 7 & 7A Nbound, Mile 58.7: Woodrow Wilson Service Area – Look for the hotel/motel boards with phones to call for reservations, and don't forget to pick up your motel coupon booklets and use the clean bathrooms.

Woodrow Wilson, the 28th President of the U.S. from 1913-1921 (during WW I), went to Princeton University in 1875. He returned as a professor in 1890, later becoming the University's president in 1902. From there he went on to become NJ's governor in 1910 and then US President.

Wilson maneuvered some major legislation through Congress. The first was one we still suffer over: a graduated Federal income tax; but he also passed the Federal Trade Commission to prohibit unfair business practices, a law prohibiting child labor and another limiting railroad workers to an 8-hour day.

He planted the seeds of the United Nations in the last of his Fourteen Points. After the Germans signed the Armistice in Nov. 1918, Wilson went to Paris and came back to the Senate with the Versailles Treaty containing the Covenant of the League of Nations, the UN's forerunner. ◗ 24 hrs. ☎ 609-585-1222.

MAP PG 24

Q. Why Did Washington Cross the Delaware?
Answer: To Get to the Other Side.

Exit 7: Here is the famous painting of George Washington crossing the Delaware. On Christmas night 1776, Washington had to take a gamble in what was the bleakest time of the war. He wrote, "I think the game is pretty near up". As his troops shivered with hunger and disease, the British and Hessian soldiers were snug in their winter quarters on the NJ side of the Delaware River. On this holiday eve, the enemy feasted on goose and tankards of rum, and the sentry guards were less alert, since they knew the poor condition of the Revolutionary troops, and besides, the river was full of ice.

Washington's many shoeless ("Some of them have tied old rags around their feet") troops crossed the icy waters in the dead of night in a snowstorm, and left bloody footprints in the snow. Even their musket powder became soaked, so they were told to use their bayonets.

About 2,400 men (including 2 future Presidents - James Madison and James Monroe - as well as future Supreme Court Justice John Marshall and famous rivals Aaron Burr and Alexander Hamilton) made it across.

They caught the Brits and Hessians in a drunken slumber; the Hessians standing guard in the storm thought the first Continentals were their relief party. The Revolutionaries managed to get them to surrender in 40 minutes. No Americans were killed, though a couple had frozen to death. They captured over 900 prisoners, 1,000 muskets and 40 horses.

The incredible victory flashed through all of the colonies, changing the minds of many battle weary soldiers, and turned the tide of the war. The army that had been on the brink of falling apart now felt that all was not hopeless, and planned for the campaigns ahead.

Exit 5: Lenni Lenape Indians – The Lenni-Lenapes were the first settlers of this land. In October, 1677 the ship Kent deposited some Englishmen and founded the town of Burlington; they were a fair enough lot, and actually bought their land. The Native Americans sold more and more to the new settlers until 1801, when there was only 100 of the tribe left. The land that they lived on was the first Indian reservation in the US.

Exit 5>: Burlington County Prison Museum – From 1811 to 1965, this was the oldest prison in continuous use in the U.S. Designed by Robert Mills, architect of the Washington Monument, the outside

and inside haven't changed much, including the original cell doors and prisoner graffiti. Mills suggested that all prisoners be taught to read (a bible was placed in each cell), write, and learn a trade. Since there was no TV or internet in those days, tickets were sold to the executions, and the first one was a female! ◐ Th-S 10-4, Sun 12-4. ☞ 2 3/4 mi. E on Rte 541 to 128 High St. *i* prisonmuseum.net ☎ 609-265-5476 or 609-265-5858.

Between Exit 4 & 5 Nbound, Mile 39.4: James Fenimore Cooper Service Area – Look for the hotel/motel boards with phones to call for reservations, and don't forget to pick up your motel coupon booklets and use the clean bathrooms. James Fenimore Cooper was the first famous American-born novelist. He wrote about the American west in his *Leatherstocking Tales* featuring Natty Bumpo, an 18th-century frontiersman. The settlers who moved in around him brought civilized ways that changed Bumpo's wilderness. Cooper wrote over 30 novels, the most famous of which is probably "Last of the Mohicans" in 1826.

Born here in Burlington County on Sept. 15, 1789, his father was a judge, a representative of the 4th and 6th Congress, and a land developer. The family moved to Cooperstown, NY (named after the family), and James roamed the forest, developing a love of nature which was later relayed into his books.

Cooper was thrown out of Yale because of his capers, one of which included training a donkey to sit in a professor's chair. He joined the Navy, and the sea experiences later inspired his sea stories.

He mostly lived his life as a gentleman farmer, and only started writing in 1820 on a dare from his wife. From 1826 to 1833 they lived in Europe while he served as the US consul at Lyons, and eventually returned to NY. ◐ 24 hrs. ☎ 856-234-4930.

Exit 4: GG's – Sometimes you want to stop, get off the road and really dine. This hotel restaurant has a piano player to soothe your road nerves and a chef to soothe your tummy. You could start with steak and crabcake and move on to Asian tuna, baby calf's liver in candied lime sauce or beef short ribs in mushrooms and wine. Leave room for the beautiful dessert tray. The lunch menu is upscale, with a sandwich of chicken salad, cranberries and onions or one with toasted brie and apple or beef medallions. Best deal is a $23 3-course meal of the day. Hey, there's a shoeshine stand here. Doubletree Guest Suites, RT to 515 Fellowship Rd., just 275 yds W of the exit. *i* mtlaurelsuites. doubletree.com ☎ 856-778-8999 (hotel), 856-222-0335 (GG).

Exit 3>: Adventure Aquarium – You just gotta see those hippos. Though Button and Genny jump and float (can't swim) and seem so playful under water, they are the most dangerous animal to man, and have no natural predators. Be awed by the the 40' shark tunnel with 2 dozen  of them and 850 other fish swimming around you. If that isn't enough, you can touch a shark or a ray or even swim with the sharks. There's daily seal, hippo, dive or shark and penguin feeding (they eat 20% of their body weight a day) shows. Our favorite exhibit was the creature lab, where we found out that it is the male sea horse that gives birth! There's a cafe, 4-D theatre and a huge gift shop. ◐ Daily 9:30-5 ☞ Right next to the Battleship NJ - see story. 1 Aquarium Dr. *i* adventureaquarium.com ☎ 856-365-3300.

Between Exit 4 & 3 Sbound, Mile 30.2: Walt Whitman Service Area – Look for the hotel/motel boards with phones to call for reservations, and don't forget to pick up your motel coupon booklets and use the clean bathrooms.

MAP PG -24-26

Walt Whitman, born on May 31, 1819, spent the last years of his life in Camden NJ. He is best known for his American classic "Leaves of Grass" (1855). Though known as the father of free verse, he was a printer, teacher, journalist, editor, Civil War hospital worker and finally a civil servant in Washington. He wound up in NJ when he had come to visit his dying mother at his brother's house. A stroke in 1873 led to life in the NJ countryside, where he lived until his death in 1892. ◗ 24 hrs. ☎ 856-429-9323.

Exit 3>: Battleship New Jersey – This is the longest battleship ever built (by 3"), America's most decorated one, and it has served in every military conflict of the 20th century. Now it's a floating museum, with exhibits on the history and design

of battleships, a 4D flight simulator ride and fascinating tours, which include the combat engagement center, where you can participate in a missile launch. We've saved the best part for last - on Fri and Sat evenings you can sleep on board in the sailors' bunks, chow down in their mess hall and wake to Reveille. ◗ Apr, Sept-Dec Daily 9:30-3; May-Sept, Daily 9:30-5; Feb & March S&S 9:30-3. ☞ Rte 168 N 3/4 mi., S on I-295 for 1 Exit to Exit 26, Rte I-76/676 N past Whitman Bridge (do not take bridge) 4.8 mi. to Mickle Blvd Exit (5A, also Martin Luther King Blvd), head W to waterfront. RT past Aquarium at Wiggins Park circle, RT at end of street and RT onto Delaware to garage on right. Take the Battleship Shuttle outside garage exit. ℹ battleshipnewjersey.org ☎ 866-877-6262 or 856-966-1652.

Exit 3: Italia Pizza Trattoria – It was the calzone that got to us - crammed with tons of gooey ricotta and mozzarella with slices of quality ham and a cup of scrumptious tomato dipping sauce - one was enough for both of us. The 2nd generation is still keeping up poppa Frank Di Fillippi's recipes, and people come from all over for the broccoli rabe or spinach in garlic and olive oil, and yes, the meatballs too. Anything you might want, from parmigiana dinners to gnocchi, sausage heros to cold hoagies or baked ravioli and fried calamari, are here and then some. The wood-fired pizza page is extensive, including white vegetable pizza, deep dish, stuffed, and pizza turnovers. ◗ M-Th 10-11, F&S 11-12, Sun 11-11. 108 S. Black Horse Pike (Rte 168). ☎ 856-931-4436.

Exit 3: Club Diner – This newly renovated 1946 silver diner shines brightly on the strip inviting you to partake. Where else would you find a liverwurst sandwich sitting side by side with jumbo shrimp,

turkey salad on a croissant, 13 kinds of chicken breast (local Bellmawr style is with

---

NEW! Drive In-ventor

The drive-in phenomenon is credited to Richard Hollingshead, a Camden New Jersey auto salesman who pegged up a bed sheet in his back yard, placed a 1928 Kodak movie projector on the hood of his car and played a movie. He applied for a patent and opened his 1st drive-in theater in Camden, N.J. in 1933.

---

broccoli and provolone), fresh oyster stew, prime rib, meat platters, franks & beans and double decker sandwiches? The home baking offers up cinnamon buns and cheesecake, breakfast includes Belgian waffles, and we were happy to see a junior platter menu for those with smaller appetites. ◐ Daily 24 hours. 20 N. Blackhorse Pike ☎ 856-931-2880.

Between Exit 2 & 1 Southbound, Mile 5.4: Clara Barton Service Area
– Look for the hotel/motel boards with phones to call for reservations, and don't forget to pick up your motel coupon booklets and use the clean bathrooms.

Clara Barton, born on Christmas Day 1821, began her work as a teacher in Bordentown, NJ in 1851. When she was only 11, she nursed her brother David for 2 yrs when he had been badly injured, and the lessons learned were of much use to her later on. As a teacher, she was so upset by the poor children who could not afford to go to school that she offered to teach for free for 3 months if the town would make the school free for all. The concept was so successful that a larger school had to be built.

In 1862, during the Civil War, she got government permission to accompany the sick and wounded as they were being moved. She heard about terrible shortages of field supplies, so she set about supplying their needs, tearing up old sheets for towels and handkerchiefs and cooking for the troops. Then, with her characteristic independence, she advertised for provisions in a newspaper, and when the public sent enormous donations, she set up a distributing agency.

For 4 years after the war, Clara supervised a Federal search for missing soldiers. By 1869 she was traveling in Europe and offered her services to help tend to civilian victims of the Franco-Prussian War. While In Geneva, she learned of the

Play Ball!

Exit 1: New Jersey Mud – If you are a baseball nut, look down at the Delaware River as you cross over it here, because this is where the famous Lena Blackburne's Baseball Rubbing Mud comes from. In 1938 when an umpire complained to Blackburne (3rd base coach for the old Philadelphia Athletics) about the condition of the balls which were rubbed with tobacco juice, shoe polish or mud made of water and dirt from whatever field they were playing on, he went looking in the Delaware River until he found some muck (the whereabouts of the mud hole is still a dark secret) with a perfect texture - a cross between chocolate pudding and whipped cold cream. Nowadays, major and minor leagues in the US still use this mud to mask the ball's shine and improve the pitcher's grip. In 1969 it was permanently enshrined in the Baseball Hall of Fame at Cooperstown. The mud's source was willed to a close friend, John Haas, who had worked with Blackburne on his mud-finding exploits. Haas eventually turned over the enterprise to his son-in-law, Burns Bintliff. Burns in turn passed it on to son Jim and his family. Other kinds of mud and even mechanical methods have been tried to de-slick baseballs, but they couldn't make the grade - only good ole New Jersey mud will do.

MAP PG 26

International Red Cross, and brought the concept back to America.

She took on the formation of this agency practically single-handedly, educating the public through brochures and speeches and paying calls to cabinet heads and Congressmen. Her efforts were successful, and it was founded in the US in 1881. She served as its first president, and for the next 23 years directed its relief activities, retiring at the age of 82 and living to the ripe old age of 91. She certainly lived up to her nickname, "Angel of the Battlefield". ◑ 24 hrs. ☎ 856-299-6051.

Between Exit 1 & 2 Nbound, Mile 5.4: John Fenwick Service area – Look for the hotel/motel boards with phones to call for reservations or ask at the travel information center for advice. Don't forget to pick up your motel coupon booklets, use the clean bathrooms or get some Dippin' Dots ice cream from the machine near the info center.

John Fenwick, a Quaker, landed in these parts in 1675 to start a settlement without fear of persecution. He named it Salem from the Hebrew word for peace, and the county is still called that. He was probably a better leader than businessman, because financial troubles led him to turn the holdings over to William Penn, who had started another Quaker colony called Pennsylvania on the other side of the Delaware River. He died only a few years later in 1683. ◑ 24 hrs. ☎ 856-299-8246 .

DELAWARE

NEW! **Rte. 9 Exit:** Our Lady Queen of Peace – You can't miss her, high on a hill with her arms outstretched in front of Holy Spirit Church, with the sun bouncing off the 33' high stainless steel statue. Father Sweeney started the

project with the power of prayer. A committee used "Rosary Checks" to record the number of rosaries that an individual prayed for the building of a statue. The goal was for 500,000 before any fund raising began. Not only did the number of rosaries prayed exceed this, but unsolicited donations came in before any formal fund raising began. Sculptor Charles C. Parks did 2 others on the same theme honoring the Virgin Mary. This one, though, is sometimes referred to as "Our Lady of the Highways" as it sits majestically on the approach to the the Delaware Memorial Bridge. *i* ourlady-de.org

Exit 14 (Rte 9 New Castle): Bowlerama – Open for over 50 years, this fun spot has just been renovated and updated for your bowling pleasure, including glow-in-the dark bowling. Ask about weekend or weekday specials (like: 2 hours bowling, 4 prs shoes, pizza & pepsi $54.95). Take a break, bowl, play in the Kids Zone and win redemption tickets. Have lunch in the Kegler's Pub and Sports Bar, Spare Rib Xpress (roast beef platter, Italian salad, Philly steak, 1/2 lb burgers, crab cakes) or dessert at Dunkin Donuts or the ice cream parlour. ◑ M-Th 9-12, F 9-12 am, Sat 9-12, Sun 9-11. ☞ N on Rte 9 thru 1st light. 3031 New Castle Ave. *i* bowlerama.us, spareribx.com ☎ 302-654-0263 or 302-654-0704.

Exit 14 (Rte 9 New Castle): Mike's Famous Harley-Davidson – Kids

young and old who have ever pined to drive a Harley-Davidson will enjoy browsing through this showroom and sitting astride one. If you can't own a Harley, you can still buy a piece of the action with Genuine Harley-Davidson MotorClothes and merchandise like helmets, jeans, jackets, pins, patches, wallets, jewelry and collectibles. And if you're already a biker, there's a service department here. For a bite to eat, there's Primo Hoagies. ◗ Sun-Th 10-6, F 10-8, Sat 9-8. 2160 New Castle Ave. *i* mikesfamous.com ☎ 800-FAMOUS-HD or 302-658-8800.

Exit 14 (Rte 9 Newcastle): **Kalmar Nykel** – You can visit or sail on a square-rigged tall ship at this exit. The original one left Sweden in Nov. 1637 under the command of Peter Minuit (former Gov. of Dutch New Amsterdam) with a companion ship, Fogel Grip. They ran into a raging storm, and each sustained major damage, losing sight of each other and believing the other sunk. Miraculously, both vessels landed one week apart on Texel Island, Netherlands. After extensive repairs, they left for the New World on Dec. 31,1637.

By March they arrived in Delaware Bay, met with the Native American chiefs and purchased land to start New Sweden. They built their fort and trading post in the log cabin style they knew from home, and started this new form of construction here. The ship was the only settler ship to make 4 successful crossings of the Atlantic. It saw battle in the Swedish-Danish war, and served Sweden for 22 years. When she is in port, you can see her 10-story

high mainmast, 7,800 sq ft of sails, 9 mi. of rigging, and 4 cannons. Tours describe the daily life onboard a17th century ship. ☞ Rte 9 (New Castle Ave) N for 2.8 mi., RT on Swedes Landing Rd, RT to 1124 E. 7th St. *i* kalmarnyckel.org ☎ 302-429-7447.

Exit 14: The Dutch sent Peter Stuyvesant to Fort Casimir, later New Castle, to take control of the river traffic. Its strategic location caused the settlement to change "hands" constantly amongst the Netherlands, Sweden and Great Britain. William Penn (of Pennsylvania fame) actually first stepped onto American soil right here in New Castle. The town prospered under his Quaker administration, but the counties here, which were well established, became dissatisfied with Penn's rule, and in 1704 he granted them a separate legislature, New Castle, which became the colonial capitol of Delaware.

Two signers of the Declaration of Independence, George Read and Thomas McKean, hailed from these parts. You can still walk the the cobblestoned streets only 3 mi. off 95 and tour Read's 1801 Federal-style 22-room mansion (42 The Strand ☎ 302-322-841) with its new technology: air roasting ovens and steam tables in his kitchen.

Exit 14>: Jessops Tavern – Around 1724 Abraham Jessops lived and worked here as the town cooper, and so the name. Situated in the heart of this authentic colonial town the pub atmosphere, with original wooden floors and muskets on the walls, adds to the fun of chowing down on shepherd's pie, fish and chips, pot pie, pot roast and mashies. The red, white and blue sandwich (flank steak, mush-

MAP PG 26-27

rooms, blue cheese on sour dough) is popular, and it all comes with their thin crisp salted and peppered sweet potato fries. Finish off the meal with a fruit cobbler or homemade bread pudding with butterscotch bourbon sauce. ☞ S on Rte 9 (Wilmington Rd) for 2.2 mi and continue on E 3rd St 2 blocks, LT on Delaware St to 114 Delaware St. *i* jessopstavern.com ☎ 302-322-6111.

Exit 13 (Rte 13 Dover): Entenmann's Bakery Outlet – Head right here if you want to load up on inexpensive (3/$5 or $2 ea) sweet snacks for the car: super cinnamons, crumb cakes, raspberry danish, chocolate donuts, lemon crunch cake, pecan danish ring, multigrain cereal bars, Welch's fruit snacks or the healthier Rold Gold pretzels. You can also buy discount bread (Arnold, Freihofer, Thomas' muffins) to make lunches.

Markdowns and overstocked items are fresh, and are there because of their appearance or incorrect weight. Market returns are unsold from regular stores, and most everything is at least 50% off (mostly 80%). Manager Specials did not sell out and are further reduced to sell quickly (usually $1). ◐ M-Sat 9-5, Sun 9-4. 1505 N Dupont Pkwy. ☎ 302-328-2510.

NEW! **Exit 5C>:** Hotel du Pont – Pierre S. du Pont opened this 12-story Italian Renaissance grand hotel in 1913. It still reflects that time, with its craftsmanship and courtesy. You can dine in the Green Room under the 6 hand-carved chandeliers, with carved oak paneling, roomy wing chairs and Versace dinnerware. If you peek into the Gold Ballroom you'll see peacocks, urns and walls created in "sgraffito", a plaster scratching technique from the Renaissance. The hotel had always made a commitment to struggling artists and dis-

played their works, so now it owns and shows a formidable collection of Brandywine artists, including 3 generations of original Wyeth masterpieces. When you walk the halls think of Joe Dimaggio, Charles Lindburgh, Eleanor Roosevelt, JFK and Warren Buffet, who also walked them. To top it off, within the edifice there's the Dupont Theatre, offering a Broadway experience with 6 shows each year and an acclaimed children's series. 11th & Market in Wilmington. *i* hoteldupont.com ☎ 800-441-9019 or 302-594-3100.

NEW! **Exit 5C>:** Deep Blue – Yup, it's a seafood restaurant with a creative chef who might have fresh shrimp ceviche, a cornmeal crusted catfish sandwich or poached tuna salad on the menu. Mahi mahi might come blackened with a fava bean salad or Key West shrimp made with fettuccine carbonara, but the menu also satisfies the landlubber, with crispy beef wontons, braised duck ragout (with polenta, arugula, goat cheese) or a filet of beef with scallion potato cakes. 111 W 11th St, Wilmington. *i* deepbluebarandgrill.com ☎ 302-777-2040.

NEW! **Exit 5C>:** Capriotti's – We kept hearing about the "Thanksgiving dinner on a bun" and followed the delicious scent here. We chomped into a fresh crusty roll piled high with chopped fresh roasted turkey, stuffing, cranberry sauce and mayo, and fell in love at first bite. Locals call it  the "Bobbie", named after Aunt Bobbie, who would make this after Thanksgiving.

Opened and in the same location since 1976, Lois and brother Alan Margolet named the store after Grandpa. Around since 1987 is cousin Diane Rizzo, who is now running the busy spot. Frankie Rizzo roasts the turkeys and roast beef daily and orders only quality meats, cheeses, and has fresh rolls and produce delivered daily. Sure, you could also order other hot and cold subs here (cheese steaks, eggplant Parmesan, Italian cold cuts, meatball), but why bother? You can find other Capriottis in about 8 states. ◗ M-Sat 11-7. 510 N. Union St, Wilmington. *i* capriottis.com ☎ 302-571-8929.

Early Branding?

Delaware River – The Native Americans had many names for this river: Poutaxat, Makiriskitton, Whitituck. The Dutch called it the Zueydt (south) River and the Swedes simply called it the New Sweden Stream. Finally the name that stuck was penned by English explorer Sir Samuel Argall, who in 1610 was bringing fish from Cape Cod to Jamestown, VA to feed the hungry colonists (pretty far for take-out!). He named it in honor of Baron De La Warr, also known as Thomas West, who was the first Governor of Virginia (the man paying the tab).

Exit 4A: Christiana Mall – There's no tax in Delaware, so take advantage while you are passing through. More than 130 stores are here, including Apple, Aldo, Lego, Forever 21, H&M, Justice, White House Black Market, M.A.C., Lucky Brand Jeans, Williams-Sonoma, Spencer Gifts, Abercrombie & Fitch and a dozen jewelry stores. ◗ M-Sat 10-9:30, Sun 11-6. 715 Christiana Mall Rd. *i* shopchristianamall.com ☎ 302-731-9815.

Mile 5 Nbound and Sbound: Delaware Welcome Center Travel Plaza – Stop in this brand spanking new and LEED certified (very green) rest stop for motel coupon booklets, sparkling clean restrooms, 3 ATMs and several Internet stations. There's a visitor center with friendly traveling advice (☎ 302-731-0430 ◗ M-F 11-7, Sat 9-5, Sun 12-8) and lots

of flyers. There's still a pet walk and picnic tables where you could enjoy the new food options: Johnny Rockets, Baja Fresh, Popeyes Chicken & Biscuits, Famous Famiglia or Jamba Juice. ◗ Daily 24 hours. ☎ 302-731-8599.

Between Mile 3 & 2: Legend has it that the Stars and Stripes were unfurled for the first time in the only Delaware Revolutionary battle. It was fought on or about September 3, 1777, and called "the Battle of Cooch's Bridge", which is about a mile to the east of here.

Exit 1B>: SAS Cupcakes – Perfect for this college town, this cupcake party store is fun fun fun. Great pitstop for everyone in the car, their 12 daily choices might include: triple chocolate (our favorite by far), red velvet, S'mores, vanilla, peanut butter, cinnamon toast and more. Want to send a gift on ahead or back to the family - they have developed a special cupcake mailer to mail them swirled and sprinkled to

anywhere in the US. ◗ M-Th 10-8, Fri & Sat 10-9, Sun 10-6. 134B E. Main St, Newark. *i* sascupcakes.com ☎ 302-368-CAKE or 888-825-8988.

Exit 1B>: Deer Park Tavern – Edgar Allen Poe fell in the mud when alighting from his carriage in front of this inn. Upset, he decried, "A curse upon this place! All who enter shall have to return!". This is really not such a bad thing. A tavern since 1851, it remains one (also had lives

MAP PG 27

as a women's seminary, polling location, barbershop and ballroom). To go with the brews, the menu offers lighter fare like Eastern shore pretzels topped with crab meat to baby burgers called sliders, tuna sashimi salad, a Cuban sandwich or a grilled bison burger, as well as steaks and bourbon grilled salmon. ● M-Sat 11-1am, Sun 9-1am. ☞ N on S College Ave (Rte 896) for 2.5 mi. and you'll be facing 108 W. Main St. *i* www.deerparktavern.com ☎ 302-369-9414.

Exit 1B>: Caffe Gelato – Ryan German started this as a University business project, went all the way to Italy to study correct techniques and created intensely flavored ices. The coconut is textured, the peanut butter surprises you - it's so cold; pineapple is light, pistachio is brown and smacks of fresh nuts, the lemon puckers your mouth, but we loved the moka capuccino the best. For a quick bite, there's creative Italian paninis and salads, but you can now enjoy a wondeful meal before (or after) your gelato: shrimp canelloni, rosemary roasted pork tenderloin with mushroom risotto, pistachio chicken or crispy polenta and short ribs. ● M-Th 11- 9:30, Fri & Sat 11-10, Sun 10:30-8. ☞ N on S College Ave (Rte 896) for 2.5 mi., RT on Main St. to 90 E. Main St. *i* caffegelato.net ☎ 302-738-5811.

Exit 1: Mason-Dixon Line – The royal charters that established MD and PA and granted them to the Calvert and Penn families did not agree as to where boundaries lay. The British court had to declare a border, so a proper survey was needed. Surveyors in the colonies were no match for the difficult job, so 2 experts from England, Charles Mason and Jeremiah Dixon, an astronomer and a surveyor, spent from 1763-1767 surveying

the N/S line now separating DE and MD, and the E/W line dividing MD and PA. Stones engraved with a "P" were placed on the northern side and an "M" on the southern. Each 5th mi. was marked with a crownstone carved with the coat of arms of William Penn and Lord Baltimore.

Fifty years later, in the Missouri Compromise of 1819-1820 (covering the slavery issue in new territories admitted to the Union), an imaginary line along the MD-PA border and beyond separated the free States from the slave States. Called the Mason-Dixon line, it came to be known as the boundary between the North and South.

MARYLAND

NEW! **Exit 109B>:** Milburn Orchards – Exactly when did farms become amusement parks? This 4th-generation one has been around for 100 years and is famous for their apple cider doughnuts and u-pick fruits in season, and for

just plain family fun. Kids love the barnyard buddies and we loved the goat walk. There's a hay maze, a wooden truck to climb in, sand box, wagon ride, bean bag throw, cutouts for picture taking and a talking outhouse. The farm stand has turned into a gourmet store with sauces, dressings, dipping pretzels, pickled eggs or beets and brown bags of cake mixes (funnel cake!). Don't forget the pies: awesome apple, apple caramel bread or Sandra's favorite coconut custard. ☞ N on Rte 279 1 mi., LT on Fletchwood Rd

(Rte 277) for 1.3 mi, to flashing light, RT on Appleton Rd. 1 mi. to 1495 Appleton Rd. ◐ June-Oct M-Sat 9-7, Sun 10-5, Nov-mid Jan M-Sat 10-6. *i* milburnorchards.com ☎ 800-684-3000 or 410-398-1349.

Exit 109>: Elk Forge B & B – What an oasis along the way; if your bones are weary from your car journey, you can try the small spa on the premises for a hot stone or deep muscle massage, body wrap or facial to soothe it all away. The B & B is nestled in 5 acres of woods, and of themed rooms (Pennsylvania Dutch, Art Deco, Victorian) most sport fireplaces and whirlpools. Breakfast is set with silver and china in the cheerful solarium overlooking the putting green and nature trail. Exercise and billiard rooms, videos and board games are

there for entertainment. *i* elkforge.com ☎ 877-ELK-FORGE or 410-392-9007.

Exit 109>: Little Wedding Chapel – In 1913, when Delaware passed a mandatory matrimonial waiting and public notification law, Elkton MD became the elopement capital of the Northeast, marrying well over 10,000 a year during the 1920s and '30s. Maryland required a church service, so "marrying parsons" used cabbies to stake out the train and bus stations to offer arrivals special package deals. At the 15 private chapels that existed, celebrities such as Debbie Reynolds, John and Martha Mitchell, Cornel Wilde, Joan Fontaine, Martha Raye and even the Reverand Pat Robertson were married here. Elkton's 25-year wedding bliss was halted in 1938 when the state (embarrassed by the tacky goings on) started to require a 48-hour waiting period. This chapel, in a 200-year-old stone building, is tiny (6 pews), is flower-ready and it's the only one which has survived and still performs 500 or so weddings a year.
142 E Main St.
☎ 410-398-3640.

Exit 100>: Fairwinds Farm – Wow, a B&B where you can go horseback riding! This farm family takes in travelers, be they the human kind or the animal kind (horses, dogs, etc). JoAnn Dawson, the "farmers' wife", was written up in the NY Times, Baltimore Sun

and was on Good Morning America for her role as a wrangler in Oprah Winfrey's "Beloved" film, and then was in "The Sixth Sense". JoAnn writes the "Lucky Foot Stable" books, perfect for kids in the car; stop and get one autographed. Enjoy a walk in the fields, visit with Jeepers the goat, gather your own eggs for breakfast in the hen house or just watch the horses graze from your window. Ask about riding lessons, horse-drawn carriages, hay rides and pony rides. Same day reservations possible. *i* fairwindsstables.com ☎ 410-658-8187 or 302-540-1852.

MAP PG 27-28

Exit 100: North East – For the charm of small town life, take a quick pit stop along South Main St. Beans, Leaves, Etc. (#33) is for specialty coffees, teas and gourmet goodies or Where Butterflies Bloom (#102) for gifts: Primal Elements soaps (buy Sandra the vanilla), Disney figurines, salt lamps, Weatherland chimes, Kitras glass ornaments, amber and a Xmas shop in back. A real hoot is Herb's Tackle Shop (#203), where you can just throw some coins in the vending machine in  front and out pops... worms! Look for the 5 &10 Antique Market (#115), with 2 floors holding about 80 invisible dealers, so you simply choose from the display cases and pay at the front. You can have a bite at Woody's Crab House (#29) (see story).

Exit 100: Woody's Crab House – For your fill of Maryland's famous crabs, you can head over to this wood-slatted "shack" for crab bisque or Maryland crab soup to start, and then crab imperial, crab au gratin or fresh jumbo lump crab salad. Their hardshell bluefin crabs were voted best by Chesapeake Bay magazine. You could go farther asea for gulf shrimp, Little Neck clams, Alaskan king crab legs, their famous Carolina shrimp burger or have a landlubbers' chicken or ribs. Big and small kids will enjoy munching on the free peanuts while they wait. ◐ M-Th 11-9, F-Sun 11-10 ☞ S on Rte 272 for 2.3 mi. til it turns into Main St. 29 S. Main St. 𝒊 woodyscrabhouse.com ☎ 410-287-3541.

NEW! **Exit 100>:** The Wellwood Country and Yacht Club – Back in the 19th century, with no phones or internet, businessmen and politicians had to meet regularly. This club, situated halfway between the Union League of Philadelphia and the Gridiron Club of Washington, was a favorite spot to talk AND go fishing, duck hunting, shooting, boating (you can still pull up at the marina across), swimming and play quoits and golf. You can still come here to dine (in or out) on crab bisque, oysters Rockefeller, crab imperial (2nd generation owner Larry Metz's mom's recipe), Maryland hard shell crabs (all you can eat with fried chicken $29.99), fresh seafood, steaks or Italian dishes like eggplant Wellwood (crab atop breaded eggplant with melted cheese & pasta) and end with fresh fruit gelati. Notice the company that came before you: Theodore Roosevelt gifted them with a wooden bald eagle from the White House, Calvin Coolidge sent a lamp, etc. ◐ May-Oct Tues-Sun 11:30-10, Nov-Apr W-Sun 11:30-10. ☞ S on 272 for 1.7 mi, RT on US 40 for 3/4 mi, LT on Wells Camp Rd to 2nd stop sign, RT on Rte 7 for 1 mi, LT onto Rte 267 to stop sign at Market St. LT for 2 blocks, LHS. 523 Water St. 𝒊 wellwoodclub.com ☎ 410-287-6666.

NEW! **Exit 100>:** Nauti-Goose – Ya gotta love the name. You can drive your car or your boat here to enjoy the waterfront views. Popular menu items are all there but you can get exotic with the Thai spiced coconut shrimp, chicken taco salad, pretzel mountain (raspberry glazed ham, tomato, cheese on a baked pretzel with balsamic honey mustard), clam spaghetti, lobster ravioli or seafood mac 'n cheese, and you can and wash it all down with strawberry goose juice. Summers F-Sun nights there's an all you can eat seafood and prime rib buffet - and a band. 200 Cherry St. 𝒊 nautigoosesaloon.com ☎ 410-287-7880.

Mile 98 Nbound and Sbound: Chesapeake House – This is a busy full service center with a food court, ATM, motel coupon booklets and clean restrooms, a picnic area and pet walk. ◐ 24 hrs.

Exit 93: Perryville Outlet Center – You can't see this from the exit, but trust us - it is hiding down in a valley. Parents will like Oshkosh B'gosh, and then there's a Dress Barn Outlet, Jones NY, Totes/Isotoner/Sunglass World, Nike for shoes and Book Cellar for vacation reading. Drop by the Cecil County Visitors Center for info on the area. ◑ (Apr-Dec) M-Sat 10-8, Sun 11-6; (Jan-Mar) M-Th 10-6, F/S 10-8, Sun 11-6. *i* perryvilleoutletcenter.com ☎ 410-378-9399.

Exit 93: Cecil County Visitors Center – This spot in the Perryville Outlet Center.is perfect for a tourism office. They have friendly staff full of information about the county and the state. They can book hotel rooms in their area, help with car trouble and you can walk your pet nearby. The motel coupon booklets are there, and there are clean restrooms and an ATM in the mall. If you have kids with you, ask for their Maryland Junior Rangers or Bay Games - a children's activity book with stickers and a card game, and then you can use the coupon savings flyer while they're busy. ◑ M-F 8-4:30, Sat 10-4, Sun 11-2. 68 Heather Lane *i* seececil.org ☎ 800-Cecil-95 or 410-996-6299.

Exit 93>: Studio 432 – Often artists have dreams of huge studio spaces

to work in or a venue to sell their own work (and those of their friends), but alas it remains a dream. Sue Eyet had a "green vision" and convinced her husband to buy an abandoned 1899

Exit 89: The Underground Railroad was neither underground nor a railroad, rather a secret network of roads, waterways, trails and hiding places called "stations" (barns, churches, basements and woodsheds). With help from anti-slavery activists (who were breaking the law by assisting), enslaved people were led from bondage to freedom.

In 1793 the US passed a Fugitive Slave Act, which allowed for the capture and return of any runaway living in a "free" state. Harford County's location near the Mason-Dixon line made it a strategic point. Rock Run Mill in the Susquehanna State Park was nicknamed "The Promised Land", since it would provide both refuge and a place to pick up provisions for the ferry journey across the river leading farther north.

Further north on I-95, Farmington CT was considered "Grand Central Station". The route ran through the New England states and ended in Ontario, Canada. If the slaves were lucky enough to make it that far, the British authorities declined to honor the US demands to return them. You can find lists of some of the safe houses at: nps.gov/history/nr/travel/underground/routes.htm

MAP PG 28-29

church and recycle it into a studio/shop for her re-cyled metal art. The 80 artists reclaim and re-purpose wood, glass silk and more: typewriter keys into jewelry; ties into tybags; buttons into bouquets; scrabble letters/beads/old greeting cards into sparkling butterflies; cutlery into herons, blue crabs and dragonflies; bottle caps into belts; metal into crabs and angels - you get the picture. ◑ Th-Sun 11-6. 432 Aiken Ave *i* studio432.biz ☎ 410-642-6749.

Exit 85>: New Ideal Diner – If you want to go back to an authentic 50's diner, this is a sunny windowed stainless steel O'Mahony model, shipped here in 4 pieces in 1952. The basic diner food served is made with meat freshly butchered right here, and the place is well known for breakfasts, which could include chipped beef with sausage gravy or corned beef hash. Daily lunch and dinner specials ($6.45-

$6.95) include entree, veggie (15 choices) and dessert. You might like to try George Engelsson's mother's recipe for spaghetti with meat sauce, or the all beef franks and beans, which taste suspiciously like Nathan's. Popular choices are the spicy crab or lobster bisque soup, fried sweet potatoes and rice or bread pudding. At

least stop and swivel on a stool at the counter for the soda fountain milk shakes, ice cream sundaes or root beer floats. The friendly waitresses seem right out of a movie; it's the kind of place where everyone knows your name and what you like to eat, and cross conversations are common. ◑ Daily 5:30 a.m. to 9 p.m. 104. S Philadelphia Blvd. ☞ 2 mi E on MD 22, RT on US 40 for 1/2 mi. ☎ 410-272-1880.

Exit 85: Durango's Southwestern Grille – Finding a Southwestern restaurant on the route is a nice change of taste, and this one comes with a twist of MD. You can't help but notice the crab

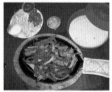

pretzel - it's the first thing on the menu - and the hearty cream of crab soup. You can also start with the tortilla eggrolls with smoked chicken, black beans, cheese and red peppers or the Cajun fried shrimp or Rio Grande salad with scallions, walnuts, pineapple and pico de Gallo. If you want steam coming out of your ears, you can opt for the black and bleu chicken dredged in cajun seasoning with bacon or the volcanic wings, but there's also burgers, Tucson tuna steak, prime rib fajitas, grilled veggie sandwich, and even if there's no room for dessert, you can still have the smallest ice cream sundae ($1.50). ◑ M-Th 6am-9pm, F-Sun

(open all night) Fri 6am-Sun 9pm. 980 Hospitality Way ☎ 800-346-3612 or 410-273-6300.

Mile 82 Nbound and Sbound: Maryland House – This is a busy full service center with a food court, ATM, motel coupon booklets, clean restrooms, a picnic area and pet walk. The upstairs info center (elevator) offers friendly tourist advice (flyers from Maine to Florida), traffic reports, a motel board with phones for reservations, fax machine, mail box, postage stamps and even meeting rooms. ◑ Daily 8-6. ☎ 410-272-0176.

Exit 77: Gabriel Brothers – Regulars familiarly refer to them as "Gabes", and expect every visit to be a treasure hunt. What you will find is a rack or two of liquidated items in recognizable name brands up to plus and tall sizing. We've seen: Liz Claiborne, Carolyn Taylor, Lane Bryant, White Stag, Erika, Wrangler, Lee, XOXO, Nautica, Polo, Izod, Timberland, Phat Farm, Disney, Carters, Pipeline, Rockport, Diesel. For over 40 years, the daily shipments with shockingly low prices for casual clothes, kitchen and bath items, linens and casual jewelry have kept them coming back. ◑ M-Th 9-9, F&S 9-10, Sun 11-7. ☞ 1/2 mi N on Rte 24. 3430 Emmorton Rd. *i* gabrielbrothers.com

Exit 77B: Stars and Stripes Grille – This fun center and restaurant takes patriotism to the max with its clever menu names. You can start right off with the star spangled steak bites (blackened on garlic toast with Cajun tiger sauce) and take a trip to the Solomon's Island cream

of crab soup. Entrees shine with rockets red glare ribs, two if by sea tuna (lemon pepper and

The Town That Fooled The British

NEW!

On August 10, 1813 during the War of 1812, the British navy attempted a nighttime bombing of St. Michaels, MD. Local tradition holds that residents of this ship building center extinguished village lights and hung lanterns in trees north of the town. Enemy guns overshot their target, hitting only 1 home (now known as the Cannonball House); a cannonball penetrated the roof and rolled down the staircase as Mrs. Merchant carried her infant daughter downstairs. The house still exists as a private residence.

Some Quackery

Exit 74: Super 8's Duck Pond – Value added is what motels try to offer, but this one goes one step beyond. The motel surrounds an old rock quarry which was turned into a lake. The water is home to Canada geese (at times there are 100's of them), Peking ducks, a crane and mallards. If you're lucky (or unlucky), you'll get to hear the yodelling geese. The fowl play a game all day with the motel desk staff, since they like to hang out around the motel entrance and the staff constantly chases them away.

There's a hot breakfast here for humans. ☞ S on Rte 152 to US 40. Motel on right. ☎ 410-676-2700.

paprika), live free or die club or the spirit of '76 spinach salad. There's a little patriot's menu with Betsy Ross spaghetti or Paul Revere shrimp poppers. After the menu fun, go play at laser tag, putt putt mini golf, batting cages or the arcade games. ◐ arcade/outside: M-Sun 10-10, food Sun-Th 11-11, F&S 11-2. 416 Constant Friendship Blvd *i* starsandstripesgrille.com ☎ 410-569-4700 or 410-569-8255.

Traffic Jam

If you're caught in traffic around Baltimore or Washington D.C. and think you're going really slowly, think about the patriots who rode horseback on this road. Thomas Jefferson complained that he could do at most 3 mph.

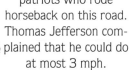

Exit 59: Broadway Diner – This is a family-run new 50's style diner (even a jukebox!) brought here from NY in 11 pieces and then put together. Guy Fieri, on Diners, Drive-Ins & Dives, featured the Hungarian goulash, potato crusted salmon, shrimp creole and Broadway festival (seafood pasta). But Mama's meatballs made it onto the menu while George's pastry creations grab your attention when you enter - macadamian cinnamon buns, baklava, dulce la leche and the kid's will love the little mouse chocolate cake. You can eat breakfast, lunch or dinner (the fresh baked cream cheese bread is divine) 24 hours a day. Don't miss the fab salads - exotic has mango, strawberries, feta and onions with creamy balsamic dressing and there's even an organic salmon one. The 24 burgers are made from angus beef and can be had on focaccia, the tortilla wraps

MAP PG 29-30

are popular, there's moussaka and pastichio, many vegetarian options, 18 omelettes, filet mignon, potato crusted salmon, shrimp creole and the crunchy fried chicken. ◗ Daily 24h. 6501 Eastern Ave., just E of the exit. *i* broadwaydiner1.com ☎ 410-631-5666.

Exit 58>: Captain Harvey's Submarines – We were told that one cheese steak sub here could feed you lunch for a week, and they were right. In a strip mall, you line up in this skinny joint, and if you can get past the abrasive counter help (think Seinfeld's soup Nazi, and be prepared to know if you want lettuce, tomato, mayo, hot peppers or pickles BEFORE you order), you will be rewarded with a sub filled a mile high with steak and onions. A half sub filled us both up to the max. There are seafood and chicken subs, but why bother? You have to eat in your car (be prepared for a mess), and don't be surprised by the seagulls circling overhead

for the leftovers. ◗ M-Th 10-10, F-Sun10-11. ☞ 2.5 mi. S off exit to 3435 Dundalk Ave (Logan Village Shopping Ctr). ☎ 410-284-7772.

NEW! Exit 58: Gunter Family Food – Here's a quick takeout spot where you can get your fix of homemade tuna, egg, chicken salad, roast beef sandwich or the popular Italian cold cut sub or BBQ sandwich. The extensive take out menu covers wings, burgers, pizza and tons of sides (old bay french fries, pizza fries, jalapeno peppers, mashies and gravy). Wash them all down with smoothies (pina colada, watermelon, banana) or milkshakes, Italian ices, gelati or soft serve. Hey, there's even homemade cakes: walnut swirl, apple dumplings, banana pudding (only $2.99). ◗ M 10:30-5, T-Th 10:30-8, F 10:30-10, Sat 12-10. 545 Dundalk Ave. *i* gunterfamilyfood.com ☎ 410-633-1756.

Broadway in Baltimore

Exit 57: Toby's Dinner Theatre (at Best Western) – Wow. Instead of a night with the boob tube, why not get energized by a live musical production - and then plop into bed upstairs in your hotel room? The quality of the performance would make NY proud. Dinner is buffet style (turkey, ham, baked tilapia, chicken picata, onion/pepper mashies, spinach casserole, fresh salad bar and ice cream sundae bar for dessert), and keep an eye on your servers, for they become the performers. Hotel has Free shuttle to Inner Harbor, Convention Center and Johns Hopkins. 5625 O'Donnell St. *i* tobysdinnertheatre.com ☎ 410-633-9500 (hotel), 866-99Tobys or 410-649-1660.

Exit 53: Oriole Park at Camden Yards – This baseball field is located in what was a railroad center, and is only 2 blocks from the birthplace of baseball's most legendary hero, George Herman "Babe" Ruth. His father operated Ruth's Cafe on the ground floor of the family residence located at Conway St. and Little Paca, which amazingly is now center field at Oriole Park! Tours of the park lasting 1 1/4 hours are given daily from mid-Feb thru mid-Dec, except on afternoon game days. ◗ M-Sat 11,12,1,2; Sun 12:30,1,2,3. *i* theorioles.com ☎ 888-848-BIRD or 410-547-6234.

Mile 56: The Star Spangled Banner – When driving through the Fort McHenry Tunnel, you are now driving under the very water that Francis Scott Key was stuck in on September 13 and 14, 1814 during the War of 1812. Key, a lawyer, had boarded the British flagship to secure the release of a friend.

He watched a gigantic flag with 15 white stars and 15 red and white stripes flutter defiantly on the ramparts of Fort McHenry. Sewn by Mary Young Pickersgill and her daughter Caroline, it was so large that it could not be stitched in their home, so they had completed it in a Baltimore brewery.

As Key waited out the 24 hours in "shock and awe", the British fired off 200-lb. bombs which were supposed to explode on impact, but instead often blew up prematurely in mid-air. At night they sent up signal rockets which burned in flaming arcs across the sky. Through all of that, at dawn Key was amazed to see Mary's flag still waving and the Fort intact.

Overcome with emotion, he wrote some phrases on the back of a letter. It was his brother-in-law who suggested singing the poem to the meter of a British drinking song, "To Anacreon in Heaven". The song was an instant hit, but it took Congress until 1931 to designate it the US national anthem. If you want to see the flag, it is still a moving sight; it is hanging in the Smithsonian Institute, which is down I-95 a bit.

Why not sing along through the tunnel in Francis' honor?:

Oh, say can you see, by the dawn's early light,
What so proudly we hailed at the twi-light's last gleaming?
Whose broad stripes and bright stars, through the perilous fight, O'er the ramparts we watched, were so gallantly streaming?
And the rockets' red glare, the bombs bursting in air,
Gave proof through the night that our flag was still there. O say, does that star-spangled banner yet wave
O'er the land of the free and the home of the brave?

Did you know there are 3 more verses? (You can find them all at our web site www.drivei95.com/images/anthem.pdf)

MAP PG 30

Exit 50: Polock Johnny's – The American basics - a hot dog and fries ratcheted up a notch, have been served here since 1921. John Kafka, with his carny background, parlayed his secret red sauce recipe, sausages and lemonade into a family empire. Son JFK Jr. perfected the roll and sausage recipes (going as far as hiring a wurst spe- cialist from Germany!), started an annual sausage eating contest and voiced humorous radio spots to continue the brand. The dog with the works is perfect even without the add-ons: onions, chili, mustard, ketchup, green peppers, fried onions, cheese, kraut or gravy, but do have it with a side of amazing OC (Ocean City) fries. If you must, there's also cheese steak, fish sub, BLT and chili. ◐ M & T 7-6, W-F 7-9, Sat 9-6. 3212 Washington Blvd., at the bottom of the hill from the S Caton Ave exit. ☎ 410-644-5997.

Exit 50: Rheb Candy – Way back in 1917 when WWI ended, self-taught Louis Rheb started making taffies, brittles, jellies and fudge in the basement of his home right here. Louis and his wife Esther went to different markets to sell them until  they converted their garage into this store in 1950. Now in its 3rd generation, Louis' many recipes include his famous vanilla or chocolate butter cream, coconut clusters, pineapple covered in dark chocolate, sponge (honeycomb & molasses), peanut butter cups, cashew bark, whipped cream filled chocolates and our personal favorites, the chocolate nut caramel. Sugar-free options can be butter crunch, marshmallow, peanut truffle or cashew clusters. Pets can crunch on the carob dog bones, and even chocolate-phobics can enjoy the sucking candies, fruit slices and peanut brittle. ◐ M-Sat 8:30-5. 3352 Wilkens Ave. *i* rhebcandy.com ☎ 410-644-4321.

Exit 49A>: G&M Restaurant – Baltimore locals know their crab cakes, and this 16-year-old joint with its new facelift is a favorite place - only lump crab meat, no filler, perfect seasoning and broiled to perfection. The menu carries Greek, Italian and daily specials, the soups are homemade, but it's the crab cakes here, ma'am. You can FedEx them to your home too. ◐ Daily 11-11. ☞ take 695 E to Exit #8 Hammonds Ferry Rd. Make LT 1/2 block. 804 Hammonds Ferry Rd. *i* gandmcrabcakes.com ☎ 410-636-1777.

Communication Revolution

Mile 48: The World's First Telegram – This was dispatched on the B&O railroad's right of way between Washington and Baltimore, which runs parallel to I-95. One telegraph unit was set up in the Supreme Court chamber and the other in the B&O's Pratt St. Station in Baltimore. On May 24, 1844 Samuel Morse's dots and dashes were received in the first telegram, which read "What hath God wrought?". Morse trained as a painter and studied at Yale, but it was a chance meeting on a ship with Dr. Charles Thomas Jackson that set him on the path toward telecommunications. Since he had sketched for so many years, he could visualize and draw ideas in his head. He realized that he would need a code for each letter to communicate. He took time to study the English language to determine the most popular letters and numbers, and it was his brilliant idea to assign the simplest patterns to the most common letters, which led to his greatest contribution: the Morse Code. His inventions began one of the most important revolutions in American history: the communication revolution.

Exit 47A>: The Elkridge Furnace Inn – Started as a tavern in 1744 and attached to the manor house (1810) this Federal/Greek revival building also  spent time as an iron smelting furnace, thus the name. The setting on the Patapsco River, graced by linden, holly and magnolia trees, now houses a special occasion French-trained chef-ed restaurant offering seasonal menus. Inside notice the staircase with tiger maple spindles, original floors and 23 fireplaces to warm your toes. Chef Daniel Wecker knows how to prepare classic veal loin blanquette or magret de canard (duck), or you can feast on pheasant, venison scallopini and seafood lasagne, but don't worry - there's always a steak du jour, chicken breast and, of course, French onion soup. Note that there's a 3-course prix fixe menu for only $34. ◑ T-F 11:30-2, 5-9, Sat 5-10, Sun 10-2, 4-8. 5745 Furnace Ave. ☞ Rte 195 East to Exit 3 Washington Blvd. (Rte. 1). RT South, then LT at 1st intersection, Levering Ave. LT at Main St. RT on Furnace Ave. *i* elkridgefurnaceinn.com ☎ 410-379-9336.

Exit 38A>: Historic Savage Mill – This was a canvas mill from 1822 to 1947

supplying sails for clipper ships, tents and cannon covers for the Civil War, backdrops for the silent movies and then cots, truck covers and bags for both World Wars. It has been adapted as a home design and crafts center in 9 buildings (30 shops) making up a fun maze, so you never know what you will find around the next bend: grandfather clocks, art, quilts, custom guitars, Xmas decor, Lucy & Ethels's cottage chic, a game store, Polish pottery and an entire level with 75 antique dealers. You can dine at the Rams Head Tavern or our favorite, Bonaparte Breads (hint: the French Embassy shopped here). ◑ M-Th 10-6, F&S 10-9, Sun 11-6. ☞ E on Rte 32, then S on US 1 for 0.7 mi, RT on Gorman Rd, RT on Foundry Rd. 8600 Foundry Rd. *i* savagemill.com ☎ 410-792-2820 or 800-788-6455.

NEW! **Exit 38A>:** Terrapin Adventures – Who said a car trip is boring? Get out of the car here for thrills on the High Ropes, with its 18 traverses (find Island in the Sky or the Heebie Jeebie), the Giant Swing where up to 3 of you are flung 40 ft. under 2G's of force or the

Climbing Tower with 12 routes, including a sky high view of the Little Pawtuxent River. Try out the vertical playpen and the cargo net or just seek the thrill of the 330' zip line, but be ready for a tightrope walk to get there. Everyone, beginners and advancers, wears a safe auto belay system. If all that wasn't enough, you can rent bikes or kayaks, go river tubing, horseback riding, geo-caching or fly fishing. 8600 Foundry St. *i* terrapinadventures.com ☎ 301-725-1313.

Mile 37 Nbound and Sbound: Maryland Welcome Center – These are full service centers with friendly tourism advice, flyers, motel coupon booklets, clean restrooms, wi-fi and a picnic area. This one can make motel reservations, and you can ask for their large print map. Don't feel guilty if you grab something from the vending machines here - revenues help support the Maryland Business Enterprise Progarm for the Blind. ◑ Th-Sun 8:30-4:30. ☎ (Nbound) 301-490-1333 or (Sbound) 301-490-2444.

Exit 23>: College Park Aviation Museum – How appropriate to house an aviation museum at the oldest continuously operated airport in the world. The

MAP PG 31-32

NEW! What racist incident marked the dedication of the Lincoln Memorial? Blacks were assigned a roped - off section, separated by a dirt road.

first person to greet you is Wilbur Wright - who else? This animatronic man tells you how he came to this airfield in 1909 to teach military officers how to fly. The gallery contains historic and reproduction aircraft associated with the history of the airfield, as well as hands-on activities for children of all ages, including a 1911 Model B Flight Simulator where you can fly over this airport using hand controls and state-of-the-art visuals. Look for exhibits on the first US Postal Air flight in 1918 and the first controlled helicopter flight by H. Berliner. The airport runway is just outside the rear glass windows of the museum, so you can watch take-offs or landings as today's pilots take to the sky. ● Daily 10-5. ☞ S. on Kenilworth Ave (Rte 201), RT at light onto Paint Branch Pkwy to Corp. Frank Scott Dr., another RT, follow signs to museum at #1985. *i* collegeparkaviationmuseum.com ☎ 301-864-6029.

NEW! **Exit 22>:** NASA/Goddard Space Flight Visitor Center – You can meet Dr. Robert Goddard's life size likeness right next to a mock-up of his famous liquid fueled rocket which fired up way back on March 16, 1926 in Auburn MA. The 2 1/2 secs of flight led to today's rockets fly-

ing to outer space and back. This small FREE interactive gallery encourages you to learn about the planets, galaxies, the Lunar Reconaissance Orbiter, black holes and James Webb's space telescope. You can sit in a rocket, take a photo in a space suit and watch a real time NOAA weather readout station. Don't miss the Science on a Sphere computer/video projector movie showing the rocky Mars surface, hurricane season on earth and you can even find out

that you can see the lights of I-95 from outer space! 8800 ICESat Rd. ● T-F 10-3, Sat&S 12-4. *i* nasa.gov/centers/goddard/visitor/home/index.html ☎ 301-286-8981 or 301-286-3978.

───※───

OOPS, IMPORTANT ERRORS

Did you know that Timothy Matlack, the calligrapher who hand-lettered the Declaration of Independence, made 3 errors in the writing of it? Two of them have been cor-

rected by the addition of a ^ with the corrections inserted above the word: the word "representative" was spelled "represtative" and the word "only" was omitted. The third error could not be changed, since an extra letter was written in the line "Nor have we been wanting in attentions to our Brittish brethren".

───※───

Exit 7: John Wilkes Booth fled through these parts after assassinating President Abraham Lincoln in Ford's Theatre in Washington, DC on April 14, 1865. With David Herold, a fellow conspirator, he stopped at the house of Dr. Samuel Mudd to get treatment for a broken leg, which happened in his leap to the stage. He arrived at Dr. Mudd's around 4 a.m. on April 15. Dr. Mudd set, splinted, and bandaged the broken leg, and they stayed until the next afternoon. Mudd's handyman, John Best, made a pair of rough crutches for Booth. Mudd was paid $25 for his services. Within days Dr. Mudd was under arrest by the US Government and was charged with conspiracy and with harboring Booth and Herold during their escape. He was sentenced to life in prison and missed the death penalty by one vote. However, because of outstanding efforts as a physician during a yellow fever epidemic at the prison, he was granted parole after only 4 years by President Andrew Johnson. See story Exit 7A about Booth's stop at Surratt House.

Exit 7A>: Surratt House & Tavern – As you enter the side door of this house you are walking in the footsteps of John Wilkes Booth the night he killed President Lincoln, since he came in here through the same door to retrieve a rifle, field glasses and supplies for his run from the law. Built in 1852, this was a tavern, an inn, a post office and a polling place. It was thought to be a safe house for the Confederate underground. The massive search for Booth led them here to Mary Surratt's house, and as a result she was tried in a military court and con-

victed of conspiracy to assassinate the President. On July 7,1865 Mary Surratt was the first woman to be executed by the federal government.

Today you can visit this famous house; a docent in 1860's period clothing walks you through the typical middle class home. You can also make reservations for the 12-hour "Escape Route" bus tour. ◑ mid Jan - mid Dec Th & Fr 11-3, S&S 12-4, or by appt. ☞ Rte 5 S for 4 mi., RT onto Woodyard Road (Rte 223W) to 2nd light, LT onto Brandywine Rd. 9118 Brandywine Rd. *i* surratt.org. ☎ 301-868-1121.

Exit 3B: Henry's Soul Cafe – With its slogan "Home of the Sweet Potato Pie", you can expect that there will be collard greens, okra, chitterlings and pigs feet on the menu as well. For the less daring, head for the meatloaf, freshly fried fish (trout or whiting), country style steak and, of course, fried chicken, all cooked to order by this second generation of Henry's. Fresh corn bread is made daily, and it is used for the turkey and chicken stuffing, or you can have your BBQ sandwiches made on it. And don't forget that sweet potato pie for dessert. ◑ Sun 12-8, M 11:30-7, T-Sat 11:30-9. 5431 Indian Head Highway. *i* henryssoulcafe.net ☎ 301-749-6856.

Exit 3A: Oxon Cove Park/Oxon Hill Farm – If you need a breath of fresh air, a picnic spot or if the kids need to blow off some steam, enjoy this FREE National Park Service site. The park varies from river shoreline to grassland, forest, marsh and swamp ecosystems. On a clear day, the 2-mile easy loop walk even offers a glimpse of the Washington Monument.

The little farm has horses, cows, sheep, goats, pigs, rabbits, a chicken coop, deer, wild turkey, lots of birds to watch, a duck pond and herb garden. If you stop at the right time, there are programs for cow milking (10am), a chicken program (11am), tractor rides (1:30pm) or ranger talks about the history of the farm (S&S 1-3). There's even a challenged people program.

The property goes back to 1811 when Dr. Samuel and Mary DeButts bought it. In 1814 they watched in horror as the War of

1812 fires from the burning of the White House and other buildings glowed on the walls of their own white house. Across the Potomac, in Alexandria Harbor, sat the British warships, and the city surrendered to them. No wonder the DeButts went off to visit their daughter in VA. In 1891 (and until the 1950's), the US Gov't bought it for St. Elizabeth's Hospital, allowing patients to work the farm for therapy

MAP PG 32-34

and to grow their own food. ◐ Daily 8-4:30. ☞ bear R on exit ramp to Oxon Hill Rd. 6411 Oxon Hill Rd. *i* nps.gov/nace/oxhi/index.htm ☎ 301-839-1176.

Hot Time in the Old Town

On August 24, 1814, during the war of 1812, the British army seized Washington D.C. and began the destruction of the U.S. seat of government, with 4,000 crack troops happily seeking revenge against the insolent former colonies. The ragtag poorly trained American militiamen were situated in Bladensberg, where Pres. James Madison and his Cabinet came to witness the defense of the city. But it was all for naught, as the American troops retreated so fast that the skirmish became called "Bladensburg Races".

Important public documents and records such as the Declaration of Independence had been stuffed into linen bags and moved to a vacant house in Virginia. Dolly Madison, calmly evacuating the "President's Palace", was adamant that the famous Gilbert Stuart portrait of George Washington must be removed. It was screwed so tightly to the wall that the doorkeeper and gardener tugged and tugged but could not move it. Finally someone found an axe and they chopped the frame off, removing the canvas, and they all sped to VA just in the nick of time.

In the Capitol, the enemy piled all the mahogany desks and chairs and set them on fire, and soon the flames went right through the roof. At the White House, they helped themselves to souvenirs: the President's shirts and hat and Dolly's chair cushion. When the troops found a banquet set in the dining room (for the victory dinner!), they toasted "little Jemmy Madison's health", then piled all the furniture and set another fire.

President Madison could see it from his vantage point in the hills of VA, and the citizens of Baltimore watched the red glow in the night sky. Luckily for us a huge rain began to fall, stopping the spread of the flames and sending the soaked British scurrying out of the city by the next nightfall.

NEW! Exit 2A: Gaylord National Resort – Sure, the 18-story atrium just wows you, but it's the attention to detail and cheerful service that keep you. The decor reflects DC architecture, with its white marble floors (even the elevator), doric columns, star-studded chandeliers with striped carpets, and even a snippet of the Constitution by each room door. There's a sound/water/light show all evening (patriotic songs, of course) and restaurants for each budget. Look for the life-sized swinging Babe Ruth greeting you at the National Pastime Sports Bar with its 30' HD wall, eat seafood dockside on the wooden boardwalk at Moon Bay or stroll the Pienza Italian market. High end is Old Hickory Steakhouse, with its tender steaks (topped with foie gras), truffle french fries (yum), intense lobster corn chowder and homemade ice cream and sorbets. What impressed us was the Maitre des Fromages - a woman passionate about her cheeses. which you can order for appetizer or dessert or just sample with a glass of wine. Outside, stroll through the shops in this new city and see if you can find the giant emerging from the sand, called "The Awakening"; kids use him as a playground. 201 Waterfront *i* gaylordnational.com ☎ 301-965-2000.

NEW! Exit 2A: Aloft National Harbor – When you walk into this hotel, it's like attending a fun party. The great room is noisy with music, a bar scene, people playing board games or computer ones, guests grabbing a bite in the re-fuel area and others checking fights on the wall screen (3 nearby airports) and printing out their boarding passes. There are outdoor sitting areas overlooking the harbor or an indoor fire pit. The hall and room designs are modern, gorgeous, pared down, efficient, offering good lighting and a computer work station with window views and a peek-a-boo shower. 156 Waterfront St. *i* aloftnationalharbor.com ☎ 301-749-9000 or 877 Go- Aloft.

VIRGINIA

Exit 177B>: Alexandria Visitor's Center – When you go up the staircase, don't be surprised if the ghost of Mr. Ramsay passes you. He and other specters may be encountered in the nightly ghost walks, or you can join spook-free walking tours, scavenger hunts or just

ask for friendly advice. Pick up the *Proclamation of The Mayor of the City of Alexandria*, proclaiming you an "Honorary Citizen for the Day", which includes 24 hours of FREE parking at the meters in town. There's a FREE Trolley from the King St. Metro to the waterfront. On Saturdays (5:30-10:30am) there's still the nation's oldest (1753) Farmer's Market in Market Square, where George Washington sold produce. ◕ Apr-Dec daily 9-8; Jan-Mar 10-5. ☞ N up S. Patrick St. (US 1) 3/4 mile to King St. RT to 221 King St. *i* visitalexandriava.com ☎ 800-388-9119 or 703-746-3301.

Exit 177A: Hampton Inn Alexandria Old Town Area South – Right near Old Town (with lots of parking), this chain motel offers a FREE hot breakfast bar, FREE high speed Internet and best of all, a FREE 24-hour shuttle service to Old Town, Reagan Airport and the Washington DC metro. Just like a chauffeur - call when you're ready and "Jeeves" comes to pick you up. Leave your car and explore both Alexandria and DC. ☞ Follow signs to US 1 So., over Potomac River; Inn will be on left. 5821 Richmond Highway. *i* hamptoninnalexandria.com ☎ 800-Hampton or 703-329-1400.

Exit 177B>: Christ Church – This church's (1767) fame rests on the fact that both George Washington and Robert E. Lee worshipped here. In the front left, notice Washington's pew (#60) - the only one remaining in its original double configuration. Confederate Gen. Robert E. Lee (# 46 on the right) was married to Washington's step-great granddaughter, Mary Custis. Regular congregants refer to the chapel's geography as the Lee side or the Washington side.

> ## George Washington Really Slept Here
>
> **Exit 177B:** George Washington really slept here, because he maintained a town house at 508 Cameron St. The building today is a replica of his 1769 home, which he used when time or weather prevented his return to Mount Vernon. While he lived here he managed to set up the Friendship Fire Co., acted as vestryman at Christ Church Parish and was a Mason of Lodge #22, becoming its first Worshipful Master in 1788.

MAP PG 34

Notice an original boot scraper outside the door (Washington side). Perhaps one of these gentlemen used it. During the Civil War, Col. Orlando Willcox of the Union Army wrote of

Washington's connection to the church, "There I could almost feel his imposing presence...". It is a tradition for each President of the US to visit here at some point during his administration, usually on a Sun. near Washington's birthday (Feb 22). Tours are given. ☞ N up S. Patrick St. (US 1) for 3/4 mile to Duke St. RT 4 blocks to Washington St., LT 3 blocks to 118 N. Washington St. *i* historicchristchurch.org

Exit 177B>: Gadsby's Tavern – Here you have 2 co-joined buildings - a 1785 Georgian-style tavern and a 1792 Federal-style hotel, which sat on the main stage coach route between Boston and Williamsburg. For almost 100 years, the tavern was the center of political, business and social life in Alexandria. It hosted everything from dances and theatrical musical performances to assemblies; merchants came in to sell wares, and traveling dentists treated patients. Just think, as you tread on these floor boards - George and Martha Washington's house was just around the corner, and they were frequent visitors. They attended the Birthnight Ball in his honor in 1798 and 1799. Thomas Jefferson had an Inaugural banquet here. John Adams and his son John Quincy, James Madison, James Monroe and the

Marquis de Lafayette all visited. Nowadays it is an early American restaurant (have Washington's favorite duck) in a tavern-like setting, and offers tours. ◑ Apr-Oct T-Sat 10-5, Sun & M 1-4; Nov-Mar W-Sat 11-4, Sun 1-4. 134 & 138 N. Royal St. *i* gadsbystavern.org ☎ 703-746-4242.

NEW! **Exit 177>:** Stabler-Leadbeater Apothecary Museum – Founded in 1792 by Quaker pharmacist Edward Stabler, this business remained in the same family for 141 years until 1933, when the

Depression forced them to close. They chose to simply lock the door, and inadvertently preserved history. Fortunately over 8,000 items, including the old account books, prescriptions, early medical wares, apothecary containers, documents and journals all remained in their original drawers, providing a living history of the city.

Everything you see now is just about the same as George Washington, James Monroe and Robert E Lee saw them. You can go upstairs to the mixing room to see the original herb drawers, labels, corks and bottles (bright blue ridged ones held poison). See if you can find the scarificators - spring-loaded blades for blood letting, and the note that Martha wrote to them for George's ail-

> **Exit 177B:** Dr. James Craik was surgeon-general, so it was his duty to accompany George Washington during every battle he fought in the Revolutionary War. Unfortunately, without modern antibiotics, he was unable to save the Father of our Country from a simple throat infection that led to his death nearby at Mount Vernon in 1799. The home of Dr. James Craik is still there at 209 Prince St.

ments. ◗ (Apr-Oct) T-Sat 10-5, Sun&M 1-5; (Nov-Mar) W-Sat 11-4, Sun 1-4. 105 S. Fairfax St. *i* apothecarymuseum.org ☎ 703-746-3852 .

Exit 177B>: Torpedo Factory Art Center – From 1918 thru WW II this building produced torpedo shell casings and other weapons. The 9920 MK-14 green torpedo you see in the main hall salutes that era. Nowadays, about 165 artists can be found here working in 82 studios which offer water views and lots of light. We, the public, are allowed to wander through and watch them work on painting, jewelry, sculpture, ceramics, wearables, printmaking, glass, photography or fiber art, and are able to buy their work on the spot without the cost of the middle man. On the 3rd floor is the Alexandria Archeology Museum, which traces the history of the city  going back 9,000 years. You can discover diagrams of 23 miles of trails in the city which can be traversed by foot, bike or car. ◗ Daily F-W 10-6, Th 10-9. 105 N. Union St., corner of King St., by the river. *i* torpedofactory.org ☎ 703-838-4565 X1.

NEW **Exit 177>:** Union Street Public House – If you want a bar scene, a seafood or steak dinner or a place to take a traveling family, this 23-year-old institution, sitting in a Colonial warehouse, fits the bill. While you wait for your meal, share a mound of spicy onion tangles or the tips and chips - piles of homemade potato chips topped with tender charbroiled steak pieces and blue cheese sauce. The menu is heavy on seafood with a N'orleans touch - Gulf Coast gumbo with smoked chicken, shrimp, Smithfield ham in a hot broth or Jambalaya penne including shrimp, Andouille sausage and chicken in a zesty tomato sauce or the Carpetbagger po' boy stuffed with steak, fried oysters, sauce remoulade or the muffuletta, and maybe throw in side of saucy creamy lobster mac 'n cheese. There's cheesecake of the day to finish it off. ◗ M-th 11-10, F&S 10:30-11, Sun 10-10. 121 S. Union St. *i* unionstreetpublichouse.com ☎ 703-548-1785.

Exit 177C>: Collingwood Library and Museum on Americanism – Originally part of George Washington's River Farm, this research library includes - amazingly - his diaries, Paul Revere's lantern from Boston's Old North Church (see poem below), 6,000 books on patriotic subjects and 600 volumes of genealogy from the Mayflower Society of Washington D.C. The wee bit of a museum is easily traversed in under an hour. Kids would enjoy the Sioux chief headdress with 87 eagle feathers, Uncle Sam's outfit, flags of all the States and Medal of Honor winners. There are replicas of The Declaration of Independence and the Magna Carta. Facing the front door there is a huge old holly tree, where you can hide inside and have a secret picnic on a bench. Entrance is FREE, or you may just want to stretch your legs walking around the grounds and go down for the water views. ◗ M, W-S 10-4, Sun 1-4. ☞ RT heading S on S. Washington St. (turns into George Washington Memorial Pkwy) for 4 1/2 mi., LT at Collingwood Rd., RT on E. Blvd Dr. to 8301 E. Blvd Dr. *i* collingwoodlibrary.com ☎ 703-765-1652.

Do you know which it was - "one if by land or two if by sea"? Here's the verse in "Paul Revere's Ride" by Henry Wadsworth Longfellow that addresses it:

"Meanwhile, impatient to mount and ride,
Booted and spurred, with a heavy stride
On the opposite shore walked Paul Revere.

MAP PG 34

Now he patted his horse's side,
Now he gazed at the landscape far
and near,
Then, impetuous, stamped
the earth,
And turned and tightened
his saddle girth;
But mostly he watched with
eager search
The belfry tower of the Old
North Church,
As it rose above the graves on the hill,
Lonely and spectral and sombre and still.
And lo! as he looks, on the belfry's height
A glimmer, and then a gleam of light!
He springs to the saddle, the bridle
he turns,
But lingers and gazes, till full on his sight
A second lamp in the belfry burns."

NEW! **Exit 177C>:** Hotel Monaco – When you see the funky red and turquoise colors, you realize that this 4-star hotel in the heart of Old Town has a quirky side. Imagine our surprise when as we walked into the lobby, and they were setting up a Wii along with apple cider to imbibe. Notice that the drapes in the rooms are based on the cuff of a Union soldier's uniform. Kids love Disney night at the indoor pool, and dog lovers gather on T & Th eves in nice weather for the Doggie Happy Hour. For luck, go rub the nose of the mascot pig in the Jackson 20 restaurant

(named for Pres. Andrew Jackson on the $20 bill). Another Jackson, James Jackson, was the owner of Marshall House, the original hotel on this corner. He became famous for killing Col. Elmer Ellsworth, who had the gall to pull down Jackson's Confederate flag, thus making Ellsworth (a friend of Lincoln) the first casualty of the Civil War. 480 King St. *i* hotelmonaco.com ☎ 703-549-6080.

NEW! **Come for the Liver and Cauliflower...**

Exit 177C>: The Majestic – Look for the original blue and pink neon sign, and you know you have found the reincarnation of "Mr. John's" famous 1932 Majestic Cafe. Nowadays the menu creates the same buzz; regulars insist certain plates stay: the choc-a-bloc full-of-onions soup, chef's creative fried green tomatoes (we had it hollandaise style), home-style meatloaf, pecan encrusted scallops, coco'a vin (chicken with chocolate), the lip smackable calves' liver (roasted onions, lardons, red wine, sauce). The tradtion is to end with the coconut cake. Sandra would come here just to eat the side order of cauliflower gratin with black truffle bechamel, and Stan would take (don't faint) the liver! ◐ Lunch

M-Sat 11:30-2:30, Dinner M-Th 5:30-10, F&S 5:30-10:30, Sun 1-9 (Nana's family dinner). 911 King St. *i* majesticcafe.com ☎ 703-837-9117.

NEW! **Exit 177B>:** La Madeleine – A country French cafe chain is an oasis for a quick bite, as everything is baked fresh every day (they have no freezer). Quiche Lorraine or Florentine and croque monsieur (ham and cheese with garlic cream sauce) are there, of course, along with puff pastries filled with creamy spinach or chicken, mushrooms and bechamel sauce. Cold salads and hot sandwiches include chicken Parisian (bacon, cheddar) or Cordon bleu (ham, swiss), pastas and rosemary rotisserie chicken (signature dish with tomato basil soup). Crepes are filled with beef, broccoli and potatoes or shrimp, tomatoes or spinach, and leave room for dessert ones: Romanoff with fresh strawberries and brandy sour cream sauce or have a chocolate almond croissant. They suggest smart choices and slim portions and healthy oatmeal and muesli for breakfast, but we didn't opt in. 500 King St. ☀ Sun 7-10, M-Th 7-10:30, F&S 7-11:30 *i* lamadeleine.com ☎ 703-739-2854.

Exit 177>: George Washington Masonic Memorial – Opened in 1932, freemasons from around the country helped build this memorial to George Washington and to the history of American Freemasonry. When you enter there

are murals of Washington and a colossal statue of him wearing his Masonic apron and ornaments. On the 4th floor, you can see the trunk he carried during Revolution, family paintings, his game box, a list of his slaves and try to find the lock of his hair. This is one of the places mentioned in Dan Brown's "The Lost Symbol". At the top there is an Observation Deck with a panoramic view of Alexandria and Washington DC. ☀ M-Sat 10-4, Sun 12-4. 101 Callahan Dr. *i* gwmemorial.org ☎ 703-683-2007.

Slave Breeding

Exit 177C: Freedom House Museum – In 1808, a US law outlawed the importation of slaves. Still so necessary for plantation life, clever entrepreneurs did not let this stop the sale of slaves - they simply bred them! The slaves were encouraged to have as many children as possible so they could be auctioned off. This building was once headquarters for the Franklin and Armfield Slave Pen, the largest and most successful domestic slave trading firm in America. "We will give Cash for one hundred likely YOUNG NEGROES", read one of their ads in the Alexandria Gazette in 1828. "Persons who wish to sell, would do

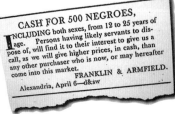

well to give us a call, as the negroes are wanted immediately. We will give more than any other purchasers that are in the market or may hereafter come into the market."

Between the 1830's and 1860's Virginia exported more than 10,000 slaves a year to the Deep South, and the total may have reached 300,000, tearing families apart forever. The FREE museum is a must to absorb the personal stories of this black mark on the country's history. ☀ M-F 9-5, Sat 10-12 (by appt). 1315 Duke St. *i* freedomhousemuseum.org ☎ 703-836-2858.

A notice that appeared in the March 16, 1801 edition of the Alexandria Advertiser & Commercial Intelligencer advertised 4 slaves to be sold at the Market Square on March 26. Enslaved African Americans (as well as local farmers) came to the square to sell their handiwork or produce, skimping and saving to buy their freedom. Sophia Browning Bell was allowed to use a corner of her master's yard to grow tomatoes and vegetables to sell at market. In 1801 she bought her husband George for $400 and freed him. In 1807, George Bell was able to buy Sophia's freedom for $5; Sophia Bell's low price, was probably due to her being very ill at the time. In 1807, George Bell helped establish the 1st school for African American children in Washington D.C.

MAP PG 34

Exit 173>: The Tailored Man – Get measured on your way down South at this family shop and pick up your custom finished suit on your way home. This is where you can be fitted for the famous made-to measure Hong Kong suit. Since the 1960's, these garments have been stitched by Chinese tailors and sold by Indian owners to travelers from all over the world in pretty much the same way. They fit taking 19 measurements, offer suits in a myriad of fabrics and have them ready in a couple of weeks (or 7  days if you must have it!) at affordable prices. This is a US beachhead for one of these tailors. Shirts can be custom-made too. ◐ M-F10-6:30, Sat 10-5. ☞ LT off exit, 1.5 mi N on Van Dorn St, RT on Duke St 0.4 mi to 5243 Duke St. on LHS. *i* tailoredman.com ☎ 703 751-7868.

Exit 163 - Fairfax County Visitor Center – located in the Comfort Inn at this exit. Helpful advice from Nancy, Jean or Linda, informative flyers, coupon books and clean bathrooms in the motel await you. ◐ Daily 9-5. 8180-A Silverbrook Rd. *i* fxva.com ☎ 800-732-4732 or 703-550-2450.

Exit 160B>: Occoquan and Prince William County Tourist Information Center – Captain John Smith of Jamestown fame made it all the way to this town, just 5 min. off an exit. The river setting made it a natural choice for early tobacco farming, forges, grist mills, saw mills and cotton mills, with cargo leaving for Europe and the West Indies - until the river silted up. Merchant's Mill, the first automated grist mill in the nation, lasted here for 175 years before being damaged by fire. This was quite a bustling city up to the early 20th century when, in 1916, a fire devastated much of the town and then, in 1972, Hurricane Agnes hit hard again. At that point, a merchants association rejuvenated the place with artsy types who have opened over 50 charming shops in all the ups and downs and alleyways. Look for everything from folk art to flax clothing, quilting supplies, cook books, Americana, braided rugs, custom-fit bras, jewelry, tin lamps and yummy home-made pies. Please note that the town is haunted by ghosts (pick up the guide in the visitor's center) who rearrange things in stores, tread footsteps, leave behind flowers, flicker candles or show up as a Confederate soldier. ☞ Gordon Blvd (Rte 123) 3 lights N for 3/4 mi. to Historic Occoquan sign. LT onto Commerce, 1st RT onto Washington St., to 200 Mill St. at the bottom. ◐ Daily 9-5. *i* visitpwc.com or www.occoquan.org ☎ 703-491-4045 or 800-432-1792.

NEW! **Exit 160>:** Madigans Waterfront – This is a mostly surf and some turf kind of place for lunch

---

Sunday in the Park with War

In July of 1861, Washingtonians traveled in their "Sunday best" to Judith Henry's farm in Manassas Junction. They brought their picnic lunches, blankets and fans to loll away the afternoon 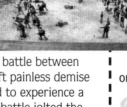 watching, through binoculars, a battle between North and South. Expecting a swift painless demise to the South, they were horrified to experience a bloodbath killing 900 men. This battle jolted the North and Washington leaders into realizing that a Civil War had really begun. A year later, in one of the US's bloodiest days, 24,000 men died in yet another Confederate victory here.

(seafarer's salad with shrimp and scallops, and fried calamari on top or soft shell crab sandwich) and dinner (seafood trio - crab cake, salmon, grilled shrimp or scallops au gratin), which you can enjoy on the waterfront decks. Sunday brunch is popular with its omelet, waffle and carving stations and there's entertainment F& S nights and karaoke Wed. Be careful - there's a resident ghost. ◗ M-Th 11-10, F&S 11-11, Sun 10-9. 201 Mill St. *i* madiganswaterfront.com ☎ 703-494-6373.

Exit 160>: Workhouse Arts Center – For 80 years, this was a prison

designed for Pres. Teddy Roosevelt's progressive vision to provide non-violent criminals with fresh air, natural light and purposeful work for rehabilitation. Agricultural operations began in 1912, and then prisoners produced bricks to construct the buildings you now see. A Women's Division held famous prisoners: about 168 women, most from the National Women's Party who were jailed for picketing at the White House for women's voting rights. Lucy Burns, who, along with Alice Paul, founded the National Women's Party, was one of them. Eventually it became a medium security prison with watch towers, cells and wired fences. It closed in 1997. Think of this as you now see The Lorton Arts Foundation's new vision, with 100 artists in residence in open studios and gallery exhibitions of local, regional and international artists. Other arts are covered as well: film, performing arts, theatre,

> **Shop til you Drop?**
>
> For women, this could be the ultimate resting place. In the Potomac Mills mall parking lot, if you look for the small grassy knoll in front of IKEA, you will notice the cemetery plot with gravestones for the Nash family, among others.

music, so every w e e k e n d there's something going on here. ◗ W-Sat 11-7, Sun 12-5.

☞ N on Rte 123 (Gordon Blvd) over bridge for 2 mi. Center is on right at 9601 Ox Rd. *i* workhousearts.org ☎ 703-495-0001.

Exit 156: Potomac Mills – This enclosed mall has over 200 stores, and you can grab a bite in one of the 25 eateries. There are outlets here that you don't find much elsewhere on I-95: Benetton Outlet, JC Penney Outlet, H&M, As Seen on TV, Charlotte Russe Outlet, Designer Suit Factory, Smithsonian Catalog Outlet, Vans Outlet, Neiman Marcus Last Call, Saks OFF 5TH, BCBG MaxAzria Factory store, XXI Forever, Off Broadway Shoe Warehouse, Modell's Sporting Goods, Banana Republic Factory Store and Children's Place Mega Outlet. ◗ Mon-Sat 10-9, Sun 11-6. *i* potomacmills.com ☎ 703-496-9330.

Exit 152>: Weems-Botts Museum – Parson Mason Locke Weems, a bookseller from Dumfries, wrote the biography "Life of Washington", in which he mentions a story about Washington as a young lad "barking" a cherry tree and then confessing to his father, "I cannot tell a lie". This story took on a life of its own. The book was the 2nd best selling book in America (after the Holy Bible) for years, and was in continuous publication from 1800 to 1927.

His original book shop is now this museum. The name Botts refers to Benjamin Botts, who purchased the building from Weems in 1802 and who was on the team defending Aaron Burr in his treason trial.

MAP PG 24-36

They were successful, and Burr was not convicted. Botts and his wife Jane were killed, along with the Gov. of VA and other prominent state leaders, in a theater fire in Richmond in 1811. You can picnic here, but I don't think there's a cherry tree to sit under. ● T-Sat 10-4. ☞ Rte 234 E. to Dumfries, RT at US 1. Continue 1 mi, keep right at split, RT onto Duke St. at museum sign. Museum is 2 blocks up hill. Pkg on rt of Cameron St along sidewalk; please don't park in the apt. bldg's lot. 3944 Cameron St. *i* historicdumfries.com/weemsbotts.html ☎ 703-221-2218.

Exit 150A: Iwo Jima Statue – If you take a short detour to the entrance to the Quantico Marine Base you can see a recreation of this famous WW II statue created by Felix de Weldon (lit up at night). In a 35 day fight for Iwo Jima, an island that was crucial for US bombing raids on Japan's main islands, 6,821 marines were killed. On February 23, 1945 U.S. Marines from the 28th Regiment, 5th Division, raised the U.S. flag atop Iwo Jima's Mount Suribachi. After being cast in Brooklyn, NY the original statue actually was driven down I-95 headed to Arlington National Cemetery, where you can still see it.

Semper Fidelis

VA Exit 150A>: National Museum of the Marine Corps – Adjacent to the Marine Corps base in Quantico VA, this soaring design evokes the image of the flag-raisers of Iwo Jima. Go through marine boot camp and follow interactive exhibits through the WWII Pacific Theatre.

Learn about fighting the Korean war on the streets of Seoul and then to the hamlets, jungles and rice patties of Vietnam, where helicopters meant the difference between life and death. Irreplaceable artifacts, including aircraft and tanks (A-4 Skyhawk is a movie screen) immerse you in the sights and sounds of Marines in action. Grab a bite of Colonial cuisine (venison fricasse, peanut soup) in the replica Tun Tavern, the birthplace of the Corps, and buy some cool gifts at the store (Marine Monopoly, gung ho sauce). ● Daily 9-5. FREE

i usmcmuseum.org ☞ E off the exit, RT on US 1 (Jefferson Davis Hwy) to 18,900 Jefferson Davis Hwy. ☎ 877-635-1775 or 703-784-2607.

───────◆───────

Exit 148>: Globe and Laurel – Major Rick Spooner and his wife Gloria are the hosts at this pub, which is located close to the entrance to the Quantico base and to the Marine Corps museum. If you are fascinated by military people and paraphernalia, come here to rub shoulders with Marines, Navymen and FBI agents. The walls and ceiling are plastered with with their emblems and civil police patches too; the rooms are dedicated to each: Belleau Wood (marine), The Bridge (naval), FBI room and the Ward area with lounge chairs.

The pub was intriguing enough for Patricia Cornwell to use it as a location in 2 of her mystery novels. Food is reasonably priced, with the popular Maryland crab cakes, roast prime rib of beef, Norwegian salmon with a garlic, ginger and white wine marinade or duck a l'orange. A cute Marine salute: desserts are called Ruffles & Flourishes, and there is no charge for " y o u n g recruits" under 5. ◐ M-Sat 11:30-10pm

☞ E on Russell Rd, bearing right when it splits in 0.3 mi, RT on Rte 1 for 0.7 mi to 3987 Jefferson Davis Hwy on right side. *i* theglobeandlaurel.com ☎ 703-221-5763.

Exit 143: Five Guys – Hamburger lovers like Sandra will adore the fresh meat burgers prepared daily (3.3 oz. for only $2.69) loaded up with free toppings: relish, onions, pickles, tomatoes, fried onions, sauteed mushrooms, jalapeno peppers, green peppers and sauces. The perfect side - hand cut and twice fried potatoes - are Five Guys style or Cajun (vinegar too, if you wish) and scrumptious. The burger-laden menu also has kosher-style beef hot dogs, veggie burgers or grilled cheese. Pres. Obama likes to eat these too. 1525 Stafford Market Pl., 1/4 mi W of exit. *i* fiveguys.com ☎ 540-288-8266.

Mile 132 Southbound: Virginia Welcome Center – This brand new center has a walking loop, interactive kiosks for info in the rest area and inside, flatscreens for weather, news and tourism info. There are more clean bathrooms (and a family one now) and the FREE motel discount coupon booklets, as well as flyers from places to visit all around the State. Don't forget to chat with the friendly and helpful staff who can answer many questions. ◐ Daily 8:30-5. ☎ 540-786-8344.

Exit 130>: Fredericksburg and Visitor Center – Walk in the footsteps of George Washington and James Monroe, just a cannon shot from I-95. In the vibrant 40 sq. block "Old Town" you'll discover more than 350 18th and 19th century hous-es, with cannonballs still embedded in the sides of a few. Check out the Hugh Mercer Apothecary shop, an 18th century doctor's office where blood draining was a common occurrence, or the Rising Sun Tavern, where you will learn about Colonial twice-a-year bathing habits. The city goes back to pre-Colonial times, and has a Civil War legacy of 4 battles claiming over 100,000 casualties, so it is no wonder that it is haunted.

Until the last decade of his life, George Washington spent alot of time here. From the ages of 6 to 20 he lived across the river at Ferry Farm (burned down in 1740, but you can still visit) and attended school for a term or two. He would break up his long journey to Williamsburg with a stop at his brother Charles, his mother's, his sister Betty's beautiful Kenmore Plantation, attend church services and BBQ's, or hoist a few with friends at Weedon's Tavern.

Ask at the Visitor Center (marked as CVB on the map below) about the Timeless Ticket (40% off 9 historic sites, museums and battlefields) and a 2-hour parking per-

mit for the city garage, or it's free in municipal lots. There's a 14-min film and a walking tour map of 26 sites, and for kids by kids, "Walk with Me". If you like antiques and locally owned shops, here's a little stroll along Main St.: **1**. #708 Beck's; **2**. #710 Twinkle Toes; **3**. #726 Deborah's Place; **4**. #717 Collector's Den (540-373-2430); **5**. #804 A Place in Time; **6**. #814 The Toy Store; **7**. #822 Silver Spider; **8**. #803 The Rocking Horse Gallery; **9**. #805 (our favorite name) Sorry Mom Tattoo shop; **10**. #807 Made in Virginia Store (540-371-2030); **11**. #829 Civil War Life Museum Store (540-834-1859); **12**. #904 Blue Shark Antiques (540-373-5873); **13**. #914 Car-

MAP PG 36-37

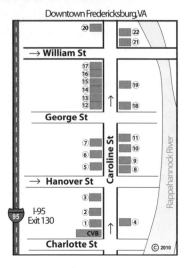

Downtown Fredericksburg, VA

The railways and highways get covered, too (find the I-95 chevron!). Read the signs and see photos of the African American experience during the Civil Rights era or just oogle some decorative arts. Find out what a yee-hawkawn is. The beautiful gift shop sells tea sets, candle snuffers, Melissa and Doug

license plate games, military chess sets, books, etc. ◐ Apr-Oct 10-5, Sept -Nov & Mar 10-4. 1001 Princess Anne St. *i* famcc.org ☎ 540-371-3037.

oline Square Antiques; **14**. #916 Antique Court of Shoppes; **15**. #918 Way Back When; **16**. #920 Market Square Antiques; **17**. #922 Upstairs Downstairs; **18**. #901 Goolrick's Pharmacy (540-373-3411); **19**. #925 River Run Antique Mall (540-371-4588); **20**. #1022 Fredericksburg Clock Shop & Antique Gallery; **21**. #1001 Antique Court Shops; **22**. #1017 Re-Run Shop.

Don't forget to stop at Goolrick's (#18 on map): opened in 1867, it's the oldest continously operated soda fountain (since 1920). ◐ M-Sat 9-5, Sun 11-5, 1st Fri ea. month 5-8. For Visitor's Center: ☞ E on Plank Rd (Rte 3) for 1 1/4 mi. LT onto William St. (Business Rte 3), 1 1/4 mi. to Princess Anne St. RT 3 blocks to Charlotte St., LT til corner. 706 Caroline St. *i* visitfred.com ☎ 800-678-4748 or 540-373-1776.

NEW! **Exit 130>:** Fredericksburg Area Museum – Housed in the 1927 Planter's Bank, it's fitting to find an exhibit about currency in their vault. We learned why coins have ragged edges - to prevent shaving them for bits of silver. In the first room, you find out about personal experiences of Frederickburgers during each war, like Jane Beale's diary of an,1862 battle. We don't realize the role of a river - here the Rappahannock - in people's lives.

Exit 130>: Mary Washington House – In 1772, George Washington bought this house for his Mom. This is where he told her he was to become our first President, and he also left for the inau-

guration from here after receiving her blessing. Some of her favorite possessions are still here: the sundial was hers, the "best dressing glass" that she willed to George, and she planted the 238 year-old boxwoods in the back garden. She lived here for 17 years until she died in 1789, and never saw him as President. There's an adorable gift shop where you can buy frilly cards, kids' tea sets, pineapple trivets, tea cozies, Spode blue dishes and candles from VA beeswax. 1200 Charles St. ◐ Mar-Oct M-Sat 11-5, Sun 12-4; Nov-Feb M-Sat 11-4, Sun 12-4. *i* apva.org/marywashingtonhouse ☎ 540-373-1569.

NEW! **Exit 130>:** kybecca – Rebecca just couldn't find good cheeses in the area, so along with husband Kyle (thus the name) she opened up a cheese and wine

Exit 130>: Rising Sun Tavern – Washington's brother Charles had this place built around 1760 as his home, so George was a frequent guest here. Later on it was a tavern and a stagecoach stop. Enjoy the delightfully funny costumed wenches who give living history tours in which you will learn how these sayings got started: "Not playing with a full deck" - The King put a tax on the ace of spades, so if you played without that card, you avoided the tax

"Here's looking at you" - Mugs had glass bottoms so when you were getting to the end of your drink, you could see your drinking partner through the little bit of liquid left

"Bar tenders" - The liquor and rum was stored in a barred little cage in the corner of the room and the owner would sit in there and tend to his stock

"Caught with fingers in the till" - You sometimes paid for your drinks by yourself using a box which had a locked money drawer. Unsavory characters would try to pry it open, so the owners put a bell in there to catch them with their fingers in the till. The bell ringing in a cash register came from this idea

"Bite off more than you can chew" - A ring of chewing tobacco was passed around the table and you bit off a piece to chew. If you took too much, you'd spit it out on the floor

"Mind your P's and Q's" - This stood for pints and quarts. You'd have to make sure you ordered enough before last call.

◗ Mar-Oct M-Sat 10-5, Sun 12-4; Nov-Feb M-Sat 11-4, Sun 12-4. 1304 Caroline St. *i* apva.org/risingsuntavern ☎ 800-678-4748 or 540-373-1776.

shop to cure her mouse urges. This eventually led to the hangout next door with wine-by-the-glass from their cool machine and tapas-like homey food. You can taste

and slurp and make your own pairings, or just chow down on the lobster mac 'n cheese (it bites!), bison blue cheese sliders (salute to White Castle), beet chips, lamb shank stew with dumplings or ravioli frito with bison marinara. We loved the sparkly Fentiman Mandarin and Seville orange soda and Vignette Chardonnay soda. ◗ M-Th 5-11, F&S 3-12am, Sun 11-9. 400-402 William St. *i* kybeccawinebar.com ☎ 540-373-3338.

Exit 130>: Bistro Bethem – This is an oasis for gourmet food lovers on the road, it's upscale but casual - live music Tues eves and art on display for sale. Husband (and chef) and wife team Blake and Aby Bethem serve bistro cuisine with a daily chalkboard of fresh specials. Usually there's a steak/frites plate, but you might see bronzini, a roasted sea bass or lamb loin with ricotta dumplings in roasted garlic sauce, shrimp and grits or even braised veal cheeks. Starters could include mac 'n cheese, a smoked blue fish plate and grilled romaine salad. ◗ T-Sat 11:30-2:30 and 5-10, Sun 11:30-2:30, 5-9. 309 Williams St. *i* bistrobethem.com ☎ 540-371-9999.

Exit 130>: James Monroe Museum and Memorial Library – This site restoration was begun in 1927 by Monroe's great-granddaughter, Rose Gouverneur Hoes and her 2 sons. For more than 50 years, her son Laurence catalogued these unique objects which belonged to the 5th President (and 4 term Governor of Virginia) and his family. Everything is here, from Monroe's kitchen utensils to the jew-

MAP PG 37

elry his wife brought back from Europe (he was minister to France, England and Spain), including furniture, artwork and his clock collection. Monroe's own library is here, and his writings include letters, gifts and busts of his close friend Marquis de Lafayette. ◑ M-Sat 10-5, Sun 1-4, (Dec-Feb M-Sat 10-4, Sun 1-4). ⓲ umw.edu/jamesmonroemuseum 908 Charles St. ☎ 540-654-1043.

Exit 130>: Hugh Mercer Apothecary Shop – Mercer was a friend of George Washington, a physician and a General in the Continental Army. Back then, if

you came to visit him at this shop, he tried to balance your black and yellow bile, phlegm and blood by: purging you, making you puke, blister, or by bleeding you. You will laugh and squirm as the wenches explain his use of herbs and potions and show you real live leeches

that were used for bleeding a quart of blood at a time. He could pull your teeth, amputate limbs or slice out your eye lenses. Upstairs, look for the door with the hole in it used for men to get their wigs powdered. ◑ Mar-Oct M-Sat 9-4, Sun 12-4; Nov-Feb M-Sat 10-3, Sun 12-4. 1020 Caroline St. ⓲ apva.org/hughmercerapothecary/ ☎ 540-373-3362.

Exit 130>: Carl's – This 2nd generation family-owned frozen custard stand is a ritual stop for native Fredericksburgers. It was opened by Carl and Margaret Sponseller in 1953 in a former gas station along US 1, at the time the busiest N/S highway in the US.

Frozen custard takes soft ice cream, mixes it with eggs, and then the mixture is cooked before it is frozen. The 3 flavors, vanilla, chocolate and strawberry, are still the same recipes and have been churning

out of the same machine since the 1940's. If the pale chocolate has a really familiar taste to you, that's because they use Hershey syrup in the mix. There's real malts and hot fudge sundaes, too. Though we are admitted chocoholics, Sandra actually favored the strawberry, because it tasted like you were biting into a real strawberry - because it IS made with fresh fruit. ◑ Sun-Th 11-11, F & S 11-11:30 (end Feb-end Nov). ☞ E. Plank Rd (Rte 3) 1 1/4 miles, LT on William St. (Business Rte 3), 1 1/4 miles to Caroline St. LT 7 blocks to Herndon St., LT for 1 block and RT onto Princess Anne. 2200 Princess Anne St.

Move over Starbucks, We have Wawa

Exit 130: Wawa's mini-mart/gas bars offer both inexpensive freshly brewed coffee and gas, a surcharge-free ATM, hoagies in 4 sizes, ciabatta melts, the Sizzli™ hot breakfast sandwich, quality dairy products, Wawa brand juices and teas, ready-to-go salads (chicken cherry walnut or turkey BLT), fresh fruit cups and daily soups.

Over 100 years ago in Wawa PA, George Wood's original dairy business enjoyed a reputation for quality, superior fresh products and customer service. Coffee is brewed using filtered water, and comes in original, dark roast, decaf, cappuccino and flavors (english toffee, hazelnut, and fat-free french vanilla or apple cinnamon). You can buy the beans to go or enjoy a chai tea latte. Bring your own mug in and they will refill it for the low price of $1.21 for a 12 oz size, $1.31 for 16 oz, $1.42 for 20 oz, up to $1.56 for 24 oz. (now that'll keep you awake on the road for awhile!) ◑ Daily 24 hrs ⓲ wawa.com

Exit 130B: Central Park – This is one of the new types of separate-store centers.

If you have the patience to keep driving around, you might find Funland for a break or Game Stop and Teach 'n Stuff for the kids. Ten Thousand Villages is there for gifts, scrapbookers will like Scrapdoodle, and if the trip has really been rough: Healthy Back Store and perhaps, Massage Envy. Dozens of restaurants of all flavors can be found. *i* shopatcentralpark.com

Exit 130B: Fun-Land – If your seat-mates are driving you crazy in the car, kids from 3 to 93 will enjoy this indoor/outdoor amusement area located in Central Park Mall, from its indoor roller coaster right up to the challenge of a rock climbing wall. There's  laser tag, bumper cars, a soft play area and over 100 arcade games (not for those sensitive to noise) where you can win coupons and redeem them for prizes. Outside, in decent weather there's go karts, bumper boats, miniature golf and batting cages. Parents can retire to the cafe and the simple delight of funnel cakes and slushies. Okay, we'll admit that we had fun here and spent far too long choosing our silly prizes (candy, slinky, rings, hair clips, pencils). ◕ Sun-Th 12-9, F 12-11, S 10-11. 1351 Central Park Blvd. *i* centralparkfunland.com ☎ 540-785-6700.

Exit 126B>: Spotsylvania County Visitors' Center – Ask your questions about the area, Fredericksburg, Stafford (or the rest of Virginia), have them go on the net for you, use the clean restrooms, pick up flyers, motel coupon booklets and see a 10-min video. ◕ Daily 9-5. ☞ Rte 1 S for 1/2 mi. to Southpoint Pkwy. LT, office is on LHS at 4704 Southpoint Pkwy *i* www.spotsylvania.va.us ☎ 877-515-6197 or 504-507-7090 or 540-891-8687.

Exit 126: Spotsylvania Towne Center – Anchors here are Macy's, Costco, Sears, JC Penney, Belk, and Dick's Sporting Goods. There are no less than 17 jewelry stores and then fun Dippin' Dots ice cream treats. How about a Guitar Center for music in the car, Michael's (arts & crafts), Speedway Collectibles, Lids, Wiggle Worms and Victoria's Secret for fun? ◕ M-Sat 10-9:30, Sun 11-6. 137 Spotsylvania Mall. *i* spotsylvaniamall.com ☎ 540-786-6660.

Mile 108 Southbound: Petersburg Area Information Center – In the rest area you will find this quick (unmanned) pit stop to pick up information about the area. Don't forget to look for your booklets with motel discounts. It's a good time to use rest rooms, and there's a picnic area.

Exit 104A: Caroline County Visitor Center – This spanking new center is worth a stop just to see the 14,000,000-year-old 28 ft. eobalaenoptera harrisoni whale fossil suspended in the window - even creepier lit up at night. If you need it, they will call motels for you (or you can use the coupon booklets found here), offer wi-fi, ATM, vending machines and a screen with

MAP PG 37-38

Civil War FREEbies

For battle buffs, the Civil War can keep you interested for a lifetime. The state of VA feeds your need by offering a FREE package all about the different civil war trails throughout the state. These colorful brochures cover the marches chronologically, then go on to write about the battles, the leaders, the technology used, supply and logistics, and even acknowledging the black troops and civilians involved. *i* civilwartraveler.com/virginia ☎ 888-Civil War.

weather info. Hey, there's FREE postcards and brand new clean restrooms. The gift shop features county artists: woven purses, ceramics, paintings, metal art, jewelry, aprons and tea towels, cornbread, gingerbread or sweet potato biscuit mixes, and a bit of collectibles. ☻ Sun-Fri 10-5, Sat 9-5. 23724 Rogers Clark Blvd. *i* visitcaroline.com ☎ 804-633-3490.

Exit 104A>: Russell Stover Candies Factory Outlet – What heaven: discount chocolate! Ask for a FREE taste of a "tile" when you walk in to whet your appetite. There are first quality boxes (Whitman Samplers, Truffle Assortment, Cherry Cordials), intermediates (left wall) and the "seconds" (left front aisle), mostly in gray boxes or white bags. These have only slight imperfections or are overstocks - believe us, they taste exactly the same as the firsts. You can even buy just your favorite ones (raspberry parfaits, coconut creams, nut delights) without having to rummage though a whole assorted box.

Look on the right wall for sugar free, low carb, net carb, Weight Watchers, holiday boxes and small packs for car snacks. The kids' (any age) corner sports pop rocks, Starburst, jaw breakers, Sour Patch, Skittles and a Jelly Belly wall (36 flavors). The staff will happily create-a-gift with

your personal selections. Room for RV parking. Yum! (Another fancier location - ice cream parlor, candy kitchen and little corner in the right back for sale boxes - at Exit 98, Santee, SC). ☻ M-S 10-5, Sun 12-5. ☞ 1.1 mi. E on Rte 207, RT on Enterprise Pkwy (in the Carmel Church business park),

LT at intersection. 23361 Business Center Court. *i* russellstover.com ☎ 804-448-1169.

Exit 98: All Faith's Chapel – Sitting incongruously on the side of a truck stop, this miniature little white steepled church is always open. With four underutilized little pews ready for you, and the bible open on a pulpit, you can stop, rest and think holy thoughts.

Exit 92>: Ashland/Hanover Visitor Center/Train Station – Built in 1923 by the Richmond Fredericksburg and Potomac RR by W. Duncan Lee, it's worth a mention for its embarrassing historical value. Still functioning as an Amtrak train stop, its divided floor plan is a reminder of the segregated South. There were separate ticket windows, waiting areas, restrooms and water fountain for whites and African Americans. An original baggage cart sits outside and 3 three of the original benches are here. The station has been used as a set for the filming of the movie "Major Payne" and the television series "Legacy". A sign outside explains Ashland's role during the Civil War. ☻ Daily 9-5. ☞ W. along England St (Rte 54) 1 1/4 mi. til train tracks, RT to station. *i* town.ashland.va.us ☎ 800-897-1479 or 804-752-6766.

Exit 92>: Ashland Walk – Go to the Visitor Center (#1 on the map and see story) and pick up the walking tour map of 22 buildings that run on both sides of the train tracks - there is no wrong side of the tracks in this town. The exciting part of a stroll is that if you are here at least an

hour, you will be within 12 feet of a real live moving train. Highlights of your walk might include Traintown Toy & Hobby (#4), which appropriately sells toy trains. And if you yearn for the

olden days, Cross Brothers General Store (#5) has been open since 1912 and is still run by someone in the Hawthorne/Willis families (who knows when someone is infirm and delivers to their door). Notice the Henry Clay Inn (#2), a Georgian Revival B&B - rest your weary bones in the rocking chairs on the porch. By now you should be hungry, so head over to Homemade by Suzanne (#3) or Ashland Coffee & Tea (#6) (see stories). *i* town.ashland.va.us

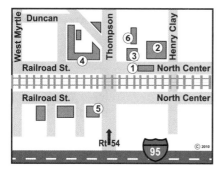

Exit 92>: Henry Clay Inn – Take your mind off the hurried pace of your drive at this Georgian Revival (re-built in 1992) Inn. Most of the 14 bedrooms sport doors to a porch. The rooms are dressed with antiques, and have sleigh, pencil post, canopy, acorn post and cannonball beds, and there's a quiet central sitting room with books and games.

Downstairs you can sit on the rocking chairs and become a trainspotter.

There's a gift shop with train items and works by local artists.

Henry Clay was an orator and statesman who was born here in Hanover County in 1777. He was known as "the Great Compromiser", and was a candidate for President in 1824, 1832 and 1844. ☞ head W (Rte 54) for 1 1/4 mi., RT and inn is facing the Vis. Ctr in the train station (#2 on the map). 114 N. Railroad Ave. *i* henryclayinn.com ☎ 804-798-3100.

Exit 92>: Homemades by Suzanne – Here's a perfect spot to pick up the fixings for a picnic lunch which you could eat inside, or better yet outside, so you can watch the trains go by. Everything, even the bread and rolls, is made from scratch. You could stoke up on vegetable soup or have one of 18 salads (country ham, blackeyed pea, seafood, Waldorf, chicken, succotash, angel hair pasta), quiches or crab cakes. and please wash them down with strawberry lemonade. Save room for authentic chess pie in chocolate (brownie lovers will adore this one) or lemon, Anne's cream puff (save one for Sandra), pecan pie or key lime cookie. Don't despair, you can taste them all, since they are sold by the piece. ◗ M-F 9-2, Sat 9-3. 102 N. Railroad Ave. (#3 on map). *i* homemades bysuzanne.com ☎ 804-798-8331.

Exit 92>: Ashland Coffee & Tea – There are times when you need a real cup of coffee. Not only can you find that here, but also tea and munchies (bagels, quesadillas, chicken chile, panini, desserts), comfy couches to stretch out on, books to read (and swap), games to play and music on Tues-Sun nights. Coffee can be as fun as: pufferbelly (a toasted toffee hazelnut latte) to Celtic caboose (an Irish cream cappuccino), racehorse latte (5 shots), or an espresso shake. Other varieties include: Southern pecan, margogype, estate coffees and there's a blend your own

MAP PG 38-39

tea bar: Chai, Japanese Sencha, Sunshine Roobos and more. 100 N. Railroad Ave. (#6 on the map). ☀ M 7am-7:30, T-Sat 7-9, Sun 8-3. *i* ashlandcoffeeandtea.com ☎ 804-798-1702.

One House to Go, please

Who would've thought that back in 1908-1940 Sears, Roebuck and Co. was selling a mail order catalog of blueprints, and even the building materials for houses, called "Book of Modern Homes and Building Plans". At 203 Berkley St. you can see an example of "The Maytown", thought to have

been assembled here in 1918. It sports most of its original ornamental features, including a corner turret with decorative overhang, full front porch, beveled plate glass in the front door and a bay window with patterned panes. Since the original house did not have running water, the pump still sits in the back yard.

Virginia Shelton, who lives here, is older than the house at 105 years, still does her own cooking and cleaning and drove until she was 99.

NEW! **Exit 86A:** Sansbury's Bakery – Sometimes a wrong turn turns into a right story. We made a u-turn at the home of the "World's Best Cheesecake", stopped the car and investigated. Best news is that you can buy it by the slice

for the car ($1.99): chocolate chip, brownie nut, marble, praline, caramel pecan, or whole cakes: key lime,

Reese's, Snicker's, cookies 'n cream, pb&j, or Sandra's hometown fave: NY style. A 4-pack of chocolate lava cake is $10.99 and

you can combine that with some ice cream from the freezer. There's also tubs of cookie dough to bake at home. 10440 Leadbetter Rd. ☀ M-F 8-5, Sat 8-4. *i* worldsbestcheesecake.com ☎ 804-550-7660.

Exit 83B>: Lewis Ginter Botanical Garden – This is an oasis on a driving trip - 82 magnificent acres which started life as Powhatan hunting grounds and was at one time owned by patriot Patrick Henry. In 1884, Lewis Ginter, who was orphaned at 17 and later became a millionaire from tobacco and real estate, developed a Club House here for Richmond bicyclists. His niece, Grace Arents, developed the gardens, and her original design is still here. There are more kinds of gardens than we ever knew existed: four season's, heal-

ing, sunken, Asian, Rose, wetland, perennial, conifer and a children's garden (with a treehouse and an activity center). For walkers, there's a "walk on the wild side" and a woodland walk and a bird trail, and as if all that wasn't enough, there's a huge lush indoor conservatory with exotic and unusual plants from around the world. You can stop for a bite at the pretty cafe or Robins Tea House overlooking a lake. Do leave some time and money for the extensive gift shop. ☀ Daily 9-5. ☞ W one block on E. Parham Rd (Rte 73), LT on Brook Rd (Rte 1) for .9 mi., RT at Lakeside Ave. 3/4 mi. to 1800 Lakeside Ave. *i* lewisginter.org ☎ 804-262-9887.

Exit 83: River City Diner – For a slice of the 50's, this diner fits the bill, with a juke box, Howdy Doody on the wall, a TV airing the Dick Van Dyke Show, and stools at a counter for your milkshakes (chocolate peanut butter, pineapple).

They're known for breakfast all day (eggs on horseback or seafood omelet with crab, shrimp, tomatoes, scallions and 2 cheeses, or banana pecan pancakes). You can build-your-own burgers, try fabulous chili or chow down on the signature Rochester Garbage plate: hot dogs, chili, cheese, baked beans, home fries, cole slaw and potato salad, but you can also enjoy salads, Mom's meatloaf with 15 sides to choose from and fried chicken salad (now that's the way to eat salad!). They offer a "cruise 'n carry-out" service - check out the menu online and order from an exit away. ◑ Sun-T 6:30-9, W&Th 6:30-10, F&S 6:30-11. 803 E. Parham Rd. (Other location ndear I-95 in Richmond: 7 N.17th St. 514-644-9418) *i* rivercitydiner.com ☎ 804-266-1500.

Exit 78: Buz and Ned's – It took a NYC guy to literally work his way thru kitchens in BBQ havens in Texas, Kansas City, Memphis, and Lexington KY, and then merge all that expertise with Ned's 150-year old family recipe into his own scrumptious BBQ. For the past 16 years, his ribs

(baby back, spare or beef) have been a hit, there's hearty Brunswick stew (chock full of corn, string beans, carrots, and potatoes), killer chili, Sandra's favorite: beef brisket and you-could-eat-alone sides of chunky smokey baked beans, cukes & onions, sweet potato fries and, of course, hush puppies. Wash 'em down with root beer and Cheerwine. ◑ M-Th 11-8:30, F&S 11-9:30, Sun 12-8 (summer: daily closes 1 hr later). 1119 N Boulevard. (Other location: Exit 83>: 8205 W.Broad St ☎ 804-346-4BBQ (4227) *i* buzandneds.com ☎ 804-355-6055.

Exit 78>: Science Museum of Virginia – Who would ever think you could watch rats play basketball right on I-95? We did and you can. Though this building was a grand old rail station, the exhibit area is not overwhelming and it can be an educational break. You can check how the drive is affecting your blood pressure, see a visual of your heart beat, or calm down watching fish in aquariums or snakes and lizards slither. Wanna see a tarantula up close?

In Newton in Space you can try a zero gravity ride and try a segway. At the building station, little ones can build an arch and actually walk on it. Outside there's an aluminaut, an aluminum submarine, while inside you can watch an Imax movie or the planetarium. Besides a gift shop, there's Starbucks in the Cafe Portico. ◑ (Sept-May) T-Sat 9:30-5, Sun 11:30-5; (May-Sept) M-Sat, 9:30-7, Sun 11:30-5. 2500 W. Broad St. *i* smv.org ☎ 800-659-1727 or 804-864-1400.

MAP PG 39

Exit 78>: Maymont – This park, mansion, children's farm and nature center, with 13 aquariums showcasing the James River, is the most visited site in Richmond. The mansion remains just as Major Dooley (a lawyer and railroad baron who married Sallee Dooley) left it. Since they had no children, they spent all their time and money on this grand home, built in 1893 with indoor plumbing (even a servant's toilet), electricity (borrowed from the streetcars nearby!) and an immense Tiffany window. An excellent exhibit on the lower level explains how the servants (with input and video from descendents of the staff) ran a house like this. Add to this the amazing gardens (Japanese with 45' waterfall, Italian, herb, ornamental lawn, arboretum) an aviary, carriage house, foxes, deer, gift shop and tram rides, make this an interesting stop for everyone. FREE (with suggested donation). ☞ S on N Boulevard through town for 2 1/4 mi to its end, RT and curve left onto Trafford Rd and follow it around the lake to 2201 Shields Lake Dr. ◑ Daily 10-5 for grounds, wildlife & visitor center, T-Sun 10-5 for house, nature center, farm, carriage rides. *i* maymont.org ☎ 804-358-7166.

NEW! Exit 78: Kitchen 64 – This successful restaurant family really knows how to keep their customers: the food is so scrumptious and plentiful that you'll have enough for lunch tomorrow - and the next day. The boisterous crowd may start with the shrimp and gorgonzola in a garlic cream sauce or the crab cake bruschetta, and go on to the Southern fried chicken salad or the lamb with spinach greens, roasted peppers, onions and dried cranberries, the fish tacos, or head for one of the 17 sandwiches with sweet potato fries. You can build-a-burger or a pizza. A hugely popular main is the roasted chicken, but you can get a leg of lamb, miso salmon or even the home run - meatballs with spaghetti. How about fried green tomato lasagna? We loved the chicken penne with mushrooms, tomatoes, pancetta, peas, caramelized onions in a roasted garlic Parmesan cream sauce. For breakfast, there's grits with veggies and cheese, crispy potato cakes or crab cakes eggs benedict. 3336 N. Boulevard. ◑ M-Th 11-11,

F 11-12am, Sat 9:30-12am, Sun 9:30-11pm. *i* kitchen64.com ☎ 804-358-0064.

Soul Searching

Exit 76>: Hollywood Cemetery in Richmond has the largest pyramid in the United States. If you visit  it, you can also check out the graves of 2 US presidents (James Monroe and John Tyler), Confederate Pres. Jefferson Davis and thousands of Civil War soldiers. Designed in 1847 as a garden-style cemetery, it has paths through hills and valleys and offers a fabulous view of the James River. ◑ Daily 8-6 FREE ($1 map in office M-F til 4:30). 412 S. Cherry St. *i* hollywoodcemetery.org ☎ 804-648-8501.

Exit 75>: Richmond Visitor Center – A quick drive off the exit will get you into Richmond, where you can get all the info you need right inside the Convention Center, which has free visitor's parking spots at  the curb. Ask about the wow segway tours of the city - we loved them (804-343-1850). There's a gift shop with Virginia inspired offerings and, of course, there's clean bathrooms. ◑ Daily 9-5; Summer 9-6. 405 North 3rd St. *i* visit.richmond.com ☎ 1-888-RICHMOND or 804-783-7450.

Fall of Richmond

Exit 74: Richmond was the capitol of the Confederacy during the Civil War. On April 2, 1865, Pres. Jefferson Davis was attending services at St. Paul's Episcopal Church when a courier handed him a note. Gen. Robert E. Lee was telling him to evac-

Did He Get Liberty or Death?

Exit 74C>: St. John's Church – We know the famous words "I know not what course others may take; but as for me, give me liberty or give me death!", which were uttered by Patrick Henry and lit the fires of revolution in 1775. St. John's Church in Richmond was the site of the clandestine 2nd Virginia Convention, where he called his comrades (Benjamin Harrison, Thomas Jefferson, Richard Henry Lee, Edmund Pendelton, Peyton Randolph, George Washington, George Wythe and others) to arms in a rousing speech. Re-enactments of the convention are held on Sundays at 2 pm (tickets at 1pm) from Memorial Day to Labor Day (FREE). Buried in the graveyard are one signer of the Declaration of Independence, George Wythe, and Edgar Allen Poe's mom, Elizabeth Arnold Poe. So, did Patrick Henry get liberty or death?

◐ M-S 10-3:30 Sun 12-3:30. 2401 E. Broad St.
𝑖 historicstjohnschurch.org ☎ 804 648 5015.

Answer : Liberty

uate the government immediately. Davis quietly put on his overcoat, and slipped out to find his cabinet and plan the withdrawal. While the Confederate army set fire to the tobacco and cotton warehouses and burned the bridges behind them, the streets filled with drunken looting mobs. The fire spread, exploding an arsenal and powder magazine, and the city burned through the night. By 8 am, the Northern blue-coats filed into the ruined capitol.

Exit 74C: Virginia State Capitol – This imposing Classical Revival capitol was built in 1788, designed by Thomas Jefferson (see his builder's model

in the Jefferson room), who based it on Maison Caree in Nimes, France. The statue of George Washington standing under the hidden dome is by Jean-Antoine Houdon, and is the only one he posed for - including having done a life mask for it. It is life size (all 6'2 1/2", 210 lbs of him) and made of Italian Carrera marble. If you look closely you can see he is missing 2 buttons from his vest (oh Martha!). Before the Civil War, Robert E Lee was asked by both the North and the South to lead their forces. He supposedly stood in the rotunda, having to make peace with this statue of his hero, George Washington, before walking the paces into the legislature and declaring that he could never take a sword against his fellow Virginians. ◐ M-Sat 8-5, Sun 1-4. FREE tours. 𝑖 virginiacapitol.gov ☎ 804- 698-1788.

Exit 62>: Half Way House – "Go down 3 steps and back 3 centuries in time" to this 1760 stagecoach stop located 1/2 way between Richmond and Petersburg. With the kitchen still in the back outbuilding and the bathrooms "outside", you can really imagine George Washington, Thomas Jefferson, Patrick Henry, Lafayette and Gen. Robert E. Lee dining here in this low-ceilinged, dim, stone-walled room. But the pricey food you will enjoy is far better

MAP PG 39-40

than the fare they ever ate: black Angus tenderloin, salmon picatta (artichoke hearts and capers), Cajun pasta, scallops au gratin, and for lunch perhaps chicken pie, pot roast or fried chicken salad

(smoked bacon, spiced pecans, onions, roasted red peppers and pecan pie. ◑ M-F 11:30-2, dinner 5:30-9pm daily. ☞ W on 288 a short 1/4 mi, N on US 301 1/2 mi to 10,301 Jefferson Davis Highway. *i* halfwayhouserestaurant.com ☎ 804-275-1760.

Exit 54: Southpark Mall – There is a huge circular access road surrounding this mall (Dillard's, JCPenney, Sears, Macy's) with additional satellite shopping. For your vacation you might need the Beach Reads, Lids, Game Stop, Shoe City, and maybe even Victoria's Secret. For fun, Paint & Play, Spencer Gifts, and for the road - Coffee Beanery. ◑ M-Sat 10-9, Sun 12-6. *i* southparkmall.com ☎ 804-526-3900.

Exit 52: The Crater – On June 25, 1864 Union soldiers of the 48th PA volunteers, mostly coal miners, began digging a 511 ft. tunnel toward a Confederate fort at Pegram's (or Elliott's) Salient. It took a month to dig, and the plan was to explode 4 tons of gunpowder under the area, creating a large gap in their defense line, then pouring troops through the hole. On July 30 at 4:45 am the mine was detonated, and it created a crater about 170 ft. long, 60 ft. wide and 30 ft. deep. The Union troops rushed forward into the tunnel, instead of going around it. They got stuck in it because of the high walls created at the end, and Confederate troops inflicted more than 4,000 Federal casualties. Major Houghton

of the 14th NY Heavy Artillery reported that the hole was "filled with dust, great blocks of clay, guns, broken carriages, projecting timbers and men buried in various ways - some up to their necks, others to their waists, and some only with their feet and legs protruding from the earth.", and then "blood was streaming down the sides of the crater to the bottom, where it gathered in pools for a long time before being absorbed by the hard red clay." The crater can still be seen at the Petersburg National Bat-

tlefield through short trails or a 4-mile drive. ◑ grounds: 8-dusk, Vis Ctr: 9-5. 1539 Hickory Hill Rd. *i* nps.gov/pete ☎ 804-732-3531 X200

Exit 52>: Old Blandford Church – Built in 1735 in a parish founded by Peter Jefferson (Thomas' father!), it is one of only 6 churches in the US with a full set of 15 Tiffany windows. During the siege of Petersburg it was used as a Confederate hospital, and in 1901 it became a Confederate memorial to the 30,000 soldiers buried there in the 189 acres of cemetery. Each Confederate state donated money for one of the windows representing the 12 apostles, which were personally and magnificently designed and installed by Louis Comfort Tiffany; the one of St. Peter he handcrafted himself. The windows glow with light no matter what time of day, and are rich in 3-dimensional colors, fabrics, nature

and meaning. ◐ M-Sat 10-5, Sun 1-5 (Oct-Mar closed M, Jan-Mar T 1-5). 111 Rochelle La. in Blandford Cemetery. *i* petersburg-va.org/tourism/blandford.htm ☎ 804-733-2396.

Exit 52>: Siege Museum – Imagine a war happening all around you in your own city. In this Greek Revival building (which once was a commodities market), follow the circular wooden-floored room and balcony to see how the people of Petersburg coped. Ladies used their hooped skirts to hide supplies which they carried to the fields to their loved ones, slaves delivered letters, "coffee" was made from corn, and "tea" was blackberry leaves, while a chicken cost $50. Notice the bible which sat in a pocket over a man's heart and saved his life, the "office" wagon with its outside desk and pigeon holes, and there's General Lee on his favorite horse "Traveller". Children of all ages can enjoy the scavenger hunt - pick up a FREE guide at the front desk. ◐ Daily 10-5. 15 W. Bank St. *i* petersburg-va.org/tourism/siege.htm ☎ 804-733-2404.

Exit 52S or 50D N>: The Brickhouse Run – Why not stop at a British-style pub (with a British-style couple as owners) stashed in an 18th century building on a cobblestone street, and get your fill of classic shepherd's pie (with traditional ground lamb), bangers and mash (with local Surry sausages and Merlot onion gravy - yum!) and fish and chips (of course). American favorites might be a ham steak, duck breast, gnocchi or prime rib. Besides pub brews, there's a Brit treat - Pimm's Cup, served in a traditional style with fruits and cucumbers. Do not leave without tasting the chocolate pot dessert, which is like a silky brownie pudding. ◐ lunch W-Sat 11-2:30, dinner T-Th 5-9, F& S 5-10. 409 Cockade Alley *i* brickhouserun.com ☎ 804-862-1815.

Exit 52>: La Villa Romaine – While they lived in Europe, Ken and Francois Roy collected 18 crates-worth of furniture and collectibles for the moment when they would open this B&B. The 1856 home has 4 sumptuous guest rooms (Louis XVI, Renaissance, etc.) which are so  bedecked that you can't find a surface to put your glasses down. Check out their murder mystery weekends. 29 S. Market St. *i* lavillaromaineva.com ☎ 800-243-0860 or 804-861-2285.

IN A NUTSHELL

Peanuts probably originated in S. America, but took the long way round to get here. Early Spanish explorers discovered them there, and learning of their versatility, carried them back to Europe. Other traders took the peanuts to Africa and Asia. From Africa they arrived back  here on slave ships. During the 1700's and 1800's there was only a small amount of commercial peanut farming, because the peanut was regarded as food for the poor (as they were found mostly around slave cabins), and the growing and harvesting techniques were slow and difficult. There is a mention of them being harvested commercially in 1844 in Sussex County, VA. Up to the Civil War, the peanut remained a regional Southern food.

MAP PG 41

Exit 47: The King's Highway (King's Road, Post Road) – This section of I-95 follows one of the first highways in the US, which started in New England and went to Charleston, SC and then on through GA and FL. It started out as an Indian trail called the Potomac Trail, since it followed the course of the Potomac River. Try to imagine this as a wide dirt road, often muddy, strewn with tree stumps and boulders. Thomas Jefferson wrote that the fastest he could traverse it was at 3 miles per hour. The Highway was the link between all the colonies, which gave them a sense of unity. It enabled the movement of mail, newspapers and goods from one end of the New World to the other. It connected with the Boston Post Road in the North - see the story in CT, Exit 39.

Its name was derived from the 18th century order by King George I to build a road "to be used for the subjects of said Lord and the King with their horses and carriages to go and return at their will and pleasure".

Mile 36 Northbound: Petersburg Area Information Center – In the rest area you will find this quick pit stop to ask the friendly staff for information about the area and Virginia. Don't forget to pick up the booklets with motel discounts. It's a good time to use rest rooms, walk your pets and you can picnic here. ◗ Daily 9-5. ☎ 434-246-2145.

Exit 8>: Anderson's Pharmacy – The bags of pork rinds and gingerbread cookies you see when you enter obscure the lunch counter and the pharmacy in the back, which haven't changed a bit since Spencer Anderson took over here. People come in just for the chicken salad, but it's probably Norma Jean's sassy comments to her regulars (Hollywood, Scooter, Droopy, Patsy, Eddie in the photo) that entertain y'all. Daily specials like chicken 'n dumplings, fried bologna sandwich, country ham with navy beans,  country-style burgers and lemon pound cake round out the fare. ☞ just follow US 301 North off the exit for 1.5 mi to 334 S. Main St. ◗ M-F 7-2, Sat 7-11; pharmacy M-F 8-6, Sat 8-12. ☎ 434-634-3131.

Exit 4: The Good Earth Peanut Company – Sitting right on a 1650's Tuscarora Indian trail which is now a railroad junction, in an old time (circa 1854) general store, this family business roasts and sells peanuts. Lindsey and Scott Vincent go beyond the ordinary nut to sell cashew brittle, wasabi flavored peas and almonds, nut berry thrill, diet trail mix, chocolate covered peanut brittle (Sandra's favorite) and maple covered nuts, as well as pecans like key lime ones (we're addicted to the butter toasted pecans in our salads). Sweet treats are amongst the 31 offered  (you can taste any): we'll take the dark chocolate covered cherries and natural peanut butter. A bit of groceries still line the walls, like Shawnee Spring preserves and Virginia hams. ◗ M-F 8-6, Sat 9-4. 5334 Skippers Rd. ☞ 1 mi E on 629, cross RR track. *i* goodearthpeanuts.com ☎ 800-643-1695 or 434-634-2204.

Mile 1 Northbound: Virginia Welcome Center – It always pays to stop off at these centers for clean bathrooms, to walk a pet, have a picnic and to pick up the booklets with motel discounts as well as flyers from places around the State. You can see a screen with traffic travel time, and don't forget to chat with the friendly and helpful staff who can answer many questions, including help with motels or car trouble. ☀ Daily 8:30-5. ☎ 434-634-4113.

NORTH CAROLINA

Mile 181 Southbound: North Carolina Welcome Center – Rest a bit in front of the crackling fireplace, check out the weather station or attractions on the internet. Pick up your booklets of motel discount coupons, and this is a good moment to take advantage of clean bathrooms, to walk your pet, have a picnic or ask the friendly staff for help with NC sites, motels or even car problems. ☀ Daily 8-5. ☎ 252 537-3365.

Exit 173: Halifax County (Roanoke Rapids) Visitor's Center – The friendly staff will answer your questions and even hand you a free bag of peanuts. There's motel coupons, a pet walk, RV parking, clean bathrooms, wi-fi, and they will help with motels, car trouble or mailing letters. 260 Premier Blvd. in the mall on W side of I-95. ☀ M-F 9-5, (June-Aug Sat 10-3). *i* visithalifax.com ☎ 800-522-4282 or 252-535-1687.

Exit 173: New China Restaurant – Located in the Plaza Shopping Center W of the exit, this buffet-style mostly Cantonese restaurant is perfect when you want a fast lunch or supper on the road.

A real deal is the 6 lunch specials-to-go for as little as $3.75 (11-2:30 p.m.), which include rice and egg roll. Menu dishes include ginger prawns, lake tung ting shrimp marinated in a wine sauce, hunan chicken and beef in 2 sauces. ☀ Lunch buffet 11-4, Dinner Sun-Th 4-9:30, F & S 11-10. 1556 Julian Allsbrook Hwy. ☎ 252-535-2818.

Exit 173: Ralph's Barbecue – We're up to the 3rd generation of Ralph Woodruff's family (granddaughter Kim) running this busy restaurant, which uses 5,000 lbs a week of selected pork. The lunch and supper buffets are a deal, but you can also order from

the menu. Their NC dry-smoked style bbq is made daily and is served pulled and minced (vinegar, crushed red peppers, sugar, salt), along with delicious Brunswick stew, fried chicken, fluffy hush puppies, coleslaw, potato salad and collard greens. Locals wash it down with a Mr. Pibb. If you don't have time to stop, at least do takeout; we can't pass by without a Brunswick

Halifax Resolves – In the Spring of 1776, NC representatives convened near here, far enough away from the British ships gathering on the coast. Cornelius Harnett headed the committee "to take into consideration the usurpations and violences attempted and committed by the King and Parliament of Great Britain against America". The group took 3 days, and finally unanimously declared on April 12, 1776, "that the delegates for this Colony in the Continental Congress be impowered to concur with the delegates of the other Colonies in declaring Independency, and forming foreign alliances...". These bold colonists in NC were America's first to call for independence, 3 months before the Declaration of Independence. April 12th is celebrated as Halifax Day, with people in period costumes doing Colonial activities, re-enactments of encampments, military drills, etc.

MAP PG 42-44

stew fix. ◐ Daily 9-8:30. 1400 Julian Allsbrook Hwy (Rte 158). FB: ralphs-barbeque ☎ 252-536-2102.

Exit 173>: Roanoke Canal Museum and Trail – To get past what the Native Americans called Moratuck, or the "river of death", the colonists built a canal. Even Patrick Henry, in 1783, wrote that they needed "proposed internal improvements of Roanoke River navigation". This tiny museum explains how, without modern machinery, 2,000 lb. stones were placed, and how 16,000 lbs of tobacco or cotton were moved in flat bottom "bat-

teaus". The canal enjoyed a second life as a water power source for the 5 mills nearby (Rosemary, Westpoint Stevens, Patterson, etc.). For a scenic walk along the canal, you can start at the museum (go there or to the Halifax Visitor Center to pick up the Canal Trail brochure), noticing culverts, dams, ducks, locks, hawks, herons, foxes, ponds, an aqueduct and water falls. ◐ T-Sat 9-4. 📍 E on Rte 158 for 2.3 mi, RT on Roanoke Ave for 2.8 mi to 15 Jackson St. Ext. *i* roanokecanal.com ☎ 252-537-2769.

NEW! **Exit 138>:** Nash County (Rocky Mount) Visitors Bureau – Ask the friendly staff if you need to find a motel in the area and they will give you a list, help you find one close to where you're going and then offer you a phone to call. If you have car trouble, they know where to point you. You can use wi-fi here, and there's an ATM nearby. Pets can have a nice walk outside. Here a first: after dark, there's a screen you can see with

info on attractions, activities and weather reports. ◐ M-F 10-6. 107 Gateway Blvd. *i* rockymounttravel.com ☎ 800-849-6825 or 252-972-5080.

NEW! **Exit 138>:** City Lake Park – You can take a nice walk or have a picnic in this park which is only ? miles straight off the exit. In the middle of the small park is a pretty man-made lake (a 1933 WPA project) with a spraying fountain, gazebo, observation platforms and often geese and ducks. 📍 2.4 mi E on US 64 to BUS 64 Exit (Sunset Ave,), then 1.4 mi to Lake on right.

Exit 138>: Gardner's Barbecue 'n' Chicken – Okay we'll admit it, we ate fried gizzards and actually liked them. But if you're not game, you can have the fried

chicken, fried fish, chicken 'n collards and of course, the yummy barbecue with some of the 15 sides - collards, yams, butter beans, slaw, squash, etc. Don't miss the little corn sticks or the hush puppies. You can take out for a car picnic.

NEW! Some might ask why NC towns have such odd names. But Tar Heel folks would probably respond, "Why not?", especially the residents of Whynot, a small town in Southern Randolph County. The moniker is said to be the last resort of early residents, who finally put an end to a lengthy discussion about why not to call the place this or that. A man asked "Why not name the town Whynot and let's go home?".

◗ Sun-Th 11-9, F & S 11-9:30. ☞ Rte 64 E for 3.4 mi. to US 301 Bypass Exit (N. Wesleyan Blvd). LT 1.4 mi. to 1331 N. Wesleyan Blvd. on RHS. ☎ 252-446-2983.

NEW! **Exit 121:** Wilson Visitors Bureau – Here's a brand spanking new center (for exits 121-116) that offers up a kiosk for you to call motels and B&B's in the area, or you can use the WiFi. They can assist with car problems, there's a mailbox, pet walk, and sure, there's clean bathrooms. If you arrive after dark they leave brochures outside the door. ◗ M-F 9-5. 4916 E. Hayes Pl. *i* wilson-nc.com ☎ 800-497-7398 or 252-243-8440.

NEW! **Exit 121>:** Jac's Grill – A diner with specific tastebuds will love the set-up of this menu. There's a list of meats (filet, chop, chicken breast), starches (loaded potato cake, roasted sweet potato, risotto), veggies (broccolini, hay stack onions, stir fry) and sauces (bearnaise, smoked gouda cream, roasted garlic) with

which you create your own plate. The chef has his own ideas too: salmon Oscar with lump crab meat, veal piccata or marsala, sesame ahi tuna with ginger mashed potatoes and wasabi cole slaw or shrimp and grits. Starters whet the appetite, like parmesan fried oysters over corn relish or buttermilk battered green tomatoes with sweet red onion chutney and a chipotle aoli buzz. ◗ lunch T-Fri 11:30-2; dinner, T-Sat 5:30-10. 2341 Madison Dr. *i* jacsgrill.com ☎ 252-291-9199.

NEW! **Exit 121>:** Whitehead Inn – Capture the feeling of the gracious South sitting on a veranda in one of the 4 historic homes set down here amongst majestic trees and gardens. The Main house was built in 1858, and was expanded in 1872 to what you see today, with its curved stair-

case, original hardware, etc. Expect a 3-course breakfast (ours was poached pear, quiche and lemon curd cake) and wine service on Fri and Sat nights. You can even request an in-room massage. Ahhhh. ☞ E. on Alt 264 (Raleigh Rd) 5.3 miles, LT on College Dr, RT on Nash to 600 W. Nash St. NE. *i* whiteheadinn.com ☎ 252-243-4447.

NEW! **Exit 121>:** Quince – In an unassuming shopping center, you would not expect this food oasis. The owner Peter Edgar graduated from CIA and has sailed the world cooking on yachts. He has anchored here serving up Southern bistro cooking with fabulous upmarket twists and textures:

fried quail on wild mushroom risotto with frizzled onions, pot roast manicotti, rib-eye with crunchy-on-the-outside mashed potatoes, sweet potato ravioli, hush puppy battered sausage - even the salad comes with grit croutons. Doug Hackney the pastry chef learned at his mother's knee in Wilson, and bakes with passion. ◗ M-F 11-2:30, M-Sat 5-10. 2801-3D Ward Blvd. *i* quincenc.com ☎ 252-237-6463.

Exit 116>: Whirligigs – Local folk artist Vollis Simpson's claim to fame are his welded painted moving sculptures. He has about 30 on his property (which you can visit, about 15 mi. away), but the downtown of Wilson is lucky to have 5 twirling and whirling about. Take a pit stop for a scavenger hunt to see if you can find them. If you want to see more, head to Hickory Grove Park near Kenan and Pine St. for 4 smaller ones. The State has recently announced plans for a Vollis Simpson Whirligig Park in the vicinity of Golds-

MAP PG 44-46

boro and Barnes St downtown, opening in Fall of 2012, with 32 full-sized and 57 smaller ones. If your timing is right, you may be able to see some of these being erected. *i* wilson-nc.com ☎ 800-497-7398.

Exit 107 or 119>: Parker's Barbecue – Finally, we found a barbecue where the pulled pork wasn't too vinegary for our Northern tastebuds. It paired beautifully with the original cole slaw, which seemed to have a bit of a relish flavor. The small combo we ordered (enough for the 2 of us to share) also included a fried chicken breast,
y u m m y
s t e w e d
potatoes
with a
paprika-

cayenne bite, spicy Brunswick stew and both hush puppies and corn sticks (we liked the puppies). There's tons of indoor and outdoor seating. ☞ Sbound: Exit 119, 5.1 mi S on US 264, LT north on US 301 to 2514 Highway 301 S. Nbound: Exit 107, US 301 N for 13.6 mi. ◐ Daily 9-8:30. ☎ 252-237-0972.

Exit 107: Tobacco Farm Life Museum – Stretch your legs walking around Iredell Lueazer Brown's farmhouse (bedspreads and rugs made out of used tobacco twine), kitchen, smokehouse, schoolhouse and tobacco barn, all of which have been furnished with period artifacts to re-create farmstead life revolving around the Golden Leaf of tobacco. Start with the video "Year in the Life of a Farmer", and then get a glimpse into the social and community life of tobacco farmers and their families.

Exhibits showcase a typical kitchen, toys, home remedies, school life, rural doctors, a store, the Tuscarora Indians (1st tobacco farmers), farm machinery, and a kids' hands-on gallery. ◐ T-S 9:30-5. ☞ Rte 301 N. thru town toward Lucama/Wilson for 1 1/4 mi. 709 Church St. *i* tobacco-farmlifemuseum.org ☎ 919-284-3431.

Exit 98>: Selma Uptown Antique District – Antique Alert! If you're a forager, you might as well take a nearby motel, because there's 100,000 sq. ft. of antiques within walking distance of each other. It is very easy to park the car on the street. and you can stop for a soda fountain treat at Creech drugstore when you finish. The shops (refer to the map): 1. Keepsake Corner, 110 N. Raiford St. 919-975-0407. 2. Reid's Country Sampler and Bishop's Emporium, 109 N. Raiford St. 919-965-7299. 3. Cheap Thrills Thrift Shop, 103 N. Raiford St. 919-965-4740. 4. Antique Wish 110 W. Anderson St. 919-202-4900. 5. The Treasury, 100 S. Raiford St. 919-965-5335. 6. His 'n Hers Antiques, 126 S. Raiford St. 919-202-8007. 7. Visual Pleasure, 107 S. Raiford St. 919-965-0030. 8. Precious Memories, 117 S. Raiford St. 919-202-4777. 9. Railroad Antiques, 107 E. Railroad St. (919) 965-9659. 10. TWM Antique Mall, 112 S. Pollock St. (US301). 888-494-8069 or 919-965-6699. 11. Flea Market: Selma Cotton Mills, 1105 W. Anderson St. 919-202-0794. 12. Larry's Antiques, 202 N. Raiford St. 919-796-9147.

While shopping for collectibles, you may want to stop for some refreshments at 13. Creech Drug Co. (#126) opened in 1939 by Joseph Arnold Sr. and is now run by Jr. (and sister Cindy). Their most famous drink is the cherry smash, made with maraschino cherry juice, crushed cherries and ice. But you can have a freshly squeezed orangeade or lemonade, coke float or malted or ice cream cone: moose tracks, cotton candy,

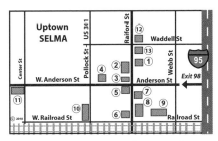

white house cherry, Reese's peanut butter, sugar free strawberry pecan. ◐ M-F 8:30-6, Sat 8:30-2 *i* johnstoncountync.org ☎ 919-965-2316.

Exit 97: Smithfield/Johnston County Visitor's Center – Located in a stately old home, this lovely center covers Exits 79-107. Stop in for the advice and clean restrooms as well as the flyers and motel coupon booklets. ◐ M-F 8:30-5. 1115 Industrial Park Dr. in front of the Carolina Premium Outlet Center. *i* johnstoncountync.org ☎ 800-441-7829 or 919-989-8687.

NEW! Exit 97: DeWayne's Home Garden Showplace – Would you believe this amazing gift and garden decor shop started out as a pumpkin stand? DeWayne persevered with his produce stand after having to move it 3 times,

and finally landed on this corner. After growing and growing, nowadays beyond the trolls, birdbaths, gargoyles, trellises, fountains, bears and benches outside, you can buy (inside) paper goods, soap, John Deere items, candles, flags, Crocs, Webkinz and don't miss Santa's Attic, the Christmas shop upstairs. ◐ M-Sat 9-6 (later in summer), Sun 10-6. 1575 Industrial Park Dr. *i* dewaynes.com ☎ 919-202-8471.

Exit 97: JR's Tobacco & Fragrance Outlet – Much more than a tobacco outlet, this store is a whole city block of bargains in perfume, books, makeup, garden ornaments, housewares, biker gear, jewelry, toys, Western wear, junk food, towels, casual clothes and a doll section, etc. Across the back of the store is one of the largest cigar emporiums you'll ever see. You can only exit the store through one door, so make sure to park near there. ◐ Daily 8-9. *i* jrselma.com ☎ 919-965-5055.

Exit 97: Carolina Premium Outlets – Eighty stores should be enough to keep you happy. Some names to help empty your bank account might be: Brooks Brothers Factory Store, Nike, Aeropostale, Le Creuset, OshKosh, Bose, Rockport, Lucky Brand Jeans and now Catherines Plus Sizes. On Tuesdays, there's 50+ shopper perks, and you can join their VIP club for discounts. ◐ M-S 10-9, Sun 11-7. *i* premiumoutlets.com/ carolina ☎ 919-989-8757.

And to think it all started with a kiss...

Exit 95>: Ava Gardner Museum – This little museum has film-worn costumes, 33 of Bert Pfeiffer's incredible paintings (hunt for little fun oddities - mouse, bird etc.), MGM publicity photos, movie posters, original scripts and a movie short all about this prolific movie star born right here near Smithfield.

The museum's collections were preserved due to a local fan, Tom Banks, who at 12 was kissed on the cheek by a young secretarial school girl. Two years later, in 1941, Banks saw a photo of Ava and learned her identity for the first time. In the years following, he and his wife began collecting Ava memorabilia from every imaginable source. In the early 80's Dr. Banks bought the house where Ava

lived from age 2 to 13 to exhibit his collection, and finally the museum moved to this location. ◐ M-S 9-5, Sun 2-5. ☞ W on E. Market St (Rt 70) 1 1/4 miles

MAP PG 46-47

to 325 E. Market St. *i* avagardner.org ☎ 919-934-5830.

Exit 95>: Gandolfo's NY Deli – It was so much fun to find a NYC-themed menu (Brooklyn Bridge, Damned Yankee, South Hampton, Holland Tunnel, Shea Stadium, Bronx Barbecue, NYPD bleu, Coney Island Gyro (yikes where's the hot dog?) in the middle of NC. The 60 creative sandwiches (and a couple of salads) are piled high onto oven fresh NY style hero or kaiser rolls or rye. There's bagel breakfasts, and if you are in a rush call for a box lunch to go. The wall is covered with authentic NYC baseball memorabilia - what else? ◑ M-S 7-9. 224 E. Market St. *i* gandolfosdeli.com ☎ 919-934-9100.

Exit 95>: Smithfield's Ham Shop – Cure Master Jesse Brown passed his techniques, inspired by the American colonists, onto his son Rufus, who runs this shop with its window view of the final "drying" process. Recognized  by many as the best ham in America, the store is filled with dry cure and salt cured smoked hams (bone-in, boneless, sliced, bacon, smoked turkeys). You can also buy Jake and Amos pickled watermelon rind or beets, Wind Willow dessert mixes (coconut cream pie), jams, sauces, cheeses and a cast iron bacon press - to keep bacon flat and crisp (who knew?). ◑ M-F 9-5. 204 N. Bright Leaf Blvd. *i* countrycuredhams.com ☎ 800-543-HAMS or 919-934-8054.

Exit 79: The Pound Cake Company – We heard rumblings for a few years about the Pound Cake lady (Jan Matthews-Hodges) and her blue ribbon awards (Best in Show NC State Fair), and we finally found her baking in a former school. We are drooling just remembering the taste (moist and buttery with

a slight crunchy sugar crust) of the pound cake we ate right out of the oven. Sure, you can buy the cake in lemon, orange, chocolate or the new sweet potato flavor, or shortbread cookies or brownies, but why bother when the original is to die for? The cake comes in 2 sizes - one just right for a snack in the car ($6.95). If you don't get it here, they are also available at Whole Foods, Earthfare, The Fresh Market and A Southern Season. ☞ West on W Main St for 3 blocks, LT on S Lee St to 310 S. Lee St. ◑ M-F 9-5:30, Sat 10-2. *i* thebestcake.com ☎ 919-894-8448.

Exit 73: Dunn Area Tourism Authority – Stop in for a candy, hot chocolate (winter) and friendly help for eats, sleeps, directions or car help for Dunn, Harnett County and even guidebooks for VA and SC. Yup, there's bathrooms and a screen for road/weather info. ◑ M-F 8:30-5. 103 E. Cumberland St. *i* dunntourism.org/ ☎ 910-892-3282.

Exit 73>: Simply Divine B & B – This gorgeous stately house, with its spacious simply decorated guest rooms (with new baths), just cries out for visitors to see its interior architectural details. The newby owners try to make you feel like a guest in  their own home. Hey, there's even an inground swimming pool in the warm months! *i* simplydivinebedandbreakfast.com ☎ 910-892-2296 or 910-897 3330.

Exit 73>: General William C. Lee Airborne Museum – This house was the home of the "Father of the Army Airborne", so the museum charts his personal life as well as the growth of Army 101st and 82nd airborne divisions. He was a relentless lobbyist to make them a formidable part of our military might.

At tank school in Versailles, France in the '30's he observed German military airborne experiments. He saw the promise of this, and started with test platoons doing parachute jumps (practiced from parachute towers in Hightstown, NJ). By August 1942, in 26 months, he shepherded the airborne from a test platoon of 50 men to 2 divisions of 8,300 men, and was in charge of the sky: parachutes, air landing battalions and eventually the glider units. He suffered a major heart attack on the eve of D-Day, and missed his chance to lead it. You have probably heard of his famous saying "the 101st has no history, but it has a rendezvous with destiny". ◑ M-F 8:30-5, Sat 11-4. 209 West Divine St. *i* generalleeairbornemuseum.org ☎ 910-892-1947.

Exit 73>: Yamato Steak and Seafood – This is the 2nd Asian restaurant from Koon Hai and Mieng Wang (Chinese down the street), so they really know how to keep local diners happy. The authentic Japanese menu cooked in an open kitchen covers the gamut from delish teriyaki chicken or hibachi steak to grilled shrimp or flounder, tempura and a large sushi menu with 64 choices on it. If you can't decide, they even have combination plates, and

the bento boxes are overflowing with value and taste (we especially loved the candied side carrots). ◑ lunch T-Sat 11:30-2:30, dinner T-Th 4:30-9:30, F&S 4:30-10, Sun 11:30-9. 1903A W. Cumberland *i* yamatoofdunn.com ☎ 910-892-3378.

Exit 71>: Averasboro Civil War Battlefield Museum & Chicora Cemetery – The cool thing about the museum of the Battle of Averasboro (Mar 15-16, 1865) is that it is inside one of the buildings which was used during the actual battle. The battle was fought on the plantation lands of the John Smith family, and two other buildings (which still stand) were used as hospitals, and blood stains are still apparent on the floor. The point of the fight (which succeeded) was to delay and dis-

rupt the advance of General Sherman's left wing. There's a gift shop. FREE. ◑ T-Sat 10-4, Sun 1-4. 3300 HIghway 82 South. *i* averasboro.com ☎ 910-891-5019.

Mile 54 Northbound: You can't miss this upside down tractor trailer lying on the side of the road looking very

much like a big dead bug with its wheels in the air. It's an ad for a truck towing school. *i* wreckmaster.com

Exit 52>: Cape Fear Botanical Garden – Sometimes you just gotta get off the road and smell the flowers. The 79 acres here give you the opportunity to choose paths through oaks, on a river, an urban trail or enjoy formal gardens, a children's garden or a camellia garden. You can also see farming tools and techniques of yesteryear which explain how Southern crops like tobacco and cotton were grown. We'll send you or the kids on a scavenger hunt: see if you can find the

MAP PG 48-49

crane in the lily pond and a hand water pump. ◖ M-Sat 10-5, Sun 12-5 (no Sun Dec-Feb). 536 N. Eastern Blvd. ☞ 3.5 mi W on Rte 24, RT on US 301 (N. Eastern Blvd.) for 1/8 mi. *i* capefearbg.org ☎ 910-486-0221.

Exit 52>: Fayetteville Convention & Visitors Bureau – Good for lazy motorists: located in a former bank, you can still use the drive-thru window to pick up your maps and ask questions about what to do or where to stay between exits 65-40. You do have to get out if you want to use the rest room, though. If you want to hear details about the city, tune the Visitor Information Network at 1680 AM. ◖ M-F 8-5. 245 Person St. (Other office: Fayetteville Area Transportation Museum, 325 Franklin S. ◖T-Sat 10-4. ☎ 910-323-9739 *i* visitfayettevillenc.com ☎ 888-98-HEROES or 910-483-5311.

NEW! **Exit 52>:** Soffe – Young girls love this line of casual athletic wear, but there's apparel for everyone else here too,

in sizes toddler 2T to 3XL. It's an outlet store, so pricing can go from $5 clothes piled in giant cardboard boxes to $16.99 on the racks. In solid colors, there's varsity pants, jackets, hoodies, T-shirts, sweatshirts, running shorts, windbreakers, cheer clothing, ranger shorts and more. There's another location at Exit 95 next door to JR (919-965-0062). ◖ M-Sat 9-5:30. 1005 Dunn Rd. *i* soffe.com ☎ 910-483-1776.

NEW! **Exit 52>:** Docks at the Capitol – Stuff about $10 of credit on a Docks card and let the fun begin. There's a bowling alley here, billiards, simulated games like a roller coaster, golf and flight pod (for 2 people), water guns, Deal or No Deal, skee ball and a sports bar. ◖ M&T 11-8, W, F, Sat 11-2, Th 11- 12, Sun 12-8. 126 Hay St. *i* docksatthecapitol.com ☎ 910-42DOCKS.

NEW! **Exit 52>:** The Climbing Place – Everyone 2 and up can have fun indoors climbing walls, roofs, corners, cracks, arches and slabs with help from the professionally trained staff, at NC's largest indoor climbing center. The wall configurations have been changing daily for the past 15 years. ◖ M-Th & Sat

10-10, F 10-11, Sun 12:30-6:30. ☞ West on Rte 27 (Grove St) 4.3 mi., LT on Ray Ave 5 blocks, RT on Russel St to 436 W. Russel St. *i* theclimbingplace.com ☎ 910-486-9638.

Exit 46>: Airborne & Special Operations Museum – The legends of those who jump into battle are covered through this museum in artifacts and film. The impressive 5-story glass walled lobby sets the stage with 2 fully deployed parachutes: a WW II era T-5 round chute and a modern MC-4 square chute. You learn the story of Lieutenant Bill Ryder, leader of the Test Platoon, who on August 16th, 1940 became the first American soldier to jump.

You can walk through a section of a C-47, sit on crates in a WW II Army briefing hut, learn about gliders that landed jeeps and bulldozers, see a famous UH-1 (Huey) helicopter from 'Nam days and a Desert Storm hide-site. Another exhibit traces the development of the Special Forces, or "Green Berets", from the summer of 1952 to today's

Operation Enduring Freedom. FREE museum (fee for movie or motion simulator).

◗ T-Sat 10-5, Sun 12-5. ☞ Nbound: Exit 46 Rte 87 N 6 mi., exit at Hay St. RT, museum on LHS at Bragg Blvd. Sbound: Exit 52B Rte 24, Grove St for 5 mi., becomes Rowan St., LT on Bragg Blvd. 100 Bragg Blvd. *i* asomf.org ☎ 910- 643-2766.

Exit 46: Museum of the Cape Fear Historical Complex – You can easily do this 3-part FREE complex in an hour. A fast slice of history is covered with civil war artifacts, an exhibit on the cotton industry, European settlement, pottery-making, slavery, a kid's touch corner and you'll find out all about plank roads. Try to find the human hair jewelry, the arrowhead collection and learn where the song "Pop Goes the Weasel" came from. Next door is a typical late Victorian 1897 residence where you learn how the Poe family lived (find out how the women achieved a "puffy hair" look). Across a walking bridge is the skeleton of the 1836 US Arsenal which stored arms and made ordnance goods. During the Civil War, NC seized it and produced the Fayetteville rifle. Gen. Sherman had it destroyed in 1865. ◗ T-Sat 10-5, Sun 1-5. ☞ Rte 87 into town, exit 104B, RT 1 block, then RT on Bradford Ave. 801 Arsenal Ave. *i* ncmuseumofhistory.org/osm/mcf.html ☎ 910-486-1330.

Exit 46>: Drop Zones – Just being on a military base is exciting for some, and Fort Bragg is special, because not only can you visit 2 FREE military museums, but you can, if you are there at the right time, get to observe the breathtaking sight of paratroopers billowing through the sky during training, perhaps at the Sicily Holland, Normandy, St Mere Eglise, Salerno, or All American Zones. See the 82nd/JFK description for directions. Visitors who are not US citizens must have pre-approval to visit. For drop schedule ☎ 910-396-6366.

Exit 46>: 82nd Airborne Division War Memorial Museum and JFK Special Warfare Museum – Two for the price of FREE is what you can discover inside Fort Bragg, where there is a big museum housing 82nd Airborne weapons, uniforms, aircraft, parachutes, a movie and more from 1917 to the present. This division "owns the night", and does most of its training and all of its work in the dark. There is an outdoor display of old aircraft where you can get up close and personal with them and a gift shop. ◗T-Sat 10-4:30. *i* https://82ndairbornedivisionmuseum.com /contact_us.html ☎ 910-432-3443 or 910 432-5307.

The other smaller museum, JFK Special Warfare Museum, gives a behind-the-scenes look at all sorts of fascinating sneaky unconventional means that have

been used to assist war efforts, with emphasis on Special Operations units. There are fascinating weapons, military art and items belonging to Colonel Nick Rowe, one of the only 2 soldiers to have escaped from a N. Vietnam POW camp. You will be surprised to find out that the wearing of the Green Berets was illegal from 1952-1961. ◗T-Sun 11-4. ☞ Rte 87 N 6 mi., exit at Bragg Blvd. LT for 8 mi. to Main gate. Note: Visitors who are not US citizens must have pre-approval to visit. *i* jfkwebstore.com ☎ 910-432-1533 or 910-432-4272.

NEW **Exit 31:** Joe Sugar's of St Paul' s – In 1916, Joe and Allan Sugar started this family business, and now the 3rd and 4th generation are dishing out the same helpful customer service. It's a men's store for every size - 32S to 78L - and shape of man - short (5' to 5' 7"), tall, thin, big, portly, extra big and tall. Customers drive from 1 1/2

MAP PG 49-50

hours away to buy the short rise pants (no hanging crotches), portly suits, short suits and shirts, extra big and tall 10XL shirts, underwear, socks and belts, up to 80" jeans, 24" neck shirts, shoes to 6E and even tall ties. You can find mismatched sized suits for the 6-pack chested slim waisted guy. On the left side there's a clearance room for $9.99 & up shirts and $19.99 & up pants. Alterations are free on the 70 brands of regular priced merchandise, and are usually done while you wait. ◑ M-Sat 9-6. 119 West Broad St. *i* joesugars.com ☎ 800-367-8427 or 910-865-5149.

Exit 20: Lumberton Visitors' Bureau – "When you stop here, you're halfway there" is this center's motto, because they are located halfway between NYC and Miami. Even if their office in the strip mall is closed, you can still find flyers and booklets of motel coupons outside. You can get info for NC or local info like this one: Comfort Inn, Fairfield Inn, Super 8, Comfort Suites, Hampton Inn, Best Western, Holiday Inn and Ramada Hotel and Suites have an alliance with the Lifestyle Fitness Center, so if you stay in one, you can exercise for FREE. There are no bathrooms in the info center - you have to head a few doors down. 3431 Lackey St. (Service rd on W side of I-95 between Exits 19 and 20). ◑ M-F 9-5. *i* lumberton-nc.com ☎ 800-359-6971 or 910-739-9999.

NEW! **Exit 20:** Fuller's Old Fashioned BBQ – Fuller Locklear's family certainly knows how to lay out a buffet. Theirs is the most wide-ranging Southern one that we've come across. Start out with the (unknown to us) johnny bread - fried rounds of corn bread on which you pour some molasses - and then you can go gently in to the fried chicken, fried fish, crab, corn beef hash, mac 'n cheese and pulled and minced BBQ. Or you can go whole hog and try some liver pudding, fried quail (Sandra's favorite), chicken 'n dumplings,

chicken gizzards, chitlins, chicken livers and fatback. There's lots of healthy sides: turnip and collard greens, rutabaga, succotash, okra, candied yams and chow chow and hot peppers on the table. If there's no time to stop, take it to go. ◑ M-Sat 11-9, Sun 11-4. 3201 N. Roberts Ave. *i* fullersbbq.com ☎ 910-738-8694.

Exit 17>: Lumberton Riverwalk/ Britt Park – If you want to take an easy 3-mi. loop walk through a park and around a lake, or make a pit stop to canoe or swim (W-Sat 11-6, Sun 1-6 in season), fish (anytime), throw a frisbee or run the dog, here's a park close to an exit. There's plenty of rest rooms, too. You can try your hand here at disc golf - a mix between frisbee and golf, with chain baskets to catch them. ☞ S. towards town, LT on W. 5th St. 1 1/4 mi., LT on Branch St. into park. ◑ 8-5 pm or dusk. *i* lumberton-nc.com ☎ 910-671-3869.

NEW! **Two!**

In 1916, James Barber of Pinehurst, NC planned the first mini-golf course. Supposedly it got it's odd name, "Thistle Dhu", when Barber declared to his designer "This'll do!". The plan was a tribute to the Louvre's Tuileries garden, complete with sculptures, fountains, and elaborated terraces.

Mile 5 Northbound: North Carolina Welcome Center – Don't forget to come and and pick up your coupon booklets of motel discounts which offer great deals along the way. There's a weather TV, an area for the pets to exercise and a picnic area. Take advantage of clean bathrooms and staff help with motel reservations or car problems. ◑ Daily 8-5. ☎ 910-422-8314.

Exit 1: South of the Border – You could only have missed the billboards if you are a sight-impaired driver. This tacky 60-year-young Mexican-themed town (still

owned by a 3rd generation Shafer) is famous to every kid who has ever read the 175 billboards on the road. What you will find, if you dare to get off, is a Pedroland amusement park, 11 souvenir shops, 6 food joints, 2 gas stations, 100 campsites and 158-rooms in the motor inn sporting carports and an indoor heated or outdoor swimming pool. You play mini golf, view the new reptile lagoon or view the whole site from the ride in the glass elevator to the top of the 200-foot tall Sombrero Tower. Olé! *i* thesouthoftheborder.com ☎ 800-845-6011 or 843-774-2411.

SOUTH CAROLINA

Mile 195 Southbound: South Carolina Welcome Center – Don't forget to come and pick up your motel discount coupons booklets which offer great deals along the way. Ask the friendly staff about interesting things to do and see. They can make reservations for you, help with car problems and there's a mail drop. Take advantage of the clean restrooms, have a picnic or run your pet. ◑ Daily 9-5. ☎ 843-774-4711.

Exit 193: The Dillon Marriage Chapel – Betcha didn't know that you are now passing through the "Wedding

Capital of the East", where over 7,000 ceremonies are performed each year. With only 24 hours notice, no blood test and no witnesses needed, you could get hooked for good. They offer 14 different marriage creeds and certificates, which get printed and framed before you leave.

If you want to jazz it up, you can buy silk bridal bouquets, boutonnieres, car decorating materials, bubbles, garters, bird seed, cameras and yes, rent a wedding gown and veil. ◑ Open 7 days a week, 24 hours a day. ☞ E on Rte 9, bear right at the fork, and it becomes MLK. 1501 Martin Luther King Blvd. *i* dillonmarriage chapel.com ☎ 843-774-2671.

Exit 181: Harbor Freight Tools Outlet – Men will not mind taking time to stop here - for it's tools, tools and more tools. Look for red and orange tags for sale prices on the brands: Chicago Electric, Central and Pittsburgh. Some items for the road might be: flashlights, compact binoculars, wind-up radio, trailer jack, and ear plugs for the kids in the back. Customer service is emphasized - even the

cashier said hello when we walked in! The clearance area is in the left rear, and in March, June and Oct there's a sidewalk sale with re-furbished items. ◑ M-F 8-7, Sat 8-6, Sun 1:30-6. 224 Harbor Freight Rd. *i* harborfreightusa.com ☎ 843-841-2012.

Exit 181>: Abingdon Manor – The sensory overload of driving on a highway all day comes to a grinding halt as you pass through this 105-year-old grand columned portico into a world of gracious dining and elegant surroundings rated by AAA

MAP PG 50-53

as 4-diamonds for both.

What could be better than drifting off to sleep in a four-poster feather bed surrounded by beautiful antiques (but 21st century baths) or sipping complimentary sherry in front of a warming fire? Breakfast and dinner (dinner optional) are served on silver, crystal and china, and are in the style of a private dinner party, with one set meal surrounded by fresh flowers and soothing jazz. *i* abingdonmanor.com ☎ 888-752-5090 or 843-752-5090.

the fried chicken - ungreasy, crunchy and moist. You might want to load your plate with: chicken & dumplings, sausage, stewed beef, corn

bread, ham hocks, fat back, turkey or ham, divine yams and definitely daily greens. Of course, there's soup and a cold salad bar (perhaps try the ham and broccoli one), and for dessert you could have ice cream or red velvet, but leave room for their famous flaky doughed peach cobbler - if there's none left, regulars are known to wait 'til they cook another one. ◑ M-Sat 6am-9:30, Sun 6-10:30 & 11-9. 2004 W.Lucas St. ☎ 843-664-0082.

Exit 164: Pee Dee State Farmers Market – On land that had been a farm, the old red mule barn has been "Barn Again", and now houses a potter's studio. An open covered farmers' market offers fresh veggies (locals rush in for the butter beans and butter peas), boiled peanuts, sugar cured hams, mountain butter, peanuts, jams and jellies, seasonal flowers and lawn ornaments. Other buildings house Harvest Moon Soapworks, Southwest Pottery and Indigo Marsh Nursery for your green thumb and McCleod Farms for baked goods and ice cream . ◑ M-Sat 8-6. 2513 W. Lucas St. (Hwy 52). *i* www.pdfarmersmarket.sc.gov ☎ 843-665-5154.

Exit 170: Atomic Bomb Accident at Mars Bluff

On March 11, 1958 in the midst of the Cold War, the U.S. Air Force accidentally dropped an atomic bomb near here. The unarmed 7,600-lb. 10' 8"- long bomb was aboard a B-47E bomber on a training mission headed for England. Its high-explosive trigger detonated on impact, making a crater as large as 35' deep and 70' wide. The bomb landed in the woods behind the home of railroad conductor Walter "Bill" Gregg. Gregg, his wife, their 3 children and a niece were injured by the concussion, which destroyed their house and out-buildings and caused minor damage to buildings within a 5-mile radius. There is a historic marker on E. Palmetto St. in Florence SC.

Exit 164: Thunderbird Country Kitchen – This roadside motel is best known for its buffet restaurant. Open over 40 years, the secret is consistancy, since Miss Ruby has been cooking there for 30 of them and other cooks and staff are there 15-20 years. Do not miss

Exit 164: Young Pecan Outlet – Founded by T.B. Young in the 1920's, this is now the largest pecan sheller in the world. Pecans are a good source of fiber and full of antioxidants. Along with the 80-year local favorite (butter roasted/lightly salted) are the butterscotch, white chocolate, double dipped chocolate and a good selection of sugar-free chocolate varieties. Young's also makes pralines, almonds, cashews, peanuts, cheese biscuits, key lime cookies, preserves, soups and dressings. At this location they bake breads, pies, cakes and have sandwiches and ice cream as well as local SC foods. ◗ M-Sat 9-6, Sun 11-5:30. 2005 Babar La. *i* youngplantations.com ☎ 843-662-2452.

Exit 160: Florence Visitor's Center – Don't forget to come and pick up your booklets for motel discounts and use the clean rest rooms. Choose some brochures, use the mailbox or ask the friendly staff about interesting things to do and see in Florence. ◗ Daily 9-5. ☞ Next to Florence Civic Center, 3290 West Radio Dr. *i* visitflo.com ☎ 800-325-9005 or 843-664-0330.

Exit 160: Percy & Willie's – First we loved the baked potato soup, then we scoffed down the house salad - greens topped with eggs, tomatoes, bacon, garlic croutons with a warm honey-mustard bacon dressing. We'd go back just for the flaky croissant drizzled with honey butter

served on the side, which could easily be sold as a dessert. We should have stopped right there and been satiated, but no, we had to go on to stuff ourselves with a perfectly cooked filet mignon and fluffy baked potato dressed with butter, sour cream, mixed cheeses, chives and more bacon, and also crunchy fried shrimp with mushrooms in a garlic butter sauce. And then there was no room for the homemade chocolate pecan pie, nor the real NY cheesecake from the Carnegie Deli. No time

to dine - carry it out. ◗ M-Th 11-10, F & S 11-11, Sun 11-9. 2401 David H. McLeod Blvd. (Rte 20). ☎ 843-669-1620.

Exit 160: Hobby Lobby – This super-sized store is a combination home accent, gift (bird houses, tassled pillows, 3-D dioramas) and creative shop. Every kind of hobby, from tole painting to stained glass, scrapbooking, quilting and needlework, is covered. For fun in the car there's color by numbers, puzzle books, 200-sheet construction pads, leather moccasin kits, tons of stickers, stamping, coin collecting and even a lap desk. If you never make it to the beach, buy a basket of shells here. ◗ M-Sat 9-8. 2357 David H. McLeod Blvd. (Rte 20). *i* hobbylobby.com ☎ 843-676-9408.

Exit 160>: Redbone Alley – If you ever told me that I would pine for grits, I

would say that you are nuts, but the grits here are like comfort food, made with lots of cheese, and have strips of ham, mushrooms, spicy shrimp and chicken, or even cajun fried quail or blackened salmon mixed in.

The two-story space is a Charleston street scene complete with balcony seating, pigeons on the upper window ledges, a children's area that has an ice cream truck with FREE samples, an arcade and a play space for toddlers. Adults can play billiards or arcade games.

The menu is modern Southern cooking, with lots of steaks (have the side of cheddar bacon mashies), chicken, sandwiches and salads - they can't take the fresh fruit chicken salad off the menu (with pecans and low fat dressing). Don't miss Dale Barth's grandma's pound cake panini made with bananas and caramel sauce. The restaurant name? - it's after the

MAP PG 53

owner's dog and daughter (she's Alley). ● M-Th 11:30-10, F & S 11:30-11, Sun 11:30-9. ☞ E. along Rte 20 for 2 mi.. LT on W. Palmetto St. to 1903 W. Palmetto St. in Florence Shopping Mall. *i* redbonealleycom ☎ 843-673-0035.

NEW! Exit 160>: Starfire Grill – More of a huge Greek diner menu than a grill, this local favorite will satisfy anyone in the car. It offers up everything from Thai chicken wings or sausage dip for starters (or 20 more options), local fave pecan chicken salad (and 21 more salads) to spaghetti Mama Mia, kabobs, apricot brandy pork chops, Louisiana chicken (Rotel tomatoes, cheeses, smoked bacon with broccoli cornbread), Calabash shrimp, Philly cheese steaks, quesadillas, smothered steaks, Singapore shrimp & chicken and interesting sides like fried okra or baked potato soup. There will be no room for dessert, but be warned there's an entire dessert and coffee/float menu. Maybe start the meal backwards? ● T-Th 11-9:30, F&S 11-10. 2130 W. Palmetto St. ☎ 843-661-7827.

Exit 160>: Sexton Dental Clinic – Who would ever have thought to combine a vacation with dental work? Obviously many people do, because this clinic has been open for 87 years, and has been attracting travelers from all over the U.S. and Canada for their speed, and especially their fair prices - complete upper and lower dentures start at $198. With 6 dentists on staff and an in-house lab, one day service for dentures is their goal. If multiple extractions are done, an overnight stay for follow-up is suggested.

Appointments are preferred, so please call or write 3 weeks in advance. 377 W. Palmetto St., Florence, SC 29501. *i* sextondental.net ☎ 800-922-6303 or 843-662-2543.

There are two other clinics (Shealy Dental Clinic ☎ 843-667-0286 and Griffin,

Watford, Tepper ☎ 800-982-1843), but Sexton is the one most people have heard of.

Exit 160: Magnolia Mall – This mall has the anchors of a Best Buy, JC Penney and Sears, but also Gift Nook, Hat World and Lane Bryant, Victoria's Secret and Aeropostale for clothes. If you need it, there's a Piercing Pagoda (but only for ears!) and 8 jewelers to buy the earrings. ● M-S 10-9, Sun 1:30-6. 2701 David H. McLeod Blvd. (Rte 20). *i* shopmagnolia mall.com ☎ 843-669-0725.

The Birth of a T-Shirt

You might notice cotton fields lining the roads. In mid-summer, the flowers are white and look something like a hibiscus. As they mature, they turn to yellow, then pink and lastly to dark red. After 3 days, they fall and leave green pods called cotton bolls, which begin to grow moist fibers inside. As the boll ripens, it turns brown and the fibers continue to expand in the warm sun until they split the boll open and fluffy cotton bursts out.

The raw cotton is cleaned, removing the trash such as burrs, dirt, stems and leaves, and then it moves over to the gin stand to pull the fiber from the seed.

The ginned fiber or lint is pressed into 500-lb. bales, and sample fibers are taken to be classified as to fiber length, strength, width, color and cleanliness. Now it moves on to the textile mills, where the bales are opened and the lint is mixed and cleaned further by blowing and beating.

The fibers are then straightened and turned into a soft, untwisted rope called a sliver, which is then pulled through machines to make it thinner. The fiber is twisted and wound on bobbins as cotton yarn, then is woven on looms into fabrics called "gray goods", and must be bleached, pre-shrunk, dyed, printed and finished before being wound onto a bolt for clothing or products. If you are interested in learning more, there's a SC Cotton Trail. A cotton exhibit can be found at the Marlboro County Museum. ◗ M-F 9-5. 123 South Marlboro St., Bennettsville. *i* sccottontrail.org ☎ 843-479-5624.

Mile 139 Southbound: Sumter County Welcome Center – Pick up your booklets of motel discounts along the way, choose some brochures or ask the friendly staff about interesting things to do and see in the nearby counties. There's a display about a local hero, NY Yankee Bobby Richardson, including his bats, balls and cards. Use the clean rest rooms, picnic tables, vending machines or pet run. ◗ Daily 9-5. ☎ 803-453-5029.

The era of NASCAR super-speedway racing began at Darlington Raceway in 1950, with the inaugural running of the Pepsi Southern 500. Darlington also houses the Raceway Stock Car Museum and NMPA Hall of Fame, a priceless collection of race cars and driver memorabilia. Darlington Raceway has aged gracefully over the years, yet still retains its feisty charm.

The birth of stock car racing is tied to moonshine. Simon Wincer (director of the IMAX NASCAR documentary) stated, "There was nothing illegal about the moonshine, but the bootleggers didn't pay tax on the liquor. These guys basically built cars to outrun the IRS and the law. That's why they became so good at racing, because they built cars with strong suspensions that could slide around on dirt roads in the mountains at night with no lights, and outrun the police."

Exit 108>: Summerton Diner – Locals don't cotton much to change, so the same cook has been here since 1967. Your basics of fried chicken, fried catfish, calves liver, baked ham, beef stew and chicken pot pie are served, but some of the sides,

The One That Got Away

Between Exit 132 & 122, Mile 129-128: General Francis Marion was one of the most skilled guerrilla fighters of the Revolutionary War, undermining the British and keeping them in a constant state of confusion. He and his men knew the secret Indian and hunter's trails and the murky paths through the cypress mazes. Like phantoms, they moved in for quick surprise attacks against much larger forces, and then would melt away to hide in the swamps.

On October 25, 1780, before British Col. Samuel Tynes and his men could even find their guns, Marion and his motley crew came out of the shadows and chased them into the swamp. The attackers killed 6, wounded 14 and captured 23. They also scored food, baggage, ammunition, 80 muskets and horses with bridles and saddles. The skirmish ended the Tory uprising in the area. A tale goes that one of them tore his pretty Tory redcoat on the thick briars, and so to this day the swamp bears the name Tearcoat Swamp.

MAP PG 53-54

like squash casserole or sweet potato souffle with pineapple and pecans (Sundays
only), squash fritters or apple salad are
worth a detour. Try not to fill up with the
fresh-from-the-oven biscuits and corn
bread, because you may need room for
dessert: perhaps home-made coconut cake,
pecan pie or banana pudding. If their vegetable soup is on the menu, we loved the
fat chunks of tomatoes, turnips, pole beans,
carrots, potatoes and peas in a sweet/spicy
tomato broth, and the chile was good too.
All this for the same price as a fast food
trio! ◑ Sun -W 7am-8pm, F & S 6am-
8:30 pm., closed Th. ☞ W up Buff Blvd
3/4 mi. to its end, RT on US 15 & 301
(Church St.) to 32 Church St. on the left.
☎ 803-485-6835.

Exit 102>: Santee National
Wildlife Refuge – This 15,095 acre preserve is a fall and winter haven for thousands of ducks and an enormous gaggle
of Canada geese who fly in from Southern
James Bay. Adjacent to the Visitor Center
is an easy mile looped nature trail which
meanders through low lying swamp and
along the shores of Lake Marion. Endan-
gered/ threatened species on the refuge
include the red-cockaded woodpecker, the
bald eagle and the American alligator.
Inside the building, with views of the lake,
are animal diaramas and an aquarium with
native fish species. ◑ T-Sat 8-4. FREE
𝑖 fws.gov/santee ☎ 803-478-2217.

Mile 99 Southbound: South Carolina Welcome Center – Don't forget
to stop and ask your questions about the
State, pick up brochures, booklets of motel
coupons and use the clean restrooms. They
can make reservations for you and call

about car problems. There's weather info,
vending machines, a pet walk and a covered picnic area. ◑ Daily 9-5 (restrooms
24 hrs). ☎ 803-854-2442.

NEW! **Exit 98:** Santee Cooper
Country Tourist Information Center – If you stop here, you can get help
with motel or restaurant bookings for 5
counties (and some on 10 other SC regions)
or pick up the motel coupon booklets.
There's info on the rest of the state, including golf, fishing and hunting, and you can
send a fax from here, mail a letter, make
use of a pet walk area or use a picnic table.
◑ Daily 8:30- 4:30. 9302 Old Hwy 6.
𝑖 santeecoopercountry.org ☎ 800-227-8510
or 803-854-2131.

NEW! **Exit 98:** Thai House – Yes, you
can really get Thai and Asian food (even
sushi!) on an exit. This friendly family
warms your tummy with their home cooking - so there's the pad Thai, but also red
curry duck which is hot and soupy, Yum-

my house salads
made with beef,
shrimp or duck,
tofu with spicy
basil garlic sauce,
blackened noodles
and popular vol-
cano flounder.
There's some Chinese dumplings, egg fu
young, chicken lo mein, and sushi: 30 maki-
mono rolls, sashimi, nigiri and temaki.
◑ Mon-Fri 11-2, 4-9, Sat 11-9. 9054 Old
#6 Hwy ☎ 803-854-9060.

Exit 98>: Lone Star Barbecue &
Mercantile – This is the real deal when
it comes to buffet-style down-home cooking. Chef Chris Williams hails from these
parts, but studied at the Culinary Institute of America. He combines grandma's
cooking with gourmet know-how. So,
there's BBQ with sweet or spicy sauce, fried
chicken and hush puppies, but also catfish

stew, sweet potatoes with raisins and marshmallows, apple salad, tomato pie (our favorite), barbecue hash on rice, beans, slaw and more. You can also take it to go. There's free country music Sat nights. The 4 creaky 100+-year-old frame buildings were brought here and attached; they were

rural country stores and farm commissaries from the late 1800's until the 20th cen-

tury. Zeaglar's Store was in operation as a post office and mercantile until 1997, so you can enjoy reminiscing as you gaze at the shelves laden with old time kitchenware, spices, sports gear, duck decoys, tools, shoes in boxes, soda bottles, tins and food. We especially loved the window curtains - old underwear hanging on a clothes line. ● Th-Sat 11-9, Sun 11-4. ☞ 1 1/4 mi. W on Rte 6, RT on State Park Rd. to # 2212. *i* lonestarbbq.net ☎ 803-854-2000.

Exit 98>: Santee State Park Cabins – If you or your kids pine for the pines, just 5 minutes off the exit you can rent these heated, A/C, 2-bedroom (sleeps 6) polygon-shaped cabins with a full kitchen, TV and living room. The peace and silence are astounding - so close to all the action at the exit, yet tucked in the woods and sitting on Lake Marion. If you have a bit of time to hang out, there's 2,500 acres of fun, with fishing (striped bass, catfish to catch), boating (kayaks, canoes), tennis, swimming, nature trails, and... raccoons, possums, wild turkeys, cormorants, foxes, ospreys, bald eagles, alligators and deer for neighbors. For campers, there's 158 sites too. ☞ 1 1/4 mi. W up Rte 6, RT on State Park Rd. Straight 4 1/2 mi. to ranger's

cabin for registering. Watch out for deer on the road. *i* southcarolinaparks.com ☎ 803-854-2408.

Exit 98: Clark's Inn and Restaurant – Fried green tomatoes, Really! Enjoy Southern family cooking: fall off the bone baked chicken or mango pecan roast pork. The deep fryer is busy with real Southern fried chicken, fried catfish and crunchy fried green tomatoes with apricot/pineapple chutney. For the less brave, there are pastas, prime rib, steaks and seafood, and the low-country plate (sausage, shrimp, chicken, veggies on savory rice) is high on our list.

In 1946 Bubba Clark, fresh from WW II, "temporarily" set up his first restaurant near here in an old bus station and now, 62 years later, his kids run this gracious dining room, with Momma Helena still around to check the recipes. Don't forget to leave room for her apple crisp and homemade

pecan pie. There's a homey Inn to stay at too. ● Daily 6am-10pm. 114 Bradford Blvd. *i* clarksinnandrestaurant.com ☎ (hotel) 803-854-2141or 800-531-9658; (restaurant) 803-854-2101.

Exit 98: Maurice's Gourmet BBQ – For 64 years, Maurice Bessinger's golden BBQ sauce has been Columbia SC's claim to fame, but now you can savour it on this exit. The BBQ ham, chicken, ribs and beef are pit cooked over hickory coals, and taste mustardy, sweet, peppery and tangy. Stan enjoyed the Carolina hash (smooth saucy bbq, onions, potatoes) on rice, and especially the hush puppies, which were light and oniony. Sandra liked the tender chicken with crispy sweet skin and the fresh squeezed lemonade. If you don't want BBQ, they're also known for their fresh meat burgers. This family-run business has 17 locations, and makes sure

MAP PG 55-56

that all the food is delivered fresh every day. ◗ Sun-Th 10-8, F&S 10-9. 263 Britain St., right beside I-95. *i* mauricesbbq.com ☎ 803-854-3889.

Exit 98>: Elloree Bed & Breakfast – Why not have the pleasure of a whole house to stretch out in, one that includes a games room with a piano and guitars, a workout room, free snacks, your own fireplace and a pool in the warmer months? Jack and Cindy will make you feel welcome (home grown pecans on your pillow!), and then allow you your privacy to enjoy your stay and the grounds. Breakfast might be homemade breads (cinnamon butter), fresh fruit parfait and an egg, cheese and sausage casserole with a side of pancakes. You can easily walk to the main street of Elloree from here. 660 W. Hampton St. *i* elloreebandb.com ☎ 803-897-4323.

NEW! **Exit 98>:** Elloree Heritage Museum & Cultural Center – This museum starts with the founder W J Snider telling you how he planned the city, and

then it goes on to show you a typical bank, grocery, drug and hardware store and Snider's own log cabin home. The farm wing (don't miss the mule) covers lumbering, the railroad, tenant farming and even midwifery. Only here will you find a plantation cotton gin house with its original working gin and press. ◗ Wed-Sat 10-5 & by appt. ☞ W on Rte 6 (Old No 6 Hwy) past the State Park entrance, for 6.8 mi, LT to 2714 Cleveland St. *i* elloreemuseum.org ☎ 803-897-2225.

Exit 68: Edisto River Trail – Right here you can take a break from long days of driving and enjoy a treat for yourself and the kids. The trail is 80 miles long,

and follows the same routes used extensively by the colonists and Native Americans. It's still just as wild and undeveloped, with wetlands, fresh, brackish and salt water tidal marshes, barrier islands, finfish, shellfish, bald eagles, wood storks, ospreys, short nose sturgeon and loggerhead sea turtles. Outfitters (near Colleton State Parks) can rent you canoes and kayaks so you can slowly paddle along bordered by banks of live oaks dripping with Spanish moss. Take as long as you like, from 4 hours to sleeping overnight in a treehouse with songbirds and owls as your only neighbors! *i* sctrails.net/trails/ALLTRAILS/WaterTrails/EdistoMain.html or edistoriver.org/frames/edisto_river.htm ☎ 843-538-8206. Carolina Heritage Outfitters offers trips *i* canoesc.com ☎ 843-563-5051.

Exit 53N or 57S>: The South Carolina Artisans Center – Here's the state's official folk art and craft center, showcasing hand-made creations (blown glass, sweetgrass baskets, whimsical garden sculptures, carvings, pottery, jewelry, shawls, quilts, tatting, wooden objects, handmade paper) by over 250 artists who live and work in SC. Located in the Detreville's charming former home, the one-of-a-kind items are definitely worth the 2-mile detour off the road for anyone who loves beautiful artwork. ◗ M-S 10-6, Sun 1-5. ☞ Sbound: Exit 57, Rte 64 S. (Bell's Hwy) 1 3/4 miles until it ends. RT onto N. Jefferies

Blvd. 1/2 mi., LT on Wichman St. Nbound: Exit 53, Rte 63 E. (Sniders Hwy) to Walterboro 3 1/2 mi. til it becomes S. Jefferies Blvd. in town. RT at Wichman St. 334 Wichman St. (Rte 17Alt) *i* southcarolina artisanscenter.com ☎ 843-549-0011.

Exit 57: Olde House Cafe – For 21 years this little diner, with the same cooks all those years, has been dishing out its lunch or dinner buffet ($8 or $10 with seafood on F&S nights), which might have fried chicken, mac and cheese, BBQ & hash, chicken or pork perlo (cut up over rice), catfish stew, country fried steak, pork strips, fried squash, greens, etc. Besides the buffet, the locals love the smothered chicken breast (mushrooms, onions, peppers, cheese), the house salad (ham, tomatoes, eggs, almonds, hot bacon, honey-mustard dressing), fried green tomatoes and the sweet potato fries. Wash it all down with an old-fashioned milk shake. They're open for breakfast, with country or smoked sausages, omelets and waffles, and this being low country - shrimps, catfish and seafood too. ◑ M-Sat 6:30-9, Sun 6:30-2. 1274 Bells Hwy (Rte 54) just E of the exit. ☎ 843-538-2614.

Exit 57>: Salon 401 – We love this hair salon, because it is like a meeting place, almost a coffee shop hang-out in the neighborhood. It has a cozy ôyou're invited to our partyö feel. If you're there at lunchtime, Mitch has been known to order pizza (or mimosas) and feed everyone. If you have questions about the area, someone in here is going to be able to help you. Best of all, he is fabulous at doing hair - men's or women's. It's a full service salon (Redken products), so yes, you can have your hair colored or get foil highlights, get a perm and your manicure, pedicure or facial, but you can also get a chemical straightening, facials, microdermabrasion, hair extensions, body wraps or a make-over. Mitchell travels to NYC and around the US for salon shows and to do his customers' hair. Stop and say hello for us, and join his party. ◑ T 9-7, W 9-5, Th&F 9-9, Sat 9-4. 651 Bells Hwy ☎ 843-549-WAVE (9283).

Exit 53: Walterboro Welcome Center – This "Front porch of the

Low Country" is spanking new, so you'll get clean restrooms but also free wi-fi, a computer terminal with weather, road conditions and e-mail possibilities, along with all the info you need about this re-developing city, the county and the SC low country. ◑ Daily 9-5. 1273 Sniders Highway. *i* walterborosc.org ☎ 843-538-4353.

Exit 53>: Walterboro – Starting back In 1784, Walterboro was a summer retreat for nearby plantations. It is easy to follow Washington St.'s crushed seashell sidewalk along the newly defined antique row. You can pick up a self-guided tour map at the Visitor Center, SC Artisans Center, Colleton Museum & Walterboro-Colleton Chamber of Commerce. ☎ 803-549-9595. Get here before the place is discovered and the prices go up.

1. Downtown Books & Expresso #213 ☎ 843-549-2241 **2**. Morning Glory Antiques #225 ☎ 843-549-6300 **3**. Old Bank Christmas & Gifts #229 ☎ 843-549-6555 **4**. Bachelor Hill Antiques #255 ☎ 843-549-1300 **5**. Green Lady Gallery #259 843-782-4569 **6**. Barnes & Taylor Antiques & Collectibles #261 ☎ 843-782-4100 **7**. Veranda #263 ☎ 570-850-7648 **8**. Gallery Music & Antiques #210 ☎ 843-908-3784 **9**. Antiques & Collectibles of Walterboro #220 ☎ 843-549-7219 **10**. Sharens Antiques #244 843-782-4752 **11**. Choice Collectibles #329 ☎ 843-549-2617 **12**. Washington Street Antiques #322 ☎ T 843-549-5527 **13**. Lucas Street Antiques & Collectibles #328 Lucas St. ☎ 843-782-7070

MAP PG 56-57

14. Antiques on Wichman #334 ☎ 843-782-3080 **15**. Albert's Attic #539 Washington ☎ 843-549-9221.

16. Old Water Tower – About 133' tall and built around 1915, the tank above the windows holds about 100,000 gallons of water. The interesting parts, though, are the 3 jail cells at the base of the tower. Years ago when travellers were stranded, they were allowed to sleep here.

17. Hiott's Pharmacy #373 ☎ 843-549-7222. After your walk, set yourself on a counter stool at the 59-year-old Hiott's for a $.60 or $.80 real fountain coke (cherry or vanilla too) and a pimento cheese sandwich (If you're there on the right morning you'll even find 82-years-young Mr. Eddie Hiott as the soda jerk). ☞ E on Rte 63 (Sniders Hwy) 3.3 mi until just after the left curve, RT on Washington St. *i* walterboro.org ☎ 843-549-9595.

Walterboro, SC Antique Row

Exit 53N or 57S>: The Blarney Stone – You can always count on a pub to have good grub. Traditional shepherd's pie might be Irish comfort food, and the shrimp and grits with fresh local wild caught shrimp would be the local equivalent, all with fresh veggies. The marriage of the 2 cultures can be found in the zingy Irish nachos with cheddar, bacon, jalapenos & salsa over crispy potatoes. Unusual sandwiches are the Irish Cuban and homemade pimento cheese, and there always is bread pudding. If you must - there's alligator bites in a biting jalapeno tartar sauce. ◗ M-W

3-9, Th-Sat 1130-9. 256 E. Washington St. ☎ 843-782-4774.

Exit 53>: Blue Lagoon Restaurant/Bowling Center – What do you do when you are an ex-engineer and ex-NYC guy - well, you open up a bowling alley and restaurant in an old Piggly Wiggly store, of course. It's rare to find "dining" in an alley, so check it out. He cuts his own steaks, grinds burgers and makes homemade tomato sauce. Regulars know to ask for the potato soup or the New England clam chowder and the steak dinner: 13 oz rib eye with mushrooms, peppers and onions for $10.95. You could go for the shrimp scampi, crab-stuffed flounder or stuffed chicken breast (mozzarella, pepperoni, pepperoncini, pimientos, mushrooms, peppers) in a pesto cream sauce, chicken Parmesan hoagie or - country fried steak, of course. Bowling specials are on Tues 7-9 for $6 and Sun is family day $2 pp + $2.25 shoe rental. ◗ (restaurant) M-Fri 11:30-2:30, 5-9, Sat 5-9. ◗ (bowling) winter M&T 2-10, W 12-10, Th&F 2-1am, Sat 10-1am, Sun 1-9, summer M-Th 12-11, F 12-12, Sat 10-12am, Sun 1-9. 226 Wichman St. ☎ 843-542-9431.

Voulez-vous Creuset avec moi?

Exit 38: Le Creuset Factory Store – In 1925 in Fresnoy-le-Grand, France, artisans began producing pots by hand-casting molten cast iron in sand molds, which were polished and sanded by hand and then sprayed with 2 separate coats of durable enamel and fired after each process. Le Creuset is the leading manufacturer using this method. These pots are impervious to acids, and are popular with chefs and home cooks for their even cooking temperatures and heat retaining blanket, which keep food hot for a long time.

The pots have lids that seal in steam to braise food in its own juices, they can be used on any kind of stove top or oven, and have a lifetime guarantee. This factory store carries discontinued, 1sts, 2nds and exclusive colors, and also offers tea kettles, dinnerware, Screw-pull wine and bar accessories, Riedel wine glasses and kitchen gadgets. ◑ Daily 9-6. ☞ W along Rte 68, RT at the 1st street (Shell Station). Store is at end of street. *i* lecreuset.com ☎ 843-589-6650.

Exit 33: The Lowcountry Visitors Center & Museum – This Center is housed in the 1868 Frampton House, part of a King's grant in the 1700's. In 1865, General Sherman's troops burned down the first plantation house and all the farm buildings. Civil War earthworks, erected by Robert E. Lee's troops in defence of the important railroad supply line for the Confederacy lie under the 250 year old live oak trees (covered in Spanish moss) in the back yard.

Besides the friendly advice and visitor information from Peach and Lynn, in the recreated 1900's parlor there are objects from the 10 museums in the Lowcountry, including artwork from Walterboro's South Carolina Artisans

Caution: Men Working

If you are complaining about the slowdown of traffic as you watch people working on the highway, think about how roads were constructed in the olden days. In South Carolina, it was compulsory that all men helped to clear roads in their neck of the woods (literally!). They complained that they had better things to do and didn't want to dig up tree stumps and shovel dirt just so strangers could pass through their town. So in 1788, the state passed a law limiting road duty to 12 days a year. There was a $2 fine for a white man if he missed the work, and slave owners were fined $1 a day if slaves failed to show.

Center (see Exit 53), and things to buy like: scuppernong jelly, Sass 'n Class figurines, Civil War replica weapons, and artifacts, tin lanterns, apple, cherry and peach cidar, Lowcountry SC wines, peach pecan preserves, benne wafers, stained glass boxes, chimes, tea sets, Southern cookbooks, and the De Nyew Testament in the Gullah language. If you are lucky (or unlucky?), you will chance upon one of the house ghosts. ◑ Daily 9-5:30. ☞ Rte 17 to Lowcountry Lane on your right. 1 Lowcountry Lane. *i* southcarolinalowcountry.com ☎ 800-528-6870 or 843-717-3090.

Exit 33>: KOA Point South – Even if you are not a camper, at this park you can stay overnight in a converted caboose, a trolley car or in a little Hansel and Gretel cabin. The caboose is actually sitting on train tracks and has a front and back platform. The pine cottage has a porch and wooden swing and just enough room for the beds. The trolley came here all the way from Charleston and is glass windowed, so you have the whole outside inside during the day but can close the blinds at night. The facilities are sparse - bring your own sheets, pillows or sleeping bags to put on the double bed for the folks and 2 singles for the kids. They have heat and AC, but NO bathrooms. For those, and showers, there's the main shower building nearby. Take advantage of the whole RV park with lakes, forests, pool, hot tub, Swimming Mermaid Coffee House, etc. See our

MAP PG 57-58

Campground pages at back for directions. *i* pointsouthkoa.com ☎ 800-726-5733.

Exit 33: Sabatier Factory Outlet – In 1834, in Thiers France, Bonnet Sabatier, at the age of 29, registered the "Sabatier" trademark and began what has become  a cutlery benchmark for excellence. This outlet shop is the only one in the U.S. which has been authorized by K Sabatier (there are about 24 Sabatier brands) in Thiers to sell the "K" knives.

Ask about the different lines, as the forged and stamped (on tables), full or partial tang knives (on walls) are of different qualities. Each series has about three dozen different knives, for everything from slicing salmon to boning a pheasant. A handful of "santoku" knives, Laguiole knives, sharpeners, magnetic knife racks (we love ours) and cutting boards can be found here too. Our Sabatier knives, which we've used since we married, are the favorite tools in our kitchen. ◐ Daily 8-6. *i* sabatieroutlet.com ☎ 800-525-6399 or 843-726-6444.

Exit 33: Carolina Cider Company – Yup, there's Southern cider here, like peach and blackberry, but also black-eyed pea relish, spicey pickled garlic, peach salsa, pepper jellies and lots of tasting spoons. Local specialties from NC, SC and GA also include toasted pecan syrup for your pancakes, fried peanuts, sweet potato, pumpkin and cherry butters and dried she-crab soup mix. How about some watermelon rind pickles? ◐ Daily 8:30-7:30. *i* carolina cidercompany.com ☎ 888-746-1899 or 843-846-1899.

Exit 21: Blue Heron Nature Trail – If it's time for a little stretch for you or the the kids, here's a 1/2 mile loop around a pond constructed of lumpy recycled tires with a swing, a fountain and an observation platform.

The 3-acre lake is the home for fish, turtles, ducks, wading herons and alligators up to 4' long. Seasonally, you should come across butterflies which are attracted to flowers chosen to entice them. There are feeders to attract birds, and food dispensers on the banks of the pond to tempt ducks and turtles. The trail is FREE and is lighted to be enjoyed any time. If you arrive M-F 9-1, visit the log cabin at the end of the trail, which has one room of flora and wildlife exhibits (alligator, bobcat, fox, beaver, feral hog head, beehive) and a clean bathroom. ☞ W. on Rte 336 about 200 yds., RT at 1st gas station. 321 Bailey Rd. *i* blueheronnature.com ☎ 843-726-7611.

Exit 21: Jasper's Porch – If you've never dined on a Southern porch (on fried catfish, country fried steak or baby back ribs), here's an opportunity to take a break 1 min. from the exit and to eat overlooking a pretty lake. Work off the award-winning she-crab soup, wild mushroom chicken and liver and onions with a stroll around the Blue Heron Trail (see story). Don't miss the fried pickles, and the lunch buffet is well known in these parts. ☞ W on Rte 336 (E Main St), first RT down Frontage Rd, restaurant is on LHS. ◐ M-Sat 7am-9pm, Sun 10:30-9. *i* jaspersporch.com ☎ 843-726-9521.

Exit 18: Switzerland – Early in the 1700's, immigrants from Switzerland tried to make their fortune with a silk colony in the new world, since it was a precious commodity in Europe. They cleared the land and planted the necessary mulberry trees for the worms. More settlers were lured here by their pamphlet called "The Contented and Homesickless Swiss Settler in the New World". Jean Pierry Purry managed to get the British government to subsidize the settlement, so by 1733 about 170 French and German Swiss Protestants founded Purrysburg on the Savannah River. Alas, they had not counted on the sweltering summers, swamps and malaria. In 1772, they did manage to export 144 lbs. of raw silk, but they died by the score. The survivors, who moved to higher ground, were more successful with cattle, and named their new village Switzerland, which is why you see that sign going southbound at exit 18.

Exit 8: Golf Ball Outlet – So this is where all your balls (Titleist, Maxfli, TopFlite, Bridestone, Calloway, Shrixen, Ultra, Pinnacle) wind up after they've disappeared into the water. Pick a dozen for $4.95, $7.95 or $9.95. Recycled boxed ones are $13.95, and bagged shag balls go for 60/$9.95 or 100/$18.95 while practice balls are 72/$17.95 a bag. Golf tees are only $2 a cup, and there are tee brushes, towels, caps - and fireworks.. ◗ Daily 8-8 summer; Sept-Apr 9:30-6. 132 Independence Blvd. *i* gogogolfballs.com ☎ 843-784-5040.

Mile 4 Northbound: South Carolina Welcome Center – Stop here at

WHY ARE THERE PALMETTO TREES IN THE MEDIAN?

Mile 0: Back on June 28, 1776 the British fleet, with 9 warships and 270 heavy guns, attacked the fort on Sullivan Island. It had been built with sand and logs from the palmetto tree, whose insides contain thick elastic fibers which smothered the bombs before they could explode, frustrating the British. The Americans were so low on ammunition that they could only fire 1 shot for every 6 they received. The tide of the battle turned, literally, that day when the tide went out, since some of the British ships ran aground on the shoal where Fort Sumter now stands. The British abandoned the ship, Actaeon. After a day of heavy fighting and the loss of a ship, the Brits gave up and sailed away, giving the States their first major victory of the Revolutionary War.

Within days came the signing of the Declaration of Independence, as the victory was a favorable sign of the Americans' capacity to oppose the British. The tough palmetto tree was then given the place of honor in the middle of the SC flag, and the state's nickname eventually became the Palmetto State.

this beautifully landscaped center and ask your questions about the State, check weather updates, pick up brochures, booklets of motel discount coupons and use the clean restrooms. They can make reservations for you or help with car problems, and there's a mail drop. There are vending machines here, a covered picnic area and a pet walk. ◗ Daily 9-5. ☎ 843-784-3275.

MAP PG 58-59

GEORGIA

Mile 111 Southbound: Georgia Visitor Information Center – Don't forget to come in and pick up your booklets of motel discount coupons. Choose some brochures or ask the friendly staff about interesting things to do and see in Georgia. They are full of great advice, and can make reservations for you or help with car trouble. There are clean rest rooms, a pet walk, wifi and covered picnic tables. ◗ Daily 8:30-5:30, restrooms 24 hours. ☎ 912-963-2546.

NEW! Exit 109: Inn at Mulberry Grove – Mulberry Grove was the name of the plantation where Eli Whitney arrived as a tutor for widow Mrs. Nathaniel Greene's children. Her hubby was 2nd in command to Washington, and had been given The Mulberry Grove Plantation as a

gift from the spoils of the Revolutionary War.

Whitney was no average tutor. A Yale graduate, he tinkered with inventions, and recognized the need to speed up the process of separating cotton seeds from cotton fibers. He gained worldwide recognition for inventing the cotton gin, which revolutionized the South's cotton industry. During the Civil War, General Sherman burned down Greene's original house, but now you can stay in this Inn on the same land. There's a touch of European elegance here, with gilded mirrors and dark wood furnishings. The hot breakfast with sausage, biscuits, grits and waffles can be taken on the patio. 101 O'Leary Rd. *i* innat mulberrygrove.com ☎ 912-965-9666.

Exit 104: Sonic – This 57-year-old chain still has car hops (tray toters, curb girls).

Back when cars had running boards, servers would hop on them to direct the car to a spot, hence the nickname. In the 50's and 60's, when Americans fell in love with their cars, this type of restaurant flourished, because they could eat in their cars and show them off.

Drinks are the stars here. Sonic signature hickory smoke-flavored burgers or chicken "toaster sandwiches" and Coney hot dogs with chili and cheese can be washed down with cherry limeades, cream pie shakes (strawberry, banana, chocolate) or real malts. Any of the following flavors can be added to personalize your drink: vanilla, chocolate, cherry, grape, orange, coconut, watermelon, strawberry, pineapple, apple or cranberry, and you can have fresh lemon or lime. All are ordered via an intercom, brought to you and hung on your car window, sometimes by kids on wheels. You can cop an "ADD-itude" by adding cheese, chili, or bacon to your sandwich or you can even ask for chocolate syrup on your fries! *i* sonicdrivein.com

NEW! Exit 104: MIWA Japanese – When a local takes you to her family's favorite Japanese restaurant and they remember her kids' names, you know you've found a friendly place. Those who don't eat sushi have lots of choices amongst the grilled or teriyaki-ed seafood, steak or chicken, fried calamari, seaweed or squid salad. Vegetarians can order tempuras, edamame and age-dashi tofu, and sushi/sashimi lunch is only $8.50-$9.50. Sandra will always go with the gyozas (homemade dumplings). ◗ M-F 11-2, 5-9,

Sat 5-9. 125 Foxfield Way, Towne Plaza. ☎ 912-748-8228.

Exit 102: Fun Zone – This amusement area offers go-kart tracks, a kiddie track, paintball, radio controlled cars and boats, 80 indoor arcade games (redemption coupons for prizes) and 2 miniature golf courses with ponds, streams and waterfalls. A small snack bar has pizza, corn dogs, chicken strips, wings and funnel cake. ◐ S-Th 10-9, F & S 10am-12am. 1040 US 80 E. ☞ 1.4 mi. E on left. *i* poolerfunpark.com ☎ 912-330-9860.

Exit 102: Mighty Eighth Air Force Museum – Wow, right in the middle of their lobby you can watch volunteers restore the fuselage of a B-17 bomber. It was unnerving to find out that the alu-

minum is so thin that your finger can make it wiggle. Hear first-hand stories of brave men and women who were not only pilots, but navigators, ground crew, radio operators or even POW's from 1942-1945. You can set the stage watching a 20 min. movie depicting the perils of a World War II strategic bombing mission over Nazi Germany, where at times 60% of the flights were one way (Now that's bravery). Find the story about Tyre C. Weaver, who was so badly wounded that he asked to be thrown from his plane to parachute into enemy territory hoping to receive medical treatment, and of the 10-year old girl who found him. Learn about Jacqueline Cochran who founded the women's air force and flew every plane, and Nancy Harkness Love, who delivered planes, tested them and towed targets, and Ann Baumgartner Carl, the first woman to pilot a jet. Peer into a MIG 21 nose section. See if you can find the dollar bill signed by Clark Gable or what tora tora tora means. There's a museum store, and outside you can view an F-4C Phantom, MiG-17A and B47 bomber. ◐ Daily 9-5. 175 Bourne Ave. *i* mightyeighth.org ☎ 912-748-8888.

Exit 99>: Savannah and Visitor Center – Savannah was the 1st planned city in the US, and is now the largest national Historic Landmark District (1,600 restored structures), with a reputation as one of America's most haunted cities. You can take tours by foot, by car, horse-drawn carriage, hearse, riverboat or in the popular continuous trolleys, which will take you

---

Hail to the Chief

When James Oglethorpe arrived to settle Savannah he was greeted by Tomo-chi-chi, Mico (chief) of the Yamacraw Indians. Unlike many other areas, the Native Americans here were hospitable. Tomo-chi-chi greatly helped Oglethorpe in establishing a British settlement in GA. From the beginning, Savannah was a good neighbor. In fact since there was so much interest in England to see a real "Indian", Oglethorpe took Tomo-chi-chi, his wife, nephew and other Yamacraws to England to visit the King. In 1739 Tomo-chi-chi's grave was placed in the center of Wright Square. It is possible that this is the only memorial erected for a Native American by descendants of European settlers.

MAP PG 59-60

through Savannah's canopy of live oaks and around many of its grid of 24 original squares (21 remain) called greens. James Edward Oglethorpe arrived in these parts in February 1733, and named GA after England's King George II, with Savannah becoming its first city. Its citizens were given the freedom to worship as they pleased, but laws forbade rum, slaves, Catholics and lawyers (nothing changes!). The town flourished without Native American warfare or hardship, because Oglethorpe pledged only friendship and good will towards the Yamacraw chief, Tomo-chi-chi.

The economy boomed with the exportation of cotton, allowing the building of the lavish homes and churches that we can still see today. The cotton warehouses on River St. are still there (sitting on the cobblestones made from the ballast left by the old sailing ships), and world cotton prices

were set in the halls of Savannah's Cotton Exchange (built in 1887), still there at Drayton and Bay St. Ask at the visitor center or a hotel about the Visitor DayPass, which for $7 allows you 24H of parking at 1-hr+ meters, city lots and parking garages. There's a FREE CAT Shuttle to transport passengers from downtown hotels and the Visitor Center to many historic sites, and also a FREE Ride on the Savannah Belles Experience, which goes across the river. Tour trolleys leave from here. Main Visitor Center: ◑ M-F 8:30-5, S & S 9-5. ☞ I-16 E. past I-516 to exit 167. LT to 301 Martin Luther King Blvd. (Other location: Hospitality Center at 1A W. River St. ◑ Daily, M-F 8:30-5, S & S 9-5. ☎ 912-651-6662.). *i* visitsavannah.com. ☎ 877-SAVANNAH or 912-644-6401.

Exit 99: First African Baptist Church - Oldest in America, this Congregation was established in 1775 and the building was built in 1859 by slaves and free blacks who built it brick by brick by lantern light in their meager time off.

One of the first ministers, Andrew Cox Marshall, asked blacks who were saving up to buy their freedom ($1,500) to put the money towards buying the land. To build this structure, men made the bricks down by the river in the overnight hours, and women carried them up to this spot. Many of the church's original pews bear the tribal markings of the African slaves. If you get to see the basement, you might notice air holes in the floorboards - this was for the Underground Railroad. The Sunday school started here in 1826 is supposed to be the oldest in N. America. 23 Montgomery St. ☎ 912-233-6597.

Exit 99>: Planters Inn – The Savannah that you imagine is still alive in this 200-year-old gracious hotel, where your car gets whisked away by the friendly valet. A genteel glass of wine awaits you in the afternoon after your stroll around the city from this centrally located inn overlooking Reynolds Square. Be warned that you share the building with resident ghosts. 29 Abercorn St. *i* plantersinnsavannah.com ☎ 800-554-1187 or 912-232-5678.

Exit 99>: ShopSCAD – It is rare that a college (in this case, Savannah College of Art and Design) changes the architectural and social face of a city. When Savannah real estate was cheap, the school embedded itself everywhere, becoming a patchwork quilt downtown, with these artistically gifted people creating a buzz everywhere. Finally, the college decided to open up a shop to highlight student, faculty and alumni creations. You might find: jewelry, children's books, totes, clothing, stationery, journals, dishes, serving pieces, soap, candles and bibs. ◑ M-W 9-5:30, Th & F 9-8, Sat 10-8, Sun 12-5. 340 Bull St. *i* shopscadonline.com ☎ 912-525-5180.

Exit 99>: Vinnie Van Go Go's – Sometimes you just crave a slice of pizza. With the chef spinning the dough in the window, you know it's fresh, at this cash-only City Market joint which has been drawing crowds for years. The 22 toppings

(artichoke to feta) can satisfy any urge, and the spinach salad will round out your meal (try a local taste - dunk the pizza in your salad dressing). The only other items on the menu are white or pesto pizza, calzones and 2 dozen beers. ◑ M-Th 4-11:30, F-Sun 12-12. 317 W. Bryan St. *i* vinnievangogo.com ☎ 912-233-6394.

Exit 99>: Leopold's – In 1919, 3 Greek brothers, George, Peter and Basil Leopold, started a Savannah ice cream tradition that is continued today by Stratton (Peter's youngest), now a Hollywood producer. Besides the popular malts and shakes, there's black and white or cherry smash sodas, huckleberry sundaes and unique ice cream flavors: chocolate raspberry swirl, lemon custard, bee honey

almond, rum bisque and their popular tutti frutti. While scarfing it all down, enjoy the walls decorated with Stratton's movie posters (The Big Chill, The Sum of all Fears, Close Encounters), the case of

collectibles from M:I 3 and a real live Panavision R-200 movie camera. 212 E. Broughton St. ◑ M-Th 11-10, Fri&Sat 11-11, Sun 12-10. *i* leopoldsicecream.com ☎ 912-234-4442.

Exit 99>: The Roundhouse Railroad Museum – This is a real roundhouse with an operating turntable, which was used from 1838 to 1963 by the Central of Georgia Railway. Trains pulled in here,

at the end of the line, to turn around or get repaired. You can get up close and personal with 7 engines, 9 kinds of cars and 3 cabooses, and can wander the yard to where the machine shops were (some still do restoration), see exhibits on steam engines, railroad rolling stock, a model railroad layout of Savannah, a short movie about the site and don't miss the the hard hat behind-the-scenes tour. This is no spiffy interpretive museum - it's the real McCoy. ◑ Daily 9-5. 601 W. Harris St. ☞ 1 block S of Visitor Ctr off MLK Blvd. *i* chsgeorgia.org ☎ 912-651-6823.

Exit 99>: Mansion on Forsyth Park – The Cirque du Soleil decor, both whimsical and dramatic, makes you want to whip out your camera and start snapping photos of the drop dead lobby, 400 works of art in the hallways and to-die-for chandeliers. A luxury oasis en route, your over-the-top Hollywood room in raspberry or lime is swathed in velvet, a candelabra gracing the desk. Don't miss the ladies' antique hat display outside the Viennese Ballroom and the decor in the restaurants. You can plan your stay

MAP PG 60

to take advantage of cooking classes or undo your traveling tension at the Poseidon Spa. Or even better, have an in-room massage and then fall right into your pillowtop, pillow laden bed. 700 Drayton St. *i* mansiononforsythpark.com ☎ 912-238-5158.

Exit 99>: The Lady & Sons – When some people are handed a lemon they turn it into lemonade, but Paula Deen (with Jamie and Bobby) turned it into Lemon Meringue Pie. Despite personal setbacks, including family deaths, a mental disorder, financial ruin and divorce, at age 42 she beat the odds and started a successful

cooking career, which includes restaurants, cook-books and a TV show. Their popu-larity has let to a reservation system: at 9:30 am you must appear in person in front of the restaurant. People think it is worth it for the cheesy corn muffin, hoe cakes, shrimp and tasso ham on grits in a white wine sauce, her chocolate gooey butter cake and that buffet (crispy fried chicken and catfish, creamy mashed potatoes, candied yams, ribs, pot roast, lima beans, black-eyed peas, green beans, macaroni and cheese) all ratcheted up a notch from the ordinary. ◑ Lunch 11-3, Dinner 5-9:30, Sun 11-4:30 buffet only. 102 W. Congress St. *i* ladyandsons.com ☎ 912-233-2600 (must have reserva-tions a day ahead).

Exit 99>: River Street's Waving Girl Statue – Romantics amongst you will love this leg-

end, which recounts the story of Florence Martus and of her sweetheart who left town on a ship. She promised to greet and wave to every ship that sailed into port until he came home. Sailors all over the world knew about her, but he never did show up.

Exit 94>: Ogeechee Barge Canal Museum & Nature Center – You can leave the whir of traffic behind and walk this quiet tow path alongside the canal for a short walk or take the full mile loop to the river, noticing frogs, snakes, alligators, crayfish and marsh birds, and enjoy the swampy woods and wooden foot bridges perhaps spotting semi-aquatic plants, such as lizard's tail, pickerel week, lobelia, and golden club. Some trees and plants are labeled (American Hornbeam, Spruce Pine, Parsley Hawthorn, Flowering Dogwood), so see if you can find the pot tree. The canal opened in 1831 and was important for the economy, aiding the transport of lumber, cotton, rice, bricks, guano, naval supplies and peaches. Indoors there are some nature displays. ◑ Daily 9-5. 681 Fort Argyle Rd. ☞ 2.3 mi. W on Rte 204. *i* savannah ogeecheecanal.com ☎ 912-748-8068.

Exit 94: Savan-nah Festival Fac-tory Stores – For those of you who need an outlet mall fix, here's a smaller do-able one where you will find: Uniform Outlet, BK Toy Outlet, Samsonite, Leggs, Hanes, Bali, Playtex, Carter's, Book Ware-

NEW! **Exit 99:** There is a Confed-erate monument in Forsyth Park which was built with money raised by women in the community. To make sure it was not tainted by the Yankees, they had it made in Cana-da of Canadian materials, and then floated it down to Savannah so that it would never touch Yankee soil. When it arrived, it didn't suit the men (the nerve!), so some of the statues were removed and the soldier hoisted to the top.

house, Dress Barn and for the guys: Bass Company Store. ◑ M-Sat 9-9, Sun 11-6. *i* savannahfestival.com ☎ 912-925-3089.

Exit 94>: Keller's Flea Market – Challenge yourself to wander through this quonset hut city and see if you can find all of these: dried flowers, dolls, belt buckles, VHS tapes, records, DVD's, cowboy boots, firewood, vacuum cleaners, suncatchers, framed paintings, leather belts, Spanish CD's, freshly squeezed lemonade, candy apples, Dixie T-shirts, kitchenware, bird cages, camouflage clothing, swords, guns, tools AND puppies! ◑ Sat & Sun 8-6. ☞ 2 mi E on Rte 204, Exit at US 17 and it's on the left. 5901 Ogeechee Rd. *i* ilovefleas.com ☎ 912-927-4848.

The Smallest Church in America (Well, Almost)

Exit 67: Christ Chapel was a vision of Mrs. Agnes Harper, a rural grocer who dreamed of a quiet sanctuary for travelers passing through Georgia. With limited funds, she managed to have erected a

10' x 15' building which seats 12, with foldaway kneelers. Mrs Harper imported the stained glass windows from England and placed a glass star in the roof to permit the midday sun to light the interior.

Prior to her death, she named the site Memory Park and deeded the church to Jesus

Unknown Revolutionary War Heros

Between Exits 94 & 90, Mile 92-91: In the evening of Oct. 1, 1779, Col. John White, Captains George Melvin and A.G.C. Elholm, a sergeant and 3 privates snared 141 British troops and 4 ships without firing a single bullet! What they did was very clever. The 7 of them built campfires scattered through the woods around the Ogeechee River bank, where the enemy had settled for the night. They then walked back and forth from fire to fire yelling orders to imaginary troops, and even going so far as challenging each other as sentinels, leading the British to believe they were surrounded.

Then, with ultimate nerve, they put into motion the 2nd part of their plan. White rode into the British camp and asked them to surrender without casualties. Captain French did so gladly, thanking them for their mercy. At that point, Captain Elholm rode in briskly asking where to place the artillery. White answered, "Keep them back, Keep them back, sir... Move your men off, and send me 3 guides to conduct them to The American post in Sunbury." He then promised he himself would go constrain his impatient "army".

Christ to prevent it from ever being sold. In 1983, the McIntosh Chamber of Commerce adopted the little church and now makes the needed repairs. Though it goes by the "Smallest" billing around here, that designation probably fits the Cross Island Chapel in Oneida, New York, at 3.5' x 6'.

Travelers continue to stop for a moment of rest, peace and tranquility. Mrs Harper once said, "It is not the dimensions of the church which is important - it is the extent of the faith." ◑ 24 hrs. ☞ Hwy 17 S. 1 mi. Church is on LHS.

Exit 42N or 58S>: The Blue Heron Inn – Okay, this B&B is in a bit from I-95, but the view from the decks and each huge room is what seems to be the entire Brunswick marsh, and the sunset moment when the water flips to golden is worth the few miles of driving. Since it's

MAP PG 60-61

halfway between exits, you are not backtracking. A popular breakfast is the sweet potato pumpkin pancakes with pecans on top. The largest room has a massive bathroom with a jacuzzi, and there's a 2-floor 3-room suite or one with a kitchenette if you need them. The helpful proprietors can assist you with your birdwatching or in getting onto nearby Sapelo Island. 1 Blue Heron Lane. *i* blueheroninngacoast.com ☎ 912-437-4304.

NEW! Exit 58>: Sapelo Station Crossing – One of our fans told us to find this place, and we're glad we did, for its hot mix of Southern and Louisiana cooking. Look for the US and Confederate flags out front, the porch rockers and a 1920's blue tenement house. The locals love the crawfish eggrolls with Asian dipping sauce, and we loved the rich alfredo-like Mardi Gras pasta with chicken in the tasso (seasoned pork) cream sauce, and the crispy/tender pecan crusted grouper in lemon butter sauce. You can wend your way through Kool's voodoo skil-

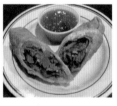

let with blackened GA shrimp, oysters, spicy LA sausage, potatoes, pepper onions, the catfish Sapelo, fried and topped with crawfish etouffee over rice or the Low Country wild GA shrimp in an Andouille creole cream sauce over cheese grits. The scratch sauces, salad dressings and desserts and sides of sweet potato casserole with hints of coconut and pecans, or the twice baked potatoes with cheese and buttermilk, show off the down home cooking. ◑ W-Sun 5:30-10. Highway 17N. *i* sapelostation.com ☎ 912-832-3555.

Exit 49: Darien-McIntosh County Chamber and Visitors Information Center – For information on local attractions from Exit 49 to Exit 67, this office is now located right in the Preferred Outlets Mall. Kids will like to see a model of "Altie" the sea mon-

ster. Pick up brochures and perhaps take a gander into town - towards the water (for a sighting?). The town was a major seaport in the 19th century, and shrimp boats still line the river, maintaining the nickname "Fisherman's Paradise". ◑ M-Sat 10-8, Sun 11-6. *i* mcintoshcounty.com ☎ 912-437-6684.

Exit 49: Preferred Outlets at Darien – Recently renovated and expanded, guys can now head to the Bass Company store or Tommy Hilfiger while the women empty their purses at the Coach Factory Store, Dress Barn, Liz Claiborne or Bath&Body Works Outlet, and the family can shop at the Gap. If you need it, the McIntosh County Visitor Center is here to help you. Ask for the coupon book there and when/where military and seniors over 55 get discounts. ◑ M-Sat 10-8, Sun 11-6. *i* outletsatdarien.com ☎ 888-545-7224 or 912-437-8360.

Exit 49>: Altamaha Coastal Tours – If you want a break in the middle of your trip, why not go out in a canoe or kayak on a river, cypress swamp or salt marsh? Rentals and tours (2-6 hours) might have you getting up close to dolphins, alligators, otters, manatees, bald eagles, ospreys, herons or egrets. Overnight camping trips are possible. Call ahead, since the tides determine the day's events. Bikes can be rented too. 229 Fort King George Dr. *i* altamaha.com ☎ 912-437-6010.

Exit 49>: Fort King George – This 1721 reconstructed fort was the southernmost outpost of the British Empire in N. America, and was abandoned in 1732. The French (from Canada) came down the Mississippi and were considered a threat from the north and west, while Spain posed a threat from Florida. This left the British colonies along the coast with the possibility of being surrounded, and thus the need for this fort.

This reconstruction has a 3-storied gabled blockhouse with a supply magazine on the lower level, a gun room on the second floor with cannon ports on the walls to fire at enemy boats in the river, and a third floor gun room with lookout posts. Also on the site are barracks, officers' quarters, the guardhouse, house of office (bathroom), a scout boat, indigenous huts (for scouts, sawyers, slaves), a blacksmith shop, bakery and molasses beer brewery (cheers!).

In addition to the Fort, there's a short film, a small museum, Scottish pioneer village, British cemetery, sawmill ruins, a nature trail and a great view of the marshlands. ◗ T-Sun 9-4. ☞ Hwy 251 E. 1 mi. to its end at Rte 17. RT for 1 mi. and turn left onto Fort King George Dr. along Rte 25 before you cross the bridge. 1 more mile to the fort. *i* gastateparks.org/info/ftkinggeorge/ ☎ 912-437-4770.

Exit 49>: Open Gates B & B – Why stay at a noisy I-95 exit motel when you can drive 2 min. and sleep in the spacious quiet of an 1876-built house that is located one block from the shrimp boats on the waterfront. You can rock on the front porch under the shade of a live oak tree, take a swim in the pool, peruse books in their large library or shop for wildlife note cards, jewelry, pottery, stained glass stars, bird houses or night lights. Owner Kelly Spratt's other job is Darien's mayor, and hubby Jeff's is birding tours, river tours or kayak, boating and fishing adventures. *i* opengatesbnb.com ☎ 912-437-6985.

Exit 49>: Skippers' Fish Camp – Just caught (on their boat) wild GA shrimp or flounder (don't miss the crispy one on the menu) should have you driving off this exit. In a glass and wood decor with a water view location and great sunsets, the menu here takes you from an oyster bar to crab and a sunset salad (marinated roasted veggies, feta, balsamic brushed pizza crust), and for land-lubbers, steaks, ribs and BBQ. Make sure to order some of the sides: sweet  potato souffle or cheddar cheese grits, and the locals love the peach cobbler for dessert. ◗ daily 11-9. ☞ Hwy 251 E. 1 mi. to its end at Rte 17. RT 1 mi. til you see the bridge ahead of you, then LT at Broad St. 85 Screven St. *i* skippersfishcamp.com ☎ 912-437-3474.

Exit 49>: Walter's Caviar – Howell Boone's family has been in the seafood business for 3 generations, owning their own shrimp boats and processing their catches. He started Walter's Caviar in 1980, farming the caviar from sturgeon,  which can live up to 50 years and weigh 1,000 pounds. Sturgeon roe is caviar. The best caviar is made when the sturgeon is processed immediately after being caught.

Boone learned the techniques used by Russian caviar processors, and is thus able to produce excellent caviar made only from true stur-

MAP PG 62

geon roe, comparable to that of Russia and Iran.

Famous Georgians who have shopped here: Pres. Jimmy Carter and Rosalyn, Ted Turner, Ed Begley, Jr. and billionairess Ann Cox Chambers. You can call to order the caviar or fresh Georgia shrimp or use: *i* georgiaseafood.com ☎ 912-437-6560.

Exit 42>: Hofwyl-Broadfield Plantation – Once you cross the pasture, the same one the Dent family strode for 167 years, you will pass the bottling house, dairy barn, commissary, pay shed and servants' quarters. Notice the 696 acres of marsh, and try to imagine it as a cypress swamp that hundreds of slaves cleared by hand, levelled for proper drainage and constructed miles of ditches and dikes and floodgates for rice farming.

William Brailsford and his son-in-law James M. Troup ran it as a rice plantation, living in the pinnacle of coastal society until the Civil War. The slaves were the foundation of rice culture, since they had the experience and tools that they brought with them from the Windward Rice Coast of West Africa, along with the ability to withstand the heat, humidity and malarial environment. After the War, much of the estate was sold off for taxes, and by the 1880's most of the wealth was gone. The East coast rice empire was over by the early 20th century. The property was turned into a dairy farm until 1942 and run by sisters Gratz, Miriam and Ophelia Dent, who were the first to free it from debt. The wonder of this old house is that Miss Ophelia Troup Dent left it as a scrapbook of generations of an entire family. All of the family furnishings, photos and mementos are still there, as if they've just left for the day. ● Th-Sat 9-5. ☞ Rte 99 E. 1 mi. to Rte 17 & 25. LT on US 17 for 1 mi. *i* gastateparks.org/info/hofwyl/ ☎ 912-264-7333.

SPANISH MOSS IS NEITHER SPANISH NOR MOSS

The silvery green veils called long moss or vegetable horsehair are a distant cousin to the pineapple!

The plant has no roots and is fed by mineral-rich cells that wash off the host tree. The more cells the tree exudes, the more for the Spanish Moss to live on, so old trees and decaying trees are a veritable feast. Rainwater is captured by scales on its small tendrils, which also keep internal moisture from evaporating. There was quite an industry in the South using Spanish  moss as mattress stuffing until synthetic materials came along. Henry Ford used it for stuffing the seats of Model T's. The moss picked directly from the trees might be bug-free, but picked up from the ground, it can harbor chiggers (mites) that burrow into the skin and cause intense itching. Treating the moss with bleach diluted with water for a minute or so in a microwave oven takes care of the critters.

Mile 40 Southbound: Brunswick & Golden Isles Welcome Center – Don't forget to come and get some booklets for motel discounts or request that reservations be made for you in the Brunswick area. Pick up some brochures or ask the friendly staff about interesting things to do and see in Brunswick or Georgia. There's wi-fi and an after hours info kiosk with local info. There are clean rest rooms, a pet walk, a mailbox and covered picnic tables. ◐ Daily 9-5, rest rooms 24 hours. *i* comecoastawhile.com ☎ 800-933-COAST or 912-264-0202.

Exit 38: Strike Zone – Bowling is back, for this is a fairly new colorful bowling alley. Wednesday is the bargain day, at only $1.50 a game. You can also play billiards or in the amusement arcade. If you're hungry, it's attached to a Denny's. ◐ M-Th 10-11, F & S 10-1, Sun 12-10. 380 Millennium Blvd. ☎ tgistrikezone.com ☎ 912-265-6600.

Exit 38>: Willie's Wee-Nee Wagon – Yup, there are 9 kinds of wieners here (kraut, bbq, slaw, bull, chili, cheese, Brunswick, etc.), but the reason the locals (and Bill Gates' pilots, golfer Davis Love, TV announcer Lee Webb) have salivated over this joint for 35 years is the pork chop sandwich with onions and mustard. Willie himself thought the cheeseburgers are something special. Any of the sandwiches (steak, fish, polish sausage, reuben) come with sweet tea.

◐ T-Sat 10-10. ☞ 2.8 mi. E on US 25, RT on Altama for 1.5 mi. 3599 Altama Ave. ☎ 912-264-1146.

Exit 36: Matteo's – Family owned and operated is what we like to hear as we look for real eats on the road. The lasagna is like "mama used to make", the eggplant rolotini is stuffed with ricotta, and you can choose your own calzone stuffing. The regular lineup of parmigiana, piccata, marsala veal or chicken are there along with spaghetti and meatballs, Italian subs, pizza, antipasto salad and even garlic rolls. You can eat in the casual front room or the more grownup back one and watch the open kitchen for entertainment or erudi-

tion. ◐ M-F 11-2:30, 5-9:30, Sat 4-9:30, Sun 11-8. In the Best Western, 100 Cary St. ☎ 912-267-0248.

Exit 36>: Brunswick Manor – The moss-draped oak setting and orchid conservatory are perfect for this 1886 Victorian B&B. The grand carved oak

staircase, crystal chandelier, and grand piano set the stage. When you enter each room it is like a museum piece, and tells a story, from a corset thrown lazily over a room divider to the accordion placed on the floor. The place is comfortable and fun - have a treasure hunt looking for the mortuary powder, Polaroid camera, beaded cocktail dress or the Donald Duck's party game. It's owned by caterers (served Angelina Jolie, Colin Powell, Jerry Seinfeld, Lily Tomlin, Pres. Jimmy Carter), so your breakfast will be lush, served with silver service under the 4-foot high silver candelabras. You can rent their house next door for family re-unions and holidays. 825 Egmont *i* brunswickmanor.com ☎ 912-265-6889.

A HUNDRED BOTTLES OF CHAMPAGNE ON THE HULL

Exit 36>: By 1942, during WW II, over 500 million tons of ships and cargo had already been lost to enemy U-boats. The U.S. Marine Commission ordered stronger 447-foot cargo vessels to be built at 16 sites, and they came to be known as Liberty Ships. Though each of them was christened with a name when launched, each operated at sea anonymously, so that the enemy could not guess its mission or cargo. The Brunswick

MAP PG 62

shipyard, manned by 16,000 people, was able to produce 4 per month, taking an amazing average of only 89 days to construct each one, reaching a grand total of 99 ships. Receiving word that they must produce 6 ships for the month of

December 1944, the J.A. Jones shipyard workers showed their dedication by guaranteeing and delivering 7! They then requested to receive no pay for the extra work done on Christmas Day, and each worker endorsed their time-and-a-half pay check back to the U.S. Government.

At the end of the war, the employee training ship, a cut-away model, was placed on display. After 20 years, it was badly rusted and was scrapped, and in 1991, after 4 years of fund-raising, a 23-foot scale model was built, which can now be seen on the grounds of the Mary Ross Waterfront Park in downtown Brunswick. It was christened, like all the others, with a bottle of champagne, and this, their 100th Liberty Ship, was duly named "City of Brunswick". The park also has an outdoor musical playscape, a Saturday farmers market, the shrimp fleet and huge ocean-going freighters.

⚬⚬⚬⚬⚬

Exit 36>: Aboard Lady Jane – You can play "Bubba Gump" and participate on the only shrimp trawler certified by the US Coast Guard. Captain Larry Credle welcomes you aboard to go out into the coastal GA waters, and then you get to

help the crew empty the net and learn about the species they caught (bonnethead, blacktip, sand shark, horseshoe crab, puffer fish, amberjack, crocker, spot, whiting, blue crab, skate). After you watch (or not) the shrimp beheading, the best of all is you get to partake in the freshest possible "shrimp boil", where you can eat as much shrimp as you can handle. 1200 Glynn Ave. (Rte 17 or Ocean Highway). *i* shrimpcruise.com ☎ 912-265-5711.

Exit 29: Steak'n Shake – Started way back in 1934 in Normal, IL with the grill in the front, because they felt that "In sight, it must be right". You can still watch made-from-steak burgers sizzling. We like the idea that you are not stuck with fries on the side, but can choose amongst: cole slaw, baked beans, salad, soup, chili or even cottage cheese. Hand-dipped milkshakes can be fun if you order them side-by-side with with 2 flavors visible vertically, or sip an orange freeze, fruit smoothie or blow the diet with a root beer float or walnut brownie fudge sundae. ◗ 24 hours. *i* steaknshake.com

NEW! **Exit 29:** GA Pig – This rundown looking shack (with wooden tables, benches and rolls of paper towels) is the kind of building you

would never walk into unless someone told you about it. We're telling you it had our favorite BBQ sandwich on the road, and Sandra especially likes it because there are women cooking BBQ here. The pungent aroma of BBQ permeates the joint, since the building was built around the hickory smokin' oven. The menu is simple: chopped pork, beef, ribs with 2 homemade sides - potato salad macaroni, cole slaw, bbq beans. You really do not need to add any of the dozens of hot sauces, and you can buy their BBQ sauce to try to make it at home. Yeah, right! ◐ M-Th 11-8, Fri & Sat 11-9, Sun 11-7 ☎ 912-264-6664.

Exit 3: Kingsland Visitor Center – Stop off at this new center for clean restrooms. Local tourist info is cheerfully provided along with GA info, and even NE Florida info (Jacksonville, Amelia Island, Fernandina Beach, etc). If you need a wi-fi hotspot, pet walk, towing services or weather screens, they're here too. ◐ M-F 8-5, Sat 10-5. 1190 E. Boone Ave. *i* visitkingsland.com ☎ 800-433-0225 or 912-729-5999.

NEW! **Exit 3:** Mango's – This review comes with a warning: be careful because their pale green house garlic sauce is addictive (it's momma's secret weapon). You will want to drizzle it on everything. A favorite was the burrito crunch - yup, deep fried burritos - this may be Venezuelan/Cuban cuisine, but this is the South after all. The arepas are like mac 'n cheese comfort food - hot crispy corn cakes stuffed with cheese and sour cream, and you can get chicken or beef empanadas. The pollo guisado (grandma's recipe) is simply chicken, potato, tomato sauce, rice, black beans with wicked candy-tasting plantains. If you like a bit of a bite, try the parilla - smoked sausage with grilled yucca. There's fish tacos, Cuban sandwiches, but also chicken cordon bleu, coconut shrimp and a local favorite - hot dogs with secret relish and potato sticks on top. ◐ M-Sat 11-3, 5-9. 112A N. Gross Rd. ☎ 912-882-6300.

Exit 3>: St. Marys Submarine Museum – Imagine an attic full of personal memorabilia of many submariners, and you get the feel of this homey museum. You can see early submarine designs (pig boats) right up to nuclear ones, consoles, periscopes, listings of boats built and lost in WW II and tons of command plaques. For the truly addicted, submarine movies play all day, and you are invited to read actual files of each U.S submarine or support commands. More than 99% of all WWII Patrol Reports and their command history files are here (even previously classified documents); these are not usually seen by the average person or submarine veteran. ◐ T-Sat 10-4, Sun 1-5. ☞ Rte 40 (Kingsland St Marys Rd) E about 9.1 mi., becoming Osborne Rd, go thru town, and it ends at St Marys St. RT to 102 St. Marys St. *i* stmaryssubmuseum.com ☎ 912-882-2782.

Mile 1 Northbound: Georgia Visitor Information Center – There are cushy couches to relax on here and those motel discount booklets. You can request that reservations be made for you. Pick up some brochures or ask the friendly staff about interesting things to do and see in Georgia. There are clean 24-hr rest rooms, wifi, the weather channel and highway incident info, a mail drop and this one has a pet walk and big airy covered picnic tables. ◐ Daily 8:30-5:30 (restrooms 24 hours). ☎ 912-729-3253.

FLORIDA

NEW! **Mile 378 Southbound:** Florida Welcome Center – Florida sunshine starts here with the FREE orange and grapefruit juices - and massage chairs ($1 3min or $5 15 min). There are tons of flyers and those motel coupon booklets. The busy tourism reps can book motels for you and help with car trouble, and sure, there's clean rest rooms. Outside use the picnic tables, vending machines and pet run. ◐ Daily 8-5. ☎ 904-225-9182.

Exit 351A N or 351D S>: House on Cherry St. – Their goal of "repose and renourishment" is met in the spacious guest rooms and in the gardens overlook-

MAP PG 62-63

ing the river. Look for the meditation areas, a rosary garden, Native American medicine wheel, seeker herb spiral, labyrinth, Buddhist alcove and fire ring.

Your hostess, a retired teacher, is great about offering info about the area. ◑ Oct-Mar. 1844 Cherry St. *i* houseoncherry.com ☎ 904-384-1999.

Exit 351A N or 351D S>: The Cummer Museum of Art and Gardens – Ninah and Arthur Cummer lost their only child, so they willed their house "To create a place of beauty and culture for all the people". One heavily paneled room, Tudor Room, remains from their original home with some of their paintings. The 7 other galleries showcase paintings from Medieval and Renaissance to folk art, with some famous names (Rubens, Van Dyke, Bernini, Velasquez, Corot, Winslow Homer, Benjamin West, Gilbert Stuart) along with a Meissen porcelain collection. Don't forget to visit the English and Italian formal gardens and say "Hi" to the Cummer oak tree that spans more than 175 ft. ◑ Tues 10-9, Wed-Fri 10-4, Sat 10-5, Sun 12-5. FREE Tues 4-9. 829 Riverside Ave. *i* cummer.org ☎ 904-356-6857.

Exit 350: Museum of Science and History – Here Tomca, the 44-year-old, 112 lb. alligator snapping turtle greets you. Can you imagine having to feed a whale up to 5,500 lbs. of food daily? You learn this and more about them and dolphins and manatees. There are planetarium shows, and kids will love the "do

touch" floor exploring energy, magnetism, gravity, light, buoyancy and how machines work. There's some history of the area. ◑ M-F 10-5, Sat 10-6, Sun

1-6. ☞ N on Hendricks Ave, which curves left onto Museum Circle. 1025 Museum Circle. *i* themosh.org ☎ 904-396-MOSH.

Exit 350B: Peterbrooke Chocolatier – Chocolate popcorn put them on the map. The combination of sweet, salty, crunchy and chocolatey is a 23-year-favorite. Taste some at the cash or try their chocolate pretzels or chocolate "fries". Pick up some sugar-free bridge mix, caramel bars or chocolate blueberries for the car. Here's some sweet

gift ideas: milk chocolate crayons in a box, chocolate pizza or they can even cover a wine bottle with chocolate. ◑ Mon-Sat 9:30-9, Sun 12-6. 2024 San Marco Blvd. *i* peterbrooke.com ☎ 904-398-2488 or 800-771-0019.

Exit 350B: Bistro Aix – What a treat to find a little bit of France tucked under an exit. Any restaurant that can take the potato chip and turn it into a signature appetizer (with peppery spices and topped

with blue cheese sauce) gets a high rating in our book. They can go Asian with crispy duck confit spring roll with pineapple "ketchup", or Italian with mushroom, fontina cheese pizza with truffle oil. The locals will not allow the grilled tuna with whipped potatoes, spinach and lemon garlic butter to be taken off the menu. Meat lovers will salivate over the filet mignon on green beans with shallots, Stilton cheese and au gratin potatoes, and Stan smacked his lips over the molten chocolate banana bread pudding. Hey - they even make brussel sprouts taste good. You can dine al fresco in nice weather, and there's a $29 prix fixe menu. 1440 San Marco Blvd.

◑ M-Th 11-10, Fri 11-11, Sat 5-11, Sun 5-9. *i* BistroX.com ☎ 904-398-1949.

Exit 350A>: River City Brewing Company – Jacksonville is a city of waterways, so you can decompress and enjoy the view of the St. John's River while scarfing down a delish meal. Try the locally caught jumbo Mayport shrimp stuffed with crab or smothered in coconut (orange horseradish mayo). The gumbo was rich with shrimp, scallops, sausage, chicken and oysters, landlubbers can have steak or lamb and the sides are interesting, like mushroom and brie bread pudding. ☞ N on Hendricks Ave, which curves left onto Museum Circle. 835 Museum Circle *i* rivercitybrew.com ☎ 904-398-2299.

Exit 350>: Kids Kampus at Metropolitan Park – This cool park, developed with local educators, offers up 10 acres of climbing, digging, splashing, sliding and soccer. In the playscapes, kids can learn how to ride a bike on city streets (bikes, helmets, balls, hoola hoops can all be borrowed for FREE) or play in dozens of little shops. They've moved a 1903 fire station here, and it's now a museum for all to enjoy (steam pumper, hydrants, helmets, extinguishers, axes, ladders and a net to jump). You can just enjoy a picnic or

use the jogging trail. ◑ M-Sat 9-6, Sun 10-6. Fire Station M-F 9-4. ☞ Head north on US 1 and 90 across the Main St bridge, keep right onto Ocean St, RT on E Bay St for 9 blocks, becomes Gator Bowl Blvd. 1410 Gator Bowl Blvd., Jacksonville. *i* jaxparks.com ☎ 904-630-5437(KIDS).

Exit 339: The Avenues – This is a large regular-price mall on 2 levels and anchored by 5 majors: Dillard's, Sears, JC Penney, Forever XXI and Belk. If you must get a coffee fix, there's a Starbucks and then 150 more stores like: Aldo Shoes,

Exit 344>: Mayo Clinic – First of all, we thought the Mayo Clinic was in Minnesota, so it was a surprise to find a campus here. The 390 acres were donated in 1986 by J.E. Davis of Winn-Dixie fame. Secondly, we never knew that anybody at all can get checked out here. Health travel is a new way to take a vacation (resting your bones) and put your mind to rest by taking care of your body. You could confuse the hospital with a hotel - it's that calm and gorgeous (art on walls, concerts, gardens, fountains and - yoiks - on-demand meal service!), but there is a Marriott here too and an ocean nearby to play in.

If you ever have to check in, there's beds for relatives, flat screen TV, wi-fi, a nurse for every 2 rooms (with a peek-a-boo window), and every room can become an ICU (don't have to move anywhere). Dr's plug in laptops at bedside to access your entire medical chart, and best of all, the specialists work as a team to heal all of you. Come here for just a check-up (they co-ordinate everything in a few days- not a few months), for a second opinion or a diagnosis. They specialize in cancer, cardio-vascular diseases and transplants. In an emergency, they never turn anyone away. 4500 San Pablo Rd. ◑ office: M-F 8-5. *i* mayoclinic.org ☎ 904-953-2000 or 904-953-7000 (International).

MAP PG 64-66

American Eagle Outfitters, Build-A-Bear, New York & Company, Justice, Spencer Gifts, Williams Sonoma and Football Fanatics. ☾ M-Sat 10-9, Sun 12-6. 10300 Southside Blvd. *i* simon.com/mall/default.aspx?ID=124 ☎ 904-363-3060.

Exit 323: World Golf Hall of Fame – As the centerpiece setting of World Golf Village, this museum celebrates golf's greatest players, showing off their personal memorabilia (Greg Nor-man's handwritten tournament notes) as well as the history and artifacts going back to 1296, when it was called Kolf and played on ice or land with a feather-stuffed ball. Videos like the one of Alan Shepard talking about his playing on the moon are there, along with an adorable Member Locker Room filled with authentic famers' clubs, bags, trophies and notebooks. You even get the opportunity to take a picture crossing the famous Swilcan Burn Bridge with the Old Course at St. Andrews in the background. There's a gift shop and cafe. ☾ M-Sat 10-6, Sun 12-6. *i* worldgolf halloffame.org ☎ 904-940-4123.

Exit 318: St. Augustine Premium Outlets – You're near the beaches here, so you can stock up at the Sunglass Hut, Crocs for sandals (and 14 others), Coach for a beach bag, Levi's for your jeans, Pepperidge Farm for snacks and to refresh afterwards, The Cosmetics Company Store. Anne Klein has opened and there's Ashworth Golf or Under Armour. When it's back to work, there's The Uniform Outlet. If you joing their VIP club you get coupons and notices about sales. ☾ M-S 9-9, Sun 10-6. *i* premium outlets.com ☎ 904-825-1555.

Exit 318: Prime Outlets St. Augustine – Here's Gucci's only outlet location

in the southeastern US, and Dooney & Bourke and Escada too. Women who (like the first lady) enjoy dresses, will like the Dress Barn, and men can head to the Hugo Boss Factory Store. The younger set will gravitate to Juicy Couture and Lucky Brand Jeans. A Disney Character store is there for the kiddies, and for tired mall-walking feet: Easy Spirit and Hush Puppies. Guest services has strollers, wheelchairs and copy machines. Join primemycloset.com for coupons, events and contests and check for 55+ prime time shoppers discounts. ☾ M-S 9-9, Sun 10-6. *i* primeoutlets.com/staugustine ☎ 904-826-1311.

NEW! Exit 318: St. Augustine Adventure Landing – Kids of all ages love amusement arcades, and this one has 80 video games, go-karts, batting cages, miniature golf and, of course, redemption prizes. Look for special deals like: M & Th 6-9 pm, $19.99 unlimited go-karting or Super Saturday $9 unlimited golf, 2 go-cart rides and 40 arcade tokens. Food hitches up a notch here, since they are smoking-on-the-spot BBQ pulled pork sandwiches ($5), and if that doesn't tempt you, they serve Starbucks coffee, cinnamon pretzels, funnel cake and cheese sticks. ☾ M-Th 12-10, F 12-12, Sat 10-12, Sun 10-10. 2780 State Rd 16. *i* adventurelanding.com/staugustine ☎ 904-827-9400.

Exit 318>: The Spanish Bakery – It was about 28 years ago when Marge and Dewey Adelsperger took over the the tiny back kitchen of the Salcedo house to serve food, and now son Gene and and daughter-in-law Julie run the

bakery. For a $5 lunch special you can have a meat empanada or smoked sausage roll or picadillo (Spanish meat sauce on rice) with homemade bread, a drink and a cookie - lemon, cinnamon or almond (from an authentic Spanish recipe using no eggs or milk). Eat them or yummy sweet potato turnovers on the picnic tables under the spreading cedar tree. ◑ 9 - 3. ☞ 5.5 mi E on Rte 16, crossing bridge over Maria Sanchez Lake, RT on San Marco Ave for 1.5 mi, RT on Orange St and park here. 42 1/2 St. George St. *i* thespanishbakery.com ☎ 904-471-3046.

Exit 318: In 1493 Ponce de Leon sailed with Columbus on his 2nd voyage. He eventually wound up living on Hispaniola, becoming a governor there and later conquering Puerto Rico, where the settlers told him of a land to the west filled with gold and a magic fountain of youth (perhaps to get rid of him?). So in 1513, this Spanish nobleman took his 3 small ships and 200 men and headed there. They landed on a white sand beach (possibly around St. Augustine), and claimed the area for King Ferdinand. Since it was Easter time, in Spanish named Pascua Florida (feast of flowers), it came to be called Florida.

Exit 318>: Old Town Trolleys – These tours are the perfect way to get around St. Augustine (parking is difficult) - they have 22 stops around town, and you can get on and off all day. Take in: Lightner Museum, Castillo de San Marcos, Old Jail, Flagler College, Florida Heritage Muse-

um, Ripley's Believe It or Not (the original one), America's oldest house and, of course, the Fountain of Youth. ◑ Daily 8:30-5. ☞ 5.5 mi E on Rte 16, crossing bridge over Maria Sanchez Lake, RT on San Marco Ave. 167 San Marco Ave. *i* http://www.trolleytours.com/st-augustine/ ☎ 904-829-3800.

Exit 318>: Barnacle Bill's – When most of the staff has been working here for over 20 years, you know this is a friendly neighborhood joint. You can't go wrong with tilapia, wahoo, cobia, mahi, and flounder caught locally, or the dozen ways of serving shrimp (Stan adored the coconut ones with the

fab orange marmalade sauce). Locals sprinkle on their famous Dat'l Do-it Hot Sauce, which you can buy here - Stan can't live without it. Start with the Minorcan clam chowder, a traditional red one with a bit of a bite, the smokin' smokin' fish dip or the gator tails. ◑ Daily 11-9. ☞ 5.5 mi E on Rte 16, crossing bridge over Maria Sanchez Lake, RT on US 1 (Ponce de Leon Blvd) for 1 1/4 mi, LT on W Castillo Dr. to 14 W. Castillo Dr. *i* barnaclebillsonline.com ☎ 904-824-3663.

Exit 318>: Schooner's Seafood House – This is one of the local favorites for basic fresh fish, and they know to order it with the famous pink spicy shrimp sauce. It is said that their award-winning Minorcan clam chowder is really the Fountain of Youth. Fried shrimp, oysters, scallops and crab cakes are paired with sides of sweet potato, squash, black-eyed peas and greens. Yup, you can score a gator tail dinner or some frog legs here. Leave room for

MAP PG 67

Grandma Bunk's peanut butter pie, carrot cake or chocolate malt pie. ◑ Daily 11 - 9. 3560 N. Ponce de Leon Blvd. *i* schooners-seafood.com ☎ 904-826-0233.

Exit 311>: Lightner Museum – Housed in the old Alcazar Hotel, built by Henry Flagler in 1887 in a Spanish Renaissance style, this building itself is worth seeing (the Russian bath is still there). Talk about the ultimate storage unit - Otto C. Lightner, Chicago publisher/editor of Hobbies magazine, converted the hotel into a museum in 1948 to contain his vast collections of art, antiques, furnishings (moving mechanical constructs, perfume bottles, vases), costumes (beaded purses), Tiffany glass and 19th century mechanical musical instruments (demos daily 11 & 2).

The enormous indoor swimming pool area showcases to-die-for antique furniture, yet there's still room for his eclectic minutiae: Edison's phonograph, marbles, Churchill's lion (stuffed, of course) and remedies for sneezing. ◑ Daily 9-5. 75 King St. *i* lightnermuseum.org ☎ 904-824-2874.

Exit 311>: Alligator Farm Zoological Park – Founded in 1893 and one

of the oldest zoos in the country, this is the only place in the world that displays all 23 living species of alligators and crocodiles. Just strolling through the lushly canopied boardwalk is a pleasure, and you might happen upon the rare albino white alligator or even an ibis, emu, monkey or egret. In the new Komodo dragon exhibit, see the Southern cassowary, the world's most dangerous bird, which looks more like a dinosaur than anything on the planet, and a 12' king cobra, a 21' reticulated python, shingleback skinks, and vipers. There are hourly shows, underwater viewing areas, and dear old preserved "Gomek" in all his 2,000 lbs. and 18 ft. glory. ◑ Daily 9-5 winter, 9-6 summer. ☞ 3.8 mi E on Rte 207, RT on Rte 312 for 3.7 mi. crossing the bridge to A1A, LT to 999 Anastasia Blvd. *i* www.alligatorfarm.com ☎ 904-824-3337.

Exit 305>: South Beach Grill – Situated on the ocean, you are looking at the water that your supper just came out of that morning. Start the meal with one of their award winning chowders, either the red Minorcan conch or the roasted corn and blue crab, and the house salad dressing was so good that we asked for the recipe. For bragging rights back home, try the Florida gator tail (yup, it tastes like chicken) with wasabi keylime mayo. Your fish can be blackened, grilled or fried, or try crab cakes or jambalaya (shrimp, fish, mussels, clams, andouille sausage, tomatoes, onions wine over red beans and rice). Landlubbers can stick to chicken, ribs or steak, wraps or a garden burger. ☞ 6 mi E on Rte 206 over the Matanzas River, RT on A1A for 250 yds, LT to 45 Cubbedge Rd. ◑ Daily 7:30-10:30, 11-9. *i* southbeachgrill.net ☎ 904-471-8700.

Exit 273: Bruce Rossmeyer's Destination Daytona – If you are a motorcycle fan, you'll think you've died and gone to heaven here. On 2 floors, it's the world's largest Harley dealership (1,500 cycles), so anything you can imagine related to cycling is here - the Harleys of course, choppers, kids' clothes, insurance, dog leashes, parts, grips, lava night lights and Harley candies. The mall includes a food court

and stores for Ness, Triumph, Ducati, American IronHorse, Rucker Performance, Rooke Customs, J&P Cycles, Trike Shop and accessories stores. Don't worry if you can't finish in a day, you can eat (Pig Stand, Houligan's, Saints and Sinners) and stay overnight at their hotel.

There's a Daytona Beach Visitor desk inside the store (◗ Daily 10-5, ☎ 386-673- 4767). 1637 N.US Highway 1. ◗ M-Sat 9-6, Sun 10-5. *i* destinationdaytona.com ☎ 866-642-3464.

Exit 268: La Crêpe en Haut – Sometimes you just want the treat of a classic French dining experience, and this one delivers beautifully, with vichyssoise, duck

a l'orange, Dover sole almondine, chateaubriand for 2 and crepes Suzette, but you can tickle your taste buds with Thai shrimp and blackened tilapia with blue cheese too. ☞ 5.1 mi E on Granada Blvd, crossing over Halifax River to 142 E. Granada Blvd. *i* lacrepeenhaut.net ☎ 386-673-1999.

Exit 268: The Cellar – After his stint as a Culinary Institute of American trained chef in NY, Sam and his wife Lina Moggio migrated South to own their own Italian

fine dining place situated in the summer home of President Warren G. Harding. You can tell he learned well in Italy, too, because the menu is studded with prosciutto di Parma, fennel, arugula, radicchio, pancetta, artichokes and shaved parmigiano. The plates are expertly executed amongst the veal, beef and seafood, and for dessert, tortas and imported gelato. ◗ T-Sun 5-10. ☞ 2.3 mi E on W. Granada Blvd, RT onto Mag-

nolia. 220 Maqnolia Ave. *i* thecellarrestaurant.com ☎ 386-258-0011.

Exit 261: Daytona Beach Visitor Information Center – Right inside the Daytona 500 Experience, there are people to help you find out more about the area, those motel coupon booklets, and an ATM machine, but there's also a full snack bar and a speedway gift shop! Ask about the Sunsaver coupons for parasailing, go-karting, free toe ring and hair braiding, food, or 2 for 1 mini golf. (Other location Exit 273: Bruce Rossmeyer's Destination Daytona (☎ 386- 673-4767). ◗ Daily 10-5. 1801 W. International Speedway Blvd. *i* daytonabeach.com ☎ 386-253-8669.

NEW! **Exit 261:** Daytona 500 Experience – Do take the narrated behind-the-scenes tour of the track (especially fun if cars are practicing) to get to the speedway's garage area, pit road and to have a

closer look at the world-famous 31-degree high banks (as high as a 3-story building). The mini-museum walks you back through time to see how Daytona came to be the "World Center of Racing". Watch an Imax movie, test your racing skills in simulators and get up close and personal with winning cars. ◗ Daily 10-6. 1801 W. International Speedway Blvd. *i* daytona500experience.com ☎ 386-947-6800.

NEW! **Exit 261>:** The August Seven Inn – The best part of this B&B for Sandra is the free twin massage chairs in their tranquility verandah. What a terrific treat to enjoy after a day on the road in the car. At this B&B, you have only a 4 min. walk to the beach, you can hang out at the Daytona Speedway or relax on the wrap-

MAP PG 67-69

around porch. Little touches such as the white noise machine, bath salts (and whirlpool tubs), wide screen TV's, DVD players and a film library in the butler's pantry (with popcorn!) are appreciated. 1209 S. Peninsula Dr. *i* jpaugust.net ☎ 386-248-8420.

NEW! PRAISE THE LORD AND PASS THE SUNTAN LOTION

Exit 261>: Daytona Beach Drive-In Church – Back in 1953 when this was still the Neptune Drive-In Theater, The First Christian Church organized the first drive-in service. Buying the property in 1957, they now welcome everyone - tourists, the physically challenged, families with kids or those looking for a unique way to worship (honking your horn = clapping). Perfect for those going to the beach on Sunday (don't need to wear your Sunday best!) - just stay in the car, tune in on your radio or listen to the speakers, and at the end Rev Larry Deitch will shake your hand through the window - then hop across the street to beach. ◑ Sun 8:30 & 10. 140 S. Atlantic Ave. *i* driveinchurch.net ☎ 386-767-8761.

NEW! **Exit 261>:** Angel & Phelps Chocolate Factory – The FREE weekday 30 min. guided tour just whets your appetite for some of the 83-year-old classics like chocolate-covered potato chips (light or dark) or pret-

zels. Other home-made favorites are the made from scratch vanilla caramels, rocco - the award winning buttercrunch toffee/chocolate topped with almonds, orange and raspberry jellies and the honeybees (turtles) with pecan pieces, caramel and chocolate. On the shelves of this 1925 company, started by 2 women - Riddell Angell and Cora Phelps - you can buy chocolate gifts like a computer, tool and hairdresser kits or chocolate greeting cards. ◑ M-F 9:30-5:30, Sat 9:30-5. ☞ 5 mi E on International Speedway Blvd, RT on S Beach St to 154 S. Beach St. *i* angellandphelps.com ☎ 800-969-2634 or 386-252-6531.

Exit 261>: Museum of Arts & Science – The menu here at this Smithsonian affiliate has something for everyone's tastes. Mom should enjoy the early American furniture, European porcelains, Batista's Cuban art collection and the quilts. Dad will like the 1948 Lincoln Continental and the Root family's coke collection, including the winning design of the 1915 perfect bottle contest, coke trucks and the 1985 coke can that

went into outer space. Kids will smile at the the 2 real trains and 800 teddy bears, and will love the new Children's Museum, where they can ride a Harley, play velcro ball, be a CSI investigator or play a laser harp. ◑ T-S 9-5, Sun 11-5. You can request a docent ahead of time (at least 24 hrs.) for your family. ☞ 3.5 mi E on International Speedway Blvd, RT on S Nova Rd, RT to 352 S.Nova Rd. *i* moas.org ☎ 386-255-0285.

Exit 261>: Racing's North Turn – If you want to rub shoulders with racing greats or their memorabilia, this beach grill sits on the location where racing history began. Chow down in the booths named for drivers or on the patio to "ignite your appetite, start your engines, or for back stretch sandwiches" (catch of the day, a  ruben with fried fish, ahi tuna wrap). Clam strips and scallops with bacon/cabbage hash share the sand with rib eye and mandarin almond salad. There's live music starting at 6 p.m. ◐ Sun-Th 11-10, Fri & Sat 11-11. ☞ 4511 S. Atlantic Ave. *i* racingsnorthturn.com ☎ 386-322-3258.

🆕 Take a Flyer and Take a Bride

Exit 249: New Smyrna Beach Visitor Center – Stop for the free postcards (with free mailing!) and the friendly help from Debbie, Pat, Lucy, Sherry and the gang. You can send a fax here,  pick up some flyers and the motel coupon books, but the best part of this one is that they can marry you - for FREE! However, you do need a licence ($56), a social security number, a photo ID and a fiance - then head for the beach to frolic. 2238 State Road 44. ◐ M-Sat 9-5, Sun 10-2. *i* nsbfla.com ☎ 800-541-9621 or 386-428-1600.

🆕 **Exit 249>:** Little Drug Co.
– If you want the feel and taste of an old time luncheonette, sitting on the stools at the large U-shaped counters here will bring you back to at least the 1950's, though the shop opened in 1922. Food specials ($4.95-$5.95) change every day, so the regulars fill the seats for the chicken pot pie, hot dog with baked beans, pot

 roast, and award winning soups: broccoli & cheese, black bean and beef steak, pasta fagioli, chicken gumbo ($2 for a cup). Many return just for the taste of their hamburger, which hasn't changed in decades. It's still a drug store too, and you can buy American Greeting cards, Russell Stover/Whitman candies, Webkins, Trail of Painted Ponies and nautical gifts. ◐ M-F 8-5, Sat 8-3 (2nd sat ea month 8-8 for oldies car show). 412 Canal St. *i* littledrug.com ☎ 386-428-9041.

Exit 249>: Riverview Hotel and Grille – Built in 1885 as a former drawbridge tender's home, Jim and Christa Kelsey attractively resurrected the property. You're near a retro 50's beach where you can still drive cars on the sand. Breakfast is served in your room on a balcony, overlooking either the tropically landscaped heated pool or the motor boats on the Indian River. Dine at The Grille with its wonderful French inspired food, and you might glimpse dolphins. You can start with escargot or French onion soup, then go on to bacon wrapped shrimp stuffed with crab and blue cheese, rack of lamb or crispy maple leaf duck or freshly caught fish, and end with a perfect creme brule or apple strudel. There's a spa to smooth out all the kinks from the car, and the lobby is adorned as a gift shop and has terrific cards. ☞ 5 mi E on Rte 44 as it becomes Lytle Ave. (don't turn when  44 veers left), 4 mi over causeway bridge, LT at 1st light, S Peninsula Ave, LT on Flagler Ave, immediate LT into #101 before bridge. *i* riverviewhotel.com ☎ 386-428-5858 or 800-945-7416, 386-428-1865 (Grille).

MAP PG 69

Dammit, Dummitt!

Exit 249>: Dummitt's Tomb – It must be very odd to live on this residential street and look out at the wee cemetery smack in the middle of

it. Charles Dummitt (or Dummett), one of the area's first settlers is still in residence here. Canova Dr. ☞ see Riverview Inn directions, but only 3 blocks along S Peninsula Ave 3 to Oakwood, LT to Canova Dr.

Exit 220: Dixie Crossroads – Rock shrimp used to be ignored as a delicacy because they were too hard to peel, so Rodney Thompson invented a shell-splitting machine to break the hard shells, and ran this restaurant specializing in them. His daughter Laurilee, after captaining her own ship for 13 years, has now taken over the helm. Though we are menu adventurers, at this place we were rock shrimp purists, eating them broiled and buttered. Forget the steak, the imported Maine lobster or mahi mahi - you can get them elsewhere. Come for the domestic wild ocean shrimp, shrimp soup, coconut shrimp with orange marmalade, famous corn fritters or sweet potato. There's all-you-can-eat options: shrimp, crab, catfish, tilapia.

We never got to the hot fudge sundae cheesecake. ◐ Sun-Th 11-9, Fri & Sat 11-10. ☞ 2 mi E on Garden St to 1475 Garden St. *i* dixiecrossroads.com ☎ 321-268-5000.

NEW! **Exit 191:** Brevard Zoo – We had one of our favorite surprises here when for a mere $6 we enjoyed the guided kayak tour around Expedition Africa and saw lemurs being fed, giraffes frolicking, and rhinos, camels, oryx and cheetahs. Afterwards we went eye-to eye with the giraffes on a feeding platform. Stan loved hand-feeding the lorikeets and we bumped into a lady holding an owl. The Wildlife Detective Training Academy sends kids off on a zoo hunt, plus

Fly Me to the Moon

Exit 215>: Kennedy Space Center – This isn't a fast pitstop, but it's worth at least a day of your life to live through the amazing feats of the Space Programs, from the first race to space in the early 60's to the Apollo project and its lunar landing in 1969 and then the Shuttle Missions. You get up close and personal with the rockets, capsules, clothing, lunar rover, a shuttle and even a live astronaut (every day, or you can lunch with him!)

Tours include one to NASA restricted areas offering a view of the shuttle launch pads from the four-story LC 39 Observatory Gantry. There are Imax movies, real movies from space, clips of the astronauts talking and you can touch both a moon rock and one from Mars. The 44,000 square foot Shuttle Launch Experience takes visitors on a simulated journey to experience launching into space from earth aboard a Space Shuttle. Crew members strap in for launch in a one-of-a-kind motion based simulator that replicates the sounds, sights, rattle and roll of lift-off to make the most realistic simulation of a launch, culminating with a breath-taking view of Earth from space. ◐ 9-6 *i* kennedyspacecenter.com ☎ 321-449-4444.

there's an indoor hands-on room where children under the age of 10 can interact with animals, and there's a train ride too. Expect a gift shop, cafe and our favorite Dippin' Dots ice cream. There's aso the vultures, jaguars, wallabies, warty pigs, giant anteaters and even a kookaburra. ◐ Daily 9:30-5. 8225 N. Wickham Rd, Melbourne. *i* brevardzoo.org ☎ 321-254-9453.

Exit 180:

Harbor City Diner – When you get a hankering for a real burger or Greek food head here, but make sure you're starving. Voted for 5 years the "best burgers in Broward County", they're massive and the fries are scrumptious - crispy on the outside and fluffy inside. The other wowees are the Greek gyro platter, chicken souvlaki or shrimp Mykonos. Dinner specials for $13.99 (soup, salad, dessert) would fill 4 tummies: blackened mahi mahi, garlic chicken, egg-

plant parmigiana, wiener schnitzel or the above dishes too, and there's 17 omelets for breakfast. ◐ Daily 7am-9pm. 1630 S. Wickham Rd. ☎ 321-952-0707.

Exit 147: Vero Fashion Outlets –

This Spanish stucco neighborhood of shops sells designer and name brand items. Walk the mall and you can buy Easy Spirit or Clark's shoes and then Izod, Banana Republic, J.Crew and Lane Bryant clothes. Swim Mart is there for beach needs, and men

---

NEW! Courageous Words of First American in Space

We all know what Neil Armstrong, the first man on the moon, said as he stepped down. What famous words did the very first American astronaut, Alan Shepard, say as he waited 4 hours for take off (with almost no room to move) in his tiny Freedom Seven Mercury spacecraft? At one point, while technicians debated over a malfunction that had halted the countdown, Shepard said over the radio, "Why don't you fix your little problem and light this candle?"

---

can head over to Bose for electronics. Ever been to a Fuller Brush store? Pick up the free coupon book at customer service. ◐ M-Sat 9-8, Sun 11-6. *i* www.vero beachoutlets.com ☎ 772 770 6097.

NEW! Exit 131A:

Dominick's Corner Grill – This local joint's kitchen is manned by a steakhouse chef and has an Italian owner, so your yearnings for both prime rib and steak and stuffed eggplant (delish) and penne Bolognese are satisfied. Daily fried egg and cheese sandwiches, kitchen sink omelettes and lunch subs are there. Dinner surprises are the fried pickles, Scoopy snacks - battered and fried prime rib morsels au jus, and the linguine with white clam sauce that included the bite of hot peppers. Though there's a 20 oz. steak on the menu, larger cuts are available - if you'd only ask. ◐ M-Th & Sat 7am-9pm, Fri 7am-10pm, Sun 7am-2pm. 5701 Orange Ave. ☎ 772-461-5097.

NEW! Exit 131A>: National Navy UDT-SEAL Museum – The ground you walk on here really really is the birthplace of Navy Frogmen - and you can see their green-faced camouflage here. Learn that Navy Combat Demolition Units (NCDU), Underwater Demolition Teams

MAP P6 69-73

(UDT) and Sea, Air and Land Teams (SEALs) are the only military areas where officers and enlist-ed men train together. Enjoy learning about World War II missions (along with a real peace treaty

from the Philippines), Apollo training crafts, a Huey helicopter, weapons and underwater gear. Outside you can imagine being submersed in water inside the small submersible. See if you can find a TV Survivor (and one in real life too!). ● Tues-Sat 10-4, Sun 12-4 (Jan-Apr also Mon 10-4). 3300 N. Highway A1A. *i* navysealmuseum.com ☎ 772-595-5845.

Exit 131A>: Manatee Observation and Education Center – This could be a quick pit stop with its 15 min. movie and 3 small areas. Learn that manatees have no natural enemies (except us), are vegetarians and hear through a hole behind their eyes. Kids can play with puzzles, watch fish in aquariums and wonder at the life-size manatee. Outdoors there's a covered observation walkway and tower with views of the Indian river, and at the right times, potential sightings of manatees in their natural habitat. If you have time, there's a

90-min eco boat tour of the Indian River Lagoon. ● T-Sat 10-5, Sun 12-4; summer Th-Sat 10-5. ☞ E on Rte 68 (Orange Ave) 4.25 mi, LT on S. Indian River Dr to 480 N. Indian River Dr. manatee-center.com. ☎ 772-466-1600 X 3333 or 3071.

Exit 121: PGA Learning Center – PGA Village is one of the only PGA facilities open to the public, and you can play

a round of golf at 3 courses. The best deal in town is $20 for an entire day to practice (100 stations) your putting, chipping and pitching greens or on 9 different bunkers - 4 kinds of sand, grass, and a fairway. You can book private instruction, a group clinic or get a computer-ized analysis of

your swing and putting. ● 8am - 10pm. ☞ W 1/4 mi to roundabout, follow signs. *i* pgavillage.com ☎ 800-800-GOLF (4653).

Exit 121: Superplay USA – With new state-of-the-art bowling lanes, laser tag, miniature golf, batting cages and 45 arcade games, this is a must stop for those with kids of all ages. Food is way beyond the usual arcade grub - there's Duffy's Sports Grille. You may see Zook, their mascot,

bowling a few games, playing laser tag, cashing redemption ticket-sor eating a burg-er. ● Sun-Th 9-11, F & Sat 9-1am. ☞ 0.4 mi E on St Lucie W Blvd, LT on NW Peacock Blvd to 1600 NW Courtyard Circle. *i* superplayusa.com ☎ 772-408-5800.

Exit 118: Sake too Japanese & Thai – Sushi aficionados will have a hard time deciding amongst the 45 rolls, udon soup, gyoza and combo dinners, while Thai lovers can feast on tom ka soup, bean thread noodle salad with shrimp, chicken, onions and lime, volcano shrimp (spicy chili-garlic) or 4 kinds of curry. Vegetarians will be thrilled with many choices, and Sandra will be back for the crispy sake duck. Everyone will feel pampered by the attentive service. ● M-F 11:30-2:45, 4:30-9:45, Sat 12-2:45, 4:30-945, Sun 4:30-9:45. ☞ W on Gatlin Blvd, RT on Village Pkwy into Tradition town,

LT to square. 10785 SW Tradition Sq. ☎ 772-345-7253.

Exit 101: Halpatiokee Park – Right off the exit you can take the opportunity to play in the baseball or soccer fields, tennis courts, batting cages, in-line hockey area or just walk or throw a frisbee. There's a 7-mile mountain bike path and primitive camping (no charge, no facilities) with only tables and fire-rings. You can rent fishing gear, bicycles and kayaks and canoes from *i* southriveroutfitters.com ☎ 772-223-1500. For park info ☎ 772-221-1420.

Exit:79: Hoffman's Chocolates – It sounds weird, but it was double-dipped chocolate (dark, milk, white) pretzels that brought this shop fame. This family businss then went on to develop melt-aways, which do just that - melt in your mouth, a bit like chocolate mousse. San-dra adored the almond butter crunch, and everyone will enjoy the pecan jitterbugs, caramel marshmallows, key lime cream, cashew clusters and covered oreo cookies. Coffee freaks - look for the Boca Latte. Sucrose-free needs are covered by 18 options (peanut butter pillows, coconut, nut clusters), and there's malt balls (mint cookie and cream), Swiss fruits and now, ice cream. ● M-Sat 9-8, Sun 10-5. 10957 N Military Trail (Garden Square Shoppes). *i* hoffmans.com ☎ 561-626-2009.

Exit 70>: CityPlace –

Inspired by the Italian concept of a town center, this center succeeds because it offers up 80 shops (Sephora, Lucky Brand Jeans, Restoration Hardware, White House/Black Market, Victoria's Secret, Bang & Olufsen), 23 restaurants, 20-screen Muvico Imax movies and a cultural arts theatre. On the weekends there's FREE entertainment on the plaza in front of the colorful dancing fountains. Everyone stops by Sloan's, their version of Willy Wonka's (cherubs on the ceiling, electric train riding the walls), for 30 flavors of ice cream (coffee & donuts, 12-scoop-with-every-topping kitchen sink, sandbox sundae including shovel), crazy chocolates (chocolate covered potato chips, cashew myrtle, heavenly hash), malts, fudge, and the do-not-miss glass-doored rest room. (Other Sloan's locations: Boca Raton, Mizner Park, 329 Plaza Real (561-338-9887), Palm Beach Gardens, 11700 Lake Victoria Gardens Ave. (561-627-4301). ● (CityPlace) M-Th 10-9, Fri & Sat 10-10, Sun 12-6. 700 S. Rosemary Dr. *i* cityplace.com ☎ 561-366-1000.

Exit 70: Palm Beach supposedly wound up with palm trees because in the late 1880's a wrecked Spanish ship's cargo of wine and coconuts floated to this barrier island. When Henry Flagler visited in 1893, the coconuts had grown into palm trees, and he was so captivated by the South Seas atmosphere that he turned the strip into one of the swankiest resort areas in the world. However, all the wealthy vacationers needed a place to stash their private railroad cars, so he also developed West Palm Beach. This was well suited as a place to live for the construction workers and servants. Each day they would all have to row across Lake Worth to serve tea in the elegant parlors, chase down croquet balls or maintain the lush grounds of those rich socialites. *i* palmbeachfl.com

MAP PG 73-76

Exit 70>: City Cellar Wine Bar and Grill – This cellar is in the attic - on the top floor of CityPlace overlook-  ing the mall action (or sometimes the action is in the resto itself, with Vince Carter, Matt Lauer, the Trumps or Celine Dion eating here) and the colorful dancing fountain. The hearty and very satisfying food could start out with the flavor-packed onion and mushroom soup or ricotta gnocchi in vodka sauce. There's veggie pizzas, or chopped bok choy chicken salad with cashews and onions and heavy duty mains: crabmeat crusted sea bass with potato pan- cakes, intensely flavorful lamb shank with fried parsnips and pop- ular rigatoni with veal and braised beef Bolognese - so thick you could call it stew. ● Sun- Wed 11:30-10, Th- Sat 11:30-10:30. 700 S. Rosemary Ave, West Palm Beach. *i* bigtime restaurants.com ☎ 561-366-0071.

Worth a Detour?

Exit 70>: Worth Ave in Palm Beach, designed by Addi- son Mizner, is the Fifth Avenue of Florida. You do not have to jet to Europe to savour

Exit 70>: Flager Museum – Henry Flagler, the son of a Presbyterian minister, left home in NY at 14, made his fortune first in Ohio in grain, then salt mining and most famously as a partner with John D. Rockefeller and Samuel Andrews in Standard Oil. In his 50's he started developing Florida's agriculture and tourism with his Florida's East Coast Railway (you can see his private rail car near the gift shop) and luxury hotels, turning Florida from a swampy wasteland into a vacation playground. Who wouldn't have liked this wedding present that Henry Flagler gave his 3rd wife, Mary Lily Kenan Flagler? It's a 55-room winter retreat built in 1902 during America's Gilded Age

the delights of: Pucci or Gucci, Valentino, Chanel, Hermes, Armani, or Jimmy Choo or 100 other merchants (or upscale resale boutiques!). Among the oldest retail- ers on Worth Avenue is Kassatly's Linens, open since 1926; Maus & Hoffman arrived in 1961, and 2nd-generation John Maus remains a stand-out retailer for men's and women's clothes. If you desire trinkets to take home, check out the 2 dozen jewel- ers. *i* worth-avenue.com

Exit 69: Hotel Biba – Who would think that smack in the middle of monied West Palm Beach, you'd find a his- which established, for the wealthy, the Palm Beach "season".

Original and period furnishings grace Whitehall - a Louis XV ballroom, Italian Renaissance library, Elizabethan dining room and Louis XIV music room. See if you can find the secret staircase or Mary Lily's 7 ft. strand of pearls. Flagler made it til age 83 and would have lived longer, if he hadn't slipped and fallen on one of the marble staircases here. ● Tues-Sat 10-5, Sun 12-5. ☞ E on Okeechobee across bridge over waterway onto Royal Palm Way, LT at 1st stop light onto Cocoanut Row for 0.6 mi., LT on White Hall Way. 1 White Hall Way. *i* flaglermuseum.us ☎ 561-655-2833.

toric-landmarked 1939 motor lodge, part of the original Mount Vernon chain? In 2001 it was converted into a '60's inspired fun, funky and affordable hotel with breakfast included and a Wed-Sat lively bar scene, and it's located only 1 mile from the beach and 1 mile from downtown. 320 Belvedere Rd. *i* hotelbiba.com ☎ 800-789-9843 or 561-832-0094.

Exit 68: Capri Bakery/Restaurant – For at least 23 years the local population has been enjoying the 8 daily Cuban lunch specials, which might be: yellow rice with chicken, "old clothes" (shredded beef), pork chunks fricasee, grilled pork steak, goat stew or fried fish. For a fast snack, grab a Cuban sandwich (pork, ham, cheese, mojo, then grilled), an empanada, pastelitos (guava, meat, cheese), croquetas or

bocaditos (sweet bread with chopped ham). Starters might be chick pea soup, stuffed yucca or corn filled with pork on a corn leaf, and end off with a teeny cup of Cuban coffee - and - a "Cuban" cigar. Look around outside and you might see a few tables of men playing dominos. ◑ M-Sat 5am-12am. 817 Southern Blvd. ☎ 561-655-1602.

Exit 66N or 68S>: Palm Beach Zoo – The walk through the lush foliage makes you feel like you are in the wilds with the animals, either in Australia, the Tropics of the Americas or in the Mayan Pyramids. There are some fun species - kangaroos, wallabies, prairie dogs, racoon, bald eagle, a butterfly and our favorite, the giant anteater. Kids of all ages will enjoy the colorful carousel, the "Wings Over Water" bird show and water play fountain. See if you can find the 26-ton ficus tree that

moved here from around the corner. ☞ Sbound: Turn E (left) off Exit 68 to Parker Ave, RT 0.7 mi to Summit Blvd, RT for 1 block; Nbound: Exit 66, turn E (right) 0.3 mi to Parker Ave, LT for 0.7 mi, LT onto Summit Blvd for 1 block. 301 Summit Blvd ◑ Daily 9-5. *i* palmbeachzoo.org ☎ 561-547-WILD (9453).

Exit 64: Fun Depot – Put on your earplugs to enter this joint, since it is buzzing, clanking and ringing with arcade games (Poker, Skee-ball, virtual roller coaster), laser storm and a climbing wall. Upstairs the Mezz is a LAN gaming center for multiplayer video gaming. Outside there are go-karts and batting cages. You have to buy tokens to play, and winning coupons are turned in for a counter-full of prizes. ◑ M-Th 12-11, Fri 12-1, Sat 10-1, Sun 10-11. 2003 10th Ave. N. *i* fundepot.net ☎ 561-547-0817.

Exit 48A>: Sports Immortals Museum and Memorabilia Mart – Sport freaks will freak out as they come face to face with 50,000 items of memorabilia of the greatest athletes, amassed by Joel Platt from his 1,000,000 piece collection. Drool over: a piano signed by the Pittsburgh Steelers, robes monogrammed for Cassius Clay/Muhammad Ali and artwork by Ali, the 1920 "death ball" which killed the only person to die in a major league baseball game, Jim Thorpe's Olympic scrapbook, Michael Jordan's signed rookie jersey, an Atlanta games Olympic torch, Jack Johnson (1st black heavyweight champion's) gloves, Dale Earnhardt's helmet, a seat from the Montreal forum, or a Honus Wagner baseball card worth $1,265,000. In the shop you can buy some of the less expensive collectibles. ◑ M-F 10-6, Sat 10-5. 6830 N. Federal Highway. *i* sportsimmortals.com ☎ 561-997-2575.

MAP PG 76-78

FLORIDA LOYALISTS

Many Americans are not aware that Florida was loyal to Britain during the Revolutionary War. In 1763 Spain had traded the area to England in return for Havana, Cuba. Then in 1776, when the 13 colonies declared independence, the loyalists from the Carolinas and Georgia swarmed down here. It was so fervently loyalist that citizens burned effigies of John Hancock and Samuel Adams, and imprisoned 3 signers of the Declaration of Independence.

NEW! Exit 32>: Xtreme Indoor Karting – You can really feel like a race car driver when you are wearing a jump suit, professional helmet and neck brace, and then lower yourself into one of the 40 European Bowman race

karts, which can reach 45 mph around the 1/2 mile asphalt track. Don't worry - there are safety marshals, and at the end you can get printed race analyses. The facility offers 120 arcade games, including Nascar race simulators, mini bowling lanes, a snack bar, sports bar and a gift shop which carries racing merchandise (race suits and helmets). 5300 Powerline Rd. ● M-Th 3-11 (arcade opens 12 pm), Fri & Sat 12-12, Sun 12-10. *i* xtremeindoorkarting.com ☎ 954-491-6265.

Exit 32: German Bread Haus – It is so rare to find a family bakery (open 24 years) these days, and especially one baking (perfect for car sandwiches) wholesome six-grain bread or Bavarian farmers' rye, and organic ones like 4-seed fruit/nut

bread or a high protein low carb jogging one. The tiny shop has European treats - cherry or apple strudels, poppy seed or cherry crumb cake, rum balls and even sugar-free desserts: rugalach and blueberry corn muffins, which make for some yummy car snacking. ● M-S 8-6. 311 E. Commercial Blvd. *i* germanbreadhaus.com ☎ 954-491-4464.

NEW! Exit 32: British Depot – How about some British tastes on the road? Shopping here, you can snack on steak and kidney or mushroom pie, cornish pasties, Scotch eggs, Shippam's crab spread with a side of Hayward's onions, and wash it down with Robinson's orange squash drink. Breakfast could be zuzzed up with Hartley's jams or Duerr's lemon curd and there's real Devon cream for tea along with Mr Kipling or Holmfield sweets and Cadbury's chocolates, of course. ● M-Sat 10-6, Sun 11-4. 1322 E. Commerical Blvd. *i* www.britishdepot.com ☎ 954-491-4920.

NEW! Exit 31: Mai-Kai Restaurant – Okay, the show is kitschy 50's, with hula girls, fire twirling dancers and birthday announcements, but patrons are still filling the 100's of seats. Don't miss the photo ops in the Polynesian garden, awash with tiki masks, gods, water falls and private dining options. The white suited

captains orchestrate the eating with the same precision as the dancers. Best deal is the $45 "Bali Hai Special" on their site, which includes the revue (show alone with no minimum is $10.95). There's 4 dozen tropical drinks to choose from. The lobster bisque was rich and perfect, the Pad Thai amazingly authentic, and for a 50's throwback, the Cantonese shrimp was there too. An a la carte menu runs around Asia: 'Nams - crab and pork wrapped in lettuce with spicy garlic sauce, Panang curry chicken with Thai coconut sauce, Singapore chili shrimp, Mandarin pressed duck or Peking duck and Javanese beef. Yet you can still find oysters Rockefeller or a surf and turf. ◐ Sun-Th 5-10:30, F&S 5-11:30 (2 shows). 3599 N. Federal Hwy *i* maikai.com ☎ 954-563-3272.

Exit 29B: Fort Lauderdale Swap Shop – Open since 1963, this flea

market is like a city with its 2,000 vendors on 88 acres. Besides the shopping (clothes, electronics, jewelry, perfume, toys, fruit and veggies), there's a 13-screen drive-in, video arcade, kiddie rides, car exhibit and weekend entertainment (1-4pm). ◐ M,T,W, F 9-6, Th 8-6:30, Sat & Sun 8-7. 3291 W. Sunrise Blvd. *i* floridaswapshop.com ☎ 954-791-SWAP.

Exit 27>: Museum of Discovery & Science – The massive sculptural gravity clock in front will stop you in your tracks. When you enter, the whole family can have fun with more than 200

interactive exhibits, plus an IMAX theater showing both creature features (think sharks and dinosaurs) and movies. Little kids can play with water, sound and gravity and can watch the scorpions,

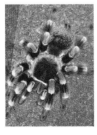

snakes and bunnies in the nature trail. Older ones (that means you, too) can fly like an astronaut on the Mars Rover, become

a human hurricane, try the brain teasers, use ultraviolet light to test fluorescent properties of minerals and pet a big green iguana. We learned here to appreciate bats, which can eat up to 1,000 mosquitoes a night! Of course, there's a gift shop. ◐ M-Sat 10-5, Sun 12-6. 401 SW Second St. *i* mods.org ☎ 954-467-6637.

Exit 26>: Fort Lauderdale Antique Car Museum – Step back in

time here to imagine a Packard (US version of the Rolls Royce) showroom of the 1920's. Arthur and Shirley Stone share with us their collection (dashboard clocks, hood ornaments, carburetors, gear shift knobs and cars, of course) and love affair with cars. All 30 Packards from 1909-1950 (including a funeral flower car, a fire truck, Calvin Coolidge's) are in working order, and their workmanship and originality can not be met even today - there are ones that have a compartment for a golf bag, a medical bag or can self-lubricate their chassis. Find out that a trunk really was a trunk, and look for the amazing FDR collection room (as a young man, in a jigsaw puzzle, election battles). ◐ M-Sat 10-4. 1527 Packard Ave. (SW 1st Ave). *i* antiquecarmuseum.org ☎ 954-779-7300.

Exit 25: Anthony's Runway 84 – You feel as if you've entered a boisterous in-flight party while you are waiting for your table (reservations necessary and you still wait).The hopping bar scene with a live piano player appears to be set inside an aircraft with plane windows depicting the world below, while the dining area has jumbo jets painted on the walls. It will not surprise you that Anthony Sr. came from a NYC nightclub background. He brought with him his Momma's cooking; Anthony Jr. now continues the tra-

MAP PG 79

ditions and the gigantic portions. Your wait staff will recite the long list of daily spe-

cials, which usually include authentic Italian Sunday feast (meatball, sausage, brasciole), ring sausage with broc-coli rabe, Sicilian rice balls and flavorful chunky minestrone soup. You can have your lasagne or eggplant or breaded veal cutlets, but do not leave without eating Anthony Sr.'s favorite cauliflower with rigatoni. ◑ T-Th 12-10, F 12-11, Sat: 4:30-11, Sun 4-10. 330 State Rd 84 (SW 4th Ave) ☎ 954-467-8484.

Exit 23>: IGFA Fishing Hall of Fame & Museum – Here's where you can learn that catfish "walk" on land, mud-skippers sit in trees, deep sea fish shine through their own lights, cave fishes swim blind and ice fish carry antifreeze. The galleries include ones about fish, tackle, places to fish and record catches. You can try your hand at 5 virtual reality simulators (hook a marlin, sailfish, bass, tarpon or trout), and on the 2nd floor research in the largest collection of reference books on fishing. Hanging in the lobby is a replica of the 1,560 lb IGFA All-Tackle record black marlin caught by Alfred C. Glassell, Jr., and out back - live alligators in wetlands. ◑ M-Sat 10-6, Sun 12-6. ☞ W on SW 48th St, LT on SW 21st Ave 1 block, LT on Gulf Stream Way to 300 Gulf Stream Way. *i* igfa.org ☎ 954-922-4212.

Exit 23>: Outdoor World – You might know this place as Bass Pro Shops, and it is a grown man's candy store. Even the entrance lobby feels like a hunting lodge. You can immerse yourself in the departments for: fishing (rods, reels, lures), fly fishing (Penn, Shimano, G-Loomis), hunting (from camo to ammo), golf (try it out on the driving net or putting green), boating, archery (indoor range), camping, a footwear department and an indoor boat show. The rest of the family can enjoy the 4-story waterfall, aquarium, trout pool and the indoor shooting range. If you get hungry there's a fresh fish market and the Islamorada Fish Company restaurant (☎ 954- 927-7377) for conch or alligator fritters, fresh dolphin, fish tacos, grouper with brandied lobster sauce or a grouper reuben, and don't miss the soft sugared bimini bread. ◑ M-Sat 9-10, Sun 10-7. 200 Gulf Stream Way (see directions for Fishing Hall of Fame). *i* basspro.com ☎ 954-929-7710.

Exit 22>: Jaxson's – In Monroe Udell's old-fashioned ice cream parlor it's fun to read the walls, with its collection of newspaper clippings, American memorabilia and license plates. For 54 years ice cream has been prepared daily on the premises using fresh cream, berries, nuts and real whipped cream, etc. in order to make gi-normous ice cream sodas, sundaes, floats (32 oz. pitcher), waffles and goblets. Sizes

are sky high (prices too, but less expensive at the outside window), as the menu goes up to a $99.95 punch bowl for 12 people who "don't want to see each other". There's 10 kinds of sundaes, like "two on a blanket" with 2 scoops on pound cake with hot fudge, marshmallow and toasted almonds. Toppings are made here too: cold ones are chocolate, marshmallow, strawberry, cherry-pineapple, chunky pineapple, black raspberry, blueberry, peach or chocolate mint, and hot ones would be fudge, butterscotch, caramel and peanut butter.

They made the Kitchen Sink famous, in which parties of 4, 6 or 8 share a mess of ice cream (chosen from the 34 flavors, including 4 sugar-free and 6 fat-free) and toppings in a stainless steel sink ($12.95 p.p). You'll also discover an old fashioned candy store with candy buttons, licorice, milk duds, peanut chews and suckers, and yes, there's food, like salads, corned beef and pastrami, mile-long hot dogs, wraps and a 1 lb. double cheeseburger, but we'd rather fill up on ice cream. ◗ M-Th 11:30-11, F&S 11:30-12am, Sun 12-11. 128 S. Federal Hwy. *i* jaxsonsicecream.com ☎ 954-923-4445.

Exit 22: Boomers – You can't miss this big amusement area with its landmark wooden roller coaster. If that makes you queasy, then you can play on an interest-ing minature golf course or try the go-kart and stock kart circuits, batting cages, bowling, kiddie rides and bumper boats/cars or go indoors for laser tag, rock walls and lots of noisy arcade games. Look online for deals on unlimited play passes. ◗ Mon-Th 12-10, F 12-1am, Sat 11-1am, Sun 11-10. 1700 NW 1st Ave. (other location Exit 45: 3100 Airport Rd, Boca Raton. ☎ 561-347-1888). *i* boomersparks.com ☎ 954-921-1411.

Exit 2A: Epic Hotel – Friendly caring service beyond your expectations is what this new slick Italian-designed hotel exudes - from the cool wet cloth and cold drink when you arrive to the thoughtful in-room computer, gold fish and embedded magnifying mirror in the bathroom. Guest suggestions and guest profiles (tall rooms for tall people) are taken seriously here. Magnificent views of Miami waters, private cabanas at the pool, 5 snack times in the business center, marina, free wine hour at 5pm, spa and a call to ask if you need a wake up call or transportation to the airport makes this a pinnacle Kimpton experience. The Area 31 restaurant highlights fresh local fish in light Mediterranean presentations. 270 Biscayne Blvd. Way *i* epichotel.com ☎ 305-424-5226 or 866-760-3742.

Exit 1B>: Versailles Cuban Restaurant – Hone your Spanish or use sign language here - it's like a visit to Havana. This 35-year-old big noisy bustling place has a bakery or lunch counter for quick meals and a take-out window for baked and fried treats: Catalan meatballs, fried plantains, fried ball of mashed potatoes stuffed with ground beef, fingers of ham and chicken or spinach empanada pastry. Or you can sit down and enjoy the Cuban samplers, dirty clothes, shredded beef, arros con pollo, black beans with rice, garlic chicken, yucca, lots of roast pork. Wash it all down with the barley malt flavored Malta Hatuey or our favorite - the smooth Cuban coffee, which tastes like toasted marshmal-lows. ◗ Daily 8am-2am. ☞ 3.25 mi W on SW 7th St., LT on SW 3t5th Ave for 1 block, to 3555 SW 8th St. (Calle Ocho) on the next corner. *i* versaillescuban.com ☎ 305-444-0240.

MAP PG 79-81

Exit 1A>: Vizcaya – James Deering (International Harvester VP) hired 3 architects to design this opulent winter home as a 400-year-old estate while he was off on European jaunts purchasing 34 rooms

worth of 16th to19th century ceilings and furnishings (Neo-Classical, Roman, Roccoco, Renaissance, Baroque). It was quite modern for its time (1916), sporting central heating, an electric telephone switch board, 2 elevators, refrigeration and even a central vac and fire control system, but he only got to enjoy it for 8 years before he died. The house is a gem, and the Baroque and Renaissance gardens are also worth the visit. ◑ Daily 9:30-5. 3251 S. Miami Ave. *i* vizcayamuseum.org ☎ 305-250-9133.

Exit 1A>: Miami Museum of Science and Planetarium – This is a small place, so it's a quick pit stop to entertain the kiddies. Outside, you can turn your body into a human yoyo and rocket yourself 10 feet in the air. You can pretend to be as strong as a giant by using the 30-ft long Giant Lever to lift as many as people as you can. Inside, there's the Energy Tracker, a trail of hands-on interactive stations to learn about wind energy, batteries, food energy and carbon footprints - and a prize for each completed ticket. Fun for all is the Energy Dance Floor, the first of its kind in the U.S., which captures energy from dancing and converts it to electricity to light up the floor. Dancers can also see the heat they are generating while they dance. The Planetarium and theatre have 4 daily shows, and there's a small wildlife center with birds of prey where you can watch a working re-hab center for them, and also alligators, crocodiles, a snake or lizard and a talking parrot. ◑ Daily 10-6. 3280 S. Miami Ave *i* miamisci.org ☎ 305-646-4200.

Bring home a Taste of your Trip

Butternut Squash Risotto

Concord's Colonial Inn in Concord, MA is an elegant 1716 restaurant sitting musket distance from "the shot heard 'round the world". It still dishes up tastes from back then: flavorful Yankee pot roast with divine mashed potatoes or yummy chicken pot pie; we sure hope Paul Revere got to taste the corn bread, which is made fresh all day long. However, the seasonal menus go well beyond that, with dishes like the butternut squash risotto below. Come here for Sunday brunch - you may bump into Louisa May Alcott. If you're too full to travel, you can sleep at the Inn, but you may share your room with ghosts. ℓ concordscolonialinn.com
☎ 978-369-9200 or 800-370-9200.

1	diced shallot
1	tbsp. unsalted butter
1 1/4	cup Arborio rice
4 1/2	cups simmering chicken or vegetable broth
2 ½ to 3	cups medium diced butternut squash
	salt and pepper to taste
2 to 3	leaves fresh sage
1/4	cup heavy cream, or more as needed
1/4	grated Parmesan cheese
1	tbsp. unsalted butter

optional garnish: shaved Parmesan cheese and/or toasted pine nuts

1. *Peel butternut squash and dice into medium cubes*

2. *In a 1 gallon pot, melt 1 tbsp. butter on medium heat. Add shallots and squash and saute for 5 to 7 minutes. Add the rice and cook for an additional 3 minutes, stirring occasionally.*

3. *Reduce heat to medium, begin adding ½ cup broth and continue to stir until you can pull a spoon along the bottom of the pot and almost no liquid remains. Add another ½ cup of the stock and stir till no liquid remains. Continue adding broth in this way until the rice is nearly done, about 20 to 25 min., stirring often. Add the cream when you put in the last 1/2 cup of broth.*

4. *To finish the risotto, add in the Parmesan cheese, sage, and remaining butter and stir until blended.*

5. *Optional: garnish with shaved Parmesan and/or toasted pine nuts*

Yield: 6 servings

Campgrounds Near I-95 Exits

State	Exit	Campground Name	Directions	Distance from Exit	# of sites	Phone
NH	2	Great Bay Camping Village	W on Rte 101 4.2 mi to exit 11, N on Rte 108 4 miles.	8.2	94	603-778-0226
NH	2	The Green Gate Camping Area	W on Rte 101 4.2 mi to exit 11, LT s on Rte 108 3 mi	7.2	109	603-772-2100
NH	2	Shel-Al Camping Area	E on 101 3/4 mi to X 13 (Rte 27), E 1.5 mi to US 1, N on Lafayette Rd 3 mi.	5.25	195	603-964-5730
NH	2	Tidewater Campground	E on Rte 101 to US 1 S.	.2	238	603-926-5474
NH	2	Wakeda Campground	W on 101 to X 12, W for 1/2 mi, LT on Ashbrook for 0.6 mi, LT on Rte 88 for 3/4 mi.	3.4	408	603-772-5274
NH	2	Hampton Beach State Park	E on Rte 101 3/4 mi to exit 13 Exeter Rd (Rte 27), E on Rte 27 3.7 mi, TR	4.5	28	603-926-3784
NH	1	The Exeter Elms Campground	W on Rte 107 6 mi, RT Rte 108, 3.5 mi	9.5	203	603-778-7631
MA	60	Black Bear Campground	E off exit, LT on Main St, 200 yds	<1 mi.	250	978-462-3183
MA	60	Rusnick Campground	S off exit along US 1 1.4 mi	1.4	200	978-462-9551
MA	54	Tuxbury Pond RV Resort (NH)	N on 150 3/4 mi, LT on Highland, becomes Lions Mouth, 1.8 mi, RT Newton 1 mi,into NH	3.5	305	603-394-7660
MA	58A	Beach Rose RV Park	E on Rte 110 2 1/4 mi, RT on Beach Rd 1.3 mi	3.75 mi.	50	800-382-2230
MA	58A	Pines Campground	E on Rte 110 2 1/4 mi, RT on Beach Rd 0.6 mi, RT on CCC Rd 1/2 mi	3.4	170	978-465-0013
MA	58A	Salisbury Beach State Reservation	E on Rte 110 2 1/4 mi, RT on Beach Rd 2 mi, RT on State Reservation Rd 1 mi.	5.25	484	978-462-4481
MA	6B	Normandy Farms Camping	W on 495, Exit 14A, 1.1 mi N on US 1, RT on Thurston St 1.25 mi	5.4	400+	508-543-7600
MA	6A	Canoe River	I-495 S to exit 10, E on Rte 123 3/4 mi., left on Newland/Mill St 2.4 mi.	3.5	200+	508-339-6462
RI	3B	Whispering Pines	1/2 mi W, left on Rte 3 1 mi, RT on Spring St 1.5 mi, RT on Sawmill Rd	2.5 mi.	200+	401-539-7011
RI	1	Frontier Family Camper Pk	South on Rte 3, left on Frontier Rd to end, left on Maxson Hill Rd.	.1	225	401-377-4510
CT	93	Holly Tree Campground	Take Rte 216 2mi. South from I-95	.2	164	401-596-2766
CT	92	M.H.G. RV Park	N on Rte 2 2.3 mi, RT on Rocky Hollow Rd .3 mi, RT Babcock Rd 300 yds.	2.7	27	860-535-0501
CT	92	Mystic KOA	N on Rte 49. Northbound: left on Rte 2 right on service rd, left on Rte 49, 1st RT	0.25	275	800-562-3451
CT	90	Seaport Campground	1 1/4 mi. N on Rte 27 then 1/2 mi. East on Rte 184	.2	154	860-536-4044
CT	74	Aces High RV Park	Rte 161 west on Chesterfield Rd.	3.5	86	860-739-8858
CT	72	Camp Niantic by the Atlantic	South to Rocky Neck Park, turn right at stop light. (Rte.156).	.1	135	860-739-9308
CT	72	Rocky Neck	S on Rocky Neck Connector 0.6 mi, LT on W Main St 1/4 mi, RT into park.	0.9	153	860-739-5471
CT	62	Riverdale Farm Campsite	N 1 block,RT on Duck Hole Rd 1/4 mi., cross cement bridge, LT on River Rd 1 3/4 mi.	2.5	250	860-669-5388
CT	62	Hammonasset Beach	S on Hammonassett Connector 1.25 mi	1.25	250	203-245-2785
CT	54	Totoket Valley RV Park	N on Rte 740 (Brushy Plain Rd) 3 mi, LT on Foxon Rd (Rte 80), 50 yds.	.3	15	203-484-0099
NJ	15E	Liberty Harbour RV Park	E on US 1 3.8 mi, curve left and RT onto Audrey Zapp Dr.3/4 mi	.4 mi.	55	201-386-7500
NJ	2	Timberlane Campground	Rte 322 E to I-295, N to exit 18.Turn right on Timberlane Rd. for 1 mi.	.11	100	856-423-6677

State	Exit	Name	Phone		Dist.	Directions
MD	109	Woodlands Camp.Resort	410-398-4414	152	6	Rte 279 South, cross Rte 40 onto Rte 7. First left on Old Elk Neck Rd.
MD	100	Elk Neck State Park	410-287-5333	258	14	South Rte 272 right to park
MD	80	Bar Harbor RV Park	410-679-0880	93	4	South 1 1/4 mi to US 40, turn right 1.7 mi to Long Bar Harbor Rd.
MD	25	Cherry Hill Park	301-937-7116	400	1	Rte 1 S. First right on Cherry Hill Rd.
MD	11A	Duncan's Family Camp	410-741-9558	270	10,3	Rte 4 South 9.5 mi to Rte 408, left on Sands Rd.
VA	161	Polick Bay Regional Park Campgrd	703-339-6104	100	5 mi	1.5 mi N on US 1, RT 3 1/4 mi on Gunston Rd, LT on Pohick Bay Dr.
VA	126B	Fredericksburg/Washington D.C.	1-800-KOA 1889	117	7 mi	3.9 mi S on US 1, LT on Guinea Sta. Rd 2.5 mi, RT on Brookside Ln.
VA	126	Fredericksburg/Washington D.C KOA	800-562-1889	117	4	S on US 1 4 mi, LT on 607 to entrance
VA	104	Hidden Acres Campground	804-633-7592	105	13 mi	11.1 mi E on Rte 207, RT on US 301 1.9 mi
VA	98	King's Dominion	800-922-6710	248	0,5	Adjacent to Kings Dominion
VA	89	Kosmo Village Camp	804-798-6689	17	2	West to US 1, turn South (right) 1 1/4 mi
VA	89	Americamps Richmond N.	804-798-5298	150	1	East on Rte 802 N Lewiston Rd. ther 1 mi south on service road
VA	61	Roadrunner Campground	804-796-5160	66	1,5	East on Rte 10, make 1st left at Jefferson Davis Hwy for 1 mile
VA	50	Picture Lake Campground	804-861-0174	175	8,25	Rte 85 W 4.5 mi to exit 63A, S on US 1 (Boydton Plank Rd) 3.75 mi.
VA	152B	Prince William Travel Trailer Village	703-221-2474	71	2,5	2 1/2 mi North on Rte 234 to campg'round on left
VA	143A	Aquia Pines Camp Resort	540-659-3447	120	0,5	1/2 mi N on Hwy 1
VA	41	The South Forty KOA	877-732-8545	112	0,5	East 1/4 mi on Rte 35 Courtland Rd, RT past Nino's restaurant
VA	17	Yogi Bear's Jellystone Park In Emporia	434-634-3115	90	1,5	1 1/2 mi south on US 301
NC	173	Interstate Inn	252-536-4111	30	200 Yds.	E on Rte 158 behind motel
NC	173	Ponderosa Campground	252-536-4741	40	1	1 mi East on Hwy 158
NC	171	The RV Resort at Carolina Crossroads	252-538-9776	95	1/2 mi	S on 125, LT at light. Right traffic circle to Wallace Fork, Resort 1/2 mile on right.
NC	154	Fayetteville /Wade KOA	252-445-5925	110	0,75	West on Rte 481 3/4 mi
NC	116	Rock Ridge	252-291-1477	117	1,9	West on Rte 42 (follow signs)
NC	98	Selma/Smithfield RVacation	919-965-5923	53	0,5	S on Pine Level Selma Rd to N on-ramp, right on Campground Rd 0.4 mi
NC	98	R Vacation Campground	919-965-5923	62	5 mi	E on East Anderson 1 block to Campground Rd, LT for 1/2 mi
NC	90	Four Oaks RV Resort	919-963-3596	20	<1 mi	N on Rte 96 1 block, LT S on Rte 301 300 yds
NC	90	Smithfield KOA	919-934-3181	104	300 yds	300 yards up US 701
NC	61	Fayetteville /Wade KOA	800-562-5350	88	0,25	East 1/4 mi
NC	44	Lazy Acres Campgrounds	910-425-9218	55	1,25	West on Claude Lee Rd (Rte 2341) 1 mi, right at Lazy Acres Drive
NC	41	Spring Valley RV Park	910-425-1505	38	2	3/4 mi N on Rte 59 (cross Hwy 301), then 1 mi N on service rd.
NC	14	Sleepy Bear's RV Park	910-739-4372	102	0,25	150 yards West on US 74, then 1/4 mi.north on Kenric Rd.
NC	1	Camp Pedro	843-774-2411	175	0,2	South on US 301 1/4 mi

Campgrounds Near I-95 Exits

State	Exit	Campground Name	Phone	# of sites	Distance from Exit	Directions
SC	190	Little Pee Dee State Park	843-774-8872	50	14 mi.	E on 34 to Rte 9 for 9 mi, RT 4 mi on State Park Rd
SC	169	Florence KOA	843-665-7007	132	1	1 block S on Rte 26, left turn on East Campground Rd. for 1 mi.
SC	157	Swamp Fox	843-665-9430	62	0.75	1/4 mi on southbound service rd., right turn on Meadors Rd.for 1/2 mi
SC	108	Taw Caw Campgrounds	803-478-2171	84	6 mi.	S 1.6 mi, LT on Bill Davis, RT at Davis Croosrds, follow signs
SC	102	Santee Lake Campground	803-478-2262	200	0.5	West 1 block to Rte 14, turn right to lakefront
SC	102	Cooper's Landing	803-478-2549	21	1	East on CR 400
SC	98	Lake Marion Resort	803-854-3083	103	2.5	East on Hwy 6
SC	98	Santee State Park	803-854-2408	158	4 mi.	1.25 mi W on Rte 6, RT on State Park Rd, follow signs
SC	98	Mill Creek Marina & Campground	803-492-7746	86	6.2	E on 6 for 4.8mi, LT on Mill Creek 1mi, RT 1/3mi to Lake Marion LN, LT
SC	77	Comfort Inn	843-563-4180	25	50 ft	I-95 & Rte 78
SC	68	Shuman's	888-533-8731	23	3	2 1/2 mi East on Rte 61, 1/4 mi. N on Hwy 15
SC	68	Colleton State Park	843-538-8206	25	3.25 mi.	2.8 mi E on Augusta Hwy, LT on US 15 0.4 mi
SC	53	Green Acres RV Park	800-474-3450	100	0.5	Rte 63 West for 1 block, then right turn at Campground Rd. for 0.4 mi
SC	33	The Oaks at Point South	843-726-5728	85	3	N on Rte 17, E on Yamassee to stop sign then N on Campground Rd
SC	33	Point South KOA	800-726-5733	52	1	N on Rte 17, E on Yamassee to stop sign then right on Campground Rd
GA	94	Savannah Oaks RV Resort	912-748-4000	100	2.5	2 1/2 mi West on Hwy 204
GA	90	Waterway on The Ogeechee	912-756-2296	32	3.5	1 mi East on Rte 144, turn North (left) on Hwy 17 2.5 mi to Kings Ferry Bridge
GA	87	KOA Savannah South	912-756-3396	125	0.25	1/4 mi South on 17
GA	58	Lake Harmony RV Park	912-832-4338	50	0.5	West 1/2 mi.
GA	58	Mcintosh Lake RV Park	912-832-6215	38	0.75	3/4 mi. West on Rte 57
GA	49	Inland Harbor	912-437-6172	50	400 ft	400 ft East on Hwy 251
GA	29	Blythe Island Regional Camp	800-343-7855	97	4	1/2 mi West on Hwy 17 then 3 1/2 mi N on Blythe Island Hwy
GA	1	Country Oaks	912-729-6212	44	0.4	0.4 mi West on St.Mary's Rd.
GA	1	North Jacksonville Kingsland KOA	912-729-3232	100	0.5	Exit 1 West to campground
FL	366	Pecan Park RV Resort	888-604-6770	183	400 yds	400 yds W on Pecan Park Rd
FL	362B	Flamingo Lake Resort	800-RV-AHEAD	288	3.5 mi.	3.4 mi W on 295, N on Lem Turner Rd 300 yds, RT on Newcombe Rd
FL	318	Cooksey's Camping Resort	904-471-3171		2 mi.	2 mi E on Rte 208, RHS
FL	318	Stagecoach RV Park (no tent)	904-824-2319	80	1/2 mile	1/2 mi W on Rte 208, LHS
FL	311	Indian Forest Campground	904-824-3574	105	2 mi	2 mi E on Rte 207, LHS
FL	311	St. Johns RV Park-call after 2	904-824-9840	15	1/2 mi.	1/2 mi E on Rte 207, LHS

State	Page	Park	Phone	Sites	Distance	Directions
FL	278	Bulow RV Resort	1-800-782-8569	387	2.7 mi	E 1/2 mi on Old Dixie Hwy, LT on Old King's Rd 2.2 mi
FL	273	Harris Village And RV Park LLC	386-673-0494	30	2.5 mi	E on US 1 2.5 mi.
FL	273	Sunshine Holiday Daytona	877-277-8737	400	0.5 mi	W on US 1 _mi.
FL	256	Nova Family Campground	386-767-0095	450	2.5 mi	E on Rte 421 2mi, LT on S Nova Rd 0.8 mi, LT Herbert St 0.3 mi
FL	256	Daytona Beach KOA Campground	386-767-9170	250	.3 miles	E on Rte 421 2mi, LT on S Nova Rd 1 mi.
FL	249	Sugar Mill Ruins Travel Park	386-427-2284	200	3.8 mi	E on Canal St 2.8 mi, RT 1 mi on Mission Dr
FL	249	New Smyrna Beach RV Park	800-928-9962	270	4.2 mi	E on Canal St 2.8 mi, RT 1.4 mi on Mission Dr
FL	244	Indian Mound Fish Camp	386-345-9845	40 RV	9.4 mi	E on W Indian River Blvd 3.6 mi, RT on US 1 5.75 mi, LT Indian Creek Rd
FL	231	Crystal Lake RV Park	321-268-8555	60	800 ft	E on exit, LHS
FL	201	Sunrise Village	321-631-0305	75	1/2 mile	280 yds W, LT on Tucker Ln 0.4mi, RT on Sandpiper Dr.
FL	201	Son Rise Palms RV Park	321-633-4335	83	1 mi	W on Rte 520 1 block, LT Tucker Ln 0.7 mi, RT on Sandy Pine
FL	195	Space Coast RV Resort	800-982-4233	259	1/4 mile	350 yds N on Fiske Blvd, RT 350 yds LT to resort
FL	173	Camelot RV Park	321-724-5396	143	4.3 mi	E on Rte 514 (Malabar Rd) 4 mi, RT on US 1 0.3 mi
FL	156	Whispering Palms	772-589-3481	571	8.4 mi	E 6.4 mi on Rte 512 East to US 1, RT for 2 mi
FL	156	Pelican's Landing of Sebastian	772-589-5188	27	7 miles	E on Rte 512 6.5 mi, RT on Indian River Rd for 1/2 mi
FL	131B	Vero Beach Kamp, etc.	877-589-5643	200	10.6 mi	E on Rte 512 6.4 mi, RT on US 1 4.2 mi
FL	118	Road Runner Travel Resort	800-833-7108	472	3.75 mi	1/4 mil E on te 66, RT 2.5 mi on Kings Hwy, RT 1 mi
FL	118	Port St. Lucie RV Resort	877-405-2333	117	10 mi	E on Gatlin 2.9 mi, LT on Port St. Lucie 5.9 mi, LT on US 1 _ mi, RT on Jennings
FL	87B	West Jupiter Camping Resort	561-746-6073	74	5.7 mi	5.6 mi E on Indiantown Rd, LT on 130th Ave
FL	70	Palm Beach RV Park	561-659-2817	31	1 mi	E on Okeechobee, 1st RT on S Australian Ave 400 yds, LT on Mercer Ave.
FL	63	John Prince Park Campground	877-992-9925	297	1.6 mi	W on 6th Ave 1.25 mi, LT on S Congress Ave 0.35 mi
FL	61	Palm Beach Traveler Park	866-927-7287	100	2.4 mi	W on Lantana Rd 2.25 mi, LT on Lawrence Rd 350 yds
FL	51	Del-Raton Travel Trailer Park	561-278-4633	60	1.8 mi	E 1 mi on Linton Blvd, RT on S Federal Hwy for 0.8 mi
FL	41	Breezy Hill RV Resort	866-340-0649	1,000	.2 mi	E 0.9 mi on SW 10th, RT on N Dixie Hwy 1 mi., RT on NE 48th
FL	41	Highland Woods RV Resort	(866) 340-0649	200	.2 mi	E 0.9 mi on SW 10th, RT on N Dixie Hwy 1 mi., RT on NE 48th
FL	32	Kozy Kampers RV Park	954-731-8570	104	3 miles	W on Commercial Blvd 3 mi
FL	31B	Sunshine Holiday RV Resort	(954) 731-1722	200	1.3 miles	W on Oakland Park Blvd 1.3 mi
FL	31B	Paradise Island RV Resort	954-485-1150	243	3/4 mi	0.7 mi W on Rte 816, LT for 250 yds on NW 21st Ave
FL	25	Yacht Haven Park & Marina	954-583-2322	250	1/4 mile	1/4 mi W on SR 84
FL	25	Twin Lakes Travel Park	954-587-0101	367	.3 miles	W on Marina Mile 2.1 mi, LT on Rte 441 mi, RT on SW 36th, RT on SW 46th
FL	20	Grice RV Park	954-983-8225	374	2.6 mi	2.5 mi W on Hollywood Blvd, RT on Rte 441 2 blocks, RT on Polk St
FL	18	Embassy RV Park	954-961-8892	67	_ mi	W on W Hallandale Blvd 0.4 mi, LT 250 yds on Lakeshore Dr.
FL	18	Holiday Park	954-981-4414	127	1/4 mile	1/4 mi W on Hallandale Beach Blvd

Golf Courses Near I-95 Exits

State	Exit	City	Course Name	Address	Phone	Pub/S/Pvt	Par	Directions
NH	3B	Portsmouth	Pease Golf Course	200 Grafton Drive	603-433-1331	P	72	W on Rte 33 (E if Sbound) to Grafton Rd, 370 yds to club
NH	3B	Greenland	Portsmouth Country Club	80 Country Club Lane	603-436-9791	SP	72	W 1 mi on 33 to Ocean Rd, RT on Portsmouth Ave to Fairway Dr.
NH	3B	Greenland	Breakfast Hill Golf Club	339 Breakfast Hill Rd.	603-436-5001	SP	72	E 1.75 mi on 33, RT on US 1 for 4.5 mi, RT on Breakfast Hill Rd.
NH	2	North Hampton	Sagamore Hampton GC	101 North Rd.	603-964-5341	P	71	E on 101 to X 13, RT on Exeter 1.5 mi, LT on US 1 3.5 mi, LT on North Rd
MA	60	Amesbury	Amesbury Golf & CC	2 Country Club Rd	978-388-5153	SP	35	Main St S for 1.75 mi, RT at Country Club Rd
MA	57	Newburyport	Evergreen Valley Golf Course	20 Boyd Drive	978-463-8600	P	35	E on Rte 113 0.9 mi, LT on Ferry Rd _ mi, LT on Boyd Dr.
MA	50	Topsfield	New Meadows Golf Club	32 Wildes Rd.	978-887-9307	P	35	N on US 1 4.9 mi, RT on Wildes St
MA	43	Lynnfield	King Rail Reserve Golf Course	427 Walnut St.	781-334-2877	P	36	N on Walnut St _ mi to Thistle Ln
MA	44A	Saugus	Cedar Glen Golf Course	60 Water St.	781-233-3609	P	35	S on US 1 2.1 mi, RT on Rte 129 for 0.7 mi
MA	33A	Woburn	Woburn Country Club	5 Country Club Rd	781-933-9880	P	34	S on Rte 3 for 2.4 mi to Country Club Rd
MA	23N, 24S	Weston	Leo J. Martin Memorial Golf	190 Park Rd	781-894-4903	P	72	W on Recreation Rd (Nbound) or South Rd (Sbound), Left on Park Rd.
MA	11A	Canton	Brookmeadow Golf & CC	100 Everendon Rd	781-828-4444	P	72	E on Neponsett St 1.2 mi, RT on Walpole St 0.9 mi, RT on Everendon Rd.
RI	8	East Greenwich	East Greenwich G & CC	1646 Divison Rd.	401-884-5656	SP	36	South on Rte.2, right on Division Rd. 1/2 mi
RI	6	Coventry	Coventry Pines	Harkney Hill Rd.	401-397-9482	P	36	North 1 1/4 mi on Rte 3, left at Harkney Hill Rd. 2mi.
RI	3A	Richmond	Meadowbrook Golf Club	163 Kingstown Rd	401-539-8491	P	72	I-95 to exit 3A. East on Rte 138 2 miles
RI	2	Hope Valley	Wood River Golf Course	78A Woodville-Alton Rd	401-364-0700	P	69	I-95 to exit 2. 3 miles down Woodville-Alton Rd on left
RI	2	Hope Valley	Lindbrook Golf Course	299 Woodville-Alton Rd	401-539-8700	P	54	I-95 to exit 2. North, bear right, south, bear left
RI	2	Hope Valley	Fenner Hill Golf Club	33 Wheeler Lane	401-539-8000	P	72	
CT	92	Pawcatuck	Elmridge	229 Elmridge Rd	860-599-2248	P	71/72	East on Rte 2 for 3/4 mi, right on Elmridge Rd.
CT	87	Groton	Shennecossett Golf Course	Plant St.	860-445-0262	P	71	Clarence Sharp Hwy S, right on Rainville, left on Benham for 1 1/2 mi.
CT	74	East Lyme	Cedar Ridge	34 Drabik Rd	860-691-4568	P	54	.1 mi N on Flanders Rd.
CT	51/52	New Haven	Alling Memorial Golf Course	35 Eastern St.	203-946-8014	P	72	High St to Laurel St., North 1.6 mi
CT	39	Orange	Grassy Hill CC	441 Clark Lane	203-795-3100	P	70/71	US 1 South 3/4 mi. to Rte 121 2 1/2 mi
CT	37N	Milford	Great River Golf Club	130 Coram Lane	203-876-8051	SP	72	North on High St./ Wheelers Farm Rd. 2 mi., left on Herbert to Coram lane
CT	13M/14S	Norwalk	Oak Hills Park Golf Course	165 Fillow St.	203-838-0303	P	71	US 1 to Richards Ave. 1.6 mi. to end, right to course
CT	6	Stamford	E.Gaynor Brennan	451 Stillwater Rd.	203-324-4185	P	71	North on West Ave. 3/4 mi., left on Stillwater 1/2 mi.
NJ	5	Willingboro	Rancocas Golf Club	12 Club Ridge Lane	609-877-5344	P	72	LT on Rte 541 0.4 mi, LT Irick Rd 3.8 mi (name changes), LT JFK, RT 626 for 0.4 mi
NJ	3	Blackwood	Valleybrook Country Club	200 Golfview Dr	856-227-3171	P	72	S on 168 1.8 mi, LT 0.8 mi on Chews Landing Rd, RT 1/2 mi

State	Exit	City	Golf Course	Address	Phone	Type	Rating	Directions
DE	4B	Wilmington	Pike Creek Golf Club	3542 Foxcroft Dr	302-737-1877	P	71	Christiana Rd N 2.1 mi, LT 3.2 mi on Limestone RTD, LT on Skyline
DE	3B	Newark	Deerfield Golf & Tennis Club	507 Thompson Station Rd	302-368-6640	P	70	Christiana Rd N 4.1 mi, RT Chapel St (Paper Mill) 2.4 mi, LT 0.5 mi on Thompson Sta Rd
MD	109A	Elkton	Brantwood Golf Course	1190 Augustine Herman Hwy	410-398-8848	P	71	S on Elkton Rd (Rte 279) 2.5 MI, LT on Rte 213 (Bridge St) 4.2 mi.
MD	109	Elkton	Bittersweet Golf Club	1190 Augustine Herman Hwy	410-398-8848	P	70	S 2.5 mi on Elkton RD, LT 4 mi on N Bridge St
MD	100B	Rising Sun	Chesapeake Bay at Rising Sun	128 Karen Dr	410-658-4343	P	71	North on Rte 272, left on Rte 274 for 2 1/4 mi
MD	100A	North East	Chesapeake Bay at NorthEast	1500 Chesapeake Club Dr	410-287-0200	P	70	South on Rte 272 for 3.75 mi.
MD	100A	Elkton	The Club at Patriots Glen	300 Patriots Way	410-392-9552	SP	72	1/4 mi S, RT on Old Baltimore Pike 3.4 mi, crossing State line
MD	89	Havre de Grace	Bulle Rock Golf Club	320 Blenheim Lane	410-939-8887	P	72	East on Rte 155 2.2 mi, right on 40 for 2 mi.
MD	85	Aberdeen	The Wetlands	740 Gilbert Rd	410-273-7488	P	72	West on 22 to Gilbert Rd, right for 1 1/2 mi.
MD	80	Aberdeen	Ruggles	Bldg 5600 Aberdeen Proving Grnd	410-278-4794	P	72	543 south, left on 7 to Hwy 40, left to 715, right thru gate
MD	74	Joppa	Mountain Branch Golf Course	1827 Mountain Rd	410-836-9600	SP	72	North on Mountain Rd. (Rte 152) for 2 mi.
MD	51	Baltimore	Carroll Park Golf Course	2100 Washington Blvd	410-685-8344	P	34	N only: left turn off exit.
MD	33	Laurel	Gunpowder Golf Club	14300 Old Gunpowder Rd	301-725-4532	P	70	West on 198 to Old Gunpowder Rd., left 1mi.
MD	33	Laurel	Patuxent Greens Golf Course	14415 Greenview Dr	301-776-5533	SP	71	East on 198 for 2 3/4 mi, right on 197, second left
VA	176A	Alexandria	Greendale Golf Course	6700 Telegraph Rd.South	703-971-3788	P	70	Exit 2 Telegraph Rd. South 31/2 mi. on right.
VA	170	Alexandria	Pinecrest Golf Course	6600 Little River Turnpike	703-941-1061	P	35	I-495 exit 52B, E on Rte.236 (Little River Tpke) 3 mi. on left
VA	166A	Fairfax	Hilltop Golf Club	7900 Telegraph Rd	703-719-6504	P	31	1.2 mi E on 7100, LT 2 mi on Telegraph Rd.
VA	163	Lorton	Laurel Hill Golf Club	8700 Laurel Crest Drive	703-493-8849	SP	71	W 1 block, RT on Silverbrook for 1 mi, LT on Laurel Crest Dr 1/2 mi
VA	160	Woodbridge	The Ospreys at Belmont Bay	13401 Potomac Path Dr	703-497-1384	P	70	S on Gordon, Right on US 1 1/4 mi, left on Dawsons Bch 1/2 mi, left to Belmont Bay
VA	160	Woodbridge	Lake Ridge Golf Course	12350 Cotton Mill Drive	703-494-5564	P	3	0.3 mi N on Gordon, LT 3.5 mi on Old Bridge, RT on Hedges Run, LT Cotton Mill 0.3 mi
VA	150B	Triangle	Forest Greens Golf Club	4500 Poa Annua	703-221-0123	P	72	Rte 619 west for 1/4 mi.
VA	140B	Stafford	Augustine Golf Club	76 Monument Dr	540-720-7374	P	71	W 3 mi on Rte 630, LT on Monument Dr (Walpole St) _ mi
VA	133B	Fredericksburg	Cannon Ridge Golf Club	9000 Celebrate Virginia Pkwy	540-735-8000	P	71	300 yds W on Warrenton, LT on Sanford Dr 1.3mi, LT on Celebrate VA Pkwy
VA	133B	Fredericksburg	The Gauntlet Golf Club	18 Fairway Dr	540-752-0963	SP	72	5.7 mi W on Warrenton Rd, FT on Hartwood Rd (Rte 612) for 2 mi, FT
VA	126B	Fredericksburg	Lee's Hill Golfers Club	10200 Old Dominion Park	540-891-0111	P	72	0.6 mi S on US 1, LT on US 17 1.3 MI, LT 1 mi on Old Dominion Pkwy
VA	110	Ruther Glen	Pendleton Golf Club	6383 Declaration Drive	804-448-4727	P	72	W 0.8 mi on Ladysmith Rd, LT on US 1 for 0.8 mi, RT to club
VA	104	Ruther Glen	Mattaponi Springs Golf Club	22490 Penola Rd	804-633-7888	P	72	.5 mi NE on Rte 207, RT 4.25 mi on Penola Rd
VA	84B	Glen Allen	Tradition at the Crossings	800 Virginia Center Pkwy	804-266-2254	SP	72	Exit 84B Rte 1 N 1 block, right on Virginia Center Pkwy.
VA	83B	Richmond	Belmont Golf Course	1600 Hillard Rd	804-501-4653	P	71	W on E Parham Rd, 1 1/4 mi S on US 1. Use X 81 Nbound

Golf Courses Near I-95 Exits

State	Exit	City	Course Name	Address	Phone	Pub/S/Pvt	Par	Directions
NC	101	Selma	Cardinal CC	363 Parish Memorial Rd	919-284-3647	SP	72	Pittman Rd.1/4 mi to stop, left 500 yds, on Batten Farm Rd 2 1/2 mi
NC	97	Clayton	The Neuse Golf Club	918 Birkdale Dr	919-550-0550	SP	72	Rte 70 W 12 mi, right on 42 to Glen Laurel Rd
NC	90	Selma	Country Club of Johnston Cty	694 Country Club Rd	919-934-4166	SP	72	N on US 301 for 1 mi to Country Club Rd, turn left
NC	81	Four Oaks	Reedy Creek	585 Reedy Creek rd	919-934-7502	P	72	I-40W to exit 319, right on 210 2.25 mi, right at Lassiter Rd onto Reedy Creek Rd.
NC	73	Dunn/Newton Grove	Sandy Ridge Country Club	211 Clubhouse Drive	910-892-6424	P	72	E 6 mi on 421, RT on Sandy Ridge 1/4 mi
NC	71	Dunn	Chicora Golf Club	495 Chicora Club Drive	910-897-7366	P	71	6 miles from exit 73
NC	58	Fayetteville	King's Grant Golf Club	347 Shawcroft Road	910-630-1111	SP	71	E on I-295 to end, LT 0.4 mi on 401, RT on Shawcroft Rd 0.6 mi to entrance
NC	55	Fayetteville	Baywood Golf Club	904 Fourwood Drive	910-483-4330	P	72	E 1.3 mi on Murphy RD, RT 3/4 mi on Baywood Rd
NC	41	Hope Mills	Cypress Lakes GC	2126 Cypress Lakes Rd	910-483-0359	P	72	E 2.5 mi on Chicken Foot Rd, LT on Bullard Rd 1.8 mi
NC	17	Lumberton	Pine Crest Country Club	110 Nigel Drive	910-738-6541	SP	72	N 1 mi on Rte 72, RT on Nigel Rd
NC	14	Lumberton	Cliffwood Golf Course	3811 Martin Luther King Dr.	910-738-9400	P	72	E on 74 3.5 mi, LT on 41 1/2 mi
SC	193	Hamer	Twin Lakes Country Club	141 W. Country Club Rd	843-774-3740	P	71	S on Rte 57 1.2 mi, LT N on Rte 301 for 2.5 mi, LT on Country Club Rd
SC	164	Darlington	Beaver Creek GC	1133 East Mciver	843-393-5441	SP	72	North on 52 2 1/4 mi. to Palmetto Rd, turn right to Mciver
SC	160	Florence	Traces GC	4322 Southborough Rd.	843-662-7775	SP	72	I-20 West 4 mi to exit 137, left on 340, 2nd left and left again
SC	157	Florence	Oak Dale Country Club	3700 West Lake Drive	843-662-0368	SP	72	From S. Exit 159 or 160, junction of I-20
SC	119	Manning	Shannon Greens Golf Club	Bloomville Hwy	803-435-8752	P	72	East on Rte 261 3mi on right
SC	119	Manning	The Players Course at Wyboo	1560 Players Course Dr.	800-538-0623	P	72	E on Rte 261 2 mi, RT on Mill St (Rte 260) 8 mi, RT on Lakeshore, then Players
SC	119	Manning	Wyboo Golf Club	2565 Players Course Drive	888-245-9300	P	72	E on Rte 261 2 mi, RT on Mill St (Rte 260) 8 mi, RT on Lakeshore, then Players
SC	108	Summerton	Foxboro Golf Club	8377 Wash Davis Rd.	803-478-7000	P	72	Exit 108, east approx. 7 miles to Goat Island
SC	90	St. Matthews	Calhoun Country Club	200 Country Club Rd	803-823-2465	SP	72	Exit 90 to HWY 176, west or exit 98 to Hwy 6 west
SC	98	Santee	Lake Marion Golf Course	9069 Old Highway 6.	803-854-2554	P	72	Exit 98 off I-95, 200 yards east on HWY 6
SC	98	Santee	Santee Cooper Country Club	300 Saluda Court	803-854-2467	P	72	Exit 98, 1/4 mile east on HWY 6
SC	98	Santee	Santee National Golf Club	8636 Old Highway 6.	803-854-3531	P	72	1.1 mi W on old hwy 6, turn left
SC	21	Ridgeland	Sergeant Jasper CC	Hwy 174.	843-726-8977	SP	36	E on Rte 336 _ mi, RT 1.6 MI on Rte 13, LT on Glover Rd (SR 174) for 2.1 mi
SC	5	Hardeeville	Pintail Creek Golf Club	261 Pintail Creek Drive	843-784-2426	P	71	Exit 5 till Rte 17S. Down 4 miles on right
GA	104	Savannah	Crosswinds Golf Club	232 James B. Blackburn drive	912-966-1909	P	72	E on Airways Ave _ mi, RT on Crossroads Pkwy, LT on James Blackburn Dr
GA	102	Savannah	Southbridge GC.	415 SouthBridge Blvd	912-651-5455	SP	72	East 1 exit to Dean Forest Rd, turn right 200 yds
GA	94	Savannah	Henderson GC	1 AL Henderson Dr.	912-920-4653	P	71	East to 1st light (Gateway Blvd. East), left 1 mile
GA	67	Shellman Bluff	Sapelo Hammock GC.	500 Marshview Dr.	912-832-4653	SP	72	East on 17 2.8 mi, left on Minton Rd.
GA	42	Brunswick	Coastal Pines GC	1 Coastal Pines Circle	912-261-0503	P	72	Rte 99 3mi on the right
GA	38B	Brunswick	Oak Grove Island GC	126 Clipper Bay	912-280-9525	SP	72	N on Rte 25/341 2.4 mi, LT on Oak Grove Rd 2 mi. To club
GA	6	Kingsland	Laurel Island Links	233 Marsh Harbour Pkwy.	912-729-7277	P	72	East on Colerain Rd 2.5mi, left on Laurel Island Pkwy

	Page	City	Course	Address	Phone	Type	Par	Directions
FL	323	St. Augustine	Slammer & Squire	2 World Golf Place	904-940-6100	P	72	1/4 mi W on International Golf Pkwy
FL	323	St. Augustine	King & Bear	1 King Bear Drive	904-940-6200	SP	72	2.4 mi W on International Golf Pkwy, RT 1.5 mi on Rte 16, LT 0.4 mi
FL	289	Daytona Beach	The Pine Course at The Grand Club	400 Pine Lakes Parkway	386-445-0852	SP	72	W on Palm Coast Pkwy 1.1 mi, LT on Belle Terre Pkwy for 0.6 mi, RT on Pine Lakes Pkwy to club
FL	278	Daytona Beach	Halifax Plantation Golf Club	3400 Clubhouse Dr	386-676-9600	SP	72	0.5 mi E on Old Dixie Hwy (Rte 4011), RT to club
FL	273	Daytona Beach	River Bend Golf Club	730 Airport Rd	386-673-6000	SP	72	S on US 1 for 2.6 mi, RT on Airport Rd to club
FL	265	Daytona Beach	LPGA International	1000 Champions Drive	386-274-5742	P	72	1/2 mi W on LPGA Blvd, LT on Champions Dr.
FL	261	Daytona Beach	Indigo Lakes Golf Club	312 Indigo Drive	386-254-3607	P	72	3/4 mi E on Int'l Speedway Blvd, LT 1/2 mi on 4009, LT on S Indigo Dr.
FL	260A	South Daytona	The Bay at Pelican Bay	550 Sea Duck Drive	386-788-4653	SP	72	0.8 mi E on Beville Rd, RT on Pelican Bay Dr 1.4 mi to Sea Duck Circle
FL	256	Port Orange	Crane Lakes GC	1790 Crane Lakes Blvd.	386-767-4653	SP	66	1.2 mi W from exit
FL	256	Port Orange	The Golf Club at Cypress Head	6231 Palm Vista Street	386-756-5449	P	72	250 Yds W, LT 2.3 on Airport Rd
FL	256	Port Orange	Spruce Creek Golf & Country Club	1900 Country Club Drive	386-756-6114	SP	72	W 2.3 mi on Taylor Rd, LT 1 mi on Spruce Crk Blvd, LT on Country Club Rd
FL	249A	New Smyrna Beach	New Smyrna Beach Municipal GC	1000 Wayne Ave		P	72	3.8 mi E on Rte 44, LT 1 mi cn US 1, LT 3/4 mi on Wayne Ave
FL	249	New Smyrna Beach	Hidden Lakes Golf Club	35 Fairgreen Ave.	386-427-4138	P	69	3.8 mi E on Rte 44, LT 1.5 m on US 1, LT 3/4 mi on Fairgreen Ave to club
FL	223	Mims	Walkabout Golf & Country Club	3950 Walkabout Way	321-385-2099	P	72	1.5 mi E on Rte 46, LT 1.25 mi on US 1, LT Glenn Rd, RT 1/2 mi on Folsom
FL	205	Merritt Island	The Savannahs Golf Club	3915 Savannahs Trail	321-455-1377	P	72	E on Rte 528 for 7 mi, LT 2 mi on Courtenay Pkwy, RT 1.75 mi on Hall Rd, RT
FL	195	Rockledge	Turtle Creek Golf Club	1279 Admiralty Blvd	321-632-2520	SP	72	N 300 yds on Fiske Blvd, RT 1/2 mi on Barnes, RT on Admiralty Blvd
FL	191	Viera	Viera East Golf Club	2300 Clubhouse Drive.	321-639-6500	P	72	E 0.3 mi on Wickham, LT on Murrell Rd 3.4 mi
FL	191	Viera	Duran Golf Club	7032 Stadium Parkway	321-504-7776	P	72	W 0.8 mi on Wickham Rd, RT on Stadium Pkwy for 1 mi, turn left
FL	173	Palm Bay	The Habital Golf Club	3591 Fairgreen Street	321-952-6312	P	72	2.5 mi E on Malabar Rd, RT 3 mi on Corey Rd, LT 1.5 mi on Valkaria Rd, RT or Fairgreen St
FL	173	Palm Bay	Majors Golf Club	3375 Bayside Lakes Blvd	321-952-8617	SP	72	W 1.1 mi on Malabar Rd, LT on Emerson Dr for 3.5 mi to entrance
FL	121	Ft. Pierce	Fairwinds Golf Course	4400 Fairwinds Drive.	772-462-4653	P	72	5.9 mi E on Indrio Rd, RT 1.1 mi on US 1, RT on Fairwinds Dr
FL	121	Port St. Lucie	PGA Village	9700 Reserve Blvd.	866-344-7899	P	74	0.6 mi W on Reserve Blvd.
FL	118	Port St. Lucie	The Saints at Port St. Lucie	2601 SE Morningside Blvd.	772-398-2906	P	72	3 mi E on SW Gatlin Blvd, LT 5.25 mi om Port St Lucie, RT on SE Morningside
FL	42A	Deerfield Beach	Deerfield Country Club	50 Fairway Drive.	954-427-6326	SP	70/63	E 0.3 mi on Hillsboro, LT on SW Natura Blvd 200 yds, RT to club
FL	38A	Pompano Beach	Pompano Beach Golf Club	1101 N. Federal Highway	954-781-0426	P	72	2 mi E on Copans Rd, RT on US 1 for 0.6 mi, RT to club
FL	33B	Pompano Beach	Palm Aire Country Club	34136 Atlantic Blvd	954-975-6244	P	72	1.7 mi W on Cypress Crk Rd, RT on Powerline 1 mi, LT on Palm Aire Dr
FL	29B	Lauderhill	Lauderhill Golf Course	4141 NW 16th St.	954-730-2990	P	30	W on Sunrise Hwy 2 mi, RT on Rte 441 for 0.7 mi, LT on NW 16th to club
FL	22	Hollywood	The Club at Emerald Hills	4100 N. Hills Drive.	954-961-4000	P	72	W on Stirling Rd 1.7 mi, LT on 45th for 0.9 mi on US 1, RT on N Hills Dr to club
FL	20	Hollywood	Eco Grande Golf Course	1451 Taft Street.	954-922-8755	P	32	1.5 mi E on Hollywood Blvd, LT 0.9 mi on US 1, RT on Taft St 1/2 mi
FL	20	Hollywood	Hollywood Beach Golf & Country	1650 Johnson Street.	954-927-1751	P	72	1.5 mi E on Hollywood Blvd, LT on US 1 7 blocks, RT on Johnson
FL	20	Hollywood	Sunset Golf Club	2727 Johnson St.	954-923-2008	P	38/35	1 block E on Hollywood Blvd, LT on 28th Ave _ mi to Johnson St, RT to club
FL	20	Hollywood	Orangebrook Golf & Country Club	400 Entrada Drive.	954-967-4653	P	72	0.4 mi W on Hollywood Blvd, LT on Entrada Dr.

Auto Mechanics Along I-95 Exits

State	Exit	Listing on our Maps	Phone	E/W of I-95	Hours	Towing
NH	15	BP Auto R	603-474-5220	E	M-F 8-6, S 8-3	
MA	58	Daaboul Sons Auto Repair	978-465-0500	E	M-S 7-7, Sun 10-3	978-465-7601
MA	57	Sunoco R	978-462-9169	E	M-F 8-5, S 8-1	yes
MA	47	Sunoco R $ RV	978-774-9191	E	M-F 8-5, S 8-3	yes
MA	44	Gaeta's Auto Service Shell 24h	978-535-3186/4762/4837	W	M-S 8-5	24h
MA	41	Shell R LP $ 24h	781-246-4054	E	M-F 8-5, S 9-2	
MA	38	Stoneham Gulf R	781-279-7766	E	M-F 8 -5, S 8-3	
MA	31	Heritage Svc M obil R D	781-862-9715	E	M-F 7-5	
MA	27	Shell R $	781-890-5525	E	M-F 7-5, S 8-2	
RI	27	Sunoco D R 24h	401-726-9272	W	M-F 8-5, S 9-7	yes
RI	27	Joe's Shell R 24h $	401-726-9345	W	M-F 8-5, S 8-1	yes
RI	24	Mario's Mobil R	401-621-9792/8606	W	M-F 8-4, S 8-12	24h, 401-621-8606
RI	15	Bob's BP D R $	401-461-7309	E	M-F 8-5	yes
CT	93	Shell D $ R	860-599-4581	E	M-F 9-5, S 9-12	yes
CT	74	Tires Plus	860-739-3485	E	M-F 8-5, S 8-1	
CT	74	Corey's D R	(860) 739-9696	E	M-F 8-5, S 8-1	
CT	67	Adelmann's Gulf D K R	860-388-4120/9461	E	M-F 7-5	yes
CT	61	Sunoco R Madison Svc Ctr	203-245-7534	E	M-F 8-5	
CT	58	Palumbo's Automotive Unlimited	203-453-1788	E	Trucks only	
CT	56	T/A Travel Ctr 24h TR	203-481-0301	W	M-F 8-5, S 8-1	yes
CT	55	Branford Auto Ctr $	203-481-6572	E	M-F 8-5	24h
CT	54	Citgo R D	203-488-0800/481-9769	W	M-F 9-5, S 9-3	
CT	54	Eagle Brothers R	203-481-5006	W	M-F 8:30-5:30, S 8:30-2	yes
CT	44	Superior Sunoco R D $ 24h	203-932-6322	E	M-F 9-5	yes
CT	37	USA Fuel R $	203-874-9926	W	M-F 7:30-6, S 7:30-1	24h, 914-698-2544
CT	37	C & G Gulf R	203-874-2893	E	M-F 8-6, S 8-4	yes
NY	21	Felipe Auto Repair - no gas	914-935-9240	W	M-F 6-6	yes
NY	20	Rye Shell R	914-967-1612	E	M-F 8-5, S 8-1	yes
NY	18	Lebrini's Sunoco D R	914-698-6444	E	M-F P-6, S 8-12, Sun 9-1	yes, 914-698-2544/5252
NY	18	Shell R 24h	914-698-1118	E	M-F 8-5, S 8-4	yes
NY	18	Vincent Gulf R	914-698-2544/5252	E	M-F 7:30-6, S 7:30-1	24h, 914-698-2544
NJ	9	Sweeney's Gulf D R 24h	732-846-0074	E	M-F 8-6, S 8-2	24h
NJ	8	Twin Rivers Exxon R D	609-448-2122	E	M-F 8-5, S 8-4	24h, 609-448-2746

State	Exit	Listing on our Maps	Phone	E/W of I-95	Hours	Towing
MA	26	Woodside Sunoco R D	781-899-4150	E	M-F 8-5	
MA	21	Daly's Sunoco R	781-235-4540	W	M-F 8-5, S 8-1	
MA	21	Wellesley Gulf R	781-235-9652	W	M-F 8-5, S 8-2	yes
MA	15	Dani's Shell R $	781-326-0760	W	M-F 9-5 S 9-2	yes
MA	11	Citgo R	781-821-1344	E	M-F 8-5, S 8-12	
MA	5	Triboro Gulf R	508-699-7344	W	M-F 8-5, S 8-12	
MA	3	Pedro's Citgo D R	508-222-6670	E	M-S 8-8	yes
RI	7	Ray's Mobil R	401-884-9814	E	M-F 7-4	
RI	7	Chevalier's Auto Service R	401-822-3500	W	M-F 8-5	
RI	6	Sunoco D R $	401-397-7865	W	M-F 8-5, S 7-2	
CT	33	Ferry Blvd Sunoco R	203-377-4753	E	M-F 8-5, S 8-12	yes
CT	31	Citgo D R	203-378-5147	W	M-S 7-8:30	
CT	24	Firestone - no gas	203-367-3674	W	M-F 7-7, Sat 7-6, Sun 9-5	yes
CT	23	Sunoco D R LP BP has R	203-255-0328	W	M-F 8-5, S 8-1	
CT	22	Benson & Post R	203-259-9017	E	M-F 7-6, S 8-4	
CT	21	J & R Service Center Inc R	203-259-5922	W	M-F 8-5:30	
CT	16	Glenn's Shell D R $ CW	203-866-6238	E	M-F 8-6, S 9-1	yes
CT	14	Conn Ave Sunoco D R $	203-855-9141	W	M-S 8-6	24h
CT	14	A-1 Auto service (C Gas) R $	203-855-1175	W	M-F 8-5, S 9-3	
CT	13	Mobil R LP $	203-655-7191	W	M-F 8-6	
CT	11	Gulf R LP	203-656-6653	W	M-F 8-5:30, S 8-3	203-327-4240
CT	10	Noroton Getty R LP	203-655-1971	E	M-Sat 6-9, Sun 7-8	yes
CT	8	Clark's Sunoco D R LP $	203-324-2575	W	M-F 8-5	
NY	17	Sunoco R	914-834-1258	W	M-S 7-5	yes
NY	13	M & B Gulf D R 24h	718-547-6106	E	M-F 8-5, S 9-3	yes
NY	11	Nor-Bay Mobil R 24h	718-379-8737/8731	E	7 days 7-7	24h, 718-423-1510
NY	5	RNS Sunoco R 24h	718-828-9482	E	M-Sat 8-7	
NY	4	Getty D R 24h	718-863-1470	E	M-Sun 8-6	yes
NJ	7	Mobil R	609-298-4001	E	M-Sun 8-6	
NJ	7	Jeff's Tire & Auto Svc R No Gas	609-298-9910	W	M-F 8-6, S 8-1	yes

State	Exit	Name	Dir	Phone	Hours	Notes
DE	3	Tangelwood Getty	W	302-738-2909	M-F 7-5, S 9-5	24h
DE	3	Exxon D R BP	E	302-453-1244	M-F 8-5, S (occasionally)	
MD	100	Abrams R NO GAS	W	410-287-5900	M-F 8-5, S 8-12	
MD	98	Sunoco D 24h $ R	B	at svc area	M-S 8-5	
MD	98	Exxon D 24h R	B	at svc area	M-F 8-6, S 8-2	yes
MD	83	Sunoco D R	B	410-272-2705	7 Days 7-11	
MD	83	Exxon D R ATM	B	410-272-8625	7 Days 8-Midnight	24h
MD	67	White Marsh Exxon 24h	W	410-931-6320	M-F 8-6:30, Sat 9-6, Sun 10-6	yes
MD	58	Dundalk Sunoco D R $ 24h	E	410-633-6444	Sat - Thurs 8:30-5:30	yes
MD	41	Shell R 24h $	E	410-799-3533	M-F 8-6, S 8-4	
MD	33	West Laurel Shell R 24h	W	301-776-6485	M-F 8-5	
VA	177	Liberty 24h R	W	703-836-5136	M-F 8-6, S 8-2	
VA	176	Telegraph Amerigo R	E	703-960-2030	M-F 8-6, S 8-2	
VA	169	Springfield Sunoco R	W	703-451-2911	M-F 8-6, S 8-1	
VA	163	Lorton Shell R $ 24h	W	703-495-8464	M-F 7-5, S 7-12	
VA	160	Stringer's Exxon D R LP $ 24h	W	703-494-4284	M-F 8-5, S (appt only)	
VA	160	Dunivin's Corner No Gas	E	703-490-1193/491-3553	M-F 7:30-6	24h
VA	156	Dale City Shell R 24h	W	703-680-5911	M-F 7-6, Sat 7-1	
VA	156	Potomac Mills Chevron R	W	703-491-6801	M-F 8-6, S 8-4	
VA	152	Dumfries Chevron R $	E	703-221-8473	M-S 8:30-6:30	
NC	90	Exxon R LP	E	919-934-9993	M-F 8-5	yes
NC	79	Woods Muffler & Auto Parts No Gas	W	919-894-8185	M-F 7:30-5, S	
NC	79	Mule City Auto & Convenience $	W	919-207-2144	M-S-7-7, Sun on call	24h
SC	169	Miller's Automotive - No Gas	W	843-679-9006	7 Days 7-6	24h
GA	29	T/A Travel D TR S 24h NO GAS	W	912-264-5530	open 24/7	
FL	347	Shell Tradewinds R	E	904-393-9006	M-F 8-8, S 8-4	24h
FL	311	Allen's Mobil R	W	904-824-8057	7 days 7am - 10 pm	24h
FL	305	Continental Truck Svc TR NO GAS	W	904-797-2665	M-F 8-5:30	yes, semis and trucks only
FL	268	DiSilva's Mobil D BP ATM R	W	386-671-9339	M-F 8-6, S 8-3	yes, DiSalvo's Auto Repair
FL	87	Jupiter Automotive Care R	W	561-744-3000	M-F 7:30-5, Sat 8-4	yes
FL	71	Firestone Complete Auto Care R	E	561-471-5861	M-F 7-7, Sat 7-6, Sun 8-5	24h
FL	57	AAA Auto (Majestic Gas) R	E	561-503-0468	M-F 8-5:30, S 8-5	24h
FL	51	Goodman's Auto Service R	E	561-276-2886	M-F 8-5:30	

State	Exit	Name	Dir	Phone	Hours	Notes
DE	1	896 Shell Friendly Auto Care		302-366-0420	M-F 8-6, S 8-2:30	yes, 302-420-0200
MD	33	Exxon D R $	W	301-498-0572	M-S 8-5	yes
MD	25	Shell R 24h $ LP	E	301-474-0215	M-F 9-4:30, Sat 9-2	24h
MD	20	Shell R $ 24h	W	301-577-1011	M-F 8-5, S 8-12	
MD	11	Sunoco R D 24h $	E	301-736-1450	M-F 8-5, S 8-3	
MD	9	Shell R $ 24h	W	301-899-9836	M-F 9-5, S 9-2	24h
MD	4	Shell 24h	E	301-894-6565	M-F 8-5, S 8-1	24h
MD	3	Oxon Hill Shell 24h	W	301-839-3377	M-F 8-6, Sat 8-5	
MD	3	Eastover Chevron R D 24h	E	301-839-1555	M-F 9-5, S 7-5	24h
VA	140	Courthouse Citgo D R	E	540-659-4034	7 Days 8-9	24h
VA	130	Greenbriar BP R D $	E	540-654-5222	M-F 8:30-6, S/S 9-4	540-350-9590
VA	126	Four Mile Fork BP D R	E	540-891-0891	M-F 8-5:30, S 8-12	24h
VA	118	Thornburg Citgo D BP 24h	W	540-532-5628	M-F 8-5	24h
VA	118	Shell R D $	E	540-532-6188	M-F 8-5	24h
VA	110	Express Exxon D R LP $ 24h	W	804-448-2100	M-F 8-6, S 8-4	24h, 804-448-2383
VA	45	Prince George Shell D R	E	804-732-9202	M-F 7-3, weekends on call	
VA	33	Davis Travel Ctr - D R LP 24h $	W	434-246-4641	M-F 8-8, S 8-4	24h
VA	31	1-stop Shell D $ K R	E	434-246-2039	7 Days 8-6	24h, 434-246-8697
NC	65	Smith's Car/Truck Repair	W	919-930-1843	M-F 8-9, Sun on call	24h
NC	17	Dobb's Mobil D R 24h $	E	910-738-6325		24h
GA	29	Glynn Diesel & RV Service	E	912-264-6466	M-F 8-5	24h, lite and medium duty trucks only
FL	48	Yamato Congress Chevron	W	954-836-6306	M-F 8-5, Sat 9-12	yes
FL	39	Gas Amp R $	W	954-735-2742	M-F 8-6, Sat 8-3	
FL	39	Shell $ R D 24h RV	E	954-943-9211	M-F 8-5	24h
FL	33	Shell R RV	W	954-771-2117	M-F 7-5, S 7-12	yes
FL	25	R & D Valero R	W	954-524-9362		
FL	25	Texaco R $	E	954-524-4776	M-F 8-6, Sat 8-2	24h
FL	18	Hallandale Auto (Ugas) $ R	E	954-454-9238	M-F 8-5:30, S 8-1:30	24h
FL	1	Citgo R 24h	E	305-856-4594	M-F 8-6, Sat 8-2	yes

We have tried to collect as complete and accurate information as we could, but repair shops unfortunately magically turn into mini-marts without any notice, so please call first to confirm.

Independent Motels and Bed & Breakfasts Along I-95 Exits

State	Exit	Name	E/W of I-95	Phone	Pets	Internet
NH	6	Anchorage Inn	E	603-431-8111	yes	yes, no $$
MA	46	Plaza Motel	W	978-535-2200	no	yes, no $$
RI	22	Christopher Dodge House	W	401-351-6111	no	yes, no $$
RI	22	Biltmore	E	800-294-7709	yes $	yes, no $$
CT	93	Stardust	W	860-599-2261	no	yes, no $$
CT	92	Cedar Park Inn & Suites	W	860-535-7829	yes, credit card on file	yes, no $$
CT	86	Groton Inn & Suites	W	860-445-9784	no	yes, no $$
CT	86	Windsor Motel	W	860-445-7474	no	No
CT	74	Hilltop Inn	E	860-739-3951	no	yes, no $$
CT	70	Old Lyme Inn & Rest.	W	860-434-2600	yes $	Only on lobby
CT	68	Liberty Inn	W	860-388-1777	yes $	No
CT	67	Executive Inn & Suite	E	860-388-3463	no	yes, no $$
CT	65	Bushnell House B&B		800-342-3162		yes, no $$
NY	10	Pelham Garden Motel	W	718-379-2300		No
NJ	9	Days Hotel	E	732-828-6900	no	yes, no $$
NJ	8	Town House Motel	W	609-448-2400	yes $	yes, no $$
NJ	7	Imperial Inn	E	609-298-3355	yes $	No
DE	14	Superlodge	W	302-654-5544	yes $	yes, no $$
MD	109	Elk Forge B&B	W	410-392-9007	some rooms, no $$	yes, no $$
MD	109	Elkton Lodge	E	410-398-9400	yes	yes, no $$
VA	177	Travelers Motel	E	703-329-1310	no	yes, no $$
VA	177	Relax Inn	E	703-329-1800	no	yes, no $$
VA	130	Fredericksburg Hospitality House	W	540-786-8321	no	yes, no $$
VA	126	Royal Inn	W	540-891-2700	no	yes, no $$
VA	92	Henry Clay Inn	E	804-798-3100	yes $	yes, no $$
VA	92	Apple Garden Inn	W	804-798-9291	yes $	No
VA	81	Town Motel	E	804-266-8781	no	No
NC	173	Orchard Inn	E	252-536-2131	yes $	yes, no $$

State	Exit	Name	E/W of I-95	Phone	Pets	Internet
NH	5	The Port Inn	E	800-282-PORT	no	yes, no $$
MA	30	Colonial Inn of Concord	W	978-369-9200	no	yes, no $$
RI	5	Classic Motor Lodge	W	401-397-6280	yes $	yes, no $$
RI	3	The Stagecoach House Inn	W	401-539-9600	3 rooms $	yes, no $$
CT	65	Westbrook Inn	E	860.399.4777		yes, no $
CT	65	Captain Stannard B&B	E	860-399-4634		yes, no $$
CT	48	A Touch of Ireland	W	203-787-7997		yes, no $$
CT	46	Premier Hotel & Suites	W	203 777 5337		yes, no $$
CT	40	Milford Inn	E	203-878-0685		No
CT	40	Mayflower Motel	W	203-878-6854		yes, no $$
CT	34	Devon Motel	E	203-874-6634		No
CT	21	Inn at Fairfield Beach	E	203-255-6808		yes, no $$
NJ	3	Bellmawr Motor Inn	W	856-931-6300		yes, no $$
NJ	1	Friendship Motor Inn	W	856-299-3700	yes $	No
MD	100	Fair Winds Farm B&B	W	410-658-8187	yes	yes, no $$
VA	64	VIP Inn (T)	W	804-271-6081	no	yes, no $$
VA	58	Interstate Inn	W	804-526-4772	yes $	yes, no $$
VA	52	Villa Romaine B&B	W	804.861.2285	no	yes, no $$
VA	50	Flagship Inns	W	860-405-1111		yes, no $$
VA	47	Heritage Motor Lodge	W	804-732-3444	yes $	yes, no $$
VA	41	Travelers Inn	W	804-733-5522	yes $	yes, no $$
VA	17	Resté Motel	E	434-535-9100	yes	No
NC	79	Preston Wordall House B&B	W	919-894-7025		No

State	Exit	Name	Dir	Phone	Pets	WiFi
NC	173	Interstate Inns	E.	252-536-4111	yes	yes, no $$
NC	145	Deluxe Inn	E.	252-446-2411	yes $	yes, no $$
NC	145	Ashburn Inn	E.	252-977-3505	yes $	yes, no $$
NC	121	Whitehead Inn	E.	252-243-4447	yes $	yes, no $$
NC	97	Regency Inn	W.	919-975-0102	yes $	yes, no $$
NC	95	Village Motor Lodge	E.	919-934-7126	yes $	yes, no $$
NC	95	Log Cabin Motel	W.	919-934-1534	yes $	yes, no $$
NC	90	Four Oaks Lodging	W.	919-963-3396	yes $	yes, no $$
NC	90	Travelers Inn	E.	919-934-4194	yes $	yes, no $$
NC	72	Valley Motor Inn	W.	910-892-2201	yes $	yes, no $$
NC	70	Relax Inn -take out?	E.	910-892-7167	no.	No
NC	49	Deluxe Inn	E.	910-484-2666	yes $	yes, no $$
NC	20	Deluxe Inn	E.	910-738-4261	yes $	yes, no $$
NC	19	Traveler's Inn	W.	910-738-2441	no.	No
NC	17	Southern Inn	E.	910-738-1502	yes $	yes, no $$
NC	17	Atkinson Inn & Suites	E.	910-674-3185	yes $	yes, no $$
NC	1	South of the Border Motor Inn	E.	800-845-6011	yes	Wifi lobby only
SC	181	Abingdon Manor	E.	888-752-5090	yes	yes, no $$
SC	164	Travel House Inn	W.	843-669-1921	yes $	yes, no $$
SC	164	Thunderbird Inn	W.	843-669-1611	yes	yes, no $$
SC	157	Tree Top Inn	E.	843-662-7712	yes $	yes, no $$
SC	157	Swamp Fox Inn	E.	843-665-0803	yes.	No
SC	146	Relax Inn	E.	843-659-4955	some rooms $	some rooms, no $$
SC	115	Sunset Inn	W.	803-473-2561	yes $	No
SC	115	M-Star Hotel	E.	803-473-2596	yes $	Wifi lobby only
SC	115	Carolina Inn	W.	843-473-7565	yes $	yes, no $$
SC	98	Santee State Park Cabins	W.	803-854-2408	no.	Wifi in office only
SC	98	Lake Marion Inn	W.	803-854-2107	yes	yes, no $$
SC	98	Elloree B&B	W.	803-897-4323	yes	yes, no $$
SC	98	Santee Inn and Suites	W.	803-854-4104	no.	yes, no $$
SC	98	Clark's Inn	W.	803-854-2141	no.	yes, no $$
SC	98	Whitten Inn	E.	803-854-2191	yes $	yes, no $$
SC	82	Peach Tree Inn	E.	843-636-9393	yes $	yes, no $$
SC	77	Southern Inn	W.	843-563-3775	yes $	yes, no $$
SC	57	Southern Inn	E.	843-538-2280	yes $	yes, no $$
SC	57	Carolina Lodge	E.	843-538-7708	yes $	yes, no $$
SC	53	Royal Inn P.	E.	843-538-2503	yes $	yes, no $$
SC	53	Rice Planters Inn	W.	843-538-8964	yes $	yes, no $$
SC	38	Econo Inn	E.	843-538-3830	yes $	yes, no $$
SC	38	Palmetto Lodge	W.	843-589-2361	yes $	No
SC	22	Plantation Inn	W.	843-726-5510	no.	
SC	21	Carolina Lodge	W.	843-726-6050	yes $	yes, no $$
SC	5	Deluxe Inn	W.	843-784-3155	yes $	yes, no $$
SC	5	Economy Inn	E.	843-784-2201	yes $	yes, no $$
GA	109	Inn at Mulberry Grove	W.	912-965-9666	no.	yes, no $$
GA	102	Magnolia Inn & suites	W.	912-748-6883	no.	yes, no $$
GA	99	Planters Inn	W.	912-232-5678	no.	yes, no $$
GA	99	Mansion on Forsyth Park	E.	912-238-5158	yes $	yes, incl in resort fee
GA	94	San's Boutique Hotel & Suites	E.	912-629-0650	no.	yes, no $$
GA	87	Royal Inn	W.	912-756-2778	yes $	yes, no $$
GA	58	Blue Heron Inn	E.	912 437 4304	yes $	yes, no $$
GA	49	Open Gates B&B	W.	912-437-6985	yes $	yes, no $$
GA	38	Guest Cottage & Suites	W.	912-264-6767	yes $	yes, no $$
GA	38	St James Suites	E.	912-280-0953	yes $	yes, no $$
GA	36	Brunswick Manor B&B	E.	912-265-6889	yes.	yes, no $$
GA	3	Magnolia Inn	E.	912-576-4777	yes $	yes, no $$
FL	358	Best USA Inn	W.	904-757-0990	no.	yes, no $$
FL	351	House on Cherry ST	W.	904-384-1999	no.	yes, no $$
FL	347	Emerson Inn	W.	904-398-6961	no.	No
FL	341	Baymeadows Inn & Suites	W.	904-739-0739	yes $	yes, no $$
FL	273	Destination Daytona Hotel & Suites	W.	386-944-1500	yes $	yes, no $$
FL	180	Budget Inn	E.	321-724-5450	yes $	yes, no $$
FL	129	Treasure Coast Inn	W.	772-466-4200	yes $	No
FL	45	Wyndham Garden Motel	W.	561-368-5200	yes $	yes, no $$
FL	42	Holiday Park Inn & Suites	W.	954-427-2200	yes $	yes, no $$
FL	32	El Palacio	W.	954-776-4880	no.	yes, no $$
FL	1	Starlite East	E.	305-857-9416	yes	yes, no $$
FL	1	Hotel Urbano	E.	305-854-2070	yes $	yes, no $$

We have tried to determine which of these accepts pets, but some information may be missing and may change without notice, so please call first to confirm.

Acknowledgements

"The journey of a thousand miles begins with one step." Lao-Tze, the Simple Way No. 64
"A journey of a thousand miles begins with a cash advance." Internet joke version

Our thanks, go to Dave and Kathy Hunter, who nudged us to take that first step on our long journey. Stan the actuary has calculated that this guide consists of 9097 items in our data base covering 1,554 miles, 609 exits, 561 stories, 295 photos, 82 maps and 2 very tired authors.

We could not possible have taken all those figures and turned them into a book by ourselves and had help from more people then we ever imagined. We are honored to show off the sum of your work.

Backstage crew: Marla Stermer, Gerry Gatien, Marissa Dulson, Brandon Posner, Barbara and Stillman Rogers, Rene and Tosh Taketomo, Roger and Sheila Marcus, Nancy and Eddie Chin, Flo Phillips, Bea and Burt Dermer, Rose and Ben Wald, Barbara and Neil Brandt

Industry Help: ibpa - Independent Publishers Association, the incredible organization where we learned about the book publishing industry in the U.S.; Dan Poynter *The Self-Publishing Manual*; Margaret Goldick, AELAQ; Norene Gilletz, gourmania.com; Sharon Castlen, Integrated Book Marketing; Dave and Jennifer Marx, PassPorter; Sam Spiegel, Partners Book Distributing; Kate and Doug Bandos, KSB Promotions.

A Tip of our Hats to the States: New England Tourism: Manny Witt, Lisa Witt; **NH** Portsmouth: Nicky Noble, Elizabeth Barcomb; Hampton Beach: Doc Noel; **MA** Greater Merrimack Valley:Deborah Belanger, Connie Morris; North of Boston: Julie Cooke, Stephen Sperandio, Bill Pickles; Boston: Larry Meehan, Stacy Shreffler; **RI** Mark Brodeur; Providence: Brian Hodge; BlackstoneValley: Bob Billington, Amanda Wood; **CT** Rosemary Bove: Coastal Fairfield: Sue Henrique; Milford: Kathleen Alagna: New Haven: Rennie Loisel, Suzette A. Benitez, Ginny Kozlowski, Amy Healy; Connecticut East, Mystic: Eliza Cole, Theresa Thesier; NJ Phyllis Oppenheimer; Camden Waterfront: John Seiter; **DE** Nicky Boone, Tina Madanat; Wilmington: Lyn Lewis; **MD** Camila Clark, Connie Yingling, Margie Long; Cecil County: Sandy Maruchi-Turner; Harford County: Wini Roche; Howard County: Rachelina Bonacci; **VA** Alisa Bailey; Julia Scott, Richard Lewis, Alexandria: Merrie Morris, Emily Hellewelle, Laura Overstreet; Prince William: Esther M. Turner; Fredericksburg: David Holder, Karen Hedelt; Caroline County Kathy Beard; Richmond: Erin Bagnell, Janene Charbeneau; Petersburg: Kevin Kirby; **NC** Lynn Minges; Wit Tuttell, Halifax County: Lori Medlin, Christina Gordon, Susan Clements; Nash County: Martha Lamm; Johnston County: Donna Bailey-Taylor, Amanda Williamson; Wilson: Sandra Homes; Dunn: Sharon Stevens; Fayetteville: John Meroski, Melody Foote, Angie Abrams; Lumberton: Mickey Gregory; **SC** Chad Prosser, Dawn Dawson-House; Florence: Holly Young; Santee-Cooper Country: Mary Shriner; Walterboro-Colleton: David Smalls, Donna Laird; Lowcountry: Jim Wescott, Brenda Wells, Peach Morrison; **GA** Kevin Langston; Carey Ferrara, Kingsland: Tonya Rosado; McIntosh County: Wally Orrel; Savannah: Erica Backus; Brunswick: Patrick Saylor; **FL** Bud Nocera; Tom Flanigan, Henny Groenendijk, Jacksonville: Jennifer Bryant, Carrie McLean; Space Coast, Palm Bay: Kalina Subido-Person, Donna Balencia; Palm Coast, St. Augustine: Jay Humphreys; Daytona Beach: Tangela Boyd, Sandy Lucania, Georgia Turner; New Smyrna Beach; Deborah Boyd, Chris Bell; Martin County, Stuart: Rozeta Mahboubi; Port Saint Lucie, Fort Pierce: Charlotte Lombard, Larry Daum, Odaly Victorio; Palm Beach: Kenneth Morgan, Melissa Gattuso; Fort Lauderdale: Fernando Harb, Jessica Taylor; Miami: Jennifer Haz, Michelle Revuelta.

Merci Beaucoup

Stan

Sandra

Driving Memories

Here's some space to jot a few notes to remember places
or people you've met along the way.

_____

_____

_____

_____

_____

_____

_____

_____

_____

_____

_____

_____

_____

_____

_____

_____

_____

_____

_____

_____

_____

_____

_____

_____

_____

_____

_____

Driving Memories

Here's some space to jot a few notes to remember places
or people you've met along the way.

EXPENSES — SOUTH

DATE	MILEAGE			GAS Gallons	DAILY COSTS								STATE	EXIT	TOWN	MOTEL	
	START OF DAY	END OF DAY	DAILY TOTAL		BR	LUNCH	DINNER	GAS	SLEEP	OTHER	TOTAL					NAME	CONF #

EXPENSES — NORTH

| DATE | MILEAGE | | | GAS Gallons | DAILY COSTS | | | | | | | | | | STATE | EXIT | TOWN | MOTEL | | |
	START OF DAY	END OF DAY	DAILY TOTAL		BR	LUNCH	DINNER	GAS	SLEEP	OTHER	TOTAL							NAME	CONF #

Drive I-95 **Mail Order Form** for yourself or for a gift

Use this to order another copy or for next year's edition so you will be the first to have one (before the bookstores even receive them). You can also order online at www.drivei95.com or over the phone from BCH company at 888-GUIDE95 (all major credit cards accepted). New editions will always be available in September or October. The book makes a **perfect gift** for a relative who will be traveling, a teacher, a secretary, a student attending college along I-95 (or their parents for visiting days), salesmen, campers and RVers, military personnel, truckers or anyone who enjoys reading about America.

If you want the gift book autographed and personalized, please fill in the lines provided below (there is no extra charge).

Your name _____

Address _____

City _____ State/Province _____ Zip or Postal Code _____

e-mail address _____ Phone _____

Please send _____ copies of *Drive I-95* to the above address.

I have enclosed my check for $_____ Checks should be made out to Travelsmart.

Credit Card type _____

Card # _____ Expiry date _____

Name on Card _____

Your signature _____

Price for books shipped: $23.95 each plus $4 shipping and handling. There is no extra shipping charge if you order up to 3 books. Add $1.50 for each additional book. Checks payable in U.S. or Canadian funds, according to your shipping address.

Personalized words_____

_____

_____

If we have missed any of your favorite spots
or you would like to comment on any of the sites in this book,
or if you have noticed any changes, please feel free to let us know.

To contact us: Travelsmart, *Drive I-95*
P.O. Box 43527 CSP Roxboro
Dollard des Ormeaux, Quebec, Canada H8Y 3P4
Phone: 514-684-4020   Fax: 866-329-2987
e-mail: orders@drivei95.com

Love Notes From our Thousands of Fans

"What an interesting and fun way to drive I-95. The kids especially enjoyed the stories and seeing what would be at the next exit as far as food etc. Even my husband joined in and we made a game out of it. Don't drive I-95 without it."

MB, NY

"I drove from New Jersey to South Florida. we did not put this book down the whole 19 hours!!! Loved it!"

B&N

"I'm not a great map reader, but this was the easiest thing ever. This book was instrumental in my having a safe, anxiety-free drive from NJ to FL. This book eliminated the guess work. Looking at the book, I could plan bathroom breaks, diaper changes, gas stops, etc. We were able to avoid the "screaming baby in the car" and navigate where to stop. I don't know how they did it. This is so worth it."

GW, NJ

"I hate being in the car. After buying your book, I couldn't wait to get on the road. I could not believe how fast the journey went just turning the pages."

E, NJ

"Don't leave home without it! In this highly informative, extremely well-organized travel book the maps are so cleverly designed that they remain impressively easy to read on the fly. The tourist information and stories are presented as if a friend had thoughtfully written a travel journal just for you - readers can't help but learn historical facts about the towns that are whizzing by. It seems as if no detail has been left overlooked. You'll never have to settle for a hastily eaten fast food burger at a rest stop again! This book is a MUST HAVE for anybody planning to drive I-95!"

MA

"The I-95 book was a great companion for our GPS.... It really came in handy..."

EC, MD

"My son is in the Army. We never leave (to visit him) without our bible on the road, Drive I-95. It's getting so marked up with little notes here and there that the trip becomes better with time. Thank you Stan and Sandra. Good bless America, God bless our Troops and God bless Drive I-95."

N.N., NJ